P9-APQ-017

The Dialectic
of Action

**Frederick A.
Olafson**

The Dialectic
of Action

*A Philosophical
Interpretation of
History and the
Humanities*

The University of Chicago Press
Chicago and London

For ALLIE

The University of Chicago Press, Chicago 60637
The University of Chicago Press, Ltd., London

© 1979 by The University of Chicago
All rights reserved. Published 1979
Printed in the United States of America
83 82 81 80 79   5 4 3 2 1

Library of Congress Cataloging in Publication Data

Olafson, Frederick A.
   The dialectic of action.

   Includes bibliographical references and index.
   1. History—Philosophy.   2. Humanities.   I. Title.
D16.8.05   901   79–10316
ISBN 0–226–62564–8

FREDERICK A. OLAFSON is professor of philosophy at the University of California, San Diego.
He is the author of *Principles and Persons*
(1967) and *Ethics and Twentieth-Century
Thought* (1973).

Contents

Acknowledgments

The intellectual debts incurred in the course of the writing of this book are too numerous to be adequately acknowledged here; but it is at least possible to indicate the two major bodies of philosophical literature from which most of the themes with which I deal derive. One of these is the literature of the analytical philosophy of history itself especially as it has developed over the last three decades or so. Although I have often taken issue with many of the positions that have been defended within that literature and have departed in quite fundamental ways from the approach to philosophical issues relating to history that has been widely shared by analytical philosophers, I have also learned a great deal even from those philosophers whose conclusions I am unable to accept. Naturally, my indebtedness is most patent in the case of those philosophers whose views, although expressed in the idiom of logical analysis, are closest to my own; and here I would mention especially William Dray, W. B. Gallie, and G. H. von Wright, and also, in a somewhat different quarter of the compass, Arthur Danto. In their different ways these philosophers have shown how theses with respect to the distinctive character of historical understanding can be formulated with a degree of rigor and precision that is commensurate with the human importance their proponents have often assigned to them; and it is my hope that my own work has benefited as much from contact with their writings as I think it has. At the same time, I have felt that it was necessary to amplify the predominantly logical or conceptual orientation of their treatment of history by introducing a conception of the historical process and of "historicity" as a dimension of human existence that is centrally implicated in generating that process. These elements in the position I present are designed, however, to give the theses about the logic of history that I share with these writers a broader and stronger philosophical foundation than such theses often appear to have and which in my view they clearly require. I hope they will be appraised in the spirit of that intention.

My second main source of philosophical insight into problems relating to history has been the literature of phenomenology and above all the work of Martin Heidegger. It is a regrettable fact that recent work in phenomenology has not moved significantly beyond the level of programmatic statements about "phenomenology" and "history" and the positive forms that a rapprochement between these two unwieldy entities might possibly take in spite of the strongly antihistorical orientation of phenomenology in its original Husserlian version. Only in the writings of H.-G. Gadamer—not himself a phenomenologist—has there been a significant development (and one that has benefited from a close relationship to actual historical materials) of the conception of history that Heidegger stated all too briefly in *Being and Time*. In these circumstances it seemed to me far more important to try to show how some of the principal concepts that Heidegger invokes could be put to work in the treatment of specific conceptual issues that arise in connection with history than to contribute yet another "interpretation" of Heidegger's thought. In the interest of general comprehension, I have also tried to keep the technical phenomenological apparatus that I employ to a minimum with the somewhat paradoxical result that in some ways the book I have written may seem more preoccupied with "analytical" themes than it is with typically phenomenological concerns. In any case, the variant of phenomenology this book represents is certainly idiosyncratic, although not as a result of any conscious attempt at philosophical hybridization; and the affinity it can claim with the classical formulations of phenomenology, whether "transcendental" or "existential," is more a matter of sharing certain quite general intuitions or "hunches" about what needs to be placed at the focus of philosophical inquiry than of commitment to specific doctrinal tenets.

Beyond this general philosophical indebtedness there are quite specific and concrete forms of assistance that I have received and would like to acknowledge. I am particularly grateful to the John Simon Guggenheim Foundation for its award of a fellowship to me for the academic year 1967–68 which enabled me to undertake the studies on which this book is based. A grant of sabbatical leave for the fall quarter of 1974 by the University of California, San Diego, made it possible for me to complete a first draft of the book; and my thanks are therefore due to that institution as well. A visit to Cornell University as a guest of the Humanities, Science, and Technology Subunit of that university's Science, Technology, and Society Program provided valuable stimulus to my work during this period; and I am grateful to Professors Max Black and Stuart Brown for the hospitality and assistance they generously afforded me.

During the period in which I have been preparing this book, I have also written a number of articles on closely related themes and some of these have been incorporated either in part or in whole into the text of the book as it now stands. I should, therefore, like to thank the presses and journals that have permitted me to reprint material that first appeared under their copyrights: *Nous,* for permission to reprint portions of "Husserl's Theory of Intentionality in Contemporary Perspective," from volume 9 (1975); Times Books, for permission to reprint portions of "Human Action and Historical Explanation," which first appeared in J. Edie, ed.,

New Essays in Phenomenology (1969); and the Prometheus Press for permission to reprint portions of my essay "Humanism and the Humanities," which first appeared in S. Hook and M. Todorovich, eds., *The Philosophy of the Curriculum* (1975).

Finally, I have received most excellent assistance during the preparation of this book from the office staff of the Department of Philosophy at the University of California, San Diego, and especially from Norma Bain and Mary French, who typed the manuscript.

1. History, the Humanities, and the "Manifest Image of Man"

I

In the course of the last three decades a considerable body of literature has come into being which deals with philosophical issues relating to history in a manner that is usually described as "logical" or "analytical."[1] The writers who have contributed to this literature share a disposition to identify the philosophy of history with the analysis of historical knowledge and to dismiss as "speculative" all or most of the earlier philosophies of history from St. Augustine's to Toynbee's. Where these speculative forerunners characteristically made independent epistemic claims with respect to the historical process, the analytical philosopher of history sees his own work in quite different terms. He is not, at least in intention, directly concerned with the historical process at all or with the ascertaining of historical fact or the interpretation of historical phenomena. That is said to be the business of the practicing historian whose finished work then supplies the datum for the analyses of the philosopher of history in much the same way as the work of the scientist is logically prior to that of the philosopher of science and that of the artist to the analyses of the philosophical aesthetician. This principle of the division of labor between philosophy and the various departments of human knowledge and culture thus defines the proper object of philosophical inquiry, in each of its branches, as the conceptual analysis of its subjacent, "first-level" discipline; at the same time it blocks the perennial tendency of the philosophical mind to venture beyond its proper sphere.

This interest in history on the part of philosophers who abjure the speculative impulse is relatively new. Indeed, it is arguable that with one or two notable exceptions the standing of history, considered as a branch of knowledge, has almost never been very highly rated by philosophers of any persuasion. The achievements of mathematics and, later, of mathematical natural science have constituted a much more impressive paradigm of knowledge than those of history, which in the view of most philosophers has seemed scarcely to rise above the level of commonsense beliefs and to be as inexact and vulnerable to error as the latter typically are. And, in fact, it was not as the result of any revision of this established view of history and of its modest epistemic standing that the attention of analytical philosophers was drawn to that discipline. As far as one can judge, the motivation of the first analytical philosophers to cross the bound-

1

ary that separates history from the natural sciences was entirely programmatic in nature. More specifically, it was a matter of showing that the
models of scientific explanation which had been developed on the basis of
an analysis of the natural sciences were applicable to history as well and
that it was therefore unnecessary to devise alternative accounts of the
way explanation proceeds in history. The brevity of most of these first
analytical treatments of history is perhaps the best indication of their
programmatic character as well as of the prevailing belief that no very
serious challenge to a unitary theory of explanation could be expected
from this quarter. It was recognized, of course, that history had a long
way to go before its finished product would conform visibly and in detail
to the proposed model of explanation in the way the products of the more
mature sciences already did; and it was further assumed that this progress
would be realized through a much closer association of history with the
social sciences. As to the appropriateness to the latter of the explanatory
model exemplified by the natural sciences, there was apparently no real
question in anyone's mind; and as regards the past achievements of history, when it was thought of as one of the *studia humaniora* rather than as
a nascent social science, an absolute silence prevailed. There was no
suggestion that an independent study of the historiographical tradition
might be called for before the conclusion was reached that the claims of
history to a certain measure of autonomy in its cognitive procedures was
simply a reflection of its undeveloped state as a science. In every meaningful respect, the first interventions of analytical philosophy in the area
of history were thus as aprioristic in character as any speculative philosophy of history has ever been.

Nevertheless, in spite of its programmatic character, the brief incursion
of these first investigators into the territory of historical knowledge
proved to have beneficial consequences. Other philosophers who shared
the broad analytical orientation of a Hempel or a Popper but who were
more interested in history than they were in natural science went over the
same terrain much more slowly and deliberately, and the maps they
brought back showed a great many more local and distinctive features of
historical inquiry than had those of their predecessors.[2] Nevertheless, the
primary focus was still on the role of explanation in history and the great
issue that dominated all these studies was whether or not the model of
explanation proposed by Professor C. G. Hempel really applied to history
or not.[3] The central element in that model was the requirement that explanations in history as elsewhere must incorporate as a major premise
the statement of a law which, together with certain pertinent factual premises, allows a particular historical fact to be deduced and thereby explained. In the course of these further inquiries, this "covering-law
theory"—more technically the nomological-deductive theory of historical
explanation—underwent a great many different revisions. The most sig-

nificant of these were the attempts that were made to do justice to the narrative character of historical explanation, which had remained almost completely obscured as long as the explanatory model was presented in the form of a syllogistic argument. The two major analyses of historical narrative that have been worked out do not, however, reject the original Hempelian account of explanation but rather translate it into narrative terms.[4] More generally, among the most widely influential contributions that have been made to this continuing discussion, there are only a few that strike one as really challenging the covering-law theory in a fundamental way rather than reformulating it. In the perspective of the three decades since its original publication, it must be acknowledged as a remarkable achievement that a single, rather brief paper—Hempel's "The Function of General Laws in History"—should not only have given rise to such a massive literature discussing its principal thesis but that this thesis should have maintained itself and controlled the terms of the continuing discussion as successfully as it has.

The reactions of professional historians to the new kind of interest philosophers have been showing in their work and to the principal theses that have emerged from the analytical philosophy of history have been at best mixed.[5] The level of abstraction from the actual circumstances of historical inquiry to which the interest of the philosopher is pitched is one that is typically uncongenial to the practicing historian; and as a result he is constitutionally predisposed to doubt whether any thesis developed at that level can accurately reflect the really significant features of the business of history as the historian knows it. Since the criteria that define what such significance is to consist in are often quite different from those to which the philosopher appeals, the exchanges between the analytical philosopher of history and the historian can easily degenerate into a *dialogue de sourds,* in which the counterinstances to a philosophical thesis that the historian draws from his familiarity with the actual procedures of historical research and writing strike the philosopher as quite irrelevant to the logical claim he is making. But if this tends to be the pattern of exchanges between the historian and the philosopher of history, it is also true that for reasons of its own, which do not have much to do with philosophical argument or the logic of explanation, history has been moving closer to the social sciences for some time now. There has accordingly been some disposition on the part of historians to look with favor on the application of the nomological thesis to their discipline in the belief that it formulates the basic epistemic demands of the social as well as of the natural sciences and that, if history seeks a rapprochement with the former, it must accept at least in principle the logical conditions that define their scientific character. To the extent that this favorable attitude toward the nomological interpretation has established itself among historians, they have tended to share Hempel's assumption that as history transforms itself into a social science concerned with past societies it will more and more visibly conform to the logical requirements which that new identity carries with it.

Thus far, however, it does not appear that either the analytical philosopher of history or the historian who doubles as a social scientist has been able to point to convincing exemplifications in actual historical work of the structures of explanatory reasoning on which the cognitive standing of history is to depend.[6] Even when the requirements of the nomological-deductive model are quite substantially relaxed, as, for example, by modifications that make it unnecessary that the law whose existence an explanation implies be actually identified and cited in that explanation, the difficulty persists.[7] In these circumstances one may well question whether actual historical practice is in reality the controlling datum for philosophical conceptualization as the metaphor of levels in terms of which the philosopher characterizes his own position in relation to other disciplines would seem to require. The truth seems to be rather that actual historical practice has been antecedently idealized in such a way that its conformity to the requirements laid down by the philosopher is virtually assured in advance and any disparities are accounted for by the undeveloped state of history itself, which can often do no better than to prefigure very indistinctly the eventual form which its understanding of events will assume. Resort to a stipulation of this kind rather clearly acknowledges the ambiguous state of the evidence that history itself offers for the set of philosophical theses that are being applied to it. But if the latter can claim only an uncertain and ambiguous grounding in actual historical practice, whatever authority it can claim must rest on general philosophical grounds which are so powerful as to rule out in advance any possibility of there being an alternative model of explanation that might prove more appropriate to the historical case. If there are such grounds and if, furthermore, what are widely regarded as the most successful branches of inquiry, for example, mathematical physics, conform to the logical requirements governing explanation which those grounds dictate, then the case for recognizing any kind of exceptional or distinct status for history or any other discipline would become extraordinarily weak. In such circumstances, it would always seem to be more reasonable to account for any anomalous features of the historical case by appealing to the postulate which declares that discipline to be in a relatively primitive and undeveloped state and thereby disqualifies it as a source of counterexamples that have to be taken seriously. At the deepest level of conviction in the minds of its proponents, the logic of the case for the nomological-deductive theory of historical explanation very often seems to move along such lines as these.

As long as the assumptions on which such a case as this depends remain unchallenged, the result is to place those who are dissatisfied with the picture of history which the nomological-deductive model yields at a serious rhetorical disadvantage. They are somewhat in the position of the critics of the Warren Report on the assassination of President Kennedy who can point to one discrepancy after another in the account that report gives of what took place in Dallas but are unable to provide any plausible alternative theory of what really took place. Similarly, the critics of the covering-law theory can show again and again how poor the fit between actual historical explanations and that theory really is: but, if they follow the logic of their own objections, they seem to have nowhere to go unless they are prepared to return to some one or other of the prescientific Weltanschauungen of a discredited philosophical past. The assumption underlying the present study is that these alternatives for the critic of the nomological-deductive theory in its application to history are in fact falsely and tendentiously construed and that the elaboration of significant alternative theories of a degree of generality comparable to that of the nomological-deductive theory itself is the only way out of the present impasse. Only when such alternatives are available will it be possible for the philosophical scrutiny of history to be something more profitable than a conflict between a logical apriorism that dismisses whatever it cannot assimilate and the instinctive hostility of the practitioner to *any* characterization in broad conceptual terms of the enterprise in which he has proprietary rights. The important thing, in other words, is not to continue casting up objections to the covering-law theory but to ask what kind of alternative theory is suggested by the features of historical inquiry to which these objections have characteristically appealed. Whether the conceptualization that thus emerges can stand the test of whatever general philosophical criteria may legitimately be applied to it is of course a further question and will have to be faced as such. But surely the resolution of such ultimate issues, if it is possible at all, will be much more convincing if the history that is called upon to respond to them is not represented only by an assortment of casual examples drawn from a handful of convenient texts but by some more adequate and considered conceptual representation of the way it goes about its business.

II

There are many clues that might be used to guide such an effort to characterize history in a way that is designed to reflect its own characteristic concerns rather than the requirements of an independent theory of explanation. One of these is implicit in the adjective "humanistic" which is very frequently used to convey the aspect of history that is scanted when it is treated exclusively in terms of the formal analogies its explanatory procedures are thought to exhibit with the procedures of the natural sciences.[8] To describe history as "humanistic" is, in the first instance, to

associate it with a number of other disciplines which compose the grouping to which we refer collectively as "the humanities"; and it is also to
impute to history and to its humanistic congeners a primary interest in and
orientation toward things human. As to the more precise character of this
interest in man, there is not any established agreement. It seems fairly
clear, however, that the humanities, by contrast with, say, physiology,
are interested in man primarily as the possessor of certain powers which
are shared, if at all, by other animals only in markedly different and
diminished form. These powers have traditionally been held to comprise
those of thought and articulate speech, of purposive action and will, as
well as of feeling that is informed by thought and purpose; and it has also
been widely supposed that these powers come together in the generic
capacity of human beings for making and recognizing distinctions of
value, including moral value. Sometimes the belief that the humanities
have a special concern with values assumes a narrowly didactic form as
when it is argued that the humanities "teach values"; but such a claim
involves a number of further assumptions which need not be made and in
fact may present some difficulties. What seems more important and less
controversial is simply the claim that history, as well as literature and
philosophy, is concerned with human beings and with human beings as
possessed of and exercising these distinctive powers; and to this may be
added the further observation that these modes of thought are themselves
exemplary deployments of these same powers.

In this connection, it may be helpful to associate this first attempt to
capture the import of the term "humanistic" with a much more ambitious
thesis which has been elaborated by Professor Wilfred Sellars.[9] This is the
interpretation he proposes of the role that has been assigned to the concept of personality or personhood in the principal phases of the history of
human thought. In the earliest of these phases—the mythic—the cosmos
as a whole was understood to be instinct with life and purpose, and
natural phenomena of various kinds were described, at least on some
occasions, in a language that imputed personality and a purposive
character to them. The first great watershed of human thought, in the
interpretation Professor Sellars proposes, was the transition to what he
calls the commonsense view of the world which denies purpose and personality to natural phenomena but continues to use teleological modes of
understanding for human beings and their actions. The resultant world
view is dualistic in the sense that it institutes a series of contrasts, as, for
example, between what happens and what is done, between intentions
and causes, and between the "inner" and the "outer," which have the
cumulative effect of portraying man as being in these important respects
different from his natural milieu and as standing in a unique relationship to
it and also to his fellow men as a result of these differences. This dualism
also generates what Sellars calls the "manifest image of man," that is, the

teleological picture of man in terms of which he has unquestioningly understood and described himself for so long now that it has assumed a virtually automatic authority in his eyes. This "manifest image" has a competitor, however, in the "scientific image of man" which has emerged in the course of the modern period and which undertakes a new integration of man with his natural world, this time under the auspices of concepts which are explicitly nonteleological in character, and which liquidate the man-world dualisms of the commonsense ontology. It is this second transition which, Professor Sellars tells us, is currently taking place or at any rate being attempted; and it will, if successful, entail even more massive shifts in our mental picture of ourselves than did the earlier breaking-up of the unitary world of myth.

The affinities between the kind of interest the humanities take in man, as it was described earlier, and the "manifest image of man" as an active and purposive being seem obvious. It is arguable, of course, that the mythic world-view is still with us, if not as a living context of belief, then at least as a sense of loss and of trauma that informs some of the poetry and even some of the philosophy of our day. But in the Western world, at any rate, the first transition noted above has been largely complete for a long time now; and it is the assumptions and the distinctions of the "manifest image of man" that have most deeply informed the language of those forms of thought to which we usually refer as "humanistic." It is, moreover, a distinctive feature of the present moment in the history of our culture that we are being made aware of certain features of those forms of thought in a way that would hardly have been possible if it had not been for the encroachments upon the humanistic domain of a contrasting and, to many minds, quite alien set of concepts. The development, for example, of ordinary-language philosophy and of the parallel phenomenological interest in what has come to be called the *Lebenswelt* can hardly be understood otherwise than as a movement of self-awareness and of self-defense on the part of a conceptual species (or, at any rate, its human sponsors) which perceives itself to be suddenly vulnerable and endangered. These references to the situation of the humanities are not intended to be ironic; if irony were appropriate at all in this connection, it could just as well characterize our perception of those humanists who are joyfully preparing themselves to be born again into the new world of the "scientific image" and are already saying their farewells to the now obsolete conceptual instruments they are leaving behind. In either case, the real point is that, whatever the future may hold, this moment in our intellectual history offers us an opportunity to gain insights into the very commonsense ontology that is now being challenged; and the suggestion being made here is that these insights may be highly pertinent to an effort to comprehend the nature of the humanities and, more specifically, the humanistic dimension of history.

It is not in fact at all difficult to make a connection between an analysis of conceptual history like the one Sellars proposes and the development of historiography and of philosophical reflection on history. Certainly the central role of teleological conceptions within historiography and philosophy is undeniable, and it is equally clear that these conceptions have often been associated with systems of thought which treat teleology in "mythic" terms as involving something larger than and in some measure independent of finite human purposes. The Christian view of history, for example, postulates the existence of a supernatural person standing outside the historical process which he arranges in a sequence that is both dramatic and cumulative. The beginning of history is the creation of man as a creature endowed with intelligence and choice and its end is the final judgment with its alternatives of salvation and damnation for individual human souls. Between these two termini the decisive event of human history is the birth of Christ, by which the whole historical field is polarized so that events preceding it take on the status of preparatory phases and events that follow it are judged by the degree to which they conform to the direction which the promise of Christ's life has imparted to human history. But Christ's life can organize history in this way and point to its end only because he is the son of God, the representative of the supernatural person who is working his will in history and who uses men for his own purposes which, of course, since men are his creatures, are really their purposes too although they cannot comprehend them. But however mysterious God's will may be, if it were not for the purpose which he pursues in human history, that history, as human beings make it by their own intelligence and will, would have no pattern of finality at all unless it were that of their natural death.

It has often been pointed out that the Hegelian theory of history is modeled on the Christian organization of history into a triad in which sin and the remoteness from God which it entails is the necessary condition for a mode of reconciliation which is the more profound precisely because it incorporates into itself the experience of evil. What is equally clear, however, is that Hegel was determined to show that history has a teleology of its own which transcends the purposiveness that human beings impart to it, and to do so without postulating the existence of a transcendent God controlling history from without. In other words, the teleology of history must be sufficiently distinguishable from the purposes of human beings so that a sense can be given to the notion of its hiddenness and its unavailability to the latter who often feel despair at the "way of the world"; and yet this same teleology must be internal to history in a way in which it could not be if it were made to depend upon a transcendent God. Hegel's solution to this dilemma was to interpret the teleology of history as a sequence in which the conceptions of selfhood, or "spirit," that are characteristic of the successive stages in the history of human civilization, approach a conception which is fully adequate. The relevant standard of adequacy is one which has to do with the overcoming of the dichotomy of subject and object and is connected with a conception of freedom understood as the coincidence of the self with the "other" with which it finally recognizes its underlying identity. What is important here is simply to point out that the cumulativeness that is essential to any teleological ordering of history is, for Hegel, a conceptual or logical cumulativeness. The latter is internal to history since it is an order within the thoughts that human beings have about themselves—thoughts that are also reflected in the whole of what we would call their "culture"—but their status as partial realizations of the fully adequate concept is what human beings do not grasp immediately but only in the course of a process that is itself cumulative. Thus one can say that the goal of this process is a conception of the self and that it is carried out by thoughts and actions that are imputable to the self; but the sequence itself and the reason why one stage follows upon another are logical in character. Only at the end of the process—that of the history and of the thought whose unity will only then be understood—will a full comprehension of the identity of the self with the historical process and of the teleology of the one with the teleology of the other be possible.

The Hegelian conception of history has had a significant afterlife within Marxism; and although it has now been substantially discredited, it still constitutes a temptation for writers of cultural history.[10] Many of the objections that brought it down may have been based on serious misunderstandings of what Hegel was about; but one criticism was decisive and that had to do with the impossibility of making actual human history run parallel with the kind of conceptual sequence Hegel envisaged or, as it might be more appropriately expressed, the impossibility of showing that the upshot or "yield" of a historical period or episode must take the form of a further contributing increment to an adequate concept of spirit. When Hegel is at his best he makes us see how this could happen and how a sequence of human actions that is not itself inspired by theoretical motives can constitute a modification in our mode of self-understanding; and on these occasions the dialectic of concepts is also a dialectic of consciousness. But on other occasions the logical sequence by itself seems to be all that Hegel cares about, and he does not even bother to suggest how it might be realized in the medium of a conscious life which is not that of a dialectical logician. To cite a particularly flagrant example, when Hegel has to characterize the cultures of the East which preceded the Greco-Roman and Germanic cultures of the West, he does so in terms of the ways in which they qualified and limited the concept of freedom as an attribute of the self; but the transitions from one culture to another, for example, the fact that India followed upon China in the movement of spirit toward full self-knowledge, are left quite unexplained.[11] Here the dialectic of consciousness seems to lapse altogether and the dialectic of concepts has to do all the work. Unfortunately, it does that work in a way that makes Hegel's thesis deeply implausible, since one civilization simply comes on stage as the bearer of a new conception of spirit, that is, on cue from the logical dialectic and without any apparent benefit from or reaction to what had taken place in its predecessor cultures or even in its own past. The only way to make sense of such a transition would be to impute a kind of agency to the concept-in-development itself whereby it could somehow impose itself upon the successive stages of the historical process without even the uncomprehending cooperation of actual participants in that process. But to the extent that this would be comprehensible at all it would seem tantamount to treating the idea as an agent and thus as functioning in a way that would not be too different from the Christian conception of the organization of the historical process by a person who is outside history.[12]

If efforts to conceive the historical process in terms of an externally imposed teleology have been discredited, that is in large part because the relationship they postulated between what might be called historical experience and the achieved form of historical understanding proved to be both tendentious and confining. And yet the aspiration to conceive history in terms of such a convergence does not seem to be less strong now than it was in the past. Historical experience—the sense we make of our own lives and undertakings—is still typically fragmented and confused; and it is not surprising if we still look to history for the expression of some larger vision in which that experience would be subsumed and reconciled with itself. But such a reconciliation would be possible, if at all, only if the interests that inform historical understanding were a purified and coherent transformation of the same, at bottom personal and moral interests that are at work in historical experience. For all their high-handed procedures, that was the kind of historical understanding that the great teleological systems sought to achieve. But with the demise of historical teleology, the possibility of this kind of convergence has become more and more problematic. After Hegel, philosophers who took an interest in history concentrated their attention on the nature of historical inquiry as it is practiced by the empirical historian and on whatever distinctive features the conceptual apparatus of the historian might possess; they left totalistic theories of the historical process more and more to speculative minds like Spengler and Toynbee. This caution has been shared by the historians themselves, and if they have not stopped trying to understand the events with which they deal in terms of long-run continuities of various kinds, they are certainly very reluctant about claiming any unique or privileged status for any one conception of the unity of the historical process. So thoroughly has this lesson been learned, in fact, that it is not uncommon for an acknowledgment of the underlying principle of interpretation in a historical work to assume the character of an avowal of the historian's "bias"—an avowal which has the purpose of putting the reader on notice as to a possible source of cognitive distortion in the account before him. Increasingly, although the intentions and characteristic mode of self-understanding of the historical agents themselves may still be thought of as at best subjective and unreliable interpretations of the events in which these agents may have been involved, the standard of "objectivity" from which this imputation of "subjectivity" derives is no longer some higher form of teleology which the agents themselves are unable to grasp but simply the statistically expressed resultant of some widely diffused process of change in which they were involved quite possibly without knowing it. As a result the gap between historical experience and historical knowledge as the historian conceives it threatens to become impassable because the terms in which historical agents have understood the events in which they were involved are in an increasingly skew relationship to the terms in which the questions which the historian brings to his materials are formulated. In these circumstances, there can be little reason to expect that the historian's interpretation of these events might constitute the "truth" of the various and often opposed "subjective" experiences of history, not just in the demanding sense in which this notion is used by Hegel, but in any more modest sense as well. The condition for such a relationship between historical experience and historical knowledge is that there be a long-run convergence between the kind of interest in the events in question that is characteristic of the one and the other side in this contrast; but when the form of the historical process as it is projected by the historian's inquiries is one to which the notions of purpose and value are largely irrelevant, the possibility of such convergence must be very dubious.

These considerations set the issue with which much of this book will be concerned. On the one hand, it is accepted that efforts to mediate between historical experience and historical knowledge by means of either of the two major instruments of traditional teleology—supernatural causal agency or a principle of logical necessitation that is allegedly inherent in events themselves—are to be rejected. But at the same time the conclusion which is usually held to follow from such a resolution—the repudiation of the concept of teleology in all its applications which transcend the sphere of purely personal and individual agency—is not to be drawn forthwith. Instead, an attempt will be made to assay the prospects for a conception of historical teleology which is internal in a stronger sense than Hegel's. It would be internal, first, in the sense of standing in a much closer and more empirical relationship to what I have called "historical experience" and, second, in the sense that it abjures any thought that such order as may be derivable from an inquiry that takes these descriptions into account is ideally separable from the agents and the circumstances that are its historical vehicle, as once again Hegel appears to have believed. The attempt, in short, is to explore those features of a personal experience of the social world and of history which may mediate the apparently insuperable disjunction of levels that was characterized above. If such features are indeed discoverable, then the further task must be to determine how they might generate and at the same time be preserved within the larger organizing structures of the historical process. And finally it will be necessary to show that a conception of the historical process generated in this way can yield a plausible interpretation of both the unity and the diversity of the historical enterprise, especially in the light of the wide range of historiographic innovations that are currently being introduced.

III

An attempt like the one just proposed to effect a linkage between the larger structures of the historical process and the teleological organization of human life is bound, in spite of all disclaimers, to arouse suspicious reactions and apprehensions that some conception of final causes is being resurrected. But, in fact, the teleology that is implicit in the concept of the person can be construed in quite different terms; and it by no means requires that one be prepared to think of the goal or terminal state of purposive action as though it were susceptible of causing such action to occur before it—the goal—has come into being.[13] When a person has a goal or a purpose, he typically casts about for suitable means for realizing that goal, which at that stage will be present only as an idea or description of the outcome that is desired. If a particular action is believed by the agent to be suitable to the production of that outcome and has no significant drawbacks of its own, it will very likely be carried into execution; and the goal may then be achieved. But it is vitally important to notice here that such a means will be chosen only to the extent it satisfies a certain prospective description by which it is tied logically to the realization of the goal that is desired. The case is thus not that the end-state is already in some mysterious way causally efficacious, but rather that the agent's performing the action which is a means to the eventual production of that end-state is explicable only on the supposition that he identifies the action in question *as* a means suitable to the end he has in mind. And because the choice of a given modality of action depends upon its satisfying such a prospective description, the explanation that is given of this action will be prima facie teleological in the sense that it involves a reference to the end-state in question via the description of the action itself that is to be explained.

The full significance of the teleological character of such an explanation does not emerge until one contrasts it with a set of logical requirements governing the kind of explanation that is typically offered in the natural sciences.[14] According to these requirements, each of the elements that is involved in the explanation of some natural process must be logically independent of the others so that the question of the relationship in which these elements stand to one another will not be begged in advance and so that the determination of that relationship can be a genuinely empirical issue. Applied to the kind of case examined above, this requirement would rule out any description that presents the action to be explained as the means to the realization of the goal. That action must instead be described in a way that leaves the question of its relationship to the end-state entirely open. The occurrence of the action would be explained through its being associated with a number of other elements which are identifiable within the history and situation of the agent in question and which are themselves to be described in a similarly noncommittal and logically independent manner as regards their relationship to the goal. These elements would be associated with one another as terms in some lawlike statement asserting that, when these elements occur in a certain relationship to one another, the action under consideration is in fact produced. In this way, it is insured not only that the relationship between these elements and the action will be empirically testable matter but also that there will be nothing in the premises of the explanation that involves an essential reference to the goal of the action. Such references must be avoided since they improperly anticipate the end-state which the action to be explained would normally produce by describing the events or states of affairs with which the premises are concerned in a way that ties them logically to that state. The governing concern of this approach to explanation is not only to block the attribution of causal efficacy to any entities that are not or are not yet actual, but also to control the descriptions occurring in the premises of the explanation in such a way that these descriptions are not themselves rendered problematic by the nonoccurrence of the end-state. The upshot is that although, when the action to be explained is successful, the goal at which, in our ordinary understanding of the matter, that action "aims" will in fact be produced and produced as a result of this action, the explanation that is constructed in accordance with these criteria will at no point depend on anything that is connected with the prospective reference which that "aiming" involves. From this standpoint, the goal will come into being, but it will do so as simply the last term in a logically segmented sequence of events and not as the consummation of the future-oriented sequence that common sense postulates.

The tangle of issues into which this brief account of teleological explanation has led us is extremely complex and there are ways of formulating the anti-teleological position which are subtler than those presented above and which permit descriptions to occur within the premises of an explanatory argument which involve references to a goal or end-state.[15]

It is not possible here to examine these formulations beyond noting that they are designed in such a way as to satisfy, at least in intention, the principle of extensionality, that is, the requirement that the validity of an explanation and the truth of the premises it contains must not be contingent upon the way the latter describe the events or states of affairs to which they refer and more specifically must not be contingent upon descriptions that incorporate a reference to the end-state the occurrence of which is to be explained. When this principle is enforced, a teleological explanation will always be treated as only a special case of the more general type of explanatory argument and one that involves no violation of the requirement that the truth-values of the statements in the explanation be independent of the descriptions they use. The opposing view is that teleological explanations in fact violate this requirement but are none the worse for it. They are in fact "intensional" in character and this means that there are connections of meaning among the factual statements in such an explanation which make it impossible to maintain the kind of logical independence of one statement from another that was required by the principle of extensionality.[16] This conflict, it should be noted, is one that arises in the analysis of explanatory arguments in the natural sciences as well as in the case of psychological and historical explanations; but it is only in the latter cases that the special problems arise that are connected with beliefs and with the logical linking of events under descriptions that reflect these beliefs. For example, if one were to infer that "X will do B" from such premises as "X desires A" and "X believes that by doing B he will achieve A" and if X were then not to do B, we would tend to assume, barring other explanations, that one or another of our premises must be false. It is in such cases as these that we also note a dependence of the truth-value of a statement on the description under which an object is referred to. In the above example, even if A and C are the same object, the statement that "X believes that by doing B he will achieve C" may be false if X does not know that A and C are the same thing. Another way of making the same point is to say that X's use of one description rather than another for the goal he seeks may be of central importance in connection with a determination of what X did. This point will be of great importance in connection with the analysis of humanistic inquiry since its effect is to block a dismissal of the way a person describes what he does as a "subjective" matter that can have no bearing on the truth-value of statements about such actions.

At this point in the argument, however, there is no need to try to settle the issues between these conflicting interpretations of teleological explanation. What is proposed instead is that this contrast serve as an instrument for expressing in logical terms certain important features of the "manifest image of man." There can, I think, be hardly any question but that the logical inhibitions that are codified in the rule of extensionality are entirely unfamiliar to the commonsense ontology by which that image is informed. That is to say, there is absolutely no evidence to indicate that in our ordinary ways of talking and thinking about human beings we feel any reluctance to refer to beliefs and desires on the part of these persons as elements in the explanation of their actions or that, when we do so, the possibility that the objects to which these beliefs and desires are addressed may turn out not to exist in any way disturbs our sense that we will nevertheless have explained the conduct in question satisfactorily. It seems, in other words, to be an established feature of such commonsense explanations of human actions that it does make a difference what people believe and how they describe the objects to which their beliefs refer. At the same time, there is nothing to suggest that common sense feels itself to be forced, as a result of these procedures, in the direction of some peculiar theory of subsistent objects. On the other hand, what one does observe in human discourse generally is an extraordinary referential freedom for which the line between the present and the future and between the actual and the nonactual appears to constitute no barrier to the various complex forms of linkage among events which this discourse effects; and it is typically just these linkages of belief that we attempt to reconstitute as best we can when it is a question of our trying to understand and explain what others have done. Nor is it only beliefs and desires that have this intensional dimension which we preserve in the accounts we give of other people's actions and our own; it is present in the case of hopes and fears and wishes and a wide range of other propositional attitudes, all of which enter freely into the accounts we give of our own and of other persons' actions. Comprehensively, one may say that the rule of logical segmentation which is designed to prevent the several elements within an explanatory argument from becoming entangled with one another appears to have no standing in the eyes of common sense. As a result, the explanations common sense gives of human actions are unabashedly teleological in form and typically rely on the *logical* connection between desiring A and doing B when B is believed to be the best means to A; and there is nothing to indicate that common sense is disposed to recognize that, in principle at least, this logical nexus ought to be broken up into discrete segments which could then be brought under some other nonteleological form of association with one another.

In the course of this discussion we have been led from the concept of the human person to that of teleology and from teleology as a feature of commonsense interpretations of human conduct to a logical distinction between extensional and intensional sentences. The underlying assumption in this movement of thought is that there may be something of great importance for the purposes of this inquiry in the distinction between the kind of case in which the way in which an object or situation is described has an effect upon the truth-value of the assertion in which it figures and the case in which it does not. But before this possibility can be further explored the concept of intension to which the discussion has led must be connected with the much wider concept of intentionality and with the much more general feature of mental phenomena which the latter denotes. This feature is not to be confused with the one we have in mind when we speak of intention in the ordinary sense which has to do with the aim or purpose of some action, although intentions in this sense will also prove to be intentional in the broader sense that is to be brought out here. In this broader sense of the term, intentionality was first carefully described by Franz Brentano and it was in fact proposed by him as the distinguishing trait of mental acts as such.[17] Brentano's account of intentionality has certain peculiar and limiting features of its own which need not be discussed here; but it was later taken up and revised significantly by Edmund Husserl.[18] In Husserl's version, intentionality remains a characteristic of mental acts and, in the first instance, of acts of belief; but it is precisely the characteristic of those acts by virtue of which they refer not to themselves or to anything that would be appropriately described as "mental" or "subjective" but rather to the objects of various kinds which make up our world. It is, in other words, precisely by virtue of their intentional character that mental acts are not self-contained in a way that would make it possible to describe them exhaustively in a purely psychological vocabulary or in terms of various mental or, as Husserl called them, "immanent" contents. They must instead be described in a manner that recognizes their orientation toward a world of objects that are independent of them and public in the sense of remaining identical not only through the references that are made to them by any one consciousness but also by an open number of such conscious beings. At the same time, it must be recognized, as it was by Husserl, that an intentional act cannot constrain or otherwise affect the objects toward which it orients itself. In other words, nothing "happens" to such objects by virtue of their being the objects of an intentional act in anything like the way it does when they are drawn into the context of human actions or activity. It is, in fact, always possible that the object or state of affairs that is "intended" does not really exist. But if the intentional act does not produce its object in the way the intellectual intuition of God has sometimes been supposed to do, and does not bring about a change in these objects, it would be equally mistaken to suppose that it is in the nature of passive contemplation of an object which, in respect of both its qualitative differentiation and its categoreal architecture, would be simply given. Husserl is saying rather that the conceptual and categoreal articulation of the objects composing our world cannot be apprehended otherwise than through the carrying out of the logical operations that are in fact the "noetic" correlatives of these "objective" or—again in Husserl's terminology—"noematic" structures. The intentional act is thus the mental act taken in its dimension of objective reference and as carrying within it the conceptual design of the object to which it is addressed, an object which it constructs through the appropriate logical operations or "syntheses." As the act of a particular consciousness at a particular datable point in its life history, the intentional act is called "noesis" by Husserl; but as the bearer of the set of semantic conditions in terms of which the identity as well as the existence or nonexistence of objects of various types is to be determined, it is the noema; and the pairing of noesis and noema, of mental functioning with the delineation and acknowledgment of a *concrete* or identical "somewhat" within the flux of experience is the central thesis of Husserl's philosophy. That philosophy thereby establishes a strict correlation between the objective and the subjective, between the elements in the object-domain—the world—and the intentional activity that constructs them through the full range of judgmental syntheses proper to them.

The relationship between intentionality as an attribute of mental acts and as a logical property of sentences has been the subject of much recent controversy. One view has been that the former reduces to the latter and that the logical property of intentionality, however objectionable it may be on other grounds, is entirely neutral with respect to issues relating to the mental/physical distinction. The more widely shared view, however, and one that has been held by philosophers taking quite opposite stands on the question of mental acts, has been that intentionality is not as innocuous a property as this suggests and that it does have a special bearing upon the analysis of mental concepts. This second body of opinion then divides into those who draw the drastic conclusion that intentionality must be expunged from the language of science, in which it represents, in their eyes, a useless survival from some earlier age of belief, and those who, in a quite different spirit, press the analysis of intentional sentences in the hope of gaining positive insights for the philosophy of mind.[19] Once again, it is necessary for the present study to skirt these controversies. It must be acknowledged, however, that in espousing, for the purposes of this study, a conception of intentionality along Husserlian lines more is involved than the use of a certain instrument for the purpose of bringing out differences between a "manifest" and a "scientific" image of man. Husserl's theory is quite clearly a philosophical defense of central elements in the "manifest image" and not simply an explication of its claims; and it should be acknowledged that such is also the standpoint of this study.[20] Nevertheless, the explicative intention retains its importance in connection with the orientation of this study toward history and the humanities since its aim is not so much to demonstrate the adequacy in some ultimate philosophical sense of any one way of conceptualizing the characteristic epistemic procedures of these disciplines as it is to expose a conceptual stratum within the humanities which has too often been ignored in contemporary analytical treatments and which, when its presence is recognized, can hardly fail to set the logical issues with which such analyses deal in a radically different perspective.

There is, however, one point of difference between contemporary analytical accounts of intentionality and the Husserlian or phenomenological account on which this study draws, which is so important that something must be said about it here. This point has to do with the linguistic character of the facts to which a theory of intentionality of whatever kind must appeal. More specifically, when such a theory is developed entirely as a thesis about the logic of certain sentence types, the conclusions reached must remain dependent upon the explicit employment of such intentional verbs as "believe" and "think" or their cognates; and if a way could be found to bypass these locutions, or to reinterpret them in an extensionalist sense by some such strategy as inscriptionalism, the case for intentionality would fall to the ground. For Husserl, by contrast, the employment of these verbs is of secondary importance because the intentional act is not identified with the linguistic act and because his conception of the intentional act treats language-use itself in all its forms, from the most complete and explicit speech acts to the most private soliloquy, as being intentional in nature. From such a perspective, moreover, there can be no question of simply identifying intentional acts with speech acts or with a certain subset of such acts. The point of making the distinction between them is not to claim that they designate parallel and distinct series of events, physical and mental, that intersect only incidentally, but rather to bring out the full range of events or acts that carry a semantic function and thus to draw attention to the way that function can persist through the most drastic variations of its physical and imaginal accompaniments. In this connection, Husserl also insists upon the looseness and variability of the bond that ties semantic functioning to the physical aspects of linguistic activity and upon the fact that it is possible to substitute word images for words and more generally to abbreviate the sensuous side of language very drastically as is typically done "in uncommunicated mental life" in which "the word floats before us in imagination although in reality it has no existence."[21] In other words, the wider intentional act that subtends language-use as such has a much broader range than the localized intentionality that is peculiar to certain verbs and is in this sense, as I have said, internal to language; and it would also be, to say the least, premature to identify it with a function of the organism or of the nervous system in any sense that would imply that it can be described exhaustively by means of concepts drawn from the sciences that deal with one or another or both of these.

Against the background of these preliminary clarifications, it should now be possible to state the underlying hypothesis which will guide this study. It is the hypothesis that the language and the mode of conceptualization of its materials that are characteristic of the humanities and thus of history are pervasively intentional in nature. In other words, the humanities are typically concerned with accounts of what human beings, whether fictive or real, have done and said and believed and desired and are therefore heavily committed to the conceptual instruments by which these human acts are symbolized. To the extent that this is so, the language of the humanities is intentional inasmuch as it incorporates the language of mental acts and with it the teleological type of explanation within which beliefs and desires function in the kind of logical inter-dependence that was described above. In its weaker sense, which is the one most familiar from current discussion, this intentional character sig-nifies merely the non-truth-functional character of certain kinds of sen-tences, for example, "the Allies will land in the Pas de Calais" need not be true in order for the whole sentence in which it occurs, "Hitler believes that the Allies will land in the Pas de Calais" to be true. But the language of the humanities is intentional in a stronger sense as well which can be elicited by reflecting on the fact that, if the *truth* of "The Allies will land in the Pas de Calais" is not itself a condition of the truth of the sentence that includes it, it nevertheless plays an essential role in the determination of the latter's truth-value. This fact becomes obvious when we attempt to substitute "The Allies will land at Copenhagen" for the original sub-sentence and note that this substitution would immediately falsify the sentence about Hitler's belief. Quite generally, the truth-value of such sentences cannot be made out at all unless the meaning of the sub-sentences which express what the person in question believed or desired is established and unless means are found for evaluating the imputation of that meaning to that person. The underlying supposition here is that mental acts of various kinds are at once noetic in the sense of being episodes in the mental history of some assignable person and semantic in the sense that they refer to objects and states of affairs in the world; and it is suggested that this dual function supplies a central clue to the mode of representation of human beings that is characteristically humanistic. In a very fundamental sense, therefore, the humanities are concerned with what has sometimes been referred to in contemporary discussions as the "agent's description" or the understanding that a given person or group of persons have of what they are saying or doing or undergoing; and the analysis of just what this emphasis on the agent's description involves and of the questions to which it gives rise will be an important focus of this study.

IV

Although the full import of this hypothesis about the humanities will emerge only in the course of the discussions in succeeding chapters, it may be helpful to put the reader on his guard from the outset against a number of plausible misidentifications of the direction in which this broad introductory statement points. These misinterpretations are the more likely to suggest themselves because they are the offspring of what must certainly be regarded as one of the most influential philosophical approaches to the generic set of issues with which the humanities are held to have a dominant concern. This approach is the Cartesian interpretation of the commonsense dualism of man and world which was discussed earlier. This is an interpretation which transforms the contrast between teleologically and nonteleologically organized beings into a contrast between two radically different kinds of substance—the mental and the material—and which assigns the methods of the mathematical natural sciences to all the forms of inquiry that relate to the domain of material substances. Since that domain includes our bodies and our actions in that aspect in which they effect changes in the one common physical milieu, the effect of this dualism is to drive back into the mind or soul everything that cannot be accommodated within the geometrical architecture of the public world. Within that residue of mental states, it was commonly supposed, the objects of primary interest to the humanistic mind must be the feelings, or *passions de l'âme;* and it was there, in the recesses of an immaterial and invisible soul, that the *esprit de finesse* would search them out by its own characteristic method of analogizing divination. As an interpretation of the function of the literary artist in particular, this account has long outlived the Cartesian philosophy from which it sprang and even now it is not without its adherents. It is, however, most emphatically *not* the tradition of thought in which the present study is to be placed and in order to underscore this difference it may be helpful to anticipate the discussions of later chapters somewhat by sketching in some of the most important respects in which the further development of the root notion of intentionality will differ from a psychological theory of the humanities with its primary interest in *états d'âme.*

The main philosophical clue to this difference has already been provided in the discussion of the parallelism of the noetic and semantic aspects of the intentional act in Husserl's philosophy. It might equally well have been presented in terms of the Heideggerian concept of Being-in-the-world—terms which are just as clearly nonpsychologistic as those of Husserl but even more clearly nonidealistic in the implications they carry.[22] In both of these formulations, the crux of the antipsychologistic argument is the attack on the Cartesian interpretation of the contrast between the "inner" and the "outer." If, in our only absolutely secure apprehension of them, our mental states are grasped as states of a substance that has at best a problematic relationship to other nonmental substances—not to speak, as Descartes in fact does not, of their relationship to other (finite) mental substances—and if these mental states are then comprehensively described as being "inner" states of that uniquely known mental substance, the polar descriptive term "outer" is virtually deprived of its conditions of application. At any rate, almost nothing that we ordinarily think of ourselves as seeing or feeling or touching could qualify as "outer," for it would first have to be broken up into the mental state of thinking that one sees such and such an object, on the one hand, and on the other the highly problematical reference that such a mental state makes beyond itself. As it turns out in the course of Descartes' subsequent reasoning, only a very few of these states turn out to be successfully referential because they satisfy the demanding criteria that Descartes lays down for such reference. Only a "clear and distinct" idea in his special sense of these terms can validly claim to represent a world that is external to the soul in the very demanding sense that is fixed by the greatly expanded range of denotation assigned to its correlative term, "inner."

Quite apart from the extraordinary hazards to which the Cartesian philosophy thus exposes any form of reference to a world that would be common to many conscious beings, its interpretation of the contrast itself between the "inner" and the "outer" conspicuously fails to do justice to the way this contrast actually functions within the commonsense scheme of things. In our normal understanding of these matters, the feelings, thoughts, intentions, and desires which make up our mental life are not momentary, logically self-sufficient states that can be described in a similarly circumscribed manner. Instead they typically carry a reference to events, states of affairs, and actions which are not themselves mental or experiential in character and to which the adjective "private"—so often used to describe mental states in the Cartesian tradition—most certainly does not apply. To cite just one example, even so elementary and common an experience as that of pleasure is subjected to serious distortion if it is represented as being an occurrent quality of feeling which is momentarily present to consciousness in the way that a vagrant and unidentified twinge of discomfort may be. Normally we are pleased *that*, for example, our child passed his examination or that the doctor's report was favorable, and these facts that supply the occasion and the reason for our pleasure are in no sense internal to our mental life. They are drawn from a world that is both accessible to many consciousnesses and the unique property of no one of them; and, if that world does not qualify as external or "outer" in the Cartesian sense, that is only because it has been decided in advance, on very questionable philosophical grounds, that very little can so qualify. And to try to isolate these elements within the mental life and to examine them in their pure state will necessarily be to run the danger of obscuring the role they play in the movement of personal existence by which a "self" comes to have a "world."

The alternative mode of interpretation of the mental life has already been sketched in its essentials but a few examples may help to clarify the differences between a Cartesian, or psychological, and an intentionalistic approach to these matters. The concept of human action, for example, will be assigned a very prominent place in the discussions of later chapters; and its centrality reflects the fact that it is at once "objective" and "subjective" and carries this dual character in a way that resists analysis into components that are univocally the one or the other. An action effects a change in the natural or social environment of the agent and thus generates a new "objective" fact; but this is at the same time a change for which the agent is responsible and which bears the imprint of his beliefs and desires to the extent that he has been able to bring the various forces and tendencies inherent in his situation under the control of his own agency. Where the Cartesian approach would require us to divide the action into the mental episode of deliberation and decision that takes place in the mind and the subsequent changes that occur in the physical milieu beginning with the innervation of the muscles of the agent, the intentionalistic approach allows the action to retain its unity and to take on dynamical and physical properties without shedding the description by which it is tied to the intentions of the agent. An action is thus an event in the public world and as such subject to the constraints set by physical law and by the limits on any given agent's powers; but as an action it is also an event that takes its place within an order of purposes and intentions. These are in the first instance those of the agent himself but they will also typically be those of others as well, whether in the mode of cooperation or of conflict; and they will accordingly be either assisted or frustrated by the actions of other agents that respond to them. In its broadest meaning, "action" is simply the generic term for those changes (in some cases, the absence of a change that might otherwise have been expected also qualifies as an action) in the world which meet the complex conditions governing the use of intentional descriptions and thus manifest the efficacious presence of the self within its world. A world without actions would be one in which a conscious being might conceivably be a spectator of the events occurring within it and might have all kinds of thoughts and feelings that relate to these events but without any possibility of intervention in such processes; and a being so circumstanced could therefore have no need or use for those concepts that would express the intentional character and import of such interventions.

Similar observations may be made with respect to the status of time and of temporal order within various conceptualizations of the human person. Just as in the case of action, so in the case of time there has been a strong disposition to effect a sharp distinction between "objective" and subjective" time and to identify the former with the abstract metric time of the natural sciences.[23] "Subjective" or "experiential" time is then described primarily in terms of its personal and indeed private character, its responsiveness to our sense of what is important or significant, and its failure to acknowledge or to do justice to the invariant and independent order of public time. It is, in effect, identified with the feeling of flow or of passage itself in much the same way as pleasure has been identified with a momentary sensation; and once again the result has been to present what is characterized as "subjective" as though it lacked any stable principle of coordination with what is really going on in the public world. In this way, the impression is created that the only time that orders events in a way that can lay claim to intersubjective validity is the metric time of the sciences; and this impression in turn gives rise to the utterly false supposition that any qualitative determinations associated with time order are necessarily the work of an imagination in the service of the individual psyche and not a shared way of ordering and interpreting events themselves. It may be that this possibility—that there are ways of registering the fact of objective succession in time other than that of the scientific metric—is so often missed because the guiding account of subjective time is drawn primarily from literary sources. These are, indeed, often concerned with features of the temporal ordering of our experiences which may be idiosyncratic or in one way or another at odds with what the subjects of such experience would themselves recognize as the real sequence of events. But there is nothing that necessarily condemns a qualitatively differentiated mode of rendering temporal sequence to be capricious or arbitrary and there have in fact been many such systems which have served as the shared or communal ordering of time in societies that had not yet worked out a mature concept of metric time. Certainly, all such systems have disadvantages if absolute precision and uniformity are the prime requisites that they become in a technological society like ours; but this fact does not suffice to demote them to the status of mere features of the inner landscape. They are rather alternative ways of ordering the *same* objective succession of events that is ordered by the scientific metric; and the distinction between the one and the other system of temporal ordering is only very tendentiously described if we treat the one as purely "subjective" and the other as being just as purely "objective." As modes of temporal ordering that human beings use, both are "subjective" and, to the degree that both serve with varying degrees of adequacy to mark out distinctions within the temporal order of the world, both are "objective," although again in varying degrees and ways.

This point has very considerable importance in the context of the remarks that were made above about the intentional descriptions of human actions. These are descriptions which identify actions in terms of the intentions they express, that is, in qualitatively differentiated terms drawn from the sphere of "subjective" or mental process. When there is an interrelated sequence of such actions within which one intention responds to another as it is manifested in action and so on indefinitely, a stretch of time will be filled with what might be called an intentional process. The participants in that process may have difficulty in arriving at a common characterization of the process for reasons which will have to be carefully examined. The point to be made here is simply that there is nothing in the kinds of descriptions that are used in the account given of such a process or in the mode of *enchaînement* among its successive episodes which is prima facie inconsistent with the claim that the account of such a process registers an objective sequence in public time. It may be the case that those who construct the account of such a process in time are in fact familiar with an abstract temporal metric and thus with the notion of temporal location that prescinds from any qualitative differentiation, whether intentional or otherwise, that might supervene upon a mathematically defined point in time; but it is equally possible that they will not be. In either case, there is nothing to indicate that the mere superadding of these qualitative differentiations or their intentional provenience need be at all prejudicial to the integrity of the objective time-order. Because such accounts do not enforce, either in actual fact or in principle, the requirement of logical segmentation that was discussed earlier, questions may be raised about their character as *explanations* and more specifically as causal explanations of the events with which they deal; but even if this question had to be resolved against them, that would not by itself establish any presumption that they violate the objective time-order. The claim being made is, in other words, that the intersubjectivity of an ordering of time should not be simply identified with the use of an abstract temporal metric and that the intentional character of the descriptions used for a process of action in time is perfectly consistent with its intersubjectivity and with its observance of an objective time-order.

There is one further feature of the mental life of human beings with which, as already noted, the humanities are often supposed to have a special concern and which has suffered grievously in the whipsaw dialectic of the "objective" and the "subjective." This is the concept of value. The term itself is a recent formation and as such belongs to a rather late stage in the evolution of that dialectic; but it seems best nevertheless to follow current practice and to speak of "values" even when referring to periods in the history of thought in which the term was unknown or carried quite different implications.[24] In any case, no concept illustrates more dramatically the treacherous slippages to which the concepts of the "objective" and the "subjective" are vulnerable. Values—the goodness and badness of things and actions—have often been conceived, in hyperobjective terms, as properties securely domiciled in re and accessible to a special kind of vision or intuition. They have also been precipitately demoted from this status to that of feelings or preferences whose native habitat is the human mind from which they are then misguidedly projected upon the objects of these feelings. The pictures that are suggested by both these ways of treating the concept of value are in fact radically defective. The "objective" picture goes wrong because of its compulsive recurrence to the analogy it postulates between evaluation and perception and its resultant inability to deal with radical moral disagreement otherwise than by an imputation of defects to the intuitional apparatus of the moral dissenter. The "subjective" picture fails just as abjectly since it is unable to move beyond the dead-level equivalence which it postulates among the feelings and preferences in terms of which it defines value, toward any authoritative principle of discrimination and priority among them, especially when the claims of many persons are involved. In the case of value, then, if anywhere, the need for a form of conceptualization that avoids both of these plausible but finally unsatisfactory alternatives seems entirely persuasive; and it may be suggested that a search for an appropriate form of objectivity for values may bear at least a formal analogy to the efforts that have been made to free the concepts of action and of time from their association with equally constricting contrasts between the "objective" and the "subjective."

It will hardly come as a surprise if any such ambitious intention is now disclaimed by the author of this study. It will, however, be necessary to make extensive use of the concept of value, and some preliminary understandings as to the way it is to be used can hardly be refused simply on the grounds that an adequate general theory appropriate to this context of use is not yet available.[25] So, to approach the matter once again from the standpoint of the "manifest image of man," it may be helpful to point out just what the connections are between the teleological elements in the latter and the concept of a value that is more than just the preference, however deliberate and well considered, of an individual human being. The point to be made here is not intended as a reinstatement of the very sort of external teleology which was expressly dismissed from consideration at the beginning of this chapter. The teleology that characterizes human action is still an internal teleology, as was stipulated earlier, and as such it is one that is essentially bound up with the beliefs and desires of individual human agents and with the way these generate an ordering of events that must be understood by reference to the logical relationship between ends and means which these beliefs and desires project. But if this were the whole story, then it would always be indefensible to interpret what a given person does by reference to any goals other than those which that person himself projects; and in the face of the wide range of differences among these goals and the pervasive fact of conflict among those who pursue such disparate or at least incompatible goals, there would be no single standpoint from which these multiple teleologies could be appraised. Presumably it was precisely to block such a radically relativistic vision of the goals in terms of which the teleological dimension of human life would have to be construed that many have felt compelled to introduce conceptions of objective value-properties as well as of final causes of the philosophically objectionable type to which allusion has been made. But there is in fact an alternative to such a problematic strategy and one that takes the form of a more careful examination of the very situation that gives rise to these counsels of despair.

That situation is the one in which human beings and groups find themselves in conflict with one another by virtue of their espousal of goals that cannot be reconciled with one another. These situations are sometimes described as though they were comparable to the collision of natural forces or to the contest between human effort on the one side and some natural obstacle on the other. It is as though each party to the conflict had been so firmly and unambiguously programmed that the fact of conflict with other human beings and with *their* conception of their own interests could raise no questions other than those that relate to the most effective means of overcoming this new obstacle in the way of a realization of an unquestioned goal. Admittedly, there is a great deal of human behavior that lends support to just such a picture as this; and if it expressed the whole truth of the matter, the conflicts of human groups would be like the conflict between two animal species which nature had constituted and situated in such a way that the one must exterminate the other in order to survive. In such a case, one might conceivably speak, by a kind of analogy with the human state, of the "values" of this species and the "values" of that; but there would be no way in which one could adopt a standpoint that would meaningfully mediate between the one and the other.

What differentiates human conflict situations from those of animals is an awareness of certain similarities between them which both parties to the conflict can hardly avoid having although they may rarely or never permit it to assume much prominence. This is not a similarity of appearance or of physical constitution, but rather a similarity between the relationships of one and the other group to the goals that each seeks. In the simplest case, the goal may be the same, for example, a certain food supply, and the conflict may be due to the fact that the supply is not large enough to meet the needs of both groups. What goes deeper than the identity of goal, however, is the perception that, in resisting or attacking its competitors, the other group is acting out of beliefs and desires that the first group either shares or would share if its circumstances were the same as those of that other group; and this perception can be extended until it becomes a recognition that the action taken by the other group is the same action that the first group might take if its situation were the same or were perceived in the same terms as that of its adversary. When these distinctively human parallelisms within the conflict situation are internalized as they are presumably not by animals, they give rise to a sense of a need to discover features of the situation which would, as it were, set aside these undeniable similarities between the claims of the two parties and thus confer some special status of legitimacy on the one or the other. In all honesty, one must add that it would presumably be mostly "on the one" —that is, on one's own claim and one's own party—but even if one takes the most cynical view of the motivation for this desire to assign a special status to one's own need, the fact remains that it is an attempt at justification and justification to the other side as well as to oneself. As such, it has to assume that the same similarities that one has noted oneself will have been noted by one's adversaries as well and, however clumsy and transparently self-interested the justification may be, it has at least to appear to take these similarities into account and then to set them aside in favor of some differentiating feature. It has to do so, moreover, in a way that ideally should be as convincing and as valid for one side of the conflict as for the other. To the extent that this happens, another and even more significant parallelism between the two sides comes to be recognized and this is a parallelism in respect of the kinds of considerations that are treated as counting one way or the other in the evaluation of claims. In this way, even in the midst of conflict and in spite of strongly partisan attitudes on both sides, a kind of ideal partnership comes into being and with it the idea of a standpoint from which the claims in conflict might ideally be adjudicated.[26] Typically, this ideal partnership will not have much practical efficacy or at any rate not enough to overcome the much stronger interests which generate the conflict to begin with; and as an ideal it will also be subjected to a great deal of manipulation by those very interests, with the result that the whole notion of such an ideal may be thoroughly discredited in the eyes of many. Nevertheless, it is never entirely absorbed by the parochial interests it is made to serve—interests which, by a Hegelian irony, have thus given birth to a judgmental standpoint which they cannot wholly control and by which they will often stand condemned.

It will not, I think, strain the meaning of the term to suggest that this notion of an ideal partnership or community of communication is one in which a central place is assigned to the concept of intentionality or to the notion of what might, more specifically, be called intentional reciprocity.[27] The parallelism on which this partnership rests is one between the self and the other in their ratiocinative and judgmental capacities and thus in respect of their abilities to interpret a situation in such a way as to bring it under a rule of action that will be at least presumptively universal. Within this kind of community, we at least implicitly recognize one another as beings capable of envisaging a situation in this light and between whom, therefore, an exchange based on the presupposition that a common resolution is possible makes sense. Within the context of implied partnership of this distinctive kind and at the level of a relationship between persons who recognize the role of the other in the constitution of what is to count as "objective" in the several domains of human inquiry, the notion of values begins to take on a very different aspect from that suggested by either of the two pictures—the "objective" or the "subjective"—mentioned above; and it is this context and the analogies it suggests between the work of intersubjectivity in science and in society that will inform the treatment of values in this study. One should, however, bear in mind not only that, as already noted, the general theory of value that would give these analogies a more secure status than these brief observations can is not available and that, even if it were, it would be a mistake to fall into any way of speaking that suggests that all questions of value are therefore in principle determinately resolved, whatever limitations there may be on our knowledge of this determinate ordering of values. An ideal partnership of the kind described above certainly looks toward and assumes the possibility of such determinate value-findings; but it cannot anticipate the outcome of the actual process of communicative exchange that proceeds on this assumption. There is, therefore, a real sense in which references to such determinate consensus should appropriately be cast in the optative mood. This would not be to revert to the subjectivistic picture or to reduce the authority of evaluative judgment to that of the hope that somehow people will in fact agree. It is rather to recognize that the effective implementation of the *idea* of a shared system of norms is an "unendliche Aufgabe" in the Kantian sense and that it faces hazards even more serious than those of the uncertain commitment to the task itself of those who participate in it.[28] It is precisely to keep us from underestimating these difficulties that it seems best to avoid using the idioms of that form of moral rationalism which is perennially disposed to speak as though it were already situated at the point where an ideal partnership of inquiry becomes a real moral order.

V

It is time now that we turn back to the humanities and to history and attempt to determine in what respects the considerations that have been derived from the examination of the "manifest image of man" can contribute to the kind of philosophical undertaking in the area of history for which the case was argued at the beginning of this chapter. For these purposes, the humanities will be understood simply as the traditional disciplinary grouping of philosophy, literature, and history. Since so much of what has been said about the "manifest image of man" has been at least implicitly philosophical in character, it may seem as though among these three disciplines philosophy would be the most likely to turn out to be "humanistic" in some especially important sense. There is, certainly, good reason to believe as Professor Sellars does that for all their hostility to common sense and their often explicit contempt for the poets and for the mythopoeic imagination generally, the great speculative systems of philosophy remained dependent in important respects upon the "manifest image" and that the picture they constructed of the cosmos was one in which notions of purpose and value that were borrowed from the sphere of human personality played a central role. Then, too, the deepest impulse of these first systems of philosophy and of many of their successors was transparently ethical in character in the sense that their aim was to lead men out of the realm of illusion and to help them to live in the light of the truth. This quality of motivation has continued to mark philosophical reflection through much of its history; and it is hardly surprising if, as a result, philosophical confrontation and exchange have often had a conspicuously dramatic character. Even in the modern period when philosophy has been moving toward a narrower and more technically demanding conception of itself, a special kind of moral significance has often attached to it on the grounds that it evinces a disposition on the part of the individual to assume full and final responsibility for all his beliefs. As such a reflective and critical consciousness and as a principle of responsibility and coherence governing the conduct of life and belief, philosophy really amounts to a radical internalization of those modalities of belief and action by which we constitute our relationship to the world and to our fellow men. As such a broadened and more explicit framework of belief, philosophy can also become an important element in the moral world with which literature and history deal; and while philosophers have not often exhibited any great interest in literature and history, since the form of knowledge they represent is not ranked very high by comparison with that of the sciences, scholars in those two fields have shown a considerable interest in philosophy as providing the background of principled belief against which the character and action of individuals and societies can be understood.

If philosophy can claim a special significance within the moral world along the lines just described, it does not necessarily follow that it must concern itself directly with the concept of the human person or that, indeed, it need take much interest in man at all. In many areas of philosophy it is in fact the case that the conceptual and logical issues that engage the philosopher's attention have almost no visible connection with the kind of interest in human beings which has been characterized here as typically humanistic. Although the results that are achieved in the course of such analyses may sometimes have a wider interest and relevance to humanistic concerns, philosophers appear increasingly to think of themselves as technical specialists who have no responsibility for the exploration of such lines of thought and certainly no commitment to any particular conception of man. Even the very conspicuous interest that philosophy currently takes in language often assumes the form of an inquiry into logical features that are, to say the least, remote from the personal and communicatory aspects of language use. To some extent, philosophical ethics may be said to maintain a primary orientation toward the active decisional powers of human beings and the rational standards governing their employment; but even here the strongly formal and logical interests of the philosophical mind tend to predominate. For the most part, only minimal contact is maintained by the students of philosophical ethics with the actual record of moral experience as this is available in literature and in history; and all too often a sense of effective detachment from the real-life context of moral problems has been the result of a one-sided predilection for conceiving such problems as if they were at bottom logical puzzles. Overall, it would hardly be an exaggeration to say that at the present time the priorities of interest that were attributed to humanism have been largely reversed within philosophy; and it is therefore a genuinely open question whether philosophy can be regarded as a humanistic discipline in any sense which would imply that it has affinities with history and literature which might be substantial enough to take precedence for purposes of classification over other affinities which philosophy may have with other disciplines.

There is of course a good deal of work being done within philosophy to which the description "humanistic" quite naturally applies; but it tends to be scholarly and historical work rather than constructive or creative philosophy. It is, in other words, "humanistic" in a much weaker sense than the one elaborated here; and in this sense the humanist is simply the scholar who preserves and restores and interprets the works of others. If this contrast of levels were to govern the interpretation of what is "humanistic" and what is not, and if the "humanistic" level were to be identified with the secondary level of criticism and commentary, one immediate result would be to identify the humanistic aspect of philosophy entirely with the history of philosophy. Important as the latter may be both in itself and in its relationship to constructive philosophical thought, this would be a very unsatisfactory resolution of an admittedly difficult issue. After all, just to the extent that first-level philosophical thought has only a problematic relevance to human concerns, the humanistic character of any second-level activity based upon it will be similarly problematic. If one is disposed to argue the case for a stronger conception of the humanistic character of philosophy, as I am but cannot undertake to do here, it seems preferable to leave the matter unresolved for the time being than to accept a view that would make philosophy a humanistic subject only in the sense in which the natural sciences are, that is, as a human enterprise that is an eligible subject for the cultural historian. In this connection, it might also be noted that the currently widespread disposition to construe philosophy as a whole as a second-level or "meta" form of analysis for which the first-level datum is the conceptual articulation of language, whether natural or artificial, does not by itself seem to cast any light on the humanistic or nonhumanistic character of philosophy. Unless an interest in language is associated with some concept of the human person and with the related notions of agency and value, it will remain perfectly neutral in respect of that issue; and this is in fact another good reason for not supposing that the humanistic character of a discipline is primarily a matter of the level at which its work is done.[29]

If the outcome of this first attempt to associate a humanistic discipline with the "manifest image of man" seems to be generally negative, the case of literature proves to be very different. It seems hardly necessary to offer proof that poets and novelists have been pervasively and centrally concerned with human beings and with their actions; nor does it seem open to doubt that the interest in human matters that has found expression in literature has been strongly marked by a concern with distinctions between good and evil. Indeed, the organization of human time and interpersonal space by means of teleological and evaluative categories has been so fundamental to literature as on occasion to obscure the possibility of any contrasting ordering of the elements of our experience of the world and thus to raise a question as to whether literature has unambiguously made the transition from a mythical to a commonsense conception of personality, that is, to one that recognizes that there is a sphere—that of nature—to which these categories do not apply at all. If we interpret "literature" in this context to mean "imaginative literature" or, in the current much expanded use of that term, "fiction," then two very important features differentiate the mode of interest in human beings that is characteristic of literature from those of philosophy and of history respectively. By contrast with the case of history, the human beings who are portrayed in literature need not have any real existence in space and time; and, unlike philosophy, literature addresses itself to individual human beings, whether imaginary or real, that is, to particulars and not to universals. This is not to say that the characters of a play or a novel may not be borrowed in part or in whole from the real world nor is it to deny that literature may enable us to learn a great deal about the lives of persons who are real rather than imaginary. It is simply to point out that the test of literal historical or factual accuracy is not one that is applicable to literature. In the case of the contrast with philosophy, it would again be a mistake to read into it a denial that the characters of imaginative literature can have a universal significance and that an Oedipus or a Lear may in some sense illustrate a truth that holds for all human beings. But, however that universal significance is to be conceived, it is one which in literature is carried by human beings who are portrayed as individuals and not as abstract types or as concepts. The form that an interest in human beings takes in the case of literature is that of putting individual human beings and their actions before the reader (or the spectator) by means of a verbal representation, which typically includes their own utterances, and of following their actions and passions to a conclusion which will normally have a relationship to the norms of desirability and of moral value which are presupposed by the author and his audience.

If this account of the humanistic character of literature had been written a decade or two ago, it could have been allowed to stand without any significant qualification. At the present time, however, one can hardly avoid acknowledging the fact that literary theory and criticism—if not as yet, in any massive way, literary practice itself—are now strongly marked by formalistic interests of the same general kind that was noted above in the case of philosophy. These interests which are usually brought together under the rubric of "structuralism" appear to have originated not so much through contact with philosophy itself as in the perception that some of the forms of analysis practiced in linguistics are applicable to literary texts as well as to a wide range of other cultural phenomena.[30] As these forms of literary analysis have developed, they have appeared to reveal both how remote the "codes" within which authors work are from those features of their productions to which the attention of the reader and for that matter of the author himself is usually directed and how considerable a degree of systematic unity these codes possess. For reasons which are not altogether clear but which probably have much to do with the special conditions of intellectual life in France and with the fact that "structuralism" had been preceded by the existentialist movement with its emphasis on the freedom and choice of the individual human being and of his sovereign control over shared structures of meaning, structuralism has correspondingly devaluated the role of the person and of the person-based teleological organization of the *Lebenswelt* in favor of an analysis of the semantic and syntactical properties of systems of discourse for which the person serves as hardly more than a contingent vehicle. This orientation has found expression not only in a disposition to dismiss the traditional notions of the "author" and the "book" as being of secondary importance by comparison with the invariant properties of the discursive system which they are now to be thought of as instantiating. It has also taken the form of a repudiation of the conceptions of agency and temporal continuity on which the older historical humanism had laid such emphasis; and a rhetoric of antihumanism has developed which proclaims "man"—the *homo humanus* who is at once the denizen and the demiurge of the *Lebenswelt*—to be a conceptual artifact of the nineteenth century and scheduled for an early demise.[31] In a general way it would appear that insofar as this antihumanism is more than a corrective to the equally exaggerated theses of existentialist humanism they express a sense that human agency and purpose are so closely circumscribed by the discursive systems within which they operate that they can hardly claim the kind of interest that has traditionally been directed to them and that the priorities of inquiry must instead focus upon the various "paradigms" and *ep-*

istemes which assign to them whatever place and significance they can validly claim.[32]

This eruption of an antihumanistic interpretation of literature from within this most steadfastly humanistic member of the nuclear humanistic triad is an event of very considerable interest. It may even be the case that it is more likely to shape the attitudes toward their own disciplines of contemporary humanists than are the theses about explanation which have assumed such prominence in recent philosophical discussions of history. It is worth remarking, by the way, that the relationship between the structuralist approach to the humanistic disciplines and the positivist approach to history is by no means clear; and there is a need for closer investigations of possible affinities and disaffinities between them especially as regards the character of the regularities which they postulate as governing human fact. Accordingly some attempts will be made in the course of this study to comment on and evaluate various features of the structuralist case against the "manifest image" of man and the person-based categories of explanation it generates. For the most part, however, "literature" as it figures within the analyses of this study will be treated as the least problematic of the domains of discourse in which the "manifest image" has been deployed and as such it will be utilized as a comparison-instance for other such deployments, most notably in the case of history, about which serious questions have also been raised.

If we now proceed to ask how the criteria of humanistic interest apply to history, certain obvious differences from the case of literature immediately present themselves. Unlike literature, history accepts the constraints of fidelity to particular fact and—no less important—the scale of the events with which history deals is typically quite different from that of literature. Both of these circumstances present obstacles to the realization within the medium of history of the dramatic and moral unities of imaginative literature. And yet it is a fact that history like literature has been primarily concerned with human beings and that it has accorded the same priority of interest to human nature as involving purpose and agency especially in its more highly developed and striking manifestations. It is, of course, also true that in history agency is divided and extended over time and generations in a way that often makes it impossible to treat the unities of history as unities realized within a single life or generation. Nevertheless, when the great Greek historians made Athens the protagonist of their histories, this was not so much a misguided tendency to personification of social events (parallel to the earlier personification of natural events) as it was a perception of the transferability to actions that have no single agent, of categories derived from a mythical and dramatic presentation of events.[33] Broadly speaking, one can say that the tradition of narrative history which they founded was one that has remained in this respect very close to literature, and even the extraordinary expansion of the evidential base of history that took place in the eighteenth and nineteenth centuries did not expel from history the concept of the story or the associated apparatus of teleological and evaluative concepts.

If a broadly humanistic character of the kind of interest in human beings that has been manifested in the main historiographical tradition seems fairly clear, this is not to say that the identification of history with these interests has been uncontested or that its present affiliation with the humanities can be taken as secure. The deepest commitment of the historian must be to evidence rather than to any particular form of unity which he may think he discerns in the materials with which he deals; and just as the textual critic may never reach the themes that make the work he studies worth studying in the first place, so the scrupulous historian may become so absorbed in the unending accumulation of evidentiary materials that the construction of a coherent representation of past human events may altogether elude him. If, in the past, large-scale narrative histories of a strongly dramatic and moral character were nevertheless constructed, that may have been because the controlling insistence upon evidence had not yet been associated with skepticism about the very concept of agency and personality in history of the kind with which we are now familiar. In the past, historians tended to conceive the momentous events with which they dealt in terms of a kind of ideal account which the various agents might have given of their own actions; and although they never confined themselves entirely to such evidence as might be afforded by statements made about these events by their agents or their contemporaries, they did attach great weight to such evidence, which perhaps significantly was called "literary evidence." To the extent that they did so, they were in effect honoring the first of the humanistic priorities noted above and recognizing the importance in any effort to understand or explain human actions of attention to the agent's own ways of describing his situation and his actions. More recently, however, with the growing availability of other kinds of evidence, ranging from price-lists to carbon-dating, there has been a strong movement on the part of many historians away from the "subjectively tainted" evidence of the agent's own utterances. At the same time, and at least partly from the same motives, historians have become more skeptical about their previous predilection for great personages and great deeds and have begun to pay a great deal more attention to sectors of historical reality that are more anonymous and less susceptible to executive direction by the leading personalities of an age than the political sphere has traditionally been thought to be.[34] This weakening of the allegiance of the historians to the traditional forms in which their interest in human beings had found expression has gone hand in hand with a strongly skeptical view of the possibility of any evaluative stance on the part of the historian that would reflect more than his personal predilections, and such a view has inevitably called into question the appropriateness to the business of history of older assumptions as to the ordering function within the humanistic study of man of certain value-beliefs. In these circumstances it is hardly surprising that there should be a temptation to conceive the conceptual structure of history in a manner that abstracts from these features of human life—purpose and value—that have grown problematic and to replace them with elements which just because they are much less closely related to the ordering of experience with which human beings are intuitively familiar may lend themselves more readily to incorporation within regularities comparable to those discovered by the natural sciences. And it seems fair to assume that it is just this temptation which gives the characteristic theses of the analytical philosophy of history such plausibility as they have achieved in the eyes of practicing historians.

It seems clear that if the application of the criteria of humanistic interest deriving from the "manifest image" of man to history is not problematic in the way that the case of philosophy proved to be, it is hardly as straightforward as in the case of literature. At the same time, it is apparent that the case of history is of special importance for any theory of the humanities since it requires a determination as to how successfully the conceptual apparatus that derives from the "manifest image of man" can be applied to real human beings and real human actions as contrasted with the postulated beings of literature. If it can be established that humanistic modes of understanding are not confined to the domain of the nonreal and can in fact accommodate themselves to the obligations of fidelity to fact that characterize a discipline like history, one perennial form of challenge to the epistemic standing of the humanities will have been successfully met. These reflections in turn suggest a strategy of dropping philosophy out of the humanistic triad for the purposes of this inquiry and of concentrating attention on the other two and especially on affinities and disaffinities between imaginative literature and history as these bear on the issue between the "manifest" and the "scientific images" of man as competing interpretations of humanistic inquiry. (This undertaking itself remains, of course, a philosophical one; the change proposed is simply that it should not also be a meta-philosophical one which attempts to characterize philosophy itself in its status as one of the humanities.) The ultimate focus of such a strategy remains history and the development of an alternative mode of conceptualization that would be more adequate to its humanistic character than are most of the currently favored philosophies of history. To put the matter somewhat differently, my hypothesis is that the humanistic character of history is best expressed in terms of a set of criteria deriving from the "manifest image of man" and if, as we are also supposing, those criteria have a secure application within another area of the humanities—literature—then it seems to make sense to conclude that most of the central issues relating to history as one of the humanities can be profitably raised in connection with the transfer from literature to history of just those conceptual modes for the representation of human fact that correspond to our criteria. Such an order of proceeding would also have the advantage of permitting a more careful elaboration of the prior assumption about literature itself as the most unchallengeably humanistic member of the humanistic triad and to take note of certain objections that can be made against it. One could thus say that the presiding point of view of this study of the humanities is philosophical; that the paradigm case for the conception of the humanities it proposes is imaginative literature; and that the problematic case to which it is hoped to extend that conception is precisely history.

In the interest of assuring that the guiding conception of the humanities, understood now as comprising literature and history, be made as unambiguous as possible, it may be helpful to conclude this chapter by taking a step beyond the considerations advanced thus far and introducing a conception which will be central to the argument of subsequent chapters. This is the conception of narrative order. The special sense in which the term "narrative" is to be used will emerge gradually in the course of the analyses to follow; but it should be said at once that the claim being made is not that narrative order is peculiar to the humanities or that all discourse within the humanities is narrative in character. What is being proposed is the thesis that literature and history share a heavy commitment to the narrative mode as the following of human action through time and that the distinctive character of the narrative order they exhibit must be understood by reference to the intentional character of the process these actions compose. It is an intentional process in the sense that its nodal points are actions which are themselves individuated by the beliefs, intentions, and desires of their agents; and this is to say that it is a process within which the human persons whom the narrative presents are assigned speaking parts, whether in the mode of the *oratio recta* or *obliqua*, and in such a way that the continuity of the narrative depends upon the "agent's description" which is to be gathered from what the agent says or thinks or even feels. The hypothesis is thus that the humanities do not follow the example of the sciences in treating such descriptions in terms of some contrast between "objective" fact and "subjective" opinion or feeling but in a manner that makes the agent's description a central element in the constitution of the very fact with which the humanist is concerned and that does not require its accommodation to the requirements of logical segmentation that are enforced within the physical sciences. What is being suggested is that the humanities in their narrative ordering of human fact construe the events with which they deal in a way that incorporates these allegedly subjective elements and that the effect of this incorporation is not the subversion of the distinction between a true and a false account of these events but the proper conceptual constitution of the objects with respect to which truth is sought.

2. Literature and Intentional Process

The relationship to one another of literature and history has often been a close one, but it has also been marked by quite serious tensions.[1] The term "literature" originally embraced both history and philosophy until the claim of history to discover and declare the literal truth about the past led to a disaffiliation which is now virtually complete. Poets, after all, had long had the reputation of being liars and had shown only a weak disposition to reform themselves, so the idea that there could be any very considerable area of conceptual overlap between forms of discourse with such sharply contrasting orientations in respect of the ideal of truth seemed highly implausible and to many still does. History, of course, continued to have its own muse who, it was hoped, would inspire her devotees to cultivate some of the pleasing graces of literature, but even those historians who urged their colleagues to write well and interestingly appear to have thought of this as a matter of externals, that is, as a way of making history attractive to a wider audience, not as an affinity of any deeper kind. In spite of this old feeling that literature somehow culpably fails to do what history is at any rate sincerely trying to do, there is at present much more interest than there previously was in the exploration of affinities between history and literature that go deeper than the quality of the prose. Nevertheless, when as in the recent book by Professor Hayden White historical writing is analyzed in terms drawn from the structuralist theory of literature, the claim of history to speak the truth about the past typically seems to go by the board and all that is left is an expressive function with its own intricate internal organization.[2] Any movement of assimilation, however tentative, of history to literature or the other way around thus seems to obliterate the most distinctive features of one or the other of them.

The deeper grounds on which this sense of incompatibility rests will emerge more clearly in the course of this chapter, but it may be useful to begin by taking note of a sharply contrasting view of the relationship between poetry and history. I have in mind, of course, the classical treatment of this matter in Aristotle's *Poetics* which is the more interesting in the present context because it draws in philosophy—the third member of the humanistic triad—as the *tertium comparationis*. Poetry is more philosophical than history, Aristotle tells us, because history deals with particulars, with "what Alcibiades did or had done to him," while poetry presents us with universals, "the kinds of things a certain kind of person will say or do in accordance with necessity or probability."[3] What is most striking about this way of making the contrast between poetry and history is not so much the rank order it establishes by setting the philosophical character of poetry above that of history, but rather the deeper parallelism it postulates between the "imitations," or mimetic representations, of poetry and history. For Aristotle, poetry (*poiesis*) was, of course, a "making," both etymologically and otherwise, and as such a "fiction" although without any of the negative connotations relating to the truth-value of what is so described—connotations that have become virtually inseparable from this term. Both poetry and history, one gathers, address themselves to the same subject matter—human actions—but poetry, like philosophy, although at a much lower level of abstraction, seeks to "imitate" human life in its universal and recurring features or, as one commentator has put it, in its "typology"; and history presents us with particular facts simply as they occurred.[4] Aristotle is not, of course, saying that poetry *is* philosophy for then its concern with particular human beings, whether real or imagined, would be at best incidental and occasional. Presumably he means that *both* history and poetry deal with particulars, but that poetry, in the interest of conveying a larger truth about human life, is released from the obligation of fidelity to the detail of the lives of *actual* individuals, an obligation to which history is held. This is a contrast between the intentions governing the way in which particulars are presented and between the kinds of truth—universal and particular—they can be made to yield. There is no suggestion at all that the nonactuality of the poet's subject matter derogates from its status as a vehicle of truth, and it seems clear that for Aristotle *both* poetry and history are forms of mimesis and in their different ways put human beings and their actions before us in the interest of truth. It is in fact a great pity that, having laid the foundation of a mimetic interpretation of both poetry and history in this pioneering way, Aristotle did not go on to add a "peri historikes" to his treatment of poetry.

In the subsequent interpretation of the relationship between poetry and history the question of truth has assumed an ever increasing importance and Aristotle's calm allocation of one form of truth to poetry and of another form to history has been progressively undermined.[5] It may be that the association of poetry with the imagination contributed as much to this result as did the growing skepticism as to the reality of universals of whatever description; but in any case the contrast between history and not only poetry but imaginative literature as a whole gradually came to be made in a way that assumes a necessary conflict between them. History was thus thought of as accepting the constraints of fidelity to particular fact to which the poet was sublimely indifferent; and the discourse of the latter very naturally came to be thought of as primarily expressive in character and as an externalization of the poet's inner life rather than as a representation of what was common and recurrent in a shared human life. It is hardly surprising, in the light of these developments, that in the eyes of contemporary philosophers of history literature has figured as a comparative instance only in a negative way, that is, as what history would be reduced to if it were unable to demonstrate any convincing affinity with the methods of inquiry of the exact sciences.

The effort of this chapter will be to show that imaginative literature can contribute to our understanding of history in a far more positive way; and to this end a number of clues drawn from Aristotle's *Poetics* will be utilized. Notable among these will be the concept of mimesis itself and more particularly Aristotle's claim that action has a special importance for mimetic representations of human life; but there will be no attempt to validate the larger philosophical framework within which Aristotle's analysis is carried out or to presuppose a theory of universals of the same general type as his. Indeed, as the preceding chapter has already made clear, I will rely heavily upon a major philosophical concept—that of intentionality—which is certainly not Aristotelian in origin. My central concern will be to characterize the kind of world that a work of imaginative literature constructs in terms of what I will call its conceptual organization and to do so with special attention to the role of human persons and their actions within that world. Although this characterization of the world of fiction will have a very wide range of application within literature as a whole, it is not required for the thesis to be established that it apply equally well to all forms of imaginative literature. If there are indeed literary modes that are truly nonmimetic in character, then these will obviously be less likely to have much relevance to the case of history.[6] On the other hand, both the narrative and the dramatic modes exhibit the characteristic forms of a mimesis of human action in a high degree and will accordingly figure prominently in this account. In an obvious way, narrative fiction comes closest to reproducing the characteristic form of a history since in both there is an explicit contrast between the voice of the narrator or historian and the speeches and actions that are attributed to the characters. But the dramatic mode can also be used, as it was by Aristotle, to illustrate features of the mimesis of action in an even more perspicuous way; and the concept of drama in a somewhat broader sense that does not turn on the ostensible absence of the author will be central to my account.

I

There is wide agreement that imaginative literature in all its traditional forms has a dominating concern with human beings. There are, of course, plenty of superhuman beings in literature and human beings with more than human powers; and there are also many nonhuman beings like the animals that are so prominent in folktales and in children's fiction. Still, whether animal or divine, in the respects that are most important for the fictions in which they appear, these beings bear a very strong resemblance to human beings as we know them from our own experience, and it seems plausible to view them as interesting variations on the familiar attributes of human personality or as projections, whether naive or sophisticated, of human powers and concerns into situations in which, in actual fact, they are not and perhaps could not be found. There are, as far as I know, no fictions that take as their subject matter inanimate objects that have not been somehow personified or humanized; nor are there any which treat of genuinely abstract entities, although there are ways of personifying abstractions. At the very least, one can say that poets and novelists and dramatists have been concerned with beings endowed in some degree with intelligence and with a capacity for action as well as with the power of expressing their beliefs and purposes so as to make them known to some fellow being who is, if not actual, then at least possible and imaginable.

This fact about imaginative literature is so fundamental that it serves as a premise, often unexpressed, for most theories of literature; but not very much in the way of interesting implications has been thought to follow from it. It specifies the subject matter to which imaginative literature addresses itself, but it has typically not been seen as imposing any particular conceptual form upon the mode of representation of that subject matter. By contrast, there has been widespread recognition of the special freedom that imaginative literature enjoys in its treatment of both human and natural fact. This freedom, which has often been confused with the irresponsibility and indifference to truth of the liar, permits the author of a fiction to assume, as has often been remarked, some of the prerogatives of a creator-god. He can give the characters he brings into being whatever mental and physical powers he chooses and he can even force nature—the nature of his fictional world—to play a cooperative part in the tale he has to tell. Within this world of his own devising he is as omniscient as he chooses to be; and since he provides his characters with whatever experiences befall them as well as with the thoughts these experiences may stimulate, neither could be in principle opaque or inaccessible to him. Of course, he might for special reasons choose to limit the knowledge he possesses in his capacity as author to what might have been gathered from the perspective of one of his characters, but even this very limitation becomes an element in the fiction he is constructing and as such it is subject to his control. More generally, the author can place his characters in a world and in a temporal process with a particular moral and teleological organization; and he thus, in effect, sets the ultimate dimension of meaningfulness that thereby accrues to the actions and the lives of his protagonists. In practice, of course, neither the moral organization of a fiction nor the governing conceptions of the characters in it are arbitrary creations, if only because the author addresses himself to an audience with which he shares many fundamental beliefs and which would not understand what he is doing if there were not broad areas of overlap between the real and the fictional worlds. Nevertheless, the "world" of a fiction can never simply be identified with the public world of everyday experience, and the difference between the two is the measure of the creative shaping power of the author.

There have been many characterizations by authors of the process in which the events and characters of a fiction emerge; and in some of these one encounters denials that the author is in fact as absolutely in control of his world as the foregoing account implies. Thus, a writer may insist that he suddenly *discovered* that one of his characters had been drinking and that he was in some sense forced by this discovery to give the story another direction than he had intended.[7] As accounts of the psychological dimension of literary creation, these objections may be allowed to stand; but they do not really affect the deeper point that was implicit in the conception of what the author's freedom involves. That point is that this kind of "discovery" is utterly different from the ones we make in other contexts of life such as science or history if only because they can be made only by the author himself and then ratified by his considered decision. There is no independent source from which someone else could obtain evidence showing that, for example, so-and-so had been drinking and thus compel the author to take this "fact" into account. One cannot in any normal way challenge the author of a novel to show *how* he knows that something that occurs in his fiction did occur in that way; and when this kind of question cannot be asked, a whole epistemic dimension that is present whenever there can in principle be more than one inquirer is necessarily absent. It may very well be the case that feelings like the one mentioned above of being compelled to recognize a certain fact about a fictional character may carry over from the one kind of case to the other, but the fact remains that such transfers do not and cannot carry along with them the epistemic machinery that would be required to complete the analogy.[8]

It suggests itself that these distinctions can be made in a way that avoids confusion with descriptive accounts of the author's experience of composing a fiction by drawing attention to the intentional character of the activity that is involved in both the writing and the reading of, say, a novel. In the sense that is relevant here and that derives of course from the earlier account of this concept, "intentional" signifies the fact that a novel will contain a great many terms that refer to individual human persons, to places, societies, material objects, and so on, and will do so in a way that may be absolutely indistinguishable from the references to such objects that occur in nonfictional accounts that are accepted as veridical.[9] Works of fiction deploy, in other words, the whole logical apparatus by means of which we construct, in words, a kind of map of the internal structure and the external relationships of the objects that collectively compose our "world"; but the world they constitute is one which lacks the dimension of actuality or of real existence. It is therefore a *purely* intentional world in the sense that it must be understood solely in terms of what is projected by the descriptive and referential language the author has used without any thought of a possible distinction between the object that is intended and this same object *as* it is intended. To approach a literary work in this purely intentional dimension is thus nothing very arcane; it is simply to concern oneself with the characters and situations and events to which the work refers in a way that recognizes at least implicitly the limitations governing the referential status of these objects. The classical case of a failure to observe these limitations and thus to grasp the purely intentional character of the character and events internal to a fiction occurs when we ask questions about the latter to which the work can supply no answer because the questions concern aspects of the lives of these characters that are left indeterminate by the intentional acts that constitute them. How many children, for example, did Lady Macbeth have?

It is not the purpose of this essay to go further into the question of the ontological status of works of fiction or of the personages and events they contain. It does need to be made clear, however, that in saying that their status is a purely intentional one I am not claiming that they are objects of some special kind but rather that certain expectations that are normally legitimized by the use of referential language are inapplicable to them. "Hamlet" is, of course, a proper name, and in sixteenth-century Denmark and in Shakespeare's play it was used to refer to one and only one individual human being. But in the play this reference does not work in the way it did in the real Denmark. Even in circumstances of actual performance, the person to whom it is applied is a person who is only notionally Hamlet, that is, the actor who takes the part of Hamlet and utters the speeches that Hamlet makes. It would not make sense to ask whether such a person who is Hamlet only by a special kind of stipulation is really Hamlet or not; and where this question cannot be sensibly raised, the normal distinction between the object as it is intended and the object that is intended cannot obtain. Where sense has been disconnected from reference in this way but referring expressions continue to be used, one might try to characterize the resulting situation by saying that these references are merely simulated or quasi references; and by this one would convey that reference has become the fiction of reference and that as such it is subsumed, together with what would normally be called the sense of the referring expression, within the work of fiction under a larger sense in which the ideality of reference and the ideality of descriptive meaning are joined with one another.[10] In other words, the references that the characters in a narrative fiction, for example, make to one another as well as the narrator's act of reference to them have a fictional character and are to be understood in an ideal or notional way rather than as a real occasion of reference. Dickens' authorship of *The Pickwick Papers* is, of course, in no way fictional; but the narrator whose voice we hear speaking in that novel is fictional or ideal in nature. When the purely intentional character of the work is understood, the reader grasps the fact that it would make no more sense to look for the narrator in the real world than it would to look there for the characters of the tale and that the referential utterances of the narrator have themselves no location in real time.

If the intentional character of the work of fiction and the predominant orientation toward persons of literature generally can be taken as established, then it can be shown that taken together they point to another feature of imaginative literature that is of very great importance. This is the presence within the fictional world of the novel or the drama of a mode of intentional functioning that is derivative and yet at the same time distinct from that of the author. The author constitutes the world of his fiction from a position which is external to that world; and he exercises an absolute control over everything he chooses to include within that world. But since he is primarily interested in human persons rather than in natural objects, he must find a place for them within the fictional setting he has contrived; and in doing so he introduces beings who will stand in an intentional relationship to the various component parts of that fictional world and also, most significantly, to one another.[11] The characters in a play or a novel will thus know with varying degrees of accuracy and completeness what is going on around them. They will know by and large what they themselves have done and said and also, though more imperfectly, what their fellow characters have done and said. They will usually know where they are and what would be required in the way of natural and contrived instrumentalities in order to act in a certain way. They will have hopes and fears and plans that relate to their futures and these expectations and intentions will stand in more or less well-defined relationships to the knowledge or beliefs they have about their own situations and about the past actions and intentions of the other persons with whom they are involved. In other words, each of the characters has his own intentional field within which the events of the story figure under the descriptions that express the character of his interest in them. These intentional fields of the several characters necessarily overlap to a very considerable extent, and the descriptions used for any given event by different characters must be sufficiently similar so that an identity of reference can be grasped by these same characters who, if this were not the case, would be living in effectively separate worlds. Finally, these fields must themselves be understood in temporal and dynamic terms since they change significantly as a result of changes in the states of affairs they encompass and also, in a quite different sense, as a result of a reappraisal of his beliefs by the character who holds them.

There are important differences between the kind of intentional function that is attributable to the author of a fiction and the kind that is attributable to the human beings who are internal to his fiction. One such difference is that it is possible to speak of the beliefs of a character about features of the world into which he has been inserted and this is possible precisely because one can contrast such beliefs with the true state of affairs in that fictional world. It is not possible to speak of an author's beliefs about his own fictional world since there is no way in which the possibility of his being mistaken about his own creation can be explained. If authors have occasionally spoken in a way that suggests that they could be so mistaken, it is surely because they were placing themselves and perhaps their readers as well within their own fictional world and then expressing uncertainty about some aspect thereof in much the same way as one of the characters internal to the fiction might do. For these characters the world in which they are situated has been preconstituted by the author as a deus absconditus; and it is indeed tempting to think of the author's relationship to his work on the analogy of the intellectual intuition which Kant attributed to God and which produces its own objects with which it is therefore in a state of perfect correspondence, error being possible only when the object somehow transcends the intuition which is addressed to it. The characters in a fiction may indeed apprehend some object in their world under one description rather than another and it will be important to know what that description is in order to understand what they do. But the intentional activity of the author is quite different in nature and cannot be represented as being in the nature of a use of one description rather than another since it is itself the stipulation of the set of descriptions from which such a choice would have to be made.

It has often been argued in the course of the past century that an author cannot incorporate even this reduced kind of intentional activity on the part of his characters into his fictional world without thereby calling into question his own sovereign control of the world of his fiction. Why, it is asked, should not the other conscious and intelligent beings who are involved in a fiction have the same rights as the author in the constitution of what the objective truth of their world is to be? Some novelists have attempted to meet these objections halfway by identifying the author with one of the characters of the story or at any rate limiting his knowledge to what that character might have been in a position to know; and other still more radical departures from the univocal authorial control over what is to count as reality within the fiction have been attempted. Some attention will be given to these experiments later in this chapter and it will be argued that in some form or other authorial control over what is to count as real and what not cannot be abandoned. In any case the implications I propose to draw from the presence within the world of a fiction of the secondary forms of intentional functioning are not limited to those forms of fiction which are self-consciously trying to come to terms with this duality, but apply equally well to the more traditional author-controlled fictions as well. It is these implications that now need to be stated.

In broad terms, the claim I wish to make is that the world that a work of imaginative literature brings into being is in the first instance a system of persons standing in intentional as well as natural relationships to one another and acting in ways that are significant not just for the author and his reader, who stand outside the fiction, but in a prior sense, which is presumably also a necessary condition for the external kind of significance, for their fellow characters as well. Another way of making much the same point would be to say that imaginative literature not only takes human or humanlike persons as its primary foci of interest within the world it constructs, but also that it so takes them primarily in the intentional aspects of their being. What this means and does not mean can be explained as follows. There are many processes that are going on in and around human beings at any given time from which imaginative literature abstracts almost entirely or which it takes into account only when there is some special reason deriving from other sources for so doing. It is normally understood, for example, that the characters of a fiction are breathing and digesting their food, that their blood is circulating and a fairly stable body temperature is being maintained and that, if this were not the case, they would not be alive and would not be eligible to serve as characters in a fiction.[12] These processes are not normally classified as actions since among other reasons they go on for the most part without the awareness of the person in question; and they are not intentional in character since they do not in any way depend upon the beliefs or intentions of such persons and a fortiori not upon the descriptions in which these would be formulated. At the level of behavioral rather than of physiological process, it is similarly understood, in the case of fiction just as in real life, that in order to perform certain actions nerves must activate muscle fibers, and limbs must be moved in certain ways, but descriptions framed in terms of these processes are also nonactional in character and abstract from *what* the agent is trying to do, for example, start his car. They are accordingly uncommon in imaginative literature in the absence of some special reason; and in their place a decided priority is given to descriptions that relate whatever physical process is occurring to the intentions and the beliefs of the agent. Literature, in other words, simply treats actions as actions and this means in their intentional aspect without bothering very much about a great many concomitant processes which may be necessary conditions for the initiation and successful completion of such actions.

This intentional character of the descriptions of persons and their actions in literature has an important bearing on the status accorded to the statements that are made by the characters in a fiction. Broadly speaking, it is through their utterances that the beliefs and intentions that supply the context within which a physical movement becomes an action are communicated, both to other characters within the fiction and to the external audience. By utterance here is meant both statements that are made to some other human being, whether reported by means of a quotation or in indirect discourse, and "statements" that a character addresses privately to himself. A drama is, for example, a sequence of such statements with only rather sketchy attempts to portray the nonverbal actions that occur in it. The intent of such speeches within a fiction is, of course, not always to convey the beliefs and intentions of the speaker as accurately as possible; and it is sometimes to deceive others with regard to just those matters. There are also difficult questions here concerning cases in which the true beliefs and intentions of an agent seem to be only imperfectly known to him or where his capacity for stating them is somehow limited; attention will be given to these later. The point to be made here, however, is that it is assumed as a matter of course in a novel or a drama that there is a connection between what a person says and what he does and that the indications of intention and belief that we gather from that person's discourse have an important bearing, however intricate and however indirect, upon our understanding of what he does.

There are two elements that need to be underscored in this characterization of the intentional character of the events portrayed in imaginative literature. One of these is the active nature of the beings portrayed; and the other is simply the fact that there is typically more than one such person and that each person is in some significant form of contact with the others. There are, to be sure, fictions in which, as we say, nothing happens and others in which there is only a single character; but it could be shown, I think, that even in these cases the idea of action or of some more significant form of action than is possible in the circumstances *is* an ingredient in the situation of the persons portrayed. Similarly, although a person may be entirely alone, he will, if he is human at all, have had some experience of living with other people or expectation of doing so again; and in that event his actions and thoughts will hardly be solipsistic in character. These two features of human personality are in fact closely related to one another, both in fiction and in real life. The sequence of events that a fiction portrays need not be one that is initiated by a human action—a death for example is not an action—but, if not, it is an event that creates the need for action and poses alternative possibilities of action. Typically, also, what is done will be such as to make a difference to some other person, and that person as an active being will be in a position to take some action in response to or in anticipation of the first agent's action. In this way, the system of persons within a fiction enters into a form of movement which that much controverted term "dialectic" perfectly describes. It is a movement which is at every step dependent upon a multitude of supporting natural processes inside and outside the protagonists and it is also the case that natural events—nonactions—may intervene in this process in highly significant ways. But the significance these natural events have for the fiction is one that they owe to the purposes and intentions of the characters and to the point in the sequences of action at which they occur; and it is in terms of that intentional sequence of actions and responses that the primary narrative movement of the fiction takes place.

Philosophers who are concerned with the analysis of causation sometimes make a distinction between the contributing causes of an event and its decisive cause.[13] In the case of a forest fire, the contributing causes would be the more or less stable background conditions such as the dryness of the vegetation, and the decisive cause is typically a supervening event, such as the tossing of a match from a passing car, which taken together with the background conditions completes a set of sufficient conditions for the occurrence of a forest fire. The decisive cause is usually thought of as one that is more or less abnormal relative to some background of expectations; and it is also very often a feature of the situation which is subject to some form of human control as in the case of the match that starts the forest fire. Whether or not this last feature always characterizes what we call the cause of an event or not is a matter over which philosophers have disagreed; but it is clear that the abnormal event itself need not always be a human action. The interests that lie behind such fixing on one kind of event or another as the decisive cause are various and there is virtually no limit to what they may treat as the abnormal feature and thus as the decisive cause of the event under consideration. At the same time, it is possible to imagine an interest that is defined in terms of the selective attention it pays to human actions as such and which treats everything else as, in effect, a background or contributing cause of the events for which human actions are regarded as the decisive causes. Such an interest, it may be suggested, is precisely the one that is characteristic of the way the novelist and the dramatist proceed; and, if such a priority of interest is legitimate in the scientific case, where it is of course defined in quite different terms, there seems to be no reason why it should not be equally so in the case of literature. In the case of literature, there is, of course, this further difference that human actions form the line of continuity through a series of events which are related to one another much more intimately than are forest fires. One action in this series is the response to the situation that has been created by the prior action and so on; and one of its motivating grounds is the knowledge that that prior action has occurred. The interest of the novelist is in following that sequence of actions in such a way as to show not only the consequences, both intended and actual, of each successive action but also the motivation which each supplies for those actions that follow it.

It seems proper to refer to such a series of events as an intentional sequence since the principle of linkage within it is intentional. Each element in the series is an action which is motivated by certain beliefs and intentions and which can be understood only if the terms in which these beliefs and intentions are formulated are understood. And among these motivating beliefs are some which refer to prior actions which have been performed by others and which introduce new elements into the action-field and oblige the agent either to take further steps to realize his goals or to modify those goals themselves. In this intentional sense, the events of a fiction are cumulative, not only for the reader who remembers the sequence of events and how each is predicated on what has gone before, but also for the characters of the fiction themselves who are progressively internalizing—with some lacunae, of course, and with varying degrees of accuracy—the widening dramatic context. From both the internal and external standpoints, the continuity of the developing story may be said to be teleological in the sense that at each stage what is done is done out of construals of the various elements in the situation and especially prior actions, in the light of certain intentions and goals. As the reader moves through the play or novel, what he wants to know at each stage is *why* the characters acted or spoke as they did and how their so doing modified the situation for their fellow-characters who are of course themselves understood in terms of their interests and beliefs and their capabilities for action. In its most abstract logical form the progress of a narrative sequence is thus a chain of practical syllogisms in which the conclusion of each prior syllogism, as modified by whatever failures of execution the agent may not have been able to avoid, provides one of the premises for its successor.[14]

It is a distinctive feature of the theory being presented here that it posits a deep connection between the structure of human consciousness and the narrative order that is characteristic of literature. It is therefore quite natural that the schema of the mimesis of human action which has been described should generate implications for the way in which the organization of time and of selfhood will be conceived within the fictional narrative. With respect to the first of these—time—it will be helpful to bring into the discussion the well-known views of Professor Frank Kermode which present very clearly and against an entirely different background of presuppositions the general expectations relating to the organization of time which we bring to fictions of various kinds.[15] Stories and fictions generally, he tells us, have beginnings and ends and thus involve a certain organization of the flow of time and more specifically the introduction of a kind of continuity and unity by which the separateness of discrete moments in metric time is overcome. It is unfortunately not altogether clear just how Kermode conceives this unity; and some of his examples suggest that it partakes of a magical quality as, for example, in those cases in which one event in and of itself announces or prefigures another event that is subsequent to it in the time order. Such forward syntheses of time always present a problem since they require that an event assume, when it occurs, a description involving a reference to a future event; and, as Professor Arthur Danto has pointed out, such descriptions are properly conferred only from a historical standpoint, that is, from a point in time subsequent to both the event that prefigures and the event that is pre-figured.[16] Nevertheless, it can be safely assumed that the unity Kermode has in mind is a unity of meaning, both in the sense in which meaning implies "fulfillment" so that the passage of time is no longer just "one damn thing after another" and in the sense which underlies the latter and which might be called the logical sense. This is the sense in which one event can fulfill or fail to fulfill another only if it bears a description which it could not bear if another prior event had not borne a certain other description to which the description of the later event is logically related. A unity within the flow of time in Kermode's sense thus appears to involve a conceptual relationship between two successive events; and if as noted such a relationship would present problems if it were to run from the prior event to the later one it is a perfectly familiar matter when it is the description of the later event which presupposes the description of the prior one.

Because he does not make a connection between narrative order and the structures of human consciousness that are familiar to us in everyday life, Kermode lacks an important motive for distinguishing between for-ward and backward syntheses in time and between those syntheses which are at least partially imputable to the characters of the fiction and those which are imputable solely to the author. Instead, all of these are lumped together and it therefore is hardly surprising if Kermode feels compelled to treat the unities of time generated within fictions as being fictional in some sense that is stronger than the one which applies by definition to the events of the story itself. Although such unities provide the necessary structural framework for fictions, their ontological status seems some-how problematic to Kermode by comparison with the discreteness of metric time, the time of science. This conception of meaningful unities within time as being fictional in some special sense reflects the influence of certain contemporary doubts as to whether events in the real world and in the lives of real persons ever truly lend themselves to this conceptually cumulative ordering of their descriptions. These doubts, which received a classic formulation in Sartre's *La Nausée*, revive in highly sophisticated form the old view of the poet or novelist as a liar, although now the basis for the charge is not the subjective irresponsibility of the poet himself but the circumstance that events themselves never compose a story in the required sense. Kermode does not, however, entirely accept these views and he suggests a defense of fiction that is based on pragmatic considerations. He argues that the postulating of fictional unities of time is our human way of sweeping the sea away from our doorstep and of maintaining such order within the human world as there is, and furthermore that such fictions become objectionable only when we lose our sense of their fictional character and by thus losing control over them permit them to become myths.

What is wrong with Kermode's otherwise valuable treatment of these matters is, in the first instance, the disproportionate prestige which he assigns to metric time and his corresponding failure to give any attention to the characteristic ordering of human time except in the context of the construction of fictions and other symbolic representations of human life. This is unfortunate since the context of human purpose and action is one that combines temporal prospect and retrospect in a way we are all familiar with and without any sense of a fiction being involved. For example, it is a part of our understanding of ourselves and indeed of the kind of selfhood we normally claim for ourselves that references to past and future events and actions will have a place in the intentions we presently formulate to ourselves. Because such and such an event took place I must now undertake to do so-and-so. When that task is done or finally fails of accomplishment, an episode in my life will be complete which can be identified only by reference to the related ways in which these two events—beginning and end—as well as other intervening events are conceptualized or described, and this means within a particular context of human concern. The presupposition of such temporal unity is that the self that looks back is the same self as the one that looked forward in time, and that the intention that was formulated at the outset is the intention that finds fulfillment or failure in the later events. The "binding" of time through forward and backward syntheses and the conceptually cumulative descriptions by which these syntheses are effected thus proceeds pari passu with the formation of a stable and continuous—though certainly not unchanging—self. It is, in other words, not just the "magic" unity of time implicit in prefiguration but the protostory character of quite ordinary human lives that resists reduction to the metric and logically extensional ordering of time, and if everything that cannot be accommodated to that ordering is to be treated as in some radical sense fictional then a good deal more will have to fall under this interdict than Kermode seems to have contemplated; and it is at the very least not clear whether for many of these ways of describing ourselves and our lives there will be any plausible replacements. It remains to be seen, of course, how the internal continuity of a human life or of many such lives figures within the special unity of a literary fiction and how in particular it finds a place within the temporal perspective of the author as the creator of such a fiction. More attention will also have to be given to the case that is made by those to whom the assumptions about selfhood and its role in the ordering of the human world, both fictional and real, are unacceptable and who propose another mode of fictional creation that repudiates these assumptions and the traditional fictional modes based on them. Nevertheless, it does seem clear that the categorization of all non-metric unities of time as per se fictional has not been adequately justified by Kermode and that these unities are crucially implicated in the kind of selfhood we impute to ourselves and others in a completely literal manner.

II

Before pursuing any of these matters further, it will be useful to develop a little more extensively some of the implications that flow from what has already been said about selfhood and the logical conditions governing its portrayal in fiction. The argument up to this point has been designed to establish that the account given of human affairs in a novel or a drama owes essential elements of its internal organization to the way in which our experience of the world is ordered for purposes of action. It should be emphasized once again that this ordering is not something subjective, if by that is meant a private or inner state, and that the organization of the self that is in question is as much the form of our commerce with things in the world as it is of inwardness and feeling. Nevertheless, it may seem that the account that is proposed of the referential and intentional dimensions of selfhood has come down too hard on the rational aspects of human agency and, as a result, has missed some of the characteristic weaknesses and vulnerabilities of human nature on which so much imaginative literature dwells. Specifically, it may be asked how a schema based ultimately on the practical syllogism can accommodate the facts of human ignorance and irrationality without violating the kind of continuity and coherence which it imputes to human action over time; and the status of unconscious motives and beliefs may also be queried since these seem hard to reconcile with the emphasis placed on the role of a character's utterances as casting light on the beliefs that inform his actions.

It is true that a certain minimum of rationality on the part of the human agents portrayed is a presupposition of narrative order as I have characterized it; but this requisite degree of rationality is not such as to exclude the possibility of error. The information on which our actions are based is often either limited or inaccurate or both; and we are therefore constitutionally exposed to the danger of acting in ways that will in actual fact bring about results quite different from those we had expected. This fact in no way negates the kind of cumulativeness and continuity running through a sequence of actions that has figured so prominently in the account that has been given; and it is indeed only because there is such a continuity that certain consequences of our actions can be experienced as "unintended." To take the most famous case of unintended consequences in literature, it is clear that Oedipus's discovery that he has married his mother and murdered his father is one that could be made only by a being whose experience of himself satisfies certain elementary criteria of trans-temporal coherence. These criteria require that a person be able to acknowledge a past action as his own and to characterize it by reference to his beliefs and intentions in performing it as well as to the range of expected outcomes with which it was associated. Quite obviously, while the beliefs and intentions one has in performing an action constitute its meaning within one's life and project a certain future course of life for the individual in question, they cannot control the true identities of the things and persons upon which that action has a bearing. When these are re-vealed, and a contrast opens up between what one thought one was doing and what one really did, the continuity of one's life stands exposed as merely notional; and there may be a temptation to regard it as an illusory appearance. The *real* meaning of one's life would then be seen as some-thing imposed on it from without; and later events might even be read back into the original action as its true, though hidden, intent. The other possibility of interpretation, however, is the one that Oedipus himself seems to adopt in *Oedipus at Colonus* and it is that of saying that the notional character of the action performed is the one that is decisive for purposes of an understanding of and judgment on the agent.[17] In either case, the tragic significance of the revelation depends upon the fact that the action had and continued to have a meaning for its agent that was then belied by the actual state of the world. To put it somewhat differently, the effort by virtue of which life takes on a measure of the cumulative and teleological order that has been described cannot by itself insure the truth of the material premises as to the nature of the world on which it depends, and it therefore is permanently exposed to the danger that the world will not bear it out and that by failing to do so it will call into question the coherence of that life itself.

The case of irrationality is quite different from that of tragic ignorance; but up to a certain point it creates no special difficulty for the representa-tion of human beings in literature or otherwise. An action may be irra-tional when it rests on beliefs which are not only false but also should have been seen to be false by the person in question. There are, in other words, certain available criteria for the appraisal of our beliefs and when we fail to make proper use of these and when we are unwilling or unable to abandon a belief that stands condemned by these criteria, our behavior is in some degree irrational. In this sense, almost everyone is somewhat irrational and the beliefs on which we act are such as may appear quite unreasonable to an observer. Nevertheless, this limited and localized kind of irrationality need not create any special problems, and it is perfectly possible to construe a person's actions in terms of beliefs which were reached and held in a way that is less than fully rational. It is, in fact, common for comedies to revolve around personalities that are irrational in the sense of stubbornly clinging to some delusive belief; and even in a more extreme case like Don Quixote's it is still possible for the novelist to say what the Don is doing, because his delusions are fairly stable and he is able to fit real persons and places into them in a way that one can follow. What is very different from this kind of irrationality that still permits a large measure of overlap and even a rough correspondence with the normal understanding of the world would be the case in which the integrity of the self is called into question by the character of the beliefs ostensibly entertained. If what a person says he believes is so wildly at variance with the shared or public understanding of the true state of affairs that it is no longer possible to establish even rough correspondences between the one description and the other, there will be no way in which any action based on these beliefs can have the same significance for others that it has for the agent and no way in which their response can have for that person the meaning intended by him. It is hard to see how one could speak of a dialectic between persons under these very abnormal conditions when the differences of belief are such that it is impossible for the one to accept anything like the other's description of what he is doing, and the other way around as well.[18] Under these circumstances it becomes impossible to integrate the person with these radically deviant beliefs into the intersubjective world of agency in which there are plenty of disagreements and conflicts of intention but also a body of shared beliefs that set limits to what a person could possibly be said to be doing. Once those limits are violated, the person in question remains an agent and a participant in transactions with others only in a very qualified sense; for purposes of most of the relationships between persons that subtend the events of a novel or drama, he has simply gone off the map. The requirement of rationality is thus one that is bound up with intersubjectivity; and it is evident that when a fiction places its characters in the world in such a way as to set up an intentional relationship to at least certain of the elements of that world, it must also assure at least a minimum of common reference with other characters that are placed in the "same" world.

Finally in regard to unconscious motivation and the possibility of its being accommodated within a representational scheme that lays such stress on the connection between motivation and some form of utterance on the part of the person in question, there is an initial difficulty as to how the concept of the unconscious itself is to be understood. If one were to think of the unconscious as though it were a kind of sealed-off compartment within the mind to which the "I" does not have access and in which all the thoughts and motives that the "I" cannot consciously entertain are somehow domiciled, then the intractable difficulties of Cartesian dualism would be compounded and it would be quite impossible to introduce such an entity into a scheme based on the notion of an intentional mode of being in the world. This is not because the conscious life of belief and intention must be wholly transparent to itself, as has often been argued, but rather because the notion of the unconscious as a black box within the mind is very ill-adapted to correct what is wrong in the picture of a mind with perfect and total access to itself. Its way of discounting the agent's understanding of his own desires and intentions is simply to set up a crude contrast between appearance and reality and to segregate his real from his specious motives within a compartmentalized model of mind. It is impossible to exaggerate the antidramatic character of such a schematization of the mind's functions which withdraws the unconscious wholly from any position in which it might assume a speaking part and also from any participation in the cumulative and teleologically organized dialectic of persons. Even though it is true that the strategies of the unconscious are themselves purposive in character, they are, in this conceptualization, so static and so isolated from the interplay of action and counteraction that the only dramatic vis-à-vis one could imagine for them would be the therapist himself.

There is, however, another and more promising way of interpreting the notion of the unconscious which does not push it out of the world in which human beings act and respond to one another's actions.[19] This interpretation turns on a distinction between having an intention and the objectification of that intention through explicit description; and the suggestion is that instead of treating the conscious and the unconscious as discontinuous and discrete sectors of the mind, we treat the level of explicit verbalization as constituting the kind of "consciousness" which can be profitably contrasted with the unconscious understood as that which has not yet reached this level. The problem has always been to understand how a person could have beliefs and motives and intentions without knowing it, as the conception of the unconscious requires; and the intentional conception of consciousness in its semantic and object-constituting function in fact intensifies this difficulty. It does so because it represents our experiences as carrying propositional import which only the self could have formulated and which must therefore be in principle available to it for purposes of self-description. What the alternative account of the unconscious does is to open up a gap not between experience as such and propositional import but between experience-cum-propositional-import and the explicit acknowledgment of that import. It does so, moreover, in a way that leaves the "unconscious" experience within the sphere in which it is in principle accessible to the kind of description such acknowledgment involves so that the possibility of a convergence between the two is not excluded. Suppose for example that Person X has what we would call an unconscious dislike or hatred for Person Y. The "black-box" theory of the unconscious would suggest that in such a case the true feelings of Person X lie on one side of a sort of opaque screen within his mind and that the possibility of access to those feelings is thus in principle denied to him. The alternative would be to claim that these feelings form a part of the conscious life of Person X in just the way other feelings and beliefs do, but that for special reasons they are not acknowledged by their owner *as* feelings of hostility. This is not because their character as feelings of hostility is somehow mysteriously hidden from the person whose feelings they are, but rather because a description of them as such would come into conflict with other beliefs he has about himself and perhaps about the person in question. One might compare such a conflict to those that occur between observation statements and some body of scientific theory and that are resolved in favor of the latter by a correction of the former in the interest of consistency with the requirements of the theory. When the superior authority of the theory is well established—in this case when we are firmly committed to the belief that we like the person in question—the potentially conflicting episode in our mental lives will probably pass very nearly unnoticed since the "correction" will take place in a more or less automatic way. This sort of editing of our mental texts is extremely common; and it must be distinguished from deliberate misdescription of our motives and feelings on the one hand and on the other from the kind of case in which the divergence between some element in our mental lives and the description it receives takes on pathological aspects.

The bearing of these remarks on the account that has been given of the rendering of human action in imaginative literature can now be stated. We rarely if ever speak of unconscious actions; instead it is the reasons or motives for action which are often said to be unconscious and the difficulty has been to understand how this could be so. But the difficulty is removed if we abandon the assumption from which it stems, that is, the assumption that the unconscious lies outside the intentional life of the agent or is segregated from that life in such a way as to be inaccessible to him. It is perfectly possible for the agent to have intentions and beliefs which he does not acknowledge either publicly to others or privately to himself; and it is equally possible for these intentions and beliefs to find expression in action which is then either not attended to at all or systematically misdescribed by the agent in terms of intentions and beliefs which he *is* willing to acknowledge both publicly and privately and which, as rationalizations of actions, are extensionally equivalent to the unacknowledged beliefs and intentions or approximately so. The difference between such a case and the case of hypocrisy is that in the latter private acknowledgment of the real reasons occurs while in the case in which we are inclined to introduce the notion of the unconscious it does not. It does not take place because the agent reinterprets the prima facie character of his attitudes in the light of other beliefs which he is willing to acknowledge to himself and to others. But this very fact indicates that the agent is not totally without access to his "real" beliefs and intentions for otherwise there would be no conflict and no sense in which one could properly speak of a (sincere) reconstrual of the character of those beliefs. What differentiates conscious beliefs and intentions from "unconscious" ones might therefore be better characterized not as the presence or absence of "consciousness" as such but rather as acknowledgment at the level of explicit self-description addressed either to others or to oneself. The unconscious is consequently not external to the intentional life of the self but one term in a conflict between levels of intention within it. Such "unconscious" intentions are imputable to individual human beings in much the same way as others are, but their specifically unconscious character has to be signalized by noting how these intentions are interpreted whenever the need for explicit self-description arises.

As long as the "unconscious" element in our lives remains accessible to redescription in the light of a corrected higher-level belief, there is clearly no obstacle in the way of a treatment of such matters within the framework of the intentionalistic scheme presented above. This is so in good part because the effect of such corrigibility and the flexibility it implies is to give an at least potential social dimension to the situation created by the fact of these unacknowledged feelings or intentions. That social dimension is typically realized when a conflict emerges between a description which is offered by an agent for his own action and the description which other persons who observe his conduct find plausible. The first description may be sincere in the sense that it is not motivated by any desire to deceive but it may nevertheless simply not tally with the description by the external observer who may for example be describing the action in a way that connects it with a broader range of consequences than the agent acknowledges or that sets it in a pattern of conduct on the part of the agent which again the latter may hardly be prepared to recognize. In such a case, a movement toward self-understanding and an acknowledgment of the true character of what one has done may take place, and such sequences have provided literature with some of its most characteristic themes. In a literary treatment of these themes, it is typically the circumstances of life itself and the personal resources of the agent that induce this evolution rather than the special environment of the therapeutic situation and the intervention of specialists, who otherwise have no relationship to the person they seek to help. In some of its most interesting and powerful forms, this evolution originates not so much in a misdescription or denial of some feature of one's feelings or intentions with which one has failed to come to terms but in a description that faithfully mirrors the deficiencies of the intention itself—the sketchiness and vagueness of its formulation, especially in those aspects that concern the implications

and consequences for others of what one does. In such a case, what is at
issue is not an epistemological puzzle, that is, how a person could misdescribe his own intentions to himself, and the movement that takes place
is an evolution pari passu of one's descriptions of one's intentions and of
these intentions themselves as a result of a modified perception of the
situation in which one acts. On the other hand, when the agent's description of what he has done or intended not only deviates significantly from
that of others around him and does so in a way that proves not to be
amenable to resolution in any of the normal ways, the relationship in
which such a person can stand to his fellow human beings must be seriously affected. In such circumstances, the person whose account of his
own actions appears both sincere and incomprehensible to sympathetic
observers may slip into a special category—that of the patient—both in
real life and in a fictional representation. In that capacity he of course
remains a member of the human community; but his eligibility for social
and moral relationships will be drastically impaired as long as there is no
possibility of a movement toward a real reciprocity of understanding between him and his fellow men. And it is this fact that constitutes the
obstacle in the way of an intentional process in which such persons would
have a full and equal part.

III

An account has now been given of fiction as the construction of a system of
persons and the following of the intentional process which they generate.[20]
A distinction has thus been made between the constitutive function of the
external, authorial intentionality and the derivative intentionality of the
persons which the latter places within the fictional world it constitutes; and
the relationship between the one and the other has been implicitly designated as the locus of the distinctive kind of interest to which fictions as a
genus can lay claim. And yet up to this point the character of that interest itself has been only very vaguely formulated; and it is time that an effort be
made to get beyond the use of such rather unhelpful terms as "following"
for purposes of describing the sort of undertaking that fiction represents on
the part of a consciousness which stands outside the events it constitutes.
Where, one might ask, is it appropriate for such "following" to begin and
end, assuming that it is not simply a blind and compulsive spinning out of
fictional events that might in principle go on indefinitely? It seems plausible to assume that if one could identify something like natural units within
such a process one would have found a clue to the motivating interest of
both the author/creator and the reader/consumer of such fictions who
communicate with one another (or, at least, the author with the reader)
from opposite sides of the stipulated world of the fiction and, so to speak,
over the heads of the characters the latter contains. There has been a wide

variety of hypotheses seeking to characterize that interest; and in this section I propose to concentrate on those that in one way or another conceive it, as Aristotle did, as having an important cognitive aspect and as connected with the desire for knowledge and the quest for truth.

Under the guiding assumptions which were adopted at the beginning of this chapter, it might seem that the question of truth could hardly be raised since to do so would be equivalent to reintroducing the very condition—that of conformity to particular historical fact—from which fiction was released by its definition. As the example of Aristotle himself shows, however, it is possible to conceive the truth of a work of art otherwise than in terms of this kind of fidelity to particular fact; and as the history of critical theory shows, there have been several other influential conceptions of what such truth might consist in. One of these would, for example, largely abandon the notion of mimesis in favor of that of expression and equate the truth of a work of art with the sincerity with which it reflects the inner state of its author. In such a theory, the contrasts on which the correspondence theory of truth relies are neatly reversed; and it is the image of the external world which the author of a fiction constructs that is to be judged by its fidelity to his inner state rather than the other way around. But not only does a conception of this kind generate its own intractable problems; it also amounts to a decisive and negative prejudgment on the parallelism between literature and history which was one of the chief attractions of the Aristotelian position. For this as well as for other reasons it seems more advisable to eschew this alternative and to persist in trying to adapt the Aristotelian line of thought to the requirements and the philosophical assumptions of this study.

What this means in practice is that the truth of a work of fiction should be tentatively conceived as a matter of a fictional state of affairs sharing a universal with a state of affairs that is actual or has been or may be. Everything of course must depend on how this universal is conceived; and it is at once clear that if the relationship of a particular to a universal is to have any bearing on truth the universal itself must have a propositional character, that is, it must not be simply an ideal term of thought such as "man" or "justice" but something more like "man is a rational animal" or "all men are mortal." It also seems clear that the universals Aristotle has in mind when he speaks of poetry are propositional in this sense and that as such they express truths of broad scope, although in the strict logical sense their scope need not be universal. To say that poetry imitates universals would accordingly not be to deny that poetry has anything to do with particulars—a point that has already been made—but rather to assert that the particulars of poetry, precisely because they are invented particulars and designed for this purpose, can exemplify a general truth more perspicuously and more adequately than does a particular state of affairs which is not invented but actual. On this interpretation, Aristotle would not be denying that the particulars of history also exemplify universals or indeed the same universals as poetry; but he would instead be pointing out that because any real individual instantiates so many attributes and properties, most of which will be "accidental" in character, and because the historian has an obligation to reproduce the actual course of events whether it was the result of the essential or accidental properties of his subject matter, the particulars that are imitated in a historical account will illustrate any given "universal" only in a very imperfect way. In other words, the Aristotelian conception would make the difference between poetry and history depend on the relationship of the one imitation and the other to a universal which is common to the materials with which each deals but which for the reasons stated can emerge far more clearly in the kind of particular that is expressly tailored to it than it can in "natural" particulars. It may be worth noting, by the way, that there seems to be no suggestion in Aristotle's account of these matters that it is through the invented particular of poetry that one first comes to apprehend the relevant universal. A characteristic "move" of certain modern philosophies of art that aspire to rehabilitate the cognitive status of art and thus of fiction has been to present art as an anticipation of the future progress of scientific inquiry; but this is something quite different from Aristotle's way of turning the flank of the Platonic attack on poetry by showing that it exemplifies (though it need not "discover") universals and thus has an important rational element within it.[21]

The question that faces anyone who wishes to develop this Aristotelian line of thought is to determine what, if any, elements of universality there are in the various kinds of fiction and how such poetic universals resemble, and how they differ from, universals that may be discoverable in other areas of thought such as, for example, natural science. Such an investigation must immediately confront a contrast that is both obvious and important between the standpoints from which it may be undertaken. That standpoint may, on the one hand, be literary in the sense that it takes literature itself as its primary datum and, drawing simply on the experience of wide and intelligent reading, seeks to bring literary works as well as the various parts and aspects of such works under a number of classificatory headings. It may very well not be easy to say just what this restriction to literature itself as a primary datum does and does not entail; but it is at least clear that, when this standpoint is adopted, one does not approach the analysis of literary works from the side of the empirical sciences of man—the sciences which like psychology and sociology and economics study human behavior directly and not in the medium of the symbolizing function itself. Instead, the effort is to see first what recurrent forms or structures that function may deploy in the fictional representation of human beings and human affairs and then to raise the further question of what further application such universals may have to human nature outside literature. The other possible standpoint does not exactly reverse this procedure and simply move from the empirical sciences of man and the universals the latter may have discovered to human nature as revealed in literature as a further instantiation of these extraliterary universals. As was pointed out earlier, it may be conceded that priority of insight often belongs to literature and that it is only later that proper scientific recognition and formulation of the universal in question takes place. In a broad sense, however, one can say that such a reversal is implicit in this conception of the universals that are to be sought in literature since the ultimate standard by which they are to be judged is that of their suitability for incorporation into the accumulating body of empirical knowledge in the sciences of man, most particularly psychology. The character of the logical constraints which the use of this standard would extend to narrative sequences has already been noted in passing and will be taken up again in this section. For the moment, however, it suffices to draw attention to the fact that the effect of the assumptions implicit in this second standpoint is to treat literature as a kind of anticipatory and intuitive apprehension through a nonactual instance of the same truths which the sciences of man will eventually recognize and integrate, through a properly rigorous mode of statement, into the corpus of exact and authenticated knowledge.

It is unfortunate that recent philosophical reflection on history and historical narrative in particular has proceeded in virtually complete abstraction from, and apparent ignorance of, the very considerable amount of work relating to literature that has been done under the auspices of the first of these standpoints.[22] As far as one can tell, most philosophers seem to be satisfied to assume that the only purely literary universals are the traditional distinctions of genre together with the equally traditional rhetorical tropes that used to be listed at the back of English textbooks. As a result, philosophical analysis of such matters as narrative structure has not had the benefit of contact with the substantial body of thought which has been developing within literary theory over the past several decades and which in this country takes its rise from the remarkably original and indeed seminal work of Kenneth Burke.[23] One should also mention here, although without any implication of a chain of influence, the more recent taxonomical enterprise of Northrop Frye and the work that is currently being done by scholars of both literature and linguistics on the structure of narrative.[24] Although it is not possible to summarize briefly the purport of all these diverse lines of inquiry, one cannot help being struck by the degree to which they converge on a common conception of the significant *units* in terms of which works of imaginative literature are to be analyzed. These units are uniformly ''actional'' in character in the sense that they either designate types of action which a human agent may undertake or situations that result from such actions or the ''passions'' that are the backlash of action for the agent and for others as well; and there are, of course, other possibilities here. It may be that this "actional" character emerges most clearly in the "dramatistic schema" elaborated by Burke with its "pentad" of categories—Agent, Act, Agency (means or instrument), Scene (the natural and social setting of the act), and Purpose—and the affinities between that schema and the conception of intentional process that has been developed here should be equally plain. But the concept of "symbolic action" as Burke uses it seems to be systematically ambiguous since it can refer to either the actions of fictional persons or the constitutive functions of the author; and it appears that for Burke it is not important that these quite different uses of the concept should be kept reasonably distinct from one another. And although it is clear from his discussions of different "ratios" between the terms of the dramatistic schema that the latter are designed to stand in certain determinate modes of association with one another by reference to which, as recurrent conceptual patterns, individual literary works could then be classified "dramatistically," Burke has not himself, to my knowledge, constructed a stable taxonomic system along these lines. For these reasons, the example I will use of a theory of intraliterary universals will not be that of Burke but the more recent and explicitly taxonomic theory of Northrop Frye.

That theory is a theory of what Frye calls "generic plot-structures"; and it is to this notion as a unit of analysis that my interest is primarily directed rather than to its further deployments within Frye's own system. It can be usefully understood as a kind of amplification of the first efforts we make to pick out "types" within works of literature that may be candidates for instantiation in real life. These are typically character types to which the literary exemplification gives its name, perhaps because it was instrumental in a recognition of the type—a name which we then apply to real persons. Odysseus is thus the man of worldly experience and guile; Hamlet, the man who hesitates and doubts; Julien Sorel, the young man on the make; and so on. But just as in the sciences the only concept-universals which can command interest in the long run are the ones that lend themselves to the formulation of a law-universal, so in literature there is a parallel danger that by abstracting a character from the fictional situation in which we find him and treating a Quixote or an Antigone as a context-independent type which we can freely instantiate in the most varied circumstances of nonfictional life, we will be entering on a sterile line of classification and also, in the bargain, flattening out and trivializing these characters themselves. A sensitivity to this danger may then suggest to us, as it presumably has to Frye, that the more significant unit within a fiction is not this or that individual character, taken as a kind of fixed and absolute essence, but the situation in which these persons find themselves vis-à-vis other human beings and in which their characters are expressed through the actions they perform. From this point of view, what is important is the transaction in which several persons are involved, even though interest may focus on one of them, rather than any one person taken separately and outside the context of this situation and his association with just these other characters. To the degree that we can compare such comprehensive transactions with one another as complex movements of action over time we can speak of generic plot-structures or story types. Here is a second type of universal which may be said to be instantiated by a fiction; and critical theory is replete with terms of classification for these plot structures. There is, however, no single agreed upon system of classification; and there is also a good deal of resistance to the idea that such a systematization can be achieved otherwise than at the expense of just those features of particular works which may be their most distinctive and valuable ones. But whether we think of such a system of plot structures as somehow ideally complete and of the author as making a selection from the repertory of types so offered to him or whether we think of this system as itself in the process of evolution so that a new work might constitute a revision or expansion of the canon, there seems little point in denying that such plot structures exist and that an understanding of them, however implicit and however inarticulate, plays a role in both the creation and the appreciation of literary works. The interesting question, at least from the point of view of the present study, is simply what kind of universals such plot structures are and also, of course, what their range of application beyond these fictions themselves may be.

In Frye's theory, generic plot-structures form a cycle which begins in and returns to myth; and the forms through which the cycle passes— comedy, romance, tragedy, and irony/satire—are described as so many displacements of myth into a human setting. To some degree, this cycle maps not just the ideal possibilities of plot structure and their logical connections with one another, but also the evolution of Western literature which in its current ironic mode rejoins myth although this time in its "demonic" rather than its "apocalyptic" mode. The world of myth in both these forms represents the imagination in its purest and freest mode of functioning which is then successively accommodated in varying degrees to the more familiar circumstances of life as we know it. In its "apocalyptic" form, myth "presents the categories of reality in the forms of human desire as indicated by the forms they assume under the work of human civilization";[25] and in its demonic version it is "the presentation of the world that desire totally rejects . . . the world as it is before the human imagination begins to work on it and before any image of human desire has been solidly established."[26] Within the framework of this fundamental distinction the different plot structures represent different kinds of possible movement. Comedy is the upward movement by which the isolation of an individual from his society is overcome and a new society comes into being. Tragedy is the downward movement, "the wheel of fortune falling from innocence toward hamartia and from hamartia to catastrophe."[27] There is also the movement of the quest which is characteristically that of romance; and there is the movement of "experience" which is the internalization of and accommodation to those aspects of the actual world which cannot be idealized and in fact may have an affinity to the demonic. Taken together, Frye tells us, these mythoi form a single quest myth of which the four major phases are the agon or conflict (romance), the pathos or suffering (tragedy), the sparagmos or "confusion and anarchy" (irony/satire), and the anagnorisis or recognition (comedy) and thus form a kind of total life-cycle of man.

Now if one attempts to distill from this very rich and in some respects idiosyncratic systematization of fictional forms a set of logical conditions which must be met by an author if he is to have composed a work which will be assignable to any one of the categories proposed, certain things are reasonably clear. The movements within the human world which the writer of a tragedy or a comedy has to follow are movements on an axis that is defined by the comprehensive conceptions of good and evil, of the desirable and its opposite, that are its termini; and it is clear that these conceptions and the organization of the fictional world they impose must be espoused by the writer in his capacity as the creator of that world. In other words, in addition to the constitutive functions which have already been discussed and which embrace the characters of the fiction, their actions, their beliefs and intentions, as well as their social and natural milieu, there is another dimension of organization which has to be introduced into the fictional world and which can best be described as its moral dimension. Just as the author in his constitutive and intentional function is the source of the standard of objectivity by reference to which it becomes possible for some of the beliefs of the characters within the fiction to be mistaken beliefs and for others to be true beliefs, so the standard by reference to which the movements of those characters take on the descriptions that place them on the axis of moral organization within the fiction is a standard that is imputable to the author as creator of that fiction. The point here is that this standard cannot be one that is simply carried or constituted within the consciousness of the fictional characters themselves as just another one of the beliefs that they hold and that may or may not be true. It must have a status which is independent of such beliefs in the sense that will permit a moral description to apply to a character or his actions even though he does not believe that it does and might even repudiate the system of values from which it derives. Within the world of the fiction, in other words, there is a distinction between the subjective and the objective, the appearance and the reality, the belief and the true state of affairs; and this distinction is one that obtains both with respect to ordinary matters of fact and to the moral attributes that accrue to agents within the fiction by virtue of their actions. The authority of this distinction, it should be noted, is a public one and it is equal for all the inhabitants of the fictional world and also for the author and his reader insofar as they may be said to be invoked as idealized spectators of the events within that world. This is not to say that no contestation of moral ideals or of the norm of the desirable can take place within a fictional world, but simply that, if the fictional transaction is to be classifiable under any of the generic plot-structures that Frye distinguishes, there must be some residual principle of moral ordering that is not contested. If that were not the case and if the issue were really to be left quite unresolved, the direction of action within the fiction would be left indeterminate and the work itself profoundly ambiguous.

The way in which the constitutive role of the author has been discussed should not encourage the misapprehension that he must himself be the creator or originator of the principle of moral organization of his fiction. Such a requirement forms no part of the case that has just been made; and in actual fact the author will typically make use of a system of evaluative distinctions which he has inherited and which he can assume to be shared by his audience. Considerations of this kind have recently led many students of literature to deprecate the importance of the author and his works in favor of the shared myth or "code" or classificatory system which he uses or, as some would prefer to put it, which uses him. But whatever merit such a view may have, and however anonymous the author may be conceived to be in his "creative" functions, this will make no difference to the distinction on which my argument here depends. That is a distinction between elements within the fictional world which are attributable directly and without mediation, to the consciousness, whether individual or collective, which constitutes that world, and those elements which are attributable to that consciousness only by virtue of the fact that the fiction it has constituted contains other consciousnesses whose beliefs and intentions are susceptible of being at variance with the norm laid down by the authorial consciousness. The distinction does not, therefore, imply any special view of the degree of originality or creativity which the author as an individual exhibits.

What kind of universals then are the generic plot-structures under which individual works are subsumed? It seems clear that they are concepts of patterns of movement involving two or more persons whose positions change both in their relationship to one another and in their relationship to the implicit norm of the desirable governing the world within which these movements take place. As Frye interprets comedy and tragedy, for example, they typically involve images of the social world as a whole and of the conflicts by which that world is divided; and the central characters represent certain substantial human interests and attitudes which are in conflict with one another. In the case of comedy, that society is initially under the control of attitudes which are in one way or another repressive and negative in character and the conflict is one between that dominant organization of human relationships and someone representing a valid human interest that is denied within the existing dispensation. The movement is a movement toward an overthrow of that order of society and the formation of what Frye calls a new society whose norms are taken from the previously suppressed interest and which effects a comprehensive reconciliation of the members of the society with one another under new and positive auspices. In this case, as in the others, the conflict between persons is not just a conflict between particular interests which the author follows, perhaps out of motives of curiosity but without any effort to place these interests in some relationship to a controlling norm. Instead, the internal space of the fiction is organized in such a way that it is possible to plot at least in a rough way the positions and the movements of the protagonists along a normative axis; and it is on the descriptions which these movements assume by virtue of their location in such a space that our understanding of what happens in a comedy or a tragedy or a satire or a romance is to rest. These generic plot-structures are thus repeatable action-patterns plotted along coordinates that are normative in character; and it follows that these patterns can be identified and understood only by a spectator or reader who can share and perhaps find analogues in his own experience for the kinds of evaluative distinctions that are constitutive of the moral world of the fiction.

One very important feature of Frye's discussion of these generic plot-structures is the place he assigns to discovery or recognition—a generalization of the Aristotelian notion of anagnorisis beyond tragedy to other plot forms. The point here seems to be that the guiding norm of a fiction cannot remain entirely external to the consciousness of the persons within the fiction in such a way that the applicability to someone within the fiction of a certain normative description could in principle be apparent to the author and the spectator, standing as they do outside the fiction, but not necessarily be accessible to the person so described. Such a dichotomy would mean that the action could be one thing and the understanding of that action in what I have called normative terms quite another so that, while the former might be the business of the persons within the fiction, the latter might be confined to those who stand outside it. That is just not the way most fictions work. As readers, we expect that the movement of the action will be a movement of understanding of that action in its normative dimension by the agents themselves or at least the most centrally important among them. A comedy in which hypocrisy is not exposed for what it is to anyone except the spectator would be a very strange comedy indeed; and a tragedy in which the tragic hero seems to develop no sense of the significance of what he has done and how his situation contrasts with any other more desirable alternative would be even stranger. It suggests itself that our rejection of such incongruities points to a characteristic feature of the action-patterns laid down in the generic plot-structures of fiction. It has been argued that these are patterns of movement between positions that are to be understood in normative terms, but the further suggestion would be that these actions would not themselves be complete if the participants were not to achieve some insight into the significance of the events that have taken place and of the place to which these events have brought them. For those who stand outside the fiction—the author and the reader—the events of the fiction form an intelligible episode and a moral whole because a movement has taken place to which a certain normative significance attaches; but one wonders whether this sense of completeness would not be subverted if, within the fiction, events simply streamed onward without anything in the way of a retrospect or recapitulation that expresses a recognition and internalization of the wholeness of the episode which ex hypothesi has taken place. When there is such a recognition, the governing norm of the fiction and the consciousness of the protagonist are brought into harmony with one another, at least in some degree, and one might even go a step further and suggest that it is only to the extent that a person within the fiction gives signs of understanding that he has reached a certain, normatively specified position that the dramatic movement is complete. If so, then the requirement of recognition is not really a second requirement added to the prior one having to do with the description of movement in normative terms but rather a stipulation of certain internal conditions defining the kind of movement or action that is in question. It should, of course, be emphasized that such a harmony is not necessarily that of compliance with the norm but of an understanding in terms of the norm of what one has done or of where one is as the result of some action. If that were to be completely absent, one would inevitably wonder whether the norm itself is really applicable to a being who apparently cannot internalize it; if that were the case we might feel that the use of the norm as the standpoint for the construction of a story involving such a being would be as inappropriate as it would be in the case of the lives of the lower animals. The point again is not that the capacity for internalization validates the norm itself but rather its application to a particular case or range of cases. Recognition in its various forms may be regarded as the signal given from within the fiction by some one of its characters that he can and does think in the terms that make our understanding of what has happened in analogously normative terms appropriate.

It should be evident from what has been said that the subsumption of fictional events exhibiting an intentional process under a generic plot-structure does not in any way violate but rather reinforces just this intentional character of the fiction. When a moral quality accrues to the action of a fictional personage, one should not think of this change on the analogy of some natural process such as gaining weight or being hit by a càr but in ideal or, as they might be called, judgmental terms. The world of the fiction has been constituted in such a way as to incorporate a rule to the effect that conduct of a certain kind bears a certain moral quality; and this means at the very least that this conduct is subject not only to the (possibly erroneous) moral judgments of the other persons in the fiction but also to a further judgment that is not relativized to the particular situation or range of knowledge of any of these persons and that is not subject to contestation otherwise than by stepping completely outside this fictional world. The proximate responsibility for that rule of judgment is, as has been said, the author's, but only in his capacity as the creator of this fiction and not necessarily in his personal life; and it matters little whether he appeals to some further authority such as God as the ultimate and infallible judge of such matters or beyond such a personal God to a metaphysic of objective value-properties. Whether or not he takes any of these further steps, he will in any case have set up a level of evaluative descriptions for the events which occur in his fictional world and by so doing he will have placed these events within a further dimension of constitutive intentionality. This form of intentionality is external to the fiction in the sense that it cannot be contested or challenged from within the fiction and so does not enter into the intentional process of the fiction itself. But operating as it does in its uniquely privileged way, from the boundary of the fictional world, it marks out distinctions within the world of the fiction which are as authoritative and as "objective" for persons within the latter as are its stipulations of milieu, natural fact, and so on, although with this difference that the evaluative distinctions apply in the first instance to activities on the part of agents within the fiction which are themselves intentional in character. In a proper sense, however, there cannot be a dialectic between the internal and the external intentionalities since even when the characters turn on the author it is only his surrogate within the fiction that is vulnerable to their attacks; the author who constitutes both these attacks and the characters who make them remains eternally out of reach. The only true dialectic into which the author as the constitutive source of the organization of the fictional world can enter is the dialectic with his reader or audience whose position in relation to the world of the fiction is, as was pointed out, analogous to his.

What then may we be said to learn from imaginative literature? Not certainly that this form of conduct is morally right or that that one is wrong, since the imparting of such a form of knowledge would require that the rational considerations by reference to which such judgments are validated be exhibited in literature itself in the form of argument; and I am assuming that this is simply not the case. This does not mean that a work of literature may not supply the occasion on which one becomes familiar with, say, a wider standard of evaluative appraisal than one had previously known and finds it persuasive to the point of accepting it. That can and does happen; but the point still holds that literature does not concern itself directly with the aspects of such beliefs that would have to be brought into the foreground if one's interest were in validating these beliefs as knowledge-claims. In this sense moral and evaluative principles may be said to be logically prior to the works of the imagination which they order. But this very priority of the moral and evaluative presuppositions of a work of literature helps us to understand the kind of knowledge which *can* be the fruit of the experience of the work itself. What such a work shows us is the sort of thing that *can* happen in the world of human agency; and it shows it to us as qualified by the moral and evaluative attributes it takes on in a world governed by these (prior) norms of the desirable and the good. It may be that what *can* happen almost always does as, for example, when two suitably characterized young people are attracted to one another; or it may happen very rarely. Even in the latter case, however, the knowledge that such a thing or one like it in the respects that make it significant to us *can* happen may be of even greater importance than the predictable recurrence of a less significant type of event. The universality that characterizes even such infrequent events will derive from the fact that they represent permanent possibilities within the life-situation which all of us share. In the supreme examples of the kind of understanding that imaginative literature can realize, that life-situation is portrayed in such a way that the aspirations and illusions and conflicts that move the action forward are of so universally human a character that every individual human life can see itself as reflected in them. But even in such cases the universality achieved is not so much one of fact deriving from some insight into what "always" happens. Instead, such universality is owed to the fact that all of us as active and social and moral beings must move within a common practical field, with its characteristic hazards and opportunities, for which works of the moral imagination supply the best and very nearly the only maps we have. This is a practical field that is ordered by the coordinates of an ideal set of values but is at the same time traversed by lives in which illusion and self-will count for at least as much as such understanding of the partnership in which these lives stand to one another; and knowledge of the world as such a practical field is the kind of knowledge that a work of imaginative literature can impart.[28]

The conclusions reached in the course of the preceding discussion can hardly fail to have quite extensive implications for the consideration of the second standpoint from which one can approach all of these issues relating to the kind of understanding and knowledge for which imaginative literature can serve as an instrument. If the internal articulation of literary works has to be understood in terms of action-patterns in the sense elucidated above and if these action-patterns in turn involve a norm of desirability in relation to which the movements of the protagonists are plotted and to an acceptance of which the author and—putatively—his reader are committed, then it becomes, to say the least, problematic whether works designed to serve the purposes of this kind of action- and norm-related understanding would also fit the paradigm of scientific knowledge. It is not as though there were some a priori impossibility that would preclude a single verbal structure from serving such disparate purposes; but it does seem unlikely that a work whose conceptual organization has to be understood in the language of what Northrop Frye calls the "myth of concern" and as such expresses an existential continuity between those who stand outside the fiction and those whose lives are internal to it, would exhibit so considerable a degree of preestablished harmony with a quite different set of logical requirements as to authorize its being taken as a potential source of scientific knowledge. And yet that is the supposition that is implicit in the thesis which has been advanced by Professor Hans Meyerhoff and Professor Monroe Beardsley—a thesis which amounts to an application of the nomological-deductive model of explanation to human conduct as represented in imaginative literature.[29]

The crucial assertion on which any such thesis turns, whether in its application to literature or to history, is the claim that we cannot avoid a reference to causal (or statistical) laws in the account we give of the explanations offered in the domain of discourse under investigation. In the account that has been given here, there has been nothing to suggest that such a requirement is honored in the explanations that are given of the actions that take place within the fictional worlds of literature. To explain an action imputed to a character within a fiction is typically to situate it within an intentional sequence by reference to the beliefs and preferences, circumstances and capabilities of that person and above all by reference to what has happened or what that person believes to have happened up to that point in the developing sequence of action. Quite obviously, these agents are understood to be situated in a natural milieu, and it would normally be understood also that that milieu is the locus of multiple causal regularities which must be taken into account by agents who are concerned to realize some purpose. As far as I can see, however, the creation of fictional agents and fictional actions does not commit the author or anyone else to the claim that the actions of such agents are or are not themselves instances of comparable (though doubtless unknown) regularities.[30] The point is rather that this whole issue is simply irrelevant to the interests that find expression in the fictional representation of human actions, and the author of such a fiction would, in that capacity, have no business taking a stand on them. It is, moreover, precisely this independence of the business of fiction from all such theoretical concerns that makes the claims of the nomological-deductive theory so problematic for that domain. It is, after all, an almost universally agreed upon result of the long consideration of these matters by philosophers of science that not every description that can be veridically applied to an event lends itself to the formulation of a causal law. To take an extreme example, if the Second World War were referred to as "the event announced in the *Times* of London on September 3, 1939" we would not expect that this description would serve the purposes of subsumption of the Second World War under a causal or statistical law at all well. The scientist's work is in good part the setting aside of precisely such superficial and unhelpful descriptions of the events with which he is concerned; and since he is dealing with *actual* objects and events which are assumed to be fully determinate he will have an inexhaustible field of alternative descriptions in which to seek replacements for those that prove unpromising for his theoretical purposes. But here a second and even more important difference between the search for laws governing actual events and for those governing fictional events must be recognized. Not only are such fictions constructed in a language which is much too close to that of everyday life to be at all likely to serve as a suitable vehicle for scientific knowledge; it is also the case that fictional events are ex hypothesi indeterminate in a whole host of respects which may not have been of any interest to the author. It simply will not be possible, therefore, to move about within a fictional world looking for the potentially law-instantiating attributes of the occupants of that world as the scientist does in the real world because the exhaustive determinacy of the object-domain which such a search presupposes does not obtain. The only way in which one could do this would be by freely integrating the fictional world with the "real" world and by then postulating a syndrome relationship between the attributes which the author *does* in fact assign to his characters and the law-instantiating attributes with which in the real world such persons would be endowed. Such a postulation cannot, however, conceal what is really happening here and that is simply that the work itself is being left behind so as to make it possible to rebuild the characters it contains on the more commodious and—from the standpoint of scientific theory—more hospitable terrain of the real world.

The effect of these observations should be to make the enterprise associated with this second standpoint look rather different from the way it did at the outset. Its original claim was that the work of imaginative literature reveals an anticipatory understanding of laws—most likely psychological laws—governing the lives and actions of human beings and that it does so, without ever leaving the level of particular (fictional) fact, through the insights implicit in its way of giving prominence to certain features of an individual case—insights which will eventually be translated into psychological laws. There is to be sure the inherent improbability that the language of imaginative literature can serve to pick out just those features of human behavior that would serve as criteria for the identification of instances of genuine scientific laws; but it turns out that that difficulty is surmounted by a very free reconstruction of the fictional situation by means of which whatever clues the fictional account may provide are supplemented by borrowings from the real world so as to piece out the kind of evidential basis for the application of the law which the fiction itself could hardly supply. There is much that is incongruous in such an imputation of a properly scientific interest to imaginative literature, even in the mode of intuitive anticipation; but one point in particular stands out. If the cognitive function of imaginative literature were really to explain human conduct in terms of nomic relationships, the best terminology for describing the characters of a fiction would be that which pointed the way most directly to their subsumption under the appropriate laws; and yet it seems quite clear that this is neither what literary fictions do nor what they try to do or are expected to do. The language that is used by the creator of literary fictions is not the language of diagnosis but the language that conveys those aspects of a wide range of situations and relationships in which they are of concern and interest to both the persons internal to the fiction and, though not necessarily in the same way, to the reader or audience. If such descriptions were to be deleted and others substituted for them that serve a quite different theoretical purpose, the locus of the matters in question within the *Lebenswelt* of the characters of the fiction would have been lost and the possibility of a response to them would have disappeared. What this view of literature must unavoidably find itself asserting is that literature will do its job better as it progressively abandons the "language of concern," in which it can express its intuitions of lawful regularities in human conduct only in a very indistinct and approximate way, for the language of science by which alone the cognitive interest that has been imputed to it can finally be satisfied.[31] It is, of course, quite possible that some kind of isomorphism between these different mappings of human experience may in fact obtain and that the locus of concern which is identified in literature may also turn out to be the locus, at another level of description, of a significant theoretical regularity. What is wrong here is not the suggestion that this may turn out to be the case, but rather the a priori decision to incorporate this assumption into the primary account that is given of the significance and value that imaginative literature has for us and thereby to tie the fictional cart to the scientific horse. Since that decision seems to be an element in all the approaches to literature which array themselves under what I have called the second or "external" point of view on the cognitive function of literature, I conclude that the latter suffer under a serious disability. If so, and if such theories do not offer any alternative analysis of what that interest might be supposed to consist in if the coincidence they postulate should not be borne out in a given case, it seems also to follow that they do not pose a substantial challenge to the conclusions that were derived from our examination of typical theories that espouse the first or "internal" point of view; and the results of the first part of this section may therefore be allowed to stand.

Before I move on to the concerns of the next chapter, however, it may be of interest to develop these observations somewhat further in a way that has a bearing on both my earlier claim that an author of a "fiction" cannot be mistaken with respect to what is the case within the world he creates and, by way of anticipation, on issues of interpretation that will be taken up in Chapter 5. I have already indicated that the reader is not under the control of the author in the way that the characters of the latter's "fiction" are and that he is free to reject the structure of norms and governing conventions in terms of which the latter has constituted his fictional world. Sometimes such a rejection will be of a type that might be called "external" since it raises no issues about the substance of the work so rejected itself. Someone may simply not be willing to go along with the kinds of stipulations that have to be accepted in a fairy story or a piece of science fiction and will accordingly throw it aside. The reason for this rejection may be that the reader finds the world of the story too "unrealistic" and is convinced that nothing of interest or value to him can be derived from following a story based on such premises. But such a reaction, however violent, may be said to leave the work itself untouched. The fact that its defining conventions are in some sense "unrealistic" is presumably just as well known to the author as it is to this disenchanted reader; and although they attach very different forms of significance to this fact, it need not reflect disagreement about the work itself that is more serious than a conflict of individual tastes. But if such a reader were not satisfied simply to go his way and let the author and his more appreciative readers go theirs, he might want to make judgments about the work in question in which in effect the author's norms of reality and value are replaced by others that the reader/critic finds more "realistic" or at least more acceptable. If this were to happen, the reader would be saying things about, for example, the characters in the work, which he regards as true, but which the author could hardly accept without contradicting what he himself has said about them; and the reader would then have to say that the author was mistaken about his own creation. The claim made by this reader would be that in the "real world" people who act or talk in the ways the author has made his characters act and talk would be candidates for certain supplementary descriptions, say, psychoanalytic ones, and that if the author has failed to stock his own fictional world with such descriptions, that is simply the measure of how mistaken he is.

In cases like that of the fairy tale or even that of science fiction in which the author has exercised to the full the right to create a world that is explicitly different in certain fundamental respects from our own, such an attempt on the part of the critical reader to "know better" than the author is more likely to be regarded as reflecting a misunderstanding on his part than on the author's. Even if one were to agree with the reader that the "real world" is more like what he supposes it to be than it is like the world created by the author, there is a serious impropriety in transplanting characters unceremoniously from the one to the other and then claiming to have told the "truth" not just about what they would have been in the real world but about them precisely as fictional creations. This is a high-handed (and wrong-headed) procedure because it amounts to a denial to the author of his power to create a world in which there just are no such things as, for example, Oedipus complexes, and in which characters can-not therefore bear descriptions that imply there are such things. The uniquely privileged ontology of the one "real" world is thus permitted to override any stipulations to the contrary that may have been established by the author; and the predictable result is that the story he has written in terms of these stipulations never really gets read. Taken in its own terms, it may in fact be a rather uninteresting and trivial story and it may even take on a good deal more interest when it *is* subjected to the kind of interpreta-tion that treats its "world" as being, say, an inversion of certain re-lationships within the "real" world and its creation as motivated in a way that can only be understood in terms of certain real-world states of affairs. But it may also be Dante's *Commedia* and its world may have such a degree of coherence and imaginative power that it can be said to illumi-nate the "real" world rather than the other way around. In neither case does it seem necessary or proper to authorize as uniquely valid a mode of interpretation that challenges in principle the integrity of the fictional world the author creates. If one is disposed to reject that world, one is free to do so and even to take up the story on one's own and tell it in a way that accords with the canons that properly define the "real." But at least in cases like the ones cited above it is not apparent what advantage would be gained by claiming that such a reconstruction of the original story is also the truth about the world of that story and the characters it contains. The disadvantages of taking that line are, by contrast, quite clear.

But if there might, as I have suggested, be a good deal of agreement that there is something wrong with such principles of interpretation when there is no doubt that the author himself is claiming and exercising the power I have attributed to him, things typically become less clear when imaginative literature itself adopts a "realistic" orientation.[32] Obviously, even when this occurs, the author must go on claiming certain pre-rogatives such as the right to populate London and New York with characters who never existed, and to recount incidents that never took place; but in most other respects, if he subscribes to one or another of the variants of realism, he is unlikely to claim any freedom that is very much more extensive or radical than that. It follows that if he agrees that there are Oedipus complexes in the one "real" world that is to be his standard of what could and might happen, he will not really be in a position to disallow in principle the application to his characters of descriptions deriving from this conception even though the story he has told is one to which they might seem to be prima facie quite irrelevant. His situation is thus much more difficult than that of earlier tellers of tales who did not have to obtain a license for their imaginative departures from the real because neither they nor their audience had such an exacting and disciplined conception of that reality. If the author has made it clear that it is his intention to create characters and situations that are realistic in the sense that they conform to the actuality of life in a particular place and time, he may feel that he has in effect already accepted in principle the possibility that he may have got it wrong and has thus licensed in advance revisionary descriptions of those same characters and situations. He cannot, after all, consistently with his realistic principles, meet every charge of inaccuracy by taking refuge in his imaginative freedom and asserting that what was taken for a mistake was instead just the respect in which he chose to make *his* New York different from the real one.

Nevertheless, even though realism may seem to render an author vulnerable to criticism and his world to revisionary description, it does not license any wholesale application of principles of reductionist interpretation to what is after all still a work of the imagination. If it can be assumed that the author does not make himself guilty of sheer errors of fact in areas where he has accepted historical fact as his standard of truth and has not, for example, misdated World War II, it would seem that in other respects the story he tells must retain a very close connection with the terms in which he has chosen to tell it, whatever the reader may think of the merits of the latter as instruments for dealing with events in any world like the real world. It may be that the reader cannot help feeling that the Stakhanovite "hero of labor" in a Soviet novel of the thirties would be more accurately described as a Stalinist stooge and would so describe him in a novel of his own on the same subject. He may even be right in supposing that the author of the novel knew that his own description of this character misrepresented the historical truth and wrote his novel under what amounted to duress. Nevertheless, if one were to convey all these judgments by simply declaring that this was a novel about a Stalinist stooge, something would have gone wrong since the terms in which the author told his story would have been replaced by others radically different from them without any prior characterization of what the former in fact were. The rectifying operation that the reader/critic would thus perform upon the novel is presented in the form of a primary description of the novel and its characters with the result that the critic's intervention is not acknowledged as such. Even if one feels sympathetic to such rough treatment of a bad book, there are ways of making the same point without such drastic telescoping of a complex judgmental operation. More generally, it may be suggested that, gross errors of fact apart, the conception of realism and of the nature of the real world to which an author "pledges" himself must be construed in accordance with the way he himself constitutes the imaginary world of his story rather than in accordance with some assumed prior definition of what is to count as real. Such a principle of interpretation no doubt reduces "realism" to the status of a rather meaningless term of description; but it has the merit of remaining at once more faithful to the intentions implicit in the "pledge" than would otherwise be the case and to the character of the story that was actually told and that was assumed by the author to be consistent with his realistic principles.

3. Historicity
and History

In this chapter I will begin the task which was outlined in Chapter 1 and for which the examination of imaginative literature in Chapter 2 served as preparation. This is the task of determining the applicability to history, understood as the veridical reconstruction of the human past, of the set of concepts which was first introduced as an explication of the "manifest image" of man and which has since been shown to be organized around the concepts of teleology and intentionality. It is these concepts that also generate the concept of an intentional process, which was utilized in the preceding analysis of literature and which must now be shown to characterize the events—once "actual," but now "past"—with which history concerns itself. At bottom, this is the problem of determining whether such a sequence of events in the real world can have a principle of colligation that is logical in some sense close to the one that has been worked out for fictional narratives. It is to be expected that the resistance to such an application of this conception to events in the real historical world will be much stronger than it was in the case of imaginative literature with its long association with various kinds of sympathetic magic. In any case, one convenient way of initiating this inquiry is simply to see whether, as some believe, the relationship between literature and history can be understood in positive terms by reference to a common role within the one and the other for the generic plot-structures that were discussed in the last chapter. The answer I will give to this question is negative; but an examination of the issues on which this answer turns will serve as a useful introduction to the wider topic of this chapter.

I

It may be helpful to begin the examination of this matter by making some observations on the more general question of the applicability of literary universals to actual human affairs, whether these fall into the special province of history or not. There can be no doubt that we do on occasion use the vocabulary of generic plot-structures in speaking of actual human situations and sequences of events, as for example when we refer to someone's death as a tragedy or a friend's amorous adventures as a comedy. A little thought will, however, raise serious doubts about these uses and their significance for the issue under consideration. Although there is nothing in the sheer actuality of real-life situations that necessarily precludes their satisfying the criteria that serve to define the tragic and the comic modes, it does substantially reduce the likelihood that they will do so unless these criteria are themselves so relaxed as to remove most of the distinctive burden of implication which they carry in their literary application. For one thing, the special kind of indeterminacy that characterizes literary creations and that proved to be one major obstacle in the way of their being assimilated to a version of the nomological theory of explanation obviously does not obtain in the case of real-life individuals and situations; and this inevitably means that, no matter how selective the interest we take in these events may be, inconvenient and incongruous features of conduct are likely to cut across almost any general line of interpretation we propose for the events we interest ourselves in. When one also bears in mind the very considerable intricacy of the interlocking levels of intentionality which the preceding analysis of fiction exposed, it becomes apparent that the conditions that have to be met if real-life situations are to be treated as exemplifications of generic plot-structures are simply too numerous and too complex and that they are far too likely to be violated by the "course of the world" which in a thousand different ways breaks in on the kind of continuity that must be maintained if a distinctively tragic or comic resolution is to be effected.

This point will bear a little elaboration. If the analysis of the generic plot-structures set forth in Chapter 2 is valid, then one of the conditions which a work of imaginative literature must satisfy in order to be brought under one or another of these structures is that it exhibit a certain movement of consciousness toward a form of understanding that can be described only in evaluative or moral terms. The achievement of such understanding is the moment of recognition or anagnorisis and without it there would be no guarantee that the consciousness of the characters within a fiction and the ways in which the situation in which they are jointly involved develops would not remain hopelessly irrelevant to one another and to the dimension of meaning that gives that situation representative value. It was pointed out in this connection that the author of a fiction enjoys certain advantages when it comes to preventing such a failure of consciousness and that he can not only discreetly arrange incidents in such a way as to insure that a latent issue will be forced to the surface but he can also confer a privileged position within the fiction on the controlling norms which are to inform the understanding of what takes place. But it is just these advantages which are not available to the author of a narrative of real-life events; and he simply must not constrain incident and character in such a way as to keep them from violating the moral unities that are characteristic of the generic plot-structures. It is just a fact of life that the world as it is portrayed within the generic plot-structures has a far more securely established and univocal thematic organization than the actual world does; and it is presumably this fact that Aristotle had in mind when he declared poetry to be more philosophical than history. For just this reason we may be disposed to see the "truth" of our fragmentary and distracted experience of life in the artificially concentrated images of action that fiction holds up for us; and the deletion of whatever incidents or circumstances would block the *prise de conscience* or anagnorisis on which the major story forms depend may be felt as a gain rather than as a loss or a distortion. Even so, it is a "truth" that is reached through a movement of events that is, as I have argued, keyed to the normative structure of the work and to which the actual world can as a result be expected to exhibit few close analogues.

When we approach history with these considerations in mind, an important contrast between history and imaginative literature must obtrude itself upon our attention. Although the classical unities of time and place have long since been abandoned, it still remains broadly true that with some exceptions, like the multigenerational family "saga," imaginative literature tends to use the span of a single lifetime or some smaller portion thereof as the framework within which the events of a story or play are contained. The most relevant implication of this fact for our purposes is that in literature it is typically possible for the initiation and the resolution of a sequence of actions to be connected within a single temporally continuous consciousness and in many instances, of course, within more than one such consciousness. There are plenty of characters in most fictions who intersect the main action of the story only momentarily or who in any case have only the kind of limited role within it that does not require that they share or understand the concerns that are of central importance to the developing action. But such "walk-through" parts are sharply contrasted with those that carry the distinctive kind of continuity that has been imputed to imaginative literature and has also been shown to be a necessary condition for the temporal referencing of events and thus for the kind of anagnorisis that the generic plot-structures typically involve. This does not mean that these central characters and their actions are necessarily confined, for purposes of representation in imaginative literature, to "private" life, that is, to the sphere of concerns that are peculiar to them as individual human beings rather than as the occupants of some considerable social position. But even in the latter case there is a strong tendency for literature to take the events it presents—even events whose public and private meanings are intimately related to one another—primarily in terms of the meaning they assume within the context of the life of some one or other of the individual human beings who are im-·plicated in the action. Even when it is understood that the consequences of such actions for the public weal are to be serious and long-lasting and when it is also understood that there is a close identification on the part of the main actor or actors with the larger community that is so affected, literature still insists on the possibility of making a distinction between the drama that has worked itself out within the limits of that singular life and the much larger sequence of events—events that precede this limited drama as well as events that follow it—within which that drama would have to be situated, if considered from the standpoint of a larger kind of interest. Because this distinction at least suggests an element of looseness in the identification of a particular life with larger social concerns and because the meaning of an individual life, when it is even partially abstracted from its larger social and historical matrix, can easily seem to take on a kind of timeless quality as just one more exemplification of some paradigmatic and recurrent motif of human life, literature has some-times been thought to be "antihistorical" and even reactionary insofar as it neglects the larger-scale and truly progressive movement of human affairs. On the other hand, the disastrous consequences for literature of the attempts that have been made to suppress entirely this kind of duality may stand as a warning to those who are tempted to reject altogether the kind of meaning that is generated within individual human lives and who deny in effect the legitimacy of the kind of special concern with that meaning which I am imputing to literature.[1]

The preceding remarks should already have signaled the respects in which the contrast between literature and history is to be made here. Quite obviously, the scale of the events with which history deals is usually much larger than that portrayed in imaginative literature; and this dif-ference of scale has to be understood not just in terms of the numbers of people involved but also in terms of the periods of time occupied by the events in question. With this movement to another order of magnitude in the events to be represented, the opportunities and occasions for the kind of disruption or discontinuity discussed above increase dramatically. In history, by contrast with literature, even the central protagonists are con-stantly being replaced and disappearing from the scene for a whole variety of reasons with the result that the distinction made above between charac-ters whose lives merely graze the action in progress and those that really carry it will not be as readily made. If Oedipus had caught a cold and died before Tiresias uttered his dire warnings and before any confirmatory evi-dence could be presented, the story of Oedipus as we know it really would have died aborning. But in a history of Thebes Oedipus would have been succeeded by another ruler; and whatever continuity that history pos-sesses as a history would have to be one that persists through even such drastic substitutions of one chief protagonist for another. The relevant point here, however, is that as a plurality of consciousnesses is introduced into even the most central areas of dramatic agency, as it is in history, the likelihood that any one of them will be able or disposed to experience it as having the mode of unity that is proper to a tragedy or a comedy becomes more and more problematic. This is not only because history deals with real people whom the historian cannot, if he is conscientious, bend to his will so as to make them the compliant agents of his dramatic purposes. It is not even entirely due to the fact that those purposes and the perceptions of events that may be connected with them are not necessarily shared by actual historical agents, although this is certainly the case. The discontinuity of historical events and their failure to achieve a recognizable dramatic structure may well simply reflect the fact that there is no single consciousness that has been so placed as to be able to internalize the relevant sequence of events and at the same time so motivated as to identify their meaning in the way that would assimilate them to one of the major plot-structures. In speaking of literature, I referred to recognition as a signal given from within the world of the work itself—a signal that the significance of what has happened has been internalized and that it is not the external observer alone who grasps that significance. What I am saying now is that it does not seem plausible to expect that such a signal will typically be given from within the world—actual rather than fictional— with which the historian deals; and I think this fact in turn must call into question any assumption to the effect that the plot structures of literature will be transferable without further ado to historiography.[2] It is true that among the historian's primary materials there are often histories or other writings that in one way or another reflect on historical events that were more or less contemporary with them; and in making use of these the later historian may indeed have the sense that at least a version of the meaning of the events he is studying is reaching him from within the world of those events itself. But what this fact implies is really that it is history *itself* that constitutes the emergence of an analogue within the real world to the kind of consciousness on the part of participants that has been noted in imaginative literature. Clearly, however, the presence of a Thucydides or a Guicciardini within the domain of the events he deals with cannot be counted on by the later historian, and of course these eminent historians themselves could not predicate *their* account of those events on the existence of any such consciousness on the part of agents that were more centrally involved than they were. "Recognition" cannot, therefore, have the kind of *structural* role in history that it has in imaginative literature and this fact is fatal to the hypothesis about the relationship of the one to the other I have been exploring.

II

The preceding discussion seems to indicate that a direct application to history of the most highly developed forms of order that characterize works of imaginative literature is not really feasible. Accordingly, an alternative approach to the conception of a historical process is needed; and it must be one that will be capable of resolving the central logical problem that arises out of such a conception. This is the problem of showing, in the face of multiple prepossessions to the contrary, that certain events in real time are of such a nature that they cannot be described without thereby also committing oneself to the claim that certain other events had occurred before the ones being described did. This kind of logical cumulativeness has already been show to characterize fictional narratives; but when one attempts to transfer such a conception to real historical time, the tolerance accorded to the imagination and its productions will not be so readily granted. The conceptual picture of time in the real world to which a great many minds are committed simply does not accommodate the kind of connectedness between an event in time and some prior event that is required by this notion of cumulativeness. In that picture events succeed one another in time and one event is often a causal condition for the occurrence of a subsequent event; but in its moment of actuality each event, so to speak, "holds the stage" on its own and this means in such a way as to be in principle describable without the inclusion in that description of anything that is not itself a feature of that same present in which it is occurring. The work that prior events have done to make it possible for such an event to take place has, one may say, been *done;* and the present event that was so produced is no mere shadow cast on the present by those prior events or a phantom with only such reality as it can borrow from its causal ancestors. To put the matter in a somewhat different way, one might say that in this picture of time all the lines of connection among events run in the same direction as the movement in which earlier events are succeeded by later events and those by still later ones and none, whether they be causal or conceptual in nature, run back from the subsequent event to its predecessors. But an event that *has* to be described in a way that entails that some other event has already taken place violates the requirements inherent in this picture as directly as anything could; and so if such events are postulated by the conception of an intentional process, the prospects of applying that conception to historical events in real time must seem very unfavorable.[3]

Arthur Danto has recently given a sense to the term "complex event" which it may be helpful to introduce here by way of further explication of the notion of cumulative description.[4] A complex event is one in which another event is imbedded; the primary examples Danto gives are events like doing and knowing. These he symbolizes as mDa (for "m does a") and mKs (for "m knows that s") so as to bring out the fact that a change in the world in the one case, and a state of affairs in the world in the other, are "proper parts" of their respective complex events in such a way that mDa entails the occurrence of a and mKs entails the truth of s. With respect to such a complex event the question arises as to whether, as Danto puts it, it can be "sundered neatly and nonresidually into [its] constituents"; and it is evident that this is the same question as the one discussed above to which the adherents of the conception of time just described would answer that this not only can but must be done.[5] In saying this they can, moreover, cite many examples of how such resolution proceeds. There are certainly plenty of locutions in ordinary language that conjugate events in the way Danto describes and also incorporate the feature of temporal distance between these events as Danto's account does not. In other words, the way they describe what occurs at one time entails that certain other events must have occurred at other points in time and this is possible both when these events precede the event being described and when they follow it. Thus, to say that an athlete broke the previous record in his event is to imply that such a record had been set; and to say that the quarterback prevented the opposing side from scoring is to imply that at some later point in time the other side did not score. It is quite easy, however, to redescribe these events in such a way as to remove these implications. In place of the original statement about the athlete who broke the record, we would now have a pair of statements about the first and the second runners, each of which would describe what took place at two discrete moments in time in such a way as to effect a separation between them and to show that the ostensible logical connection between the two events was simply a convenience of discourse for expressing a certain empirical relationship between them. In this way one removes the disconcerting appearance of a kind of temporal "action at a distance" by which what occurs at a given time would logically constrain the event which takes place at another time.

These examples concern events which can plausibly be construed as being "physical" in the sense of not involving any intentional functions—any acts of assertion or belief—on the part of those involved in them. It is at least possible that when belief and assertion *are* involved as they of course typically are in the case of history, it will become much more difficult to enforce a resolution of complex events into their constituent events; and when such beliefs are about events in the past the difficulties of pushing through the "resolutive thesis" may well be compounded. In the case of memory beliefs, for example, it is some past experience of his own that a person claims to be recalling and it may be that it is for this reason that the implications of the resolutive thesis seem more disconcerting in such a case than they otherwise might. Thus I may remember that I made an appointment with my dentist on a certain day. The making of an appointment is the kind of event that necessitates that at the time one knows what one is doing; and so, to claim to remember such an event is to claim to be in continuing contact with one's own past conscious experience. This is a claim which we would be extremely reluctant to abandon. But if the thesis in question is applied to memory, it is not clear in what form this conviction will be able to maintain itself. The reason is that, as it stands, the statement of my memory-claim logically requires as one of its truth-conditions that it indeed be the case that I made an appointment with my dentist on a certain date. But if I yoke together the truth values of two statements describing two discrete episodes in time—my present state as one who "remembers" and the past time at which I claim to have made the appointment—I am establishing a *logical* connection between a statement that describes my present state and a statement describing my prior state and this is to say that the two compose a complex event that is *not* divisible. To avoid this result, it would be necessary to weaken my memory-claim by recasting it in the form of *belief* so as to make it consistent with a denial that I made the appointment on that day. I must not only accept as a logical possibility that this memory-belief may be false; I must also be prepared to redescribe it and all my other memory-beliefs in a way that is consistent with this possibility. This means that I must be able to describe them strictly in terms of predicates whose application to my present state can be decided without raising any question as to whether or not I made the appointment I claim to have made. As a result of these precautions the appearance of a logical constraint that emanates from a thought or speech act in the present and yet governs the truth value of a state of affairs in the past is eliminated. A memory-belief is to be treated simply as an event, whether linguistic or otherwise, that occupies *its* time-slot just as unambiguously as the falling of a stone does its own, and the remainder of the utterance in which such a memory might find expression—the "that" clause that states *what* is remembered—is to be treated as nonreferential. That is, its content is bundled into the same logical form as the unambiguously dated event of remembering itself, and the difference, if there is one, being a stone's falling fast and a person's remembering that . . . is not permitted to surface in the logical grammar that is assigned to it.[6]

The most problematic feature of this whole approach to temporally complex events is clearly the treatment it accords to those elements in our language that serve to express the references we make to other times, whether past or future, and in particular the homogenizing effect of the logical classification that is imposed upon these references. If the act of reference has always to be described in terms that effect a logical separation between that act itself and the event or state of affairs that is referred to, it is not clear how this can be done without at the same time suppressing the internal relatedness that acts occurring at one moment in time may have to other moments of time. The point here is not one that primarily concerns the adoption of a logical notation in which, for example, the whole content of the "that clause" in a memory-belief is engulfed in a single predicate letter under which the act of believing is also comprehended. For certain purposes, such a notation might be both adequate and appropriate. Typically, however, a greater authority than that of convenience is claimed for such notational devices, and this means that some semantic interpretation has to be given to this use of predicate letters that will be consistent with the requirement that they describe only the state of the person who has the belief about the past at the time he has it. The features of such "present states" that have been proposed as the relevant ones for the purposes of such determinations have varied widely. Classical empiricism answered this question by postulating the existence in the mind of certain ideas or images which are the descendants of the impressions which were received there on the occasion of the event which is remembered. It has often been pointed out, however, that this account fails to explain how these memorial images take on their character as images *of* a particular past event. Their content was, after all, spelled out in terms of sensuous features all of which are rigorously present, and the empiricist could hardly resort to yet another image to explain how these sensuous features took on a reference to something that was not present.[7] At the present time, it is much more common to explicate the ontological status of these predicates in behavioral terms, whether as the molar behavior pattern associated with the production of a statement about the past or in terms of some wider neurophysiological theory. The penalty incurred by such a procedure is, of course, that one quite loses the words that make up the subsentence within the predicate, that is, one loses them in their capacity as *words* rather than as sounds or electric signals or muscle contractions; and it is certainly not clear how a reference to a particular past event could be rendered in terms of present behavior any better than it can in terms of present imagery.

The full incongruousness of the implications deriving from the picture of time with which we began should now be reasonably apparent. As applied to complex temporal events that have an intentional character as in the case of memory, these implications are such as to commit us to a model of events succeeding one another in time within which we are unable to identify in any plausible way those events that carry a reference to events that are temporally prior to them. When we seek to have such events identified for us, we are shown either imaginal or linguistic or behavioral events that are taking place at the time at which the backward reference is supposed to have been made and upon these events there has been imposed a form of description which, consistently with the requirements of the model and of the conception of time on which it is based, effects no conceptual linkage to the relevant event in the past. If we still profess dissatisfaction and insist upon the intentional character of the act of reference we are trying to locate within this model, we will be told that the most that can be allowed in that department is memory-"beliefs" since these do not have the unacceptable logical feature that the concept of remembering does and do not entail the truth of the assertion about the past. We are thus invited to conceive the life histories of intelligent organisms like ourselves as a series of events in which the first may be, as in our example, the episode of making an appointment with one's dentist and the subsequent ones are mental states of the person who made the appointment—just the states we would ordinarily describe as episodes of remembering that this appointment was made. Each one of these states, moreover, has been collapsed into its *present* constituents, however described, with the result that no one of them can itself effect anything recognizable as a reference to the event at the beginning of the series. It is as though these states were a series of snapshots such that we would ordinarily describe them as being pictures of the original transaction but which within the restrictions imposed by the model we must describe in a way that abstracts from any such identification. Any description that does persist in so identifying will be one that is made *ab extra,* that is, independently of the restrictions imposed by the model and out of resources it denies to us.

It should be evident that the model itself of events succeeding one another in time with its fussy restrictions on what can be attributed to each of the "presents" of which that series consists could be constructed only from a position to which these restrictions do not apply. Unless the model too is to collapse into its own specious present, the reference it involves to the original event in the series as well as the references to that same event that are implicit in the restrictions imposed on the description of the mental events that follow upon it cannot be bracketed or neutralized in a way that events *within* the model are. They must be taken instead at full strength or the claim they involve will be transformed into the present experience of a claim in just the way that the episodes of remembering were transformed into the contents of so many successive presents. But a model of events in time is not devised from any transcendental position but by beings who are themselves in time and to whom the model, if it is valid, should apply. The inescapable inference must be that the model assumes that at least some of these beings have a way of being in time which the model does not capture although it is dependent upon it. There must in other words be events in time—notably acts of reference to other times—that are not susceptible of being described exclusively in terms of the "present" characteristics as this notion is construed within the conception of time in which the model is rooted. At the bottom of the puzzles we have been dealing with there is thus an illegitimate denial of equivalence with respect to the capability for temporal reference as between the person within the model and the person who constructs or uses it. The latter implicitly attributes to himself a full capability for reference to past events, but the moment such a reference is made by the person spoken about, it has to be reported in a way that incorporates the reference to a past time into the predicate that signifies his present believing.

It should now be possible to turn with somewhat more confidence than before to the task of meeting the objections to any transfer to history of the conception of logical cumulativeness that was developed in the analysis of imaginative literature. It will be helpful to begin by making a distinction between importantly different senses that the word "history" bears. In English, "history" can denote either past events as such (or some portion thereof) or it can denote the recounting of such events. In some languages, there are alternative expressions for conveying the one sense or the other as for example in German where "Geschichte" is ambiguous in the way "history" is in English, but "Historie" refers only to history as the discursive account of past events. To avoid confusion, I will distinguish between the two senses by means of a notational device; and I will speak of history(e) when it is the first sense—history as past events—that I have in mind. Since the form of historiography with which I will be principally concerned is narrative history, I will use history(n) as a notation indicating that history as record is under discussion.[8]

This distinction in fact plays an important role in any application to history of the model in which the objections referred to above generate the restrictions that negate the possibility of the kind of cumulativeness described in the last chapter. It may, in other words, be conceded that history(n) is full of descriptions of events that imply conceptual connections between them; but these, it would presumably be argued, are mere conveniences of discourse and the events proper of history(e) cannot themselves be conceived in such terms. They must surely conform to the requirements of the general model of events in time that has such an irresistible attraction for us; and it is this fact that we must firmly bear in mind when we are invited to think of history and imaginative literature as congeners. And in fact there is much that speaks in favor of a strict and unambiguous contrast of history(e) and history(n) that would block any possibility that the former might turn out to be somehow conceptually dependent on the latter. There could after all be no history(n) if there had been no history(e), since the business of history(n) is to state veridically what the events composing history(e) were. The idea of a reciprocal dependence whereby those events could not occur unless there were a narrative stating that they did occur seems utterly absurd; and we are, in fact, quite sure that most past events were not only not recorded but were and remain totally unknown. Furthermore, it seems to follow just as clearly from such a construal of the relationship between history(e) and history(n) that any further conditions that have to be satisfied before history(n) can come into being, including any conditions that might have to be satisfied by the beings who construct a history(n), must be utterly distinct from whatever conditions govern the occurrence of the events themselves that are narrated. It is hardly surprising if in the light of such considerations as these many feel compelled to conclude that any appearance of cumula-tiveness in history(n) must be reconstrued so as to avoid any conflict with what is assumed to be the logic of events in history(e).

There can be little doubt that the intuition we have about the asym-metrical character of the relationship between the two senses of "history" expresses something valid and important; but this is not to say that as it stands it is wholly perspicuous. One notices, to begin with, that the word "past" that is used to delimit the set of events which history(e) denotes, inescapably involves a reference to the point in time from which just this set of events can be designated as having already taken place and as therefore being "past." The point may seem trivial; but even so it does show that there is a conceptual connection that runs from our reference to a set of events as past to the subsequent position in time from which they are referred to. This amounts to saying that the making of such a reference to a set of events as composing a history(e) sets up a relationship between those events and the subsequent point in the *same* time sequence from which that reference is made. Since such references necessarily occur in any history(n), it is clear that the production of any history(n) will entail a conceptualization of the corresponding history(e) that places its con-stituent events in a certain temporal relationship to that history(n). The position of the historian is thus very different from that of the novelist in respect of their relationship to the events which they recount since the production of a novel cannot be situated in the same time series with the events it contains and the production of a history(n) can and must be so situated. There is the further difference that there is nothing to prevent the novelist from running forward in the time of his fictional world as far as he wishes whereas the historian can move forward in the time series of the events he is describing only as far as his own present. If he were to go beyond that limit he would be writing the "history" of the future, that is, he would have ceased to write history(n). The novelist, by contrast, is in no danger of running into his own present, which either lies outside the fictional time series altogether or, if it *is* situated there, is so in a way which pulls *it* into the fictional world and thereby opens up a gap between this fictionalized present and the real present of the novel's production of his novel. To use another comparison, the situation of the historian is very different, by reason of the essential role of the notion of the past in the definition of his domain of inquiry from the physical scientist who, we are told, is concerned only with temporal relationships that can be expressed in the form of the distinction between "earlier" and "later" or "before" and "after" and thus constructs *his* object domain in a way that effec-tively prescinds from any consideration reflecting his own location in the time series of physical events in which, of course, he is in fact located. Overall, one may convey the implication of these comparisons by saying that the position of the historian in relation to the events that compose the relevant history(e) with which he is concerned is not "transcendental" in any sense that would fit either the case of the writer of fiction or that of the physical scientist, at least on the interpretation proposed above.

How significant is this interdependence that has turned up between history(e) and history(n) for our purposes? Thus far the only connection that has been shown to obtain between history(e) and history(n) is one that has to do with the temporal relationship of the one to the other; that relationship would hold no matter what *kind* of event the past event happens to be, that is, whether it were a geological event like the beginning of the Ice Age or an event of relatively recent human history like Caesar's crossing of the Rubicon. Nevertheless, this point is not without relevance to the previous discussion of models of events in time and it suggests the question whether, if the previous model were assumed to apply to history(e), history(n) or the composing of a history(n) could be treated as one event within that history(e) and thus within the model or whether it would instead have to be viewed as being comparable to the construction or use of the model itself and thus as being in principle independent of the constraints imposed by the latter.[9] Although it must be fairly clear that the answer to this question is implicit in the conclusions of the preceding discussion, it will be useful to press somewhat farther our examination of the kind of episode that the production of a history(n) represents within the time series in which the events of the corresponding history(e) are earlier episodes. The purpose this examination can serve is not that of showing that the events of history(e) mysteriously anticipate their own history(n) in some way unknown to common sense, but rather that of using the function of the historian in the production of a history(n) as a countermodel illustrating temporal relationships that can also be found, in modified form, within the historical process—that is, within history(e)—itself. It may be that in this way the whole prevailing conception of history(e) can be called into question and a criterion found for reconstruing it in a way that will at once narrow the scope of history(e) very substantially and at the same time remove the obstacles to the introduction of the concept of cumulativeness into the analysis of both history(e) and history(n).

Pretty clearly, the relevant feature of the episode constituted by the production of a history(n) is not the historian's movement of his writing hand or his prior deployment of the apparatus of "research," but the intentional act he performs. The production of a history(n) is, at the least, the making of a number of statements which refer to and describe past events in a way that claims to be literally true; and we would properly describe what the historian does as the producer of a given history(n) in a statement of the form "At time t historian x asserts that, at a prior time s, p was the case." There will naturally be all kinds of other true statements which could be made about the episode which is the production of a history(n); and among these might well be statements to the effect that the fact that historian *x* is alive at time *t* and that the fact that he is writing a history(n) at that time is causally dependent upon a host of prior events, including quite possibly the very events of which he is constructing a history(n). But if we want to convey precisely the fact that he is constructing a history(n) of a given set of past events we will have to do so in a statement which directly imputes an intentional act to him in the manner of the statement-form introduced above. And it is in connection with such statements and the interpretation we are to place on them that the same set of difficulties arises with which we are already familiar from our previous discussion of events succeeding one another in time. But now the issue they raise is whether it is possible to give an adequate account of history(n) or of the production of a history(n) as an event that takes place within a time series governed by the constraints of the earlier model of time. Otherwise expressed, the issue is whether history(n) understood as an intentional act can be domiciled within a present that is descirbed in a way that does not assume the reality of the very past that history(n) recounts.[10]

An example of the kind of statement a historian might make may facilitate the consideration of this issue. Let us suppose that the great historian Theodor Mommsen said what he in any case certainly thought, namely, that Cicero was a poseur, and that this fact was reported by a subsequent historian in some such statement as ''Mommsen thought that Cicero was a poseur.'' Now if we interpret this second statement in accordance with the requirements of the original model, we will have to make a radical contrast between the referential commitments assumed by the maker of this statement and those that are imputable to Mommsen. The second statement itself clearly makes a reference to Mommsen and thus presupposes that that historian who lived in the nineteenth century is situated within the referential domain to which the maker of the statement has access. In contrast, the reference to Cicero which is apparently attributed to Mommsen in this statement is to be treated as not being a genuine reference since to allow it that status would entail the existence of Cicero. Such an entailment would be objectionable not only because it is at least possible that no such person as Cicero ever existed, but also because, even if we have no doubts on that score, we would not want to be committed to Cicero's existence by the fact of someone's belief that he was a poseur and thus existed. In other words, the reason for saying that the statement about Mommsen does not entail the existence of Cicero is the suspicion that Cicero may turn out to be a mythical being like Pegasus; and it has been customary in recent philosophy to take the possibility of such radical failure of reference very seriously and to treat the analysis that allows for the possibility of such failure as the paradigm for understanding all such statements as these. What this comes to is the principle that when one speaker reports the beliefs of another person he does not thereby assume the existential commitments that were carried by the latter's original statement—in this case "Cicero was a poseur." But this useful precaution produces a paradoxical result in that it makes it impossible for me to express the fact that another person—in this case Mommsen—held beliefs about the same historical personality of the first century B.C. about whom I may have the same or different views. *My* capacity for such reference is not called into doubt or at any rate not as long as I refrain from reporting my own beliefs as distinct from stating them. But the moment I want to say something like "Mommsen thought Cicero was a poseur; but he was really a great statesman," it turns out that in its first occurrence "Cicero" must be treated as nonreferring while in its pronominal occurrence it is a referring expression; and I will be hard pressed to explain within the limits of such a set of assumptions what the nature of this implied identity is.[11]

There is something inherently unsatisfactory about a paradigm that does not permit us to acknowledge a referential capability in another person which we all claim for ourselves and that obliges us to interpret what *is* involved in such states of affairs as Mommsen's believing that Cicero was a poseur in a manner that gives no hint of the internal temporal complexity of the state we predicate of Mommsen as the holder of the belief in question. It also seems a good deal more plausible to suggest that "Cicero" is every bit as much a referring expression as "Mommsen" in "Mommsen thought that Cicero was a poseur." By way of corroboration for this suggestion, I submit that if it were to turn out that no such person as Cicero ever really existed, the maker of this statement about Mommsen would not simply allow it to stand unaltered on the ground that, whatever we may since have learned about Roman history, nothing about Mommsen can have been altered by such discoveries and the truth of our statements about those beliefs, therefore, remains unaffected. Instead, he would, I think, at the very least put the name within quotation marks in the sentence—"Cicero"—to convey his own reservations as to the existential commitment the use of the proper name entails or he would modify the statement to read, "Mommsen believed there was such a person as 'Cicero' and he thought that person was a poseur." In the absence of any indications such as these, we are entitled to assume that in reporting the beliefs of another person the speaker shares the existential commitments of the original speaker. And for just this reason there is no need to devise an interpretation of the "nonreferential" portion of his statement whether in behavioral or other terms. In other words, there is no need for such an interpretation because there is no way of describing Mommsen's "state" that does not itself involve a reference to Cicero, and the whole dubious business of finding equivalents that do not carry such a reference can be given up.

Even if the situation should change and we should feel compelled to conclude that there really was no such person as Cicero the situation in which we would find ourselves would not be fundamentally different in the relevant respects; and it would still not be possible to treat the historian's beliefs as being self-contained in such a way that one could describe them in abstraction from any assumption whatever about the actual past. Although something like the Pegasus case may occasionally turn up in the course of historical inquiry—Prester John, say—this typically does not happen in the arbitrary and isolated way that the philosophical example suggests but against a background of shared or convergent identification of past personalities and events. Thus, if the existence of Cicero were to be doubted, that doubt might take the form of an argument that the person who wrote the letters to Atticus and the person who delivered the Philippics were not the same person; and in that event we would have to decide which of these two persons into which the original "Cicero" would have been split was the one to which Mommsen's description should be construed as applying. But it is apparent that this modification would not have the effect of transforming that original Cicero into a bit of imagery or behavior that would be attributable to Mommsen in the way that features of his personal appearance would be. The belief we attribute to Mommsen would still be a belief about a person or persons who lived in Rome in the first century B.C. and who was related in various ways to a host of other personalities like Caesar whose existence remains uncontroversial. No doubt there is a point at which, early in human history, it becomes impossible for us to distinguish with any assurance between real historical personalities and mythical beings that have more in common with Pegasus than they do with Cicero, but even then it would be arguable that this is not a radical failure of reference since even if the beings ostensibly referred to were to lack real existence the time at which they are supposed to have existed would not be comparably mythical. It would follow that in history by virtue of its fundamental orientation toward the real-time sequence even a reference manqué is very likely to be at the same time a successful reference to a time in the past or to the past as such; and although such a reference by itself would not enrich our historical knowledge, there is no reason to think that it would be any less resistant to a rendering in terms of the historian's present state than those that fill in the temporal reference with names of persons and events. More generally, there seems to be no point in masking the fact that this past forms part of the common domain of reference of the historian—in our example Mommsen—and of anyone else, philosopher or not, who undertakes to state what the historian says, believes, and so on. Such a person is not in the kind of privileged position which I have called "transcendental" as he would be if he were allowed a capability for temporal reference enabling him to connect the historian's present statements with the events in the past and to do so in a manner for which he recognizes no analogue in the case of the historian and without himself having to give an accounting in any court of higher instance, that is, without having to fear that *his* reference to the past will be encapsulated within his own present state through being brought within the purview of some yet more "transcendental" observer and thus within the model of events in time which the latter employs.

Even if these observations were to prove persuasive, however, concern is likely to be felt about the proposal to allow existential import to be read into intentional contexts like the one in the Mommsen example. Surely, it will be said, it would be a misconceived enterprise to license such inferences to the existence of the entities one finds imbedded in the thought and discourse of others and thus to deny oneself the right to accept the assertion that Mommsen held a certain view while rejecting the existential presuppositions on which that view itself rests. Indeed it would; but that is not quite what is being proposed. The proposal is rather to block the confluence of the sound claim that we must be in a position to qualify our acceptance of a statement in this way with a quite different thesis about the status of the intentional elements in such statements that are bracketed off in these cases. The point is thus to acknowledge that it is legitimate and indeed sometimes necessary to reject a reference that someone has made to something in his past while at the same time insisting that this rejected reference retains its properly intentional character. It need not, in other words, collapse into an image or a bit of behavior simply because the object it posits turns out not to exist as though, having lost its "hold" on the world, there were nothing more for it to be than a bit of that world itself. But when the confluence alluded to above takes place, it has the effect of making it appear as though this were indeed the case. The reason is simply that beliefs like Mommsen's *and* the belief that contradicts his are placed within a world whose conceptual structure is such that the fact of reference itself and a fortiori of successful reference can be established only from outside. It is as though *within* this world there were, at the deepest level of analysis, only "beliefs" and no "knowledge," at least in those current philosophical senses of these terms in which "knowledge" may be said to "connect us with the world" while "belief" carries no such guarantee.[12] In Heidegger's parlance these would be "world-less" beliefs; but it should be clear that they can be so characterized only because a second standpoint is covertly involved here. This is the standpoint from which these "beliefs" are characterized as such, that is, as not being "knowledge"; and that standpoint cannot itself be "world-less" since, if it were, there would be no way in which such a privative characterization of the connection of "beliefs" with the "world" could be made from it. But if we are not willing, as we certainly should not be, to maintain at the same time as we conceal the distinction between these two standpoints and the commitments they carry with them, there is really no alternative but to acknowledge the second as setting the fundamental mode of conceptualization for the domain within which Mommsen's original belief, the subsequent statement about it, and whatever revisionary operations are performed upon it are to be domiciled. If we do not take this course, there will be no way in which we can do justice to the fact—surely one of great importance in history, especially—that beliefs and the references they include "meet," as it were, "in the world." By this I mean not only that intentional fields overlap but also that they do so in such a way that this overlap is explicit and essential so that one might say that the references involved are "stacked" upon one another. It seems fair to say that if the relationship between persons that is predicated upon such intentional overlap had not been permitted by the logical resources of human language, it is problematic whether anything like history(e) and thus a fortiori history(n) could have come into being at all.[13] Since they have, it seems clear that the "ontologies" of the beings who generate history(e) must themselves have overlapped sufficiently so that it is legitimate to treat radical failure of reference as the exception and the chances of successful convergent reference as sufficiently good to make unnecessary any drastic reform of the utterances that are its vehicle.

It should be apparent by now that the paradoxical effort to avoid acknowledging that there is at least one feature of the present state of human beings that cannot be described without making a reference to a prior time is destined to fail since the myth of a transcendental position can maintain itself only as long as it remains implicit. It is true that even when the defenders of the conception of time that goes with that myth are prepared to recognize that their own references to past events must be described as features of *their* present state just as those of others are, the myth may maintain itself as an (again largely implicit) imputation to language as such of the very transcendental function that permits a reference to past events without the hazard of encapsulation in some "present" state. This resolution of the matter can hardly be satisfactory since it suspends the language in which temporal distinctions are made in a kind of ontological limbo and thereby makes our ability as beings who are in time to make use of this system of distinctions even more mystifying than the original puzzle that was to be solved.[14] Unless we are prepared to accept some extremely implausible assumptions, then, we must recognize that our system of temporal distinctions is deployed by beings who are themselves in time and that, this being the case, there must be at least one feature of their present state that cannot be described without reference to any preceding state. Such an admission of course effects a grave breach in the zone of separation which so much recent philosophy has attempted to establish between language and the world.[15] But precisely for that reason it will also enable us to deal with the position of persons *within* that world—as language users and as beings who *have* a past—without a guilty sense that we are imputing a capacity for time travel to them as indeed we would be if we were to remain with the ontological presuppositions of the "present state" theory. By abandoning those presuppositions we are instead enabled to introduce a conception of "historicity" as a comprehensive designation of the opening upon the past (and the future) as a common domain of reference and thereby to reach an ontological level at which the concept of history—the historical process itself—can be satisfactorily explicated.[16]

Before embarking on a fuller account of historicity, however, it is necessary to return to the distinction between history(e) and history(n) and to draw out the implications of the foregoing analysis for an understanding of the temporal sequence that history(e) involves. The suggestion was made then that our analysis of the characteristic intentional act of the historian might provide us with clues to features of the historical process in terms of which a closer affinity to one another of history(e) and history(n) might be construed. The nature of that affinity can now be stated by reference to the conception of historicity which has just been introduced. The point here is that the historicity of the historian is only a special case of a much wider use to which that concept lends itself. To understand what that wider range of application might be, one has only to reflect that if the philosophical observer of the historian's activities is debarred from describing them in a way that effectively abstracts for the purposes of that description from the existence of the past and thus from the historian's access to it, it would be no less illegitimate for the historian to assume a similarly transcendental position in his treatment of the persons in the past with whom his history(n) is concerned. That, of course, is what he would be doing if he were to treat the position in time of the human beings who are the central figures in his account of the past as if it were governed by the same set of rules which have just been shown to have such a distorting effect upon the way we conceive his own function as a historian. That this is so may not be immediately evident since there is an obvious respect in which these persons who are the subjects of a history(n) differ from the person whose function it is to construct such a history(n): they do not have a primarily cognitive concern with either the events in which they themselves are engaged or with the events in their own pasts. Instead, they have practical concerns and interests of various kinds which lead them to act in the ways that the historian records; and it is only rarely and incidentally that these practical concerns occasion the asking of the same kind of question about the events in which they participate that a historian would typically ask. And yet this difference cannot be absolutely decisive. Even though practical concerns dominate the perspective on events of historical agents, it remains quite possible that these have their own kind of historicity and that it is no more feasible to characterize them or the actions in which they find expression in abstraction from the agent's mode of understanding of his past than it was to characterize the function of the historian while holding open the possibility that that past did not exist. What is required is clearly an examination of the way historical agents—in other words ordinary people whose interests are not defined at the outset as historical in the way the historian's are—situate themselves in time and of the difference, if there is one, that this practical and "engaged" form of historicity can make to the kind of process which they and their actions generate. If such a difference were to be identified and to prove significant, then it would offer an important clue to the way in which the domain of history(e) constitutes itself and does so in a way that is predicated on the kind of affinity between the historian and historical agents that is implicit in the historicity that both would have been shown to share.

The connection that has just been made between the concepts of historicity and human agency constitutes the central linkage between history(n) and history(e). Not only are the historian and the historical agent situated in the same time sequence, but their way of being in that temporal sequence is similar in that both have the capacity to situate themselves in it through constructing symbolic representations of events in their own past. In the one case, as has been pointed out, the context which motivates such references to the past is the quest for knowledge of that past; in the other it is the context of action. But if such actions in turn take place within a certain understanding of the events that are past in relation to them, it is no longer really feasible to construe the distinction between history(n) and history(e) on the model of contrast between, on the one hand, an activity of thought that finds expression in reasoned knowledge-claims and, on the other, an object-domain—the past—upon which this activity of inference and interpretation is exercised. The contrast is no longer tenable in this form because it turns out that the past events to which historical inquiry addresses itself, themselves incorporate a reference to *their* past. This fact at the very least deviates notably from the conception of the relationship in which thought and inquiry stand to their object-domain in the natural sciences. There the objects do not, as it were, "talk back." The historian's "objects," however, do just that, not in the sense that they address *him,* but in the sense that they have the same kind of internal semantic complexity that characterizes his own activity as a historian.[17] It thus appears that *both* the historian's characteristic activity as a historian and the actions of his subjects are "complex events" in the sense that other prior events are intentionally imbedded in them through the capacity that each has for reference to events in his own past. What precise significance for historical inquiry this parallelism between the historian and his subjects may have is, of course, not yet clear. But if it should prove to be the case that the historicity of historical agents produces its own ordering of the events with which the historian himself is concerned, then those implications may prove to be quite substantial.

To speak of historicity in this way as a common feature of the situation of the historian and of the historical agent might seem to be simply to refer to memory as a central constitutive element in our human nature. This assumption is perfectly in order as long as certain other associations obscure just those features of our way of having a past to which the term historicity is intended to draw attention. Remembering something, in ordinary parlance, has the quality of an episode in our mental life and sometimes of a kind of feat. There is a moment at which we recall a person's name or where we parked our car or the year a recent president died; and the suggestion is that when such an episode is over it is followed by other nonmemory mental episodes involving no such reference until the next memory comes along. Experience is thus a temporal series of mental episodes only some of which involve a reference to earlier members of the series. For a psychological interpretation of our access to the past as occasional and episodic, the term "historicity" would hardly have been needed. What it designates is in fact just the *constant* contribution which the dimension of pastness makes to the intelligibility of our world, a contribution which does not require the special modality of explicit recollection and is, in fact, incorporated into the primary identifications we make of objects, persons, and situations. The desk at which I am sitting and writing this is the same desk at which I have been working every day for the past week or month or year; and to identify it as my desk is to place it in a temporal process which is also that of my life. No doubt, it is always in the present that we make such identifications; but the point which is made by the use of the concept of historicity is that that present cannot be described without presupposing a past, to which the describer has access. For the latter, the past and the present and the future form a single domain of reference, and the accessibility of that domain within which the present has only a very qualified kind of priority is assumed by every psychological account of historicity in terms of episodes that take place in our (present) heads or minds. The referential field of human consciousness is thus in an irreducible sense past as well as present and future; and the idea of a logically self-contained present and especially of a self-contained psychological present whose only relationship to the past that lies outside it is a causal one must be abandoned. In Heidegger's parlance, a human life "stretches itself along" and it does so for itself and not just from the standpoint of some hypothesized observer who establishes a causal relationship between the past and the present of the human subject to take the place of the semantic relationship which the latter would be incapable of constituting, at least on the psychological assumptions noted above.[18]

It seems fair to assume that human beings are the only conscious beings whose temporality has been internalized in the way designated by the concept of historicity; but nothing in the account being offered here requires that human beings be unique in this respect. What is important is to determine what difference this capability for direct reference to what is past makes in the logical structure of the events in which human beings are involved and thus in the kind of process which human actions generate. In Chapter 2, a characterization of such intentional processes as they are represented in fictional narrative was proposed; and it may be useful now to consider the corresponding difference which would result, for purposes of narration or storytelling, from the absence of a capability for temporal reference on the part of the subject of the narrative. One such case is that of animals but it is, in an important respect, a rather ambiguous one. On the one hand, since they are without language or at any rate a language adequate to that purpose, even the higher mammals do not tell stories about themselves, but human beings do tell stories about them. These stories are often described as anthropomophic in the sense that among other things they credit these animals with the same ability that humans have to set a present occurrence in the context of some past event and to appreciate a mode of significance of the later event which depends upon its being referred back to the previous one. Animals, in short, are endowed for the purpose of storytelling with a full-blown capacity for internalizing their own temporality and with lives that "stretch themselves along" in much the same way as those of human beings do. There is not much point in condemning this anthropomorphizing tendency of the teller of animal stories and there is no need to argue that all animals are wholly lacking in the capacity in question. A dog, for example, that is left behind by his master *does* seem to appreciate, in a perfectly good sense, what has happened; and both the painful experience of waiting for his master's return and the joy the dog feels at seeing him when he does come back both seem to reflect an ability of some kind to link temporally separated events without any continuing stimuli of a practical character. It would not do, of course, to exaggerate the degree to which even the most intelligent animals possess this capacity; and there are clearly many human story types that could not plausibly be transferred to the animal domain at all. In any case, it is surely significant that storytellers feel the need to impute a form of self-temporalization to the animals that are to be characters in their stories; and it seems clear, for example, that, if it were understood from the beginning that the lion in Aesop's fable had no way of identifying Androcles as the same man that pulled the thorn from its foot, then its failing to kill him later could not possibly have the significance that is central to the story.

If the applicability of the story form to the lives of animals can be justified only in this very limited way, what about the kinds of "stories" that are constructed by geologists or astronomers or evolutionary

biologists—the "story" of the earth or of the solar system or of evolution?[19] In such stories there can be no question of any form of continuity
that depends upon the internalized temporality of the "subject" of the
story since it is understood that that "subject" is not animate or conscious and does not sustain a relationship *to* the time it is in and cannot
therefore employ a vocabulary of temporal predicates that assign positions in the time order. It has often been pointed out that in any classification of the sciences on the basis of the nomological character of their final
products it might well be necessary to associate geology and astronomy
and biological evolution with history rather than with physics since the
proximate concern of these sciences is with a spatio-temporal particular,
the earth or *the* solar system, and the process of change through which
this particular has passed over some (usually very long) period of time.
More importantly, it is argued, no claim need be made by these sciences
that such processes as a whole are subsumable under a causal (or statistical) law or that the results they achieve are such as to make possible
reliable predictions of the future course of the process in question. The
issue posed by such cases as these is not, of course, how the word
"story" is to be employed and whether its extension to these nonhuman
contexts is permissible. It is rather to determine whether, assuming such
an extension to be an accomplished and in itself noncontentious fact, it is
possible to specify clearly what the differences between the one kind of
story and the other may be. In order to raise this question in its really
significant form, it is necessary to set aside all those hybrid cases in which
a natural entity—the Grand Canyon or the Mississippi River—is announced as the subject but is then considered primarily in terms of the
"role" it has played within human history. In the strong conception of
historicity that was set forth above, there was obviously no intention of
attributing historicity exclusively to human beings at the expense of
"things," whether the latter be natural objects like rivers and mountains,
or artifacts like knives and clothing; but it was implicit in this conception
that the historicity of such objects which we examine in museums or
travel to visit, for example, the Plain of Marathon, is derivative from their
relationship to human beings and thus from the historicity of the latter.[20]
It is, therefore, only the "pure" case of geological or cosmic history
which permits one to examine a story or history that does not owe its
character as a history, whatever that may prove to be, to its association
with human history. As an example of the kind of distinction that is
involved here, it might be pointed out that in the relevant sense the recent
landing on the moon would not form a part of the (geological) history of
the moon.

The moon may indeed serve as our example of the kind of object that
has had a "history" that was entirely independent of human life; and one
way of bringing out the specific character of human historicity is to ask

what kind of a history this is and to what degree the differences between that kind of history and the life story of an individual may be traceable to the presence in the latter case of a capacity for temporal reference. First of all, what kinds of events would it be proper to include in a history of the moon? Let us agree, without making any difficulties about it, that one such event would be the formation of the moon, on the assumption that if there are any "beginnings" at all in this kind of history this must be one of them. Let us further suppose that an account of that formation has been given and also that this account might be given in either technical or nontechnical language. The question then arises as to how the story is to go on and what the next event or episode in that story is to be. We can, of course, imagine a kind of chronicle that would record year by year such events as the fact the the moon was getting steadily cooler or the occurrence of geological upheavals or meteor impacts; and we can also assume that some of these events would be causally linked to others in accordance with established physical and chemical laws. But the question still remains: how many of these events are we to include in the history of the moon? If, as is usually the case, our interest in the moon is scientific in character, we will have some criteria for making decisions about what to include and what not to include. There will be questions about the wider evolution of the solar system to which discoverable features of the moon may supply an answer; and these questions may well set the priorities on which exclusions and inclusions from our history of the moon will be based. That history would thus omit events which have no such explanatory function and would move from one event that does have such a function to another that also has that kind of causal or evidential significance. There is no reason to expect, however, that these events will, when they are set down in the time order in which they occurred, have any particular connection with one another which would make it worthwhile to present them in this form. It would seem, therefore, that the history of the moon would be either all-inclusive and thus impossible; or the principle of selection will be one which picks out events which are too heterogeneous and discrete to yield anything like a narrative. One could, of course, construct a bogus narrative in which there would be a lot of "ands" and endless repetitions of such statements as "In A.D. 203 things on the moon were pretty much the same as in A.D. 202."

When an event counts as a beginning in human life, it does so in a very different way. The reasons why it counts as a beginning at all will also be such as to indicate what the character of the next relevant event in the story might be. This is not because a given event has fewer traceable effects in human life than in lunar history, but rather because the subject of human history is of such a nature that it effects a selection from among these possibly infinite effects of any given event and it is this selection that is reflected in the description of that event which that subject—the conscious human being—uses for purposes of determining the response he will make to it. That response itself will be predicated upon beliefs and expectations and other intentions and purposes of this agent, all of which presuppose a capacity to refer to events at prior or subsequent points in the time order. Once it is placed within a context of this kind the original event takes on a meaning—as a threat, for example, or as creating an opportunity—which gives it an orientation in time as blocking or facilitating other possible events or actions. It thus initiates a sequence of events which can be selected out of the great number of events which follow upon it precisely because they are the kinds of events that are among the appropriate responses to the events that have already taken place, under the descriptions these take on in a context in which temporal relationships have been integrated in the manner described above within the lives of the subjects of the story. No such story could be told about beings without this capacity for temporal reference, either by themselves or by anyone else, because no other beings could effectuate this kind of relationship between preceding and succeeding events. More importantly, no being without such a capacity could be involved in events and processes of this logically cumulative type; and this is to say that the point at issue here is not one that concerns only the "logic" of narration but is, at least implicitly, an ontological one that bears on the character of the process itself which such narration seeks to render.[21]

In general outline, at least, a principle of differentiation within history(e) between the kind of process which we do not ordinarily think of as being specifically historical and the kind that we do so characterize should now be reasonably clear. What is being proposed is that such a specifically historical process is initiated within the larger movement of a cosmic or natural process at that point at which intentional access is gained, on some reasonably stable and continuing basis, to prior events in that same process. To express this notion in metaphorical terms, one might say that this is the point at which a process of events in time "doubles back" on itself and is thereby enabled to live off itself in the sense that the descriptions under which events henceforth prove to be efficacious are those that presuppose the kind of backward-referencing in terms of which access to the past is achieved. The danger of such metaphorical modes of expression is, of course, that by resorting to the material mode they tend to assimilate historicity as the distinguishing feature of historical process to certain hypothesized features of the wider process from which it is to be distinguished and thereby obscure its properly intentional and ideal character. In any case, if a distinction within history(e) is made along these lines, it becomes apparent that as between that portion of history(e) that is characterized by historicity, and history(n) a closer relationship does in fact obtain than appeared likely at the beginning of this discussion. What both have in common is precisely their intentional access to past events and a capability for logically cumulative description of subsequent events in the light of such past events. To be sure, historicity is not the same thing as the production of a history(n) and the difference between the two, as has already been pointed out, lies in the overwhelmingly practical character of the interest which historical agents take in the past as contrasted with the much more central role within history(n) of a purely cognitive concern with "wie es eigentlich gewesen." Even so, the connection between the two—between history(e)-cum-historicity and history(n)—is quite apparently much closer than is suggested by the usual accounts of the development of the discipline of historical inquiry out of the more informal kinds of interest in the past. At the deeper level the connection is one that rests on a capacity for self-temporalization that is, on the account I am proposing, a necessary condition for historical process as well as for history(n) and that thereby constitutes the kind of event with which the creator of a history(n) will typically concern himself.

The preceding discussion of the special character of the events that compose a historical process points quite directly to a further conclusion that bears on the relationship between history(e) and history(n). The connection between history(n) and the development of writing has often been noted and it has been taken to consist in the fact that written records of all kinds are a primary source material for the historian although not of course the only one. What is less often noticed is the role that language as such plays in the constitution of the events that have the conceptual characteristics noted above. What those characteristics involve is really the linguistic mediation of the central processes of social life. It is language that makes possible distinctively human institutions and the shared norms in terms of which these institutions are defined; and it is language that permits man to give himself an account of the world process in which his life is imbedded in a way no animal does.[22] The fact that at first this ability is used in such a way as to draw the changes that occur within an individual life and within a society into a pattern that is unchanging is no more surprising than the fact that the first human societies have much the same kind of stability as do animal societies. What is of decisive importance is rather the fact that in the human case this stability is achieved to a significant degree by means of symbolic representations of the process of social life and thus presupposes a form of intentional commerce with the temporal dimension of that life which again is unknown to animals. From that point onward, the process of social life takes on a semantic character and it becomes impossible to say what is taking place in a given society without knowing how it would be described by members of that society.[23] Historicity in its full sense will, to be sure, emerge only when it has become at once more difficult to maintain the appearance of absolute stability within a society and more interesting to attend to the significance of events that prove unassimilable to any fixed pattern or recurrence. When this happens history(n)—history as explicit record of past events—can hardly be long postponed; and when it does appear, it will have its own kind of impact on the process it records. But that influence will be only a variation within the more fundamental modification which the historical process has already undergone with the introduction of intentional elements into its order of causation.

One final point must be made if this preliminary analysis of historicity is not to seem truncated as a result of a failure to acknowledge the role of futurity in human experience and the role it plays within historicity itself. Thus far, I have been arguing that the world of human beings is one that requires complex forms of description involving transtemporal reference; and that we as human beings thus come to sustain an intentional as well as a causal relationship to our own past. But if this is the case, then it seems equally clear that the way in which we articulate the past that we carry intentionally within us cannot be described in abstraction from a context of interests and concerns which in turn involve a reference to the future. The problems raised by such references to future events and states of affairs are rather different from those connected with references to past events. It is no more possible than it was in the case of references to past events to treat a reference to a future event as though it were simply a feature of a self-contained present state of the person who makes the reference; but in breaking open the presentness of that state a reference to the future addresses itself to what has not yet taken place and is therefore very likely envisaged as a possibility rather than, as in the former case, to something that already has the status of fact. The status of such possibilities has been a much disputed point among philosophers; and adherents to the scientific image of man almost unanimously subscribe to Spinoza's view that possibility is merely the asylum of ignorance and that progress in scientific knowledge eliminates pari passu the use of the concept of possibility in application to the object domain. Nevertheless, common sense has gone on stubbornly believing that human beings often face a choice between what are genuinely alternative possibilities. Broadly speaking, common sense as reflected in ordinary language seems to embrace whatever degree of indeterminism is required to make sense of this experience of choice; but the issue of freedom versus determinism is not one that need be taken up here. It is enough to point out that possibilities and especially action possibilities are deeply entrenched in the ontology of the *Lebenswelt* and that it is therefore reasonable to assume that they will have an important place in the conceptual ordering of the historical world. More specifically, to the extent that historical process turns out to be dependent upon historicity as an essential dimension of characteristically human agency it can also be expected to incorporate this element of future reference and thus of an acknowledgment of the possible as the characteristic mode in which future outcomes and goals are envisaged by human agents.[24]

III

Historicity has been characterized as a function of self-temporalization within a human life and its effect as the imparting of what might be called a protostory character to that life. So far, however, apart from its having been shown to be transferable to a real time-sequence, this self-temporalization is indistinguishable from the unification of personal time which was discussed in connection with literature. Historicity has still another dimension and this is the social one.[25] Human beings are members of groups or communities, ranging from the family to the state; and it does not make much difference whether one treats this fact as reflecting a conceptual truth about human beings or as a rock-bottom practical necessity in the light of such circumstances as their long period of maturation or their limited physical powers. Such communities, furthermore, have some form or other of internal organization which confers upon some of its members the authority to make decisions that count as the decisions of all and that normally lead to actions that are actions of that society as a whole. These actions as well as the events that befall a society follow one another in time; and they form a context of pastness for its present situation and undertakings. This is to say that there are some modes of self-temporalization which one shares with other persons belonging to one's own society so that the story one tells oneself is the same story that they tell themselves or very nearly so. Not only does this sharing occur among members of the same generation, but to a considerable degree between generations as well since elements in the stories of earlier generations will be included in those of the later ones, but with subsequent events added to them. In any case, historicity, in its full sense, is just this dimension of shared self-temporalization among members of a continuous human society of some kind.

One can hardly effect this transfer of the notion of historicity from the individual to a community or society without running directly into a challenge to the philosophical credentials of the notion of social or collective entities that is presupposed by such a transfer. Such a challenge can assume many forms, ranging from outright denials that such collective entities, as distinguished from the individuals who compose them, have any reality at all, to the much subtler "methodological individualism" which requires that all explanations of social phenomena be couched in concepts that make the individual human being and his actions the ultimate unit of analysis.[26] Much of the controversy between holism and individualism in the domain of history and the social sciences has undoubtedly been inspired by suspicions that to recognize the reality of such entities as communities or societies is to sanction attributions to them of forms of agency that are not, on any reasonable assumptions, attributable to individual human beings. It is claimed, for example, that to allow "Germany" or "England" to *do* things is to create a form of social mythology that is objectionable on both logical and moral grounds.[27] The logical vice of such attributions of agency is said to be that they relieve us improperly of the obligation to discover how and why specific events actually took place. It is further assumed that such investigations must be concerned with the behavior of actual individual human beings (as well as with whatever natural events and circumstances may be relevant to the case in hand); and evocations of a *Volksgeist* or of any other form of transindividual agency are held to have only the merit that indolence can claim over hard work. Morally, recognition of supraindividual forms of agency is held to be objectionable because it gives a color of legitimacy to a perverted interpretation of the relationship between the individual and the larger social formations to which he belongs and thereby appears to place the functioning of these entities beyond the reach of criticism based on some realistic conception of the interests of such individuals.

To the extent that this controversy is kept alive by suspicions that supraindividual forms of agency are in some literal sense being sponsored by the holistic position, it really seems that the issue on which it turns is not a very substantial one. If there is anyone who believes that states, for example, can be said to do anything otherwise than through the actions of individual human beings or who conceives the sense of "through" that is invoked in such cases as involving a real, although very likely unconscious, psychological influence, comparable perhaps to the case of diabolic possession, then that person has not been a participant in recent philosophical discussions of these matters and for those who have there does not seem to be any need for further warnings against such views or for the rhetoric of social thought that is primarily designed to keep them at a distance. If there is a real issue in this controversy, it must lie elsewhere; and it seems plausible to assume that it will have to do with the way we are to conceive the "individual-ness" of the individual human beings who are to be the only agents recognized by a demythologized history. More specifically, much current use of the term "individual" seems to conflate two importantly different senses it can bear. In one of them, the individuality of persons has to do with such matters as their spatio-temporal location as well as the discreteness of their mental histories; and nothing is implied by such a conception as to the character of the motives that determine the desires or actions of these (in the stipulated sense) individual beings. But in a second employment of the term it is just these matters of motivation that are in question; and the force of the term's use is to suggest that the conduct of any human person can be explained solely by reference to motives that can be described in terms of the states which that person wishes to avoid or to attain. In other words, his conduct is to be accounted for in psychological terms and without stepping outside the internal economy of his desires otherwise than to take account of the opportunities and obstacles which the external world (including other human beings) presents for his efforts. Specifically, what is not required is that such explanations should take into account the norms which define and regulate the conduct of the community to which the person in question belongs; or at any rate it is not required that they be taken into account in their capacity as norms. The point here is not that either the psychologist or the person whose conduct is to be explained would be ignorant of the existence of such norms, but rather that compliance or noncompliance by the latter with those norms is assumed to be motivated by considerations that are internal to his system of satisfactions as this can be characterized independently of the social norm. Within such an interpretation of the rationale of a person's conduct, the existence of the social norm would figure in precisely the same way as any other external circumstance that has a bearing on the achievement of prospective satisfactions. This means that it would be appraised by calculating the balance of advantages and disadvantages to oneself produced by compliance and noncompliance and by the approval/ disapproval of others that are the result of such compliance and non-compliance with the norm; and the result of this calculation would constitute the sole possible ground of the validity of the norm in the eyes of this individual. From such a standpoint as this, it would always have to appear as a kind of mystification if the "individual" were to allow the social norm to infiltrate his preference schedule in such a way that it would have a primary role in determining what his conduct in a given situation was to be. If this were to happen, the internal psychological criteria for use in assessing alternative courses of conduct would no longer be distinct from the social norm and they could, therefore, not be used to give an independent determination of the advisability of compliance with the norm on a given occasion. When this happens, there would, on the construal of individuality now under consideration, be a kind of analogue to the sort of mystification of which those who set up supraindividual forms of agency are said to be guilty. In both cases the individual is prevented from treating the interests of his community as having the logical status of constructions out of his and other individuals' interests as these are defined independently of any prior acceptance of or identification with these collective norms.

When individualism is understood as a doctrine of this kind rather than as the innocuous thesis associated with the first sense of the term, it is clear that its claim to acceptance is something less than self-evidently valid and may even be highly problematic. It might be more properly described as a version of psychologism or of the logical primacy of psychological explanations of human conduct where "psychological" is construed in a sense that abstracts from the existence of social norms.[28] What makes it problematic is not the fact that it opens up a space between social norms (or more specifically their implications for conduct in a particular situation) and the attitude which an individual human being effectively adopts. Such a space often exists and it was a defect of some earlier systems of social thought that they assimilated the position of an individual within a functioning community so firmly to the norms of that community that it became difficult to acknowledge the possibility that an individual might appraise the requirements imposed by this system of norms from a standpoint that was independent of the latter, either because his criteria were much narrower and more tailored to the particular features of his own situation or, more rarely, because they were more inclusive.[29] The valid criticism that can be made of individualism in this psychologistic version is rather that it repeats this error in another form and where the older kind of theory tended to give identification with social norms a privileged and logically compulsory status, psychologism does the same for nonidentification and treats as its paradigm the case of the individual who *always* has to evaluate the requirements of the social norm in terms of his own independent calculus of satisfactions before reaching any judgment as to their validity. What this blocks out of the picture is precisely the possibility that in a given case there may be an espousal of the social norm by an individual that is not the product of mystification or of confusion as to the latter's self-interest and that really does effect an identification between individual and social interest. In such cases a correct psychological explanation of the individual's action would be a social explanation as well since it would have to acknowledge that at least on these occasions this individual is acting as a member of his community and that the attempt to drive a wedge between public and private rationales for his action must produce a distortion of the true situation.

The implications of this point for the proposed transfer of the concept of historicity to social entities can now be stated. When we say that a society is nothing but the individuals who make it up, this statement will be perfectly true and unobjectionable provided we do not smuggle the psychologistic thesis into our understanding of what an "individual" is and into the interpretation we offer of the "making up" relationship between an individual and his society. Expressed in a positive way, what this comes to is that, when an individual is considered as a member of a society, he is being taken in his capacity not only as a person who knows that he is associated with some definable body of persons and that this association carries with it the condition of being subject to a certain set of norms that define the conduct that is expected of him, but also as one to whom the presumption that these norms will have a role in determining his conduct is applicable. In this way the degree of inner identification of the individual with those norms is left open, thus avoiding both the errors discussed above since it is not required that the individual *want* to do what these norms require or that he in fact does it. But what is not left open and is in fact excluded is the possibility that an individual might be quite unaware of his affiliation and thus of the norms governing the association to which he belongs or that he could view the existence of these norms as purely external considerations that affect his own action only by reason of their influence upon other people's attitudes. Because this possibility is excluded, an expectation is established that, however a given individual may act, that is, whether he complies with or violates the norms of the society to which he belongs, the relationship in which his action stands to those norms will be one which he has at least a minimal capacity to define and which plays some role in the effective rationale he offers for the way he acts. Whatever other conditions have to be added as part of an adequate characterization of what the existence of a society involves, this condition at least must be met; and when it is, there do not seem to be reasonable grounds why any ontological squeamishness as regards the recognition of social entities should persist.

Interestingly enough, this condition that partially explicates the notion of "making up" in which individual human beings stand to societies is clearly intentional in character since it stipulates that having certain convergent beliefs is required as a condition of membership in a society.[30] This does not mean that in this domain any more than anywhere else believing makes what is believed true, that is, that to believe you are a Jew makes you a Jew. Typically, there are other criteria of group membership as well about which it is perfectly possible to be mistaken. What is being asserted, however, is that there would be no social entity if there were not a group of people who identify themselves and one another as members of that social entity and whose relevant actions are performed under the sign of that membership and the norms it entails. From one point of view, of course, the intentional status of such membership through self-identification and of the society so constituted may be taken as a sign that an acceptance of the reality of this society is not entailed by a recognition of the propositional attitudes relating to it on the part of its "members."[31] Consistently with the standpoint adopted in Chapter 1, however, this option is not open to us. Not only are these propositional attitudes to be taken as elements in the constitution of the proper object of historical study and, in this case, of a social entity of some kind, rather than as opinions about it; if the arguments developed in the course of the preceding discussion of individualism and holism are cogent, there can be little point in interpreting the intentional character of these references to a society as authorizing a skeptical attitude toward the existence of the society these references posit. Such skepticism would have a point only if it were supposed that in the case of societies existence carries some stronger sense than that of a shared self-identification on the part of its members that finds expression in common actions; and it is this supposition which has been shown to be lacking in substance and as irrelevant to the issues with which we are dealing.

The implications of this discussion for the consideration of historicity as a social or collective phenomenon can now be stated. First of all, it should be clear that the transfer of historicity from the individual to society does not involve its reassignment from individual human beings in the first sense of "individual" isolated above to some mysterious nonindividual entity; and in fact all such suggestions are simply red herrings drawn across the track of the argument. What is involved in historicity is rather a capacity of these same individual human beings for a form of self-identification and self-description which is shared in very much the same way as their underlying self-identification as members of a society and as subject to its norms. Historicity is in fact a form of intentionality that is social in the sense of being shared (or at least of being sharable) by all the members of some human community and that is directed upon the past actions and passions of that community which it typically construes in such a way as to relate them to the present situation of that community. As such, it is entirely consistent with a position of ontological individualism which treats individual human beings as the units with which a theory of society has to work; but these are individuals who recognize that they are members of a community and who are prepared to act in accordance with the norms of that community in the belief that other members will do so as well. If methodological individualism is understood as the view that society is the resultant of the actions of individuals and that these can be described in terms of the de facto convergence of the independent rationales of many individual agents and in abstraction from the norms the acceptance of which defines membership in the society, then it is doubtful whether any conception of historicity could be individualistic in this sense. The latter would require that our sense of the past be always in the first instance an individual one and that a social form of historicity be a construction out of such prior individual modes of historicity. By contrast, the assumption underlying the interpretation I propose is that fully distinct individual human beings not only can and do act in accordance with norms and for the sake of goals that are essentially and not just incidentally shared, but also that they can and do understand their past in terms of what they together with others have jointly done and suffered in their capacity as members of their community. This is not to exclude the possibility of a separate sense of one's own individual past nor indeed of a more limited but concurrent form of historicity that one shares with the members of a smaller unit—a family perhaps—within the larger community.

A number of points need to be made if serious misunderstandings of this conception are to be avoided. Here again a parallel with the under-standings on which the existence of the society itself depends may be helpful. In that case it was suggested that while it is unlikely that a society could exist at all if some of its members did not internalize its norms in the way that the psychologistic version of individualism is unable to recognize and while some awareness of these norms and of their relationship to membership in a given society is a presumptive condition of membership itself, a full spectrum of possibilities should be left open as regards the actual degree to which an individual's conduct is effectively brought under such shared norms in a given case. Similarly in the case of beliefs that refer to a common past, it should not be supposed that the degree of effective sharing of these beliefs will be uniform throughout a society. It is in fact much more likely that such beliefs will be much more fully elabo-rated and more explicitly brought into relationship with the present situa-tion by some groups within that society than by others. Within almost any society there are persons and groups that appear to have almost no in-volvement in the ways of understanding the past that may be highly de-veloped in other sectors of the same society; but this apparent lack of historicity need not express anything more than a principle of the division of symbolic labor within a society.[32] In some cases, however, a society will have severe internal divisions and then the interpretation of the past is likely to become the object of disagreements that reflect those divisions. It is even conceivable that these might become so serious that one would question whether the society as a whole really exists and whether the effective units for purposes of social and historical analysis are not the subsocieties which are in conflict with one another and each of which main-tains its own distinct sense of its past. Even in less radically divided societies there is likely to be a good deal of manipulation of the under-standing of the past by dominant groups in their own interest; and the prominence of such manipulations sometimes threatens to obscure all aspects of our sense of the past that are not the results of manipulation. In any case, it is is not the purpose of this discussion to use the concept of historicity in either an honorific or a derogatory way; but rather to note its characteristics wherever—that is, in whatever kind of community—it can be found. There are doubtless many individuals at the present time who believe that they have divested themselves of all forms of historical self-interpretation that rely on membership in some larger community; but they nevertheless live and work within communities which do maintain such a mode of self-interpretation and it is with the latter, whether ex-ploitative or not, that this discussion will be concerned.[33]

If it can be taken as established that the concept of historicity is trans-ferable from the individual to a social group in the manner and with the qualifications that have been described, the next question is to determine the nature of the difference that historicity in this social form makes to the life process of such a group or community, that is, to its history(e). In its essentials, this difference is very similar to the one that has already been described in the course of the discussion of the temporal organization of individual lives. It may be helpful, however, to amplify the account that has already been given by using the example of a nonhuman society that lacks, as far as we can tell, anything comparable to historicity. Bees, to use that case, form societies in which there is differentiation of functions and a quite intricate pattern of cooperation, but without any language that is comparable to those used by human societies.[34] They have no way of making a contrast between the particular and the general and no system of tenses which would permit a contrast between past, present, and future, although they do have ways of conveying information that guides their honey-gathering activities. In light of this fact there is no way in which bees can form any representation of the past of their swarm or make any reference to that past. Still, it may be tempting to claim that a swarm may nevertheless have a history(e) since it is obvious that things can happen to a swarm. It may be invaded by other living creatures; it may be transported from one place to another; it may be used in experiments by human beings; and one can imagine someone—a human being—setting down all these events in the order in which they took place and with the reactions of the swarm to them and this would be the history of the swarm. In one sense, this history(n) would deal with a process of successive events in time, but there is a difference between it and the processes of human history that goes deeper than the fact that the history(n) of the bees is written by a nonparticipant. When something happens to a swarm of bees that interferes with their normal activities they are capable of reacting very effectively in such a way as to reestablish that routine. When the reaction—whether in the form of a counterattack or a removal to another site—is successful, the cosmos of the hive is reestablished and the episode is complete. But, if such an incident or one like it were to occur again, there would be no way in which the bees—even supposing the same ones were still alive—could react to it differently *because* it was the second attack in a series, since they cannot make the reference to the previous one which is required if the second attack is to be apprehended *as* the second attack. The life of a swarm, however eventful, cannot have the cumulative character that becomes possible when the fact that something occurs in the past becomes an ingredient in the way a subsequent event is interpreted and responded to; and this is a difference in the process itself. No doubt the choice of bees as an example of an animal society gives somewhat different results than would be obtained if one chose a species of higher mammals whose repertory of responses may be less rigidly defined and whose capacity for grasping temporal patterns within their experience may be correspondingly greater. Even then, however, the absence of any symbolic means of transmitting from generation to generation the understanding of temporal configuration so achieved would insure that the life of a wolf pack, say, would lack on a broader scale the cumulativeness that stems from a past event entering into one's interpretation of and response to a subsequent event.

To some it may seem that this contrast between animal and human societies is much too confidently drawn; and the question will very likely be raised whether there are not human societies which are nonhistorical in a way that presents analogues to the nonhistorical character of animal societies and thus at the very least makes the flat contrast set forth above—a contrast resting on the presence in the one case of historicity and its absence in the other—seem a good deal more problematic. Such nonhistorical societies would of course be societies that lack history(n) but the more interesting aspect of the challenge that bases itself on the existence of such societies is its suggestion that they may also be altogether lacking in the perspective of pastness which I have been calling historicity and that as a result the kind of historical process—the kind of history(e)—that is mediated by such historicity will necessarily be absent in such cases. To deny that such societies have had a history(e) in the required sense would not be to deny that they have had a past, but it would be to say that they order temporal process in such a fundamentally different way that nothing like the kind of history(e) that was described above can emerge. That ordering would typically rest on a conception of the natural and social cosmos that is static in the sense that its categories can accommodate all the kinds of events that occur within the life of the society without any need for modification or revision arising; and instead of composing a single cumulative and linear order these events would be perceived as recurrences of a type of event for which provision is already made within an unchanging system of classification. To take an example of such a treatment of what from an explicitly historical point of view would be a singular and unique event in time, it appears that when in dynastic Egypt a new king was inducted and traveled around the country to perform the rites that were appropriate on that occasion, every effort was made to stress the perduring identity of the office and its occupant and to minimize the fact of change and the particularity of *this* king.[35] Obviously, there are differences between such a human society as this and an animal society, whether of bees or of wolves, since the one has a symbolic means not available to the other of representing the identities that underlie the cycles through which its life passes; but—and this is the force of the objection that is being made—it is at the very least not obvious that the two do not have more in common than either does with, say, a contemporary "historical" society. But if that is indeed the case, will not historicity itself turn out to be only a rather parochial and contingent feature of the mode of self-understanding of a number of modern societies rather than the central structural element within human consciousness generally, as the earlier account of it seemed to suggest?

There are a number of observations that need to be made in response to this line of argument. First, it seems clear that a symbolic system that stresses the identity of the type so strongly at the expense of the nonidentity of the particulars that are subsumed under the type will be workable only if the life of the society that employs this system is itself relatively uniform and static. If events that are so novel as to resist assimilation to the permanent scheme of classification were to multiply uncontrollably, one feels something would surely have to give. Second, there is the point that has been made very emphatically by C. Lévi-Strauss who is well known for his sympathetic attitude toward societies that do not use the paradigm of "history" for purposes of self-interpretation.[36] He rejects the view that the members of such societies necessarily lack a sense of the past and live in a kind of timeless now. According to Lévi-Strauss, this is simply false. Members of even very primitive societies understand perfectly well that they have had a past and they tell a variety of stories— some true but more of them not—that are supposed to explain how things came to be as they are now. What they lack is a motive for transforming this sense of their own past that they do have into a fundamental mode of self-interpretation that would present a challenge to the adequacy of their dominant and ahistorical system of classification. Finally, as the work of Mircea Eliade has shown, any process of change that would resist incorporation within the categories of that system and would thus be historical in the sense of something radically new and unprecedented is regarded as profoundly unwelcome; and so every effort is made to avoid "falling into history."[37] In practice, this means a continuing effort to maintain the conformity with the established archetype of order from which historical change would necessarily mark a declension.

These observations suggest that the differences between nonhistorical human societies and animal societies are much deeper than the objection recognizes. Instead of being simply absent as in the case of animal societies, historicity is in fact present within the human societies in question although in a distinctly subordinate position and in a context that continually threatens to assimilate the particularity of reference that historicity involves to the typifying function of the wider ordering of the cosmos. This subordinate position, in turn, would seem to rest on two further circumstances. The life of these societies is itself uniform enough so that the need for an alternative to the static ordering is not pressing; and the idea of such an alternative mode of social life in which a positive valence would attach to change is absolutely unacceptable. In the terminology of Heidegger, these might be described as societies in which historicity is present in its "deficient" and "inauthentic" mode, that is, as that which is recognized in the mode of denying it.[38] Such a way of describing this state of affairs is too strongly judgmental to be really suitable but it does point to the feature that differentiates the nonhistorical human society from its alleged animal counterpart. The latter is nonhistorical in a much more radical sense which precludes even the kind of relationship to history that is required to keep it at a distance. The significance one attributes to this historicity *à rebours* can in fact vary a good deal more than the Heideggerian formula suggests; but it is surely legitimate to view it as a form of self-interpretation that is, as it were, "waiting in the wings" and that, when the opportunity presents itself, will become much more central to the self-understanding of that group than the static circumstances of this phase in its life permit.

IV

The contrast between communities whose mode of life is essentially static and those that have "fallen into history" is one that requires more analysis if the nature of the historical process upon which the latter have entered is to be understood. The hypothesis I want to develop is that this contrast is best understood in terms of the kinds of agency that are characteristic of the one and the other types of society; and I will use the familiar terminology of "cyclical" and "linear" to designate the two main types of agency I have in mind. But before this distinction can be explained it is necessary to understand that both of these types of agency are subtypes of a still broader classification of the forms of group agency within which the two major rubrics are the "collective" and the "distributive." There can thus be cyclical and linear forms of both collective and distributive agency. The underlying assumption here is that any form of agency that remains purely individual will not be of prime interest to the historian; and it follows that it is the different forms of group agency—the forms I refer to as "collective" and "distributive"—that should be the objects of analysis.

This contrast between "collective" and "distributive" is one which is to be understood in terms of the different ways in which an action imputed to some group of persons is related to the actions of its members, who are, of course, individual human beings. In some cases, agency predicated of the class signifies merely that all or most of its members do individually perform the action in question as, for example, if one were to say that the people of a given town ride bicycles to work. In such cases, the agency of the class of persons referred to may be said to be distributive in character. Similarly, the shareholders in a certain company might all happen to sell shares on a given day; and again the agency in question—the agency attributable to the class of shareholders rather than to the company itself—would be distributive in nature in the sense that each of these actions can be described (and described in a way that incorporates the action's internal rationale) without any reference to the similar actions of other members of the group.

There is, however, another form of agency attributable to certain groups which does not require that the action in question be ascribable individually to the members of the group in question. If one says that General Motors is converting to the production of small cars, this is not a summative statement asserting that the employees of General Motors are individually converting to the production of small cars although it will presumably be the case that they are individually doing different things as a contribution to this conversion. What such an imputation of agency to an organization like General Motors does refer to is a collective action by a group of persons, that is, the kind of action that an individual human being could not sensibly be said to be performing by himself and that can be performed only by a group of people acting jointly in a number of different and complexly interrelated ways. To give another example, a country can declare war or wage war; and this will be a collective action that harnesses the energies of nearly all its citizens although no individual among them could be said to have declared war or even to be waging war in the way that he might be said to be tilling his fields in peacetime. There are, of course, a great many important differences among collective actions with respect to the kinds of authority that are required in order to initiate them and the kinds of responsibility they impose upon individual members of the community that engages in them; but these need not concern us here. What *is* important is the fact that collective actions normally require some degree of institutionalization—some structure of authority that makes it possible for certain individuals to initiate such collective actions and to give them the direction they require during their execution. In the absence of such institutionalization, there might well be actions involving all or most of the members of a community, but they would lack all but the most elementary forms of internal differentiation and it would be reasonable to expect that they would either be of short duration or that a measure of institutionalization and of hierarchy would emerge.[39]

The distinction between cyclical and linear agency is not one that turns on a point in the logic of imputation, as does the distinction between collective and distributive actions; it concerns rather *what* is done and the relationship in which it stands to previous actions on the part of the same group of persons. The notion of a cyclical action is one that rests on the multiple routines by which the life of a human community is organized and stablized. Human beings reproduce themselves from generation to generation and they observe the salient turning points in the life cycle in ways that vary rather little from generation to generation. They go on speaking the same language and deploying its resources of classification and description on the various recurrent occasions of their lives. They work the soil and harvest crops and engage in trade; and these activities, like the others that have been mentioned, are cyclical in the sense that they involve doing pretty much the same things over and over again. It has already been suggested that when these routines and others like them establish themselves securely and operate in a largely undisturbed manner over a series of generations, a fundamentally ahistorical mode of self-interpretation also develops within which the fact of time and passage, while not denied, is treated as bringing nothing with it that is not already anticipated and subsumed within the comprehensive system of classification by which the cosmos of such a society is ordered. Such a state of affairs does not exclude change, for example, in the demographic or technological areas; but it presumably would have to be change of a limited kind that is incorporable into and thus consistent with the basic schema of stability. Even after such changes have begun to occur, whether through contacts with other peoples or through natural developments that compel migration or through whatever means, and a society emerges that no longer understands itself in entirely static terms, there will tend to remain sectors of such a society in which life is still pretty much a matter of cycles—the cycle of individual life and death, the cycle of the seasons and of the work that is appropriate to each of them. And within the life of even the most highly developed and "historical" societies there will be strata of routine which seek to maintain themselves in the face of the processes of change which have replaced the stability of routine in such societies' images of themselves.

Typically, these routines of life are closely bound up with facts of the human condition that are only marginally subject to our control. These include the geographical setting of a society with all it implies in the way of opportunities for and limits on the basic economy; and they also comprehend the biological rhythms of human life itself. It would be a mistake, of course, to conclude that because as a condition of survival human effort becomes inextricably involved in the natural matrix that surrounds it, it has thereby assumed the status of a natural process itself. Plowing a field, even though it is being done for the millionth time, is still a human action and as such has to be understood by reference to the purpose it is intended to serve; and the other routines that make up the life of a static society also have a teleological structure. But the teleology of such recurring routines of action does not generate a history, in the sense developed in this chapter, because it is not cumulative. The cycle of life and of work is resumed again and again without significant change and there is as a result no "story" of such a society that is not a retelling of a story that has already been told countless times. Laid end to end, these "stories" would not have any progressive character; each of them is essentially self-contained and can be understood without reference to any particular past episode, although of course the fact that it is a repetition of what has been done countless times before may well be important for purposes of legitimation.

Linear agency is action outside the framework of such routines as these. This departure can occur in either of two ways. One possibility is that the action(s) themselves will be qualitatively identical with others that have been previously performed in a routine way; but at some point the consequence—perhaps cumulative—of these actions will prove to be different and will be such as to place the group in question in a new situation with which it will presumably have to deal by means of actions that lie outside its established repertory. Linear agency of this type will typically assume a diffuse distributive form in the way that demographic changes do, that is, through a large number of individual actions that all go in a common direction with a final result which is somehow new for the society in question. In contrast to these forms of change there are those that have the character of collective actions such as, for example, the Crusades or the creation of an irrigation system around a great river. Because of the kind of coordination that such undertakings presuppose, collective linear action clearly requires the existence not only of an organized society but also of the kind of central executive powers that can conceive and direct the common effort.[40] In such cases one would expect the linear or innovative character of the action being undertaken to be in some degree consciously realized, though not necessarily publicly acknowledged since its legitimacy may depend upon associating such an action with previously established patterns of action from which in reality it deviates.

As between actions of these two types it would, I think, be fair to say that traditional historiography has shown a decided preference for the latter—the linear collective actions that are carried out by societies having a high degree of internal institutional structure. It may be tempting to treat that preference as simply the expression of a rather arbitrary priority of interest in large-scale dramatic events; and to conclude, as many currently do, that the neglect by historians of the kinds of change in which agency conforms more to the distributive type is wholly unjustified.[41] After all, it could be argued, there is no necessity that the linear actions that break a cycle of social routine must involve institutional agency, least of all that of the state. And if departures from a routine can have a diffuse, anonymous character and proceed without central direction or attempts to direct them, it might seem that they would be best described in terms of the gradual establishment of a new routine of some kind. The element of linear sequence would survive but it would be the sequence of two routines, without any intervening moment of collective decision and action. Certainly, one can cite many changes that seem to proceed in this way, ranging from technological and economic changes (new tools, new crops) through changes in family structure (emergence of the nuclear family) to changes in belief systems (growth or erosion of a certain system of religious belief and practice). On the view under consideration, these linear distributive actions would be sharply contrasted with the kind of linear collective actions that take place within some institutional context—collective actions such as the establishment of the unified German empire in 1870; and the inference would be invited that the central importance within the historical process that has been assigned to collective action should be reassessed and a conception of history substituted in which the element of collective agency is rarely if ever invoked to explain the emergence of novelty.

Plausible as this line of thought may be, it underestimates quite seriously the importance and the scope of institutional agency. Consider, for example, the implication which is often associated with this view and which suggests that, by comparison with the subterranean movements of distributive agency, actions that are attributable to collective or institutional agency are somehow superficial in their effects. Could anyone seriously argue that the Spanish conquest of Mexico or the Bolshevik Revolution of 1917—both surely events that fall under the second type of agency—have had less momentous consequences for the societies in question than traditional historiography has attributed to them? It may well be possible to show that these events were preceded by others of a less dramatic and more anonymous character and that, if these changes had not occurred, some of the necessary conditions for the institutional enterprises that attract the historian's attention would have been missing. It is also doubtless possible to show that even in the life of a society that passes through a violent social convulsion like a conquest or a revolution there is much that remains unchanged or only marginally affected. Neither kind of discovery, however, can justify the historian in concluding that these episodes of collective agency are simply momentary surface manifestations of processes that proceed at their own level and rate of speed and largely outside the area of institutional consciousness or control. Perhaps the most important point to be made by way of rebuttal is to point out that institutional agency cannot be identified with brief episodes of activity after which the society falls back into some pattern of routine, whether the one that preceded the disruption or the one that was introduced by it or some combination of the two. The truth is rather that, although they are often identified with some series of dramatic events by which they are introduced, institutional actions have a much longer temporal reach than such a picture allows them. They are not completed, either successfully or otherwise, in the course of a few days or months or even years, as even brief reflection on such contests as those between Rome and Carthage or between the French monarchy and the nobility will make clear. In this respect, collective actions can share the *longue durée* of those seismic movements in the social infrastructure to which so much interest is currently directed.

In this connection, there is another point of great importance that needs to be made if any sort of positive case is to be made in behalf of the orientation of traditional historiography. I have in mind the fact that it is within these long-term undertakings of institutions that it becomes possible to say of one individual who works within them at one point in time that he is "doing the same thing" as some other individual whose agency may be situated at another point in time but within the framework of the same institution. The relevant sense of this expression is different from that in which one could say of two persons who use the same tool or eat the same food or even speak the same language that they are "doing the same thing"; and what is missing in these cases is simply the requirement that these qualitatively similar actions that are performed be performed within the context of the same shared task. Once again, the focal element in this notion of "doing the same thing" is that of cumulativeness and of a completion or enlargement by a subsequent action of what had been initiated or attempted by a prior one. There is, of course, a sense in which every institutional action that is linear by virtue of introducing some significant novelty into the life of a society will also be cyclical by virtue of its creating new routines; but this inevitable element of routinization does not cancel out the linear character of the institutional agency in question, provided that the enterprise in the course of which these routines emerge remains incomplete or continues to require the support of institutional agency of a noncyclical kind to remain in existence. For example, the establishment of a national system of education will as it progresses create cyclical routines within the lives of those whom it serves and in its own procedures and these will be carried out again and again in much the same way. At the same time, to the degree that that system is to be extended or defended against attack, it will require linear institutional action that will be continuous with what was done before in the sense of completing the task that was begun or of preventing its being undone. Clearly, too, in this context there will be need for a conception of a negative form of such cumulativeness for use in describing reversals and failures within a common collective undertaking.

The claim I am making is that these institutional actions, with the longer temporal reach I have been describing, make an absolutely essential contribution to the continuity of the historical process. This is not to claim that all novelty within the life of a society is ultimately attributable to collective or institutional action nor is it to deny that such novelty is often forced upon a society by events over which it has no control at all or introduced through forms of distributive agency that owe little or nothing to institutional foresight or contrivance. The point being made is rather that the relationship between these two forms of agency—the linear collective and the linear distributive—is more complex and dialectical in character than either traditional historiography or its contemporary critics seem to recognize. Neither is wholly assimilable to the other or wholly separable from it as the context within which it takes place. Thus, when a diffuse change has reached a certain point, whether it be one that takes place in the economic or social or religious-cultural area of a society's life, it may make certain collective actions possible as literacy makes the establishment of a new kind of legal system possible or wealth accumulated in early Athens made maritime power possible. The change may also make certain previously practiced collective policies unfeasible; or the diffuse change in progress may call forth reactions of a collective kind that are designed to arrest it or to further it. In such cases it is possible to say that the diffuse distributive process of change comes to a head in some institutional undertaking that may be related to it and also that that undertaking may reinforce but may also interfere with the process of diffuse change upon which it supervenes.

All of this should be fairly straightforward and uncontroversial since it is designed to correct two opposite kinds of distortion that occur when either the distributive or the collective aspect of agency is ignored or the one is assimilated to the other. What is perhaps less evident is the difference I have stressed between the kind of continuity within the historical process that can be made out in terms of institutional or collective agency and the kind that is realized solely at the level of distributive agency. If one were to try to imagine a process in which agency is exclusively of the distributive type, then certain important differences from the kind of process that involves institutional agency seem undeniable. Whatever uniformities an external observer might note in a process of change governed by distributive agency, the fact would remain that from the standpoint of those involved in this process there would be no "we" of agency behind these uniformities and each participant would be able to describe what he was doing in full independence of what was being done by others at earlier or later points in time even though their actions might be virtually indistinguishable from one another. And where there is no numerically singular enterprise from which the action of each participant receives its proper description relating it to the action of others, there would not be the kind of unification of time within the context of shared agency that was discussed under the rubric of historicity and that entails an at least partial identification of present undertakings with those of other human beings who may be quite remote from oneself in time. There would, in fact, be no distinction in principle between the kind of uniformity of behavior exhibited by the participants in a strike and by shoppers at a fire sale; and by distinction of principle here I mean one made in terms of the kind of intention that governs the actions of the agents involved and in particular their relationships to one another. Under these circumstances there would certainly still be a process of change to which the name "history" could be applied; but it would be a history without historicity and thus without the kind of continuity for which historicity has been shown to be an essential mediating condition.

In reality, of course, the attempt to separate collective and distributive agency from one another and to imagine what kind of process the one might constitute in the absence of the other cannot get very far. Quite obviously, a collective action is a coordination of the efforts of human beings who are also engaged in activities that are not collective in the same sense; and without some recognition of that subjacent stratum of distributive agency there could hardly be any sound understanding of the resources on which collective action can draw or of the limits within which it operates. But it is surely just as obvious that distributive agency almost always tends to take on some collective aspect if only in the weak form of a sense of a common interest or of a common need for regulation among persons—settlers in a new territory, for example—whose actions run parallel with one another. If it was the characteristic fault of the older historiography to neglect the distributive infrastructure in favor of the more concentrated and dramatic episodes of collective or institutional action, it would be an equally grave one to carry out the opposite kind of abstraction and to treat the largely anonymous distributive sectors of human agency as though they were not always, at least potentially, subject to intervention and revision through some collective action. Indeed, one is tempted to suggest that the movement out of the static and ahistorical condition of archaic societies has also been a movement of expansion in the opportunities and occasions for such collective action. If such a suggestion has merit, then it would follow that the initiation and development of a distinctively historical process tends to be a movement in which more and more aspects of life are progressively drawn into the arena of public or collective consideration and decision instead of being protected from such scrutiny by immemorial precedent or by their obscurity and remoteness from the centers of public consciousness. In the light of such considerations as these the intuitions of the older historiography do not seem as misguided as they are often charged with being. And if the standpoint of much current historiography continues to give a priority, though not, it is to be hoped, an exclusive one, to collective and institutional agency, it might find elements of justification for such a practice not only in the considerations relating to continuity of agency which were developed above but also in the evidence that this trend toward a progressive "voluntarization"—typically also a "politicization"—of all spheres of life is continuing in our own day.

Among the institutions which may be described as "practical" in the sense of exercising such collective agency, the state undoubtedly is the most prominent.[42] However one chooses to set the criteria by which the emergence of the state from earlier forms of association is defined, it seems clear that two of its attributes go a long way toward accounting for the extraordinary importance it assumes within the historical process. These are territoriality and the monopoly of coercive force. By virtue of the former a claim is made that within a certain territory the actions and lives of all human beings are in principle subject to a single authority. And by virtue of the latter that same authority claims to be the sole arbiter of the manner and occasion on which force is to be used on human beings. Once the world or at any rate the *oikoumene* is parceled out among states exercising this kind of authority within the territories they claim, all other communities and institutions have to maintain themselves within an environment that has been divided into so many distinct jurisdictions, that is, so many distinct systems of law and of agencies for the application and enforcement of law. This is not to say that from the beginning all states have understood themselves to be endowed with the kind of abstract and unqualified sovereign power which Thomas Hobbes was the first to describe. They have not; and their power, although considerable enough, has been circumscribed by a whole variety of beliefs and customs which could not be simply overturned by the ruler's fiat. It is also true that before the development of modern administrative methods and communications the effective control exercised by a state may often have been as shallow as it was broad; and whole strata of social life remained relatively untouched by it. For all that, the emergence of a collective entity making claims to absolute authority and making them good at least for substantial periods of time remains a fact of decisive importance for history since it preempts and subsumes the agency of all other communities—families, tribes, linguistic and religious communities—which are compelled to accept the authority of that state. That is, to the extent that the state is able to impose its authority, any action and especially any collective action that takes place within its territorial sphere depends for its legitimacy upon the relationship in which it stands to the political order. When the state can no longer make good its claim and fails in its primary obligation of maintaining internal peace and the integrity of its borders against external enemies, these subordinate forms of association resume their freedom of action; but it can also happen that one or another of them will assume the function of the weakened or defunct state as the Roman church did after the dissolution of the Western Roman Empire, thus restoring the unity of the political and the religious community but with an inversion—temporary as it turned out—of the relationship between the secular and the spiritual components.

The church was, of course, only the first of many institutions which were to contest in more or less radical ways the supremacy of the state in the sphere it claimed for itself. It is in fact tempting to read the history of institutions generally as the story of the successive emergence of a whole variety of collective entities which represent major areas of human interest and claim the right to act in behalf of these interests and which assume many of the institutional forms of the state in order to act more effectively. From such a perspective the state would be the first large-scale human community that could be described as "practical" in the sense that relates to action as such rather than the one that has to do with the satisfaction of needs or the limits which circumstance imposes on what can be done. Such emergent institutions have had to work out in both theory and practice a relationship to the state and to other such institutions; and, however docile their intentions may have been, the possibility of conflict with the state and its claims has never been wholly absent. Large-scale economic institutions—first of trade and extractive enterprises and then of banking and manufacturing—certainly did not begin under the sign of any such estrangement from the secular state as did the Christian church; and yet their subsequent history has been full of attempts by them to control the state and by the state to control them. At the same time, economic life has become something very different from what it was in the early days of the state, that is, a relatively static and decentralized, mainly agricultural pattern of labor designed to produce the necessities of life for the many and a few luxuries for the privileged. In such circumstances, economic life and the associations that are formed for carrying it on are a part of the subjacent generative order of society and as such comparable to the reproductive cycles of nature and of the human family with both of which it was in fact so closely associated. But as the scale of economic enterprise becomes greater and especially as technological innovation becomes the rule rather than the exception, economic institutions come into being that are often the prime movers within the societies they serve and exercise a degree of power that, as in the case of the Hanseatic League, can absorb the legitimacy and coercive functions of the state. When this happens, economic institutions exercise a form of collective agency that cannot be subsumed under that of the state any more than that of the medieval church could be; and, as we know, the agency of the one as of the other can cross national boundaries and decisively influence the life of peoples in remote parts of the world.

After this review of some of the principal "practical" institutions it will be useful to turn to the family as the principal "natural" community to which human beings belong in order to contrast its role in the historical process with that of states and churches. There can be no doubt, first of all, that the family is an intentional community. People identify themselves as members of families and there are circumstances in which this identity may take precedence over all others. It is also clear that at least in some limited sense families have "histories" and that, as members of families, individual human beings take their places within "stories" of what their families have suffered and done. In a more formal sense, there are histories of the Borgias and of the Rockefellers; and there are also histories of the papacy and of the oil industry in which these families serve as continuing foci of interest. What this comes to is that families may be units of agency in the sense that actions attributable to various individual persons are performed by them in their capacity as members of a specific family and reflect intentions in which they share precisely as members of that family. Nevertheless, because families are small social units and for the most part maintain themselves as families over long periods of time only with great difficulty, it seems clear that they can hardly provide the kind of continuity that a wider history—a history that is more than a family history—would require. And though there are some families, for example, the Rockefellers, whose agency is operative at a level at which it can have a significant impact on the wider life of a society and thus on the other institutions of which a society is composed, it is much more common for the agency of this family to be located at a quite different level—the level which Santayana describes as the "generative order" of society—and to be devoted to concerns of renewal and nurturance and education which are required for each new generation within that society.[43] This is not to say that the family is timeless, in the sense of being always organized and directed in the same way, and therefore extraneous to the concerns of history. It is rather to suggest that it has been a rather stable unit within human history and that its agency has not been the source of either the more significant changes in the life of the wider society or, it seems likely, of the changes which it has itself undergone. In other words, the family is in some respects the kind of unit that combines historicity and collective agency in the way that makes it potentially interesting to the historian but because it does so for the most part weakly and briefly it is typically treated as a supporting or background form of agency rather than a focal one for historical purposes.

What has been said thus far suggests a more general interpretation of the relationship in which the various communities which human beings compose as well as the forms of agency that are characteristic of these communities stand to one another within the historical process. These communities range from those based on kinship or language in which change has at best a marginally actional character and proceeds in a diffuse and largely unconscious manner rather than through anything resembling collective or individual decision, to those explicitly "practical" communities like the state that were discussed above. Some notice has already been taken of the view which treats this relationship as one in which the stratum of change that is even nominally presided over by conscious collective action is pitifully thin and ephemeral by comparison with the massive continuities that characterize the underlying strata of

cyclical and of distributive linear agency, and qualifies for historical attention mainly as a surface manifestation of these processes. Reasons have
been given for thinking that such a view substantially underestimates the
importance of institutional agency within the historical process; but these
reasons by themselves are not adequate to justify the assigning of any sort
of *priority* to such agency within history. It is just such a priority that I
now want to defend; and in order to do so it will be necessary to introduce
a new aspect of human agency into the analysis that has been developed
thus far. This aspect has to do with what I will call the critical relationship
in which human beings increasingly come to stand to the auspices under
which they act in their capacity as members of various groups and institutions; and I will argue that it is this critical relationship that provides
the key to the special importance within history of institutional agency.

The "auspices" of human action to which reference has just been made
are simply the norms of conduct and the presiding beliefs about the world
with which in a given society action, and especially social action, is expected to be in harmony. Unless what is done is broadly consistent with
such norms, it typically forfeits its acceptability and sometimes even its
intelligibility to our social partners; and this holds true whether the action
in question is one of the highly conscious and explicit kind in which the
agency of some institution like the state finds expression or whether it is a
discursive act like answering a question which we hardly think of as an
action at all. In this sense all of the types of human agency that have been
distinguished in the course of this chapter may be said to be rule-
governed. At the same time, however, it is clear that the capacity of those
who live and act under these normative auspices for any kind of explicit
formulation of the constraints on belief and on conduct which they implicitly observe varies widely. In the case of natural languages, for example, it has often been noted that a consciousness of language as such is
slow to emerge; even when it does, consciousness of linguistic rules is
usually far less highly developed than its counterpart in the area of norms
relating to political or legal or religious life.[44] And in these areas of social
life which *have* achieved a higher degree of self-objectification and thus,
one would think, a corresponding capacity for self-modification, there are
typically strong institutionalized inhibitions against such changes; among
these there is the belief that the validity of the system of norms excludes
the possibility of their being the object of such interventions.

It is obvious, of course, that neither a lack of explicit consciousness of
rules nor a principled inhibition against modifying them can in fact prevent rule changes from taking place. These changes are often the cumulative outcome of a whole variety of ad hoc adjustments that are made
without any grasp of the system of rules that is affected by them or of the
potential impact of these adjustments upon that system. A great number
of linguistic changes take place in this way and these adjustments, which

can be motivated by such considerations as the relative ease of pronouncing a given word in one way rather than another, are hardly noticed by those who make them and certainly are not thought of as choices or as actions. Such modifications can often be accounted for by reference to the inevitable imperfections in the process of transmission of the system of rules from generation to generation. More generally, one can say that such changes in systems of rules as these are changes to which any system of rules is exposed by virtue of the varying endowments and capacities of the beings who are the "bearers" of that system or rather of those endowments and capacities that the latter possess independently of their status as beings governed by the system of rules in question. Sometimes, of course, these adjustments are the consequences of other actions which are themselves collective and linear in nature, and as such indirectly attributable to collective agency or to some one of its component elements. Thus, when the establishment of Alexander's empire brought it about that Greek was spoken as a second language in parts of the world where it had previously been unknown, the Greek language unavoidably underwent major changes; and when personal mobility become a requirement first for the settlement of the vast North American continent and then for the establishment of an industrial and commercial system of national scope, the kinship system was subjected to a rather similar form of simplification. But in all these cases the adjustments by which changes in a system of rules are effected are carried out on an ad hoc basis by reason of the *force majeure* imposed by the new set of circumstances and without much if any awareness of the long-run or cumulative implications of such changes or even of the fact that they constitute a trend. The "actions" that produce them are, in other words, undertaken with intentions that do not envisage the consequences in terms of rule change that in fact follow upon them and in this respect they are typical of the kind of distributive linear agency to which many historians now look for their explanations rather than to "l'histoire événementielle" generated by institutional agency. It is perhaps worth recalling in this connection that this same animus against the kind of constitutional change that takes place in the same explicit and self-conscious manner as the first-order undertakings of an institution like the state has long characterized the position taken by classical conservatives like Burke and representatives of the historical school of jurisprudence in Germany who felt that such profound changes should not be carried out by the puny intellects of reforming statesmen or revolutionaries but by the unconscious and anonymous wisdom of mankind.

What neither the proponents of this conservative argument nor their contemporary structuralist descendants have been able to make clear, however, is how institutions can avoid assuming such responsibilities. Even religious communities and churches which, one would think, must be under the strongest inhibitions against attributing to themselves a power to modify their own constitutional ordinances and which certainly aspire to achieve a fully adequate and thus stable formulation of their beliefs, have rarely been able to do so. As a result, believers have been divided among themselves, and the proper content of religious belief and practice has had to be officially redefined again and again; and some, though by no means all, of these changes have in fact modified the dogmatic and institutional code of these churches in significant ways. Then, too, legislative bodies that originally conceived their function as being essentially like those of a court in the sense that the law they have to apply is assumed to be already in existence gradually come to think of themselves as creating new law. In such ways as these, a new kind of reflexive or "second-order" agency comes into being whose distinctive feature is precisely that it changes or attempts to change the body of rules under which "first-order" actions of the relevant institutions and individuals are performed. The introduction of the Code Napoleon or of the metric system might be cited as an example of such a mode of agency, as could, more generally, any constitutional change in the presiding rules under which an institution acts. The more highly developed a form of institutional agency becomes, the more likely it is that it will have achieved access to its own constitutive rules and that it will have claimed for itself the right and the capacity to modify them in various ways. Even more pertinently, to the degree that an understanding of the operating code of an institution becomes diffused through its constituency, that is, through the body of persons whose interests are interpreted and differentially satisfied by that institution, a disposition will almost certainly develop to use this new opportunity for what I have called "second-order" or "reflexive" agency for the purpose of redesigning that code so as to make it more responsible to interests which, in the opinion of some, it too rigidly subordinates to others. This is to say that reflexive institutional agency that is directed to the modification of its own corpus of norms takes on a *critical* character and becomes thereby the primary locus of an institution's or a society's new and more complex relationship to itself. The point here is that if there is (thought to be) something wrong with the way a society is ordered under a particular code, and if it does not simply break up under the pressures that result, the modification that is being called for must be effected by whatever centers of collective linear agency that society has at its disposal. This is as true, moreover, when what is called for is some diminution of the control over its constituency that is exercised by an institution as it is when, as is perhaps more common, the change is in the direction of increased central activity. The likelihood is in other words slight that in a society that is sufficiently well-integrated so that one can speak of a common code by reference to which a great variety of interests are ranked and differentially satisfied, readjustments could be effected by the route of distributive agency. The reason for this is simply that the effect of the code in its existing form may be to constrain just those movements within the society by which such a "spontaneous" readjustment would be brought about; and it is not likely that those who have a primary stake in the current ordering of the society would allow those movements to take place simply through inattention or failure to understand what is going on.

Against the background of considerations like these it should now be possible to offer a measure of justification for the predilection of traditional historiography for envisaging the processes of change in the human world it studies from a conceptual vantage point situated at the highest stratum of collective human action. The valid objection to that procedure is that it has too often entailed an unacceptable degree of obliviousness to whole ranges of historical phenomena that are situated below this level of conceptualization. In the picture of group agency that has now emerged, however, it is expressly acknowledged that collective linear agency in both its forms—the one directed to the production of changes in the natural and social environment in accordance with an established body of norms and the other directed to the effecting of changes in that body of norms itself—stands in a complex dialectical relationship to the subjacent strata of cyclical agency, both distributive and collective, as well as of distributive linear agency. But the importance of these strata of agency must not be allowed to obscure the fact that the very human societies that the historian studies have organized themselves in such a way as to make the processes of social life and work at these levels subject to a supervening institutional authority; and it is arguable that traditional historiography, whatever its other failures, at least did not lose sight of this all-important fact. It is true, as has already been acknowledged, that the form which this higher institutional authority assumes is for a long time that of ratifying the actual ordering of life in a society rather than that of modifying it; it is also true that recognition and acceptance of the potentially *critical* and revisionary function of collective linear agency in its relationship to established forms of life come very slowly. Nevertheless, they do come; and the thin stratum of collective linear action that is constituted by the *res gestae* of kings has expanded immensely until today virtually the whole business of modern society is typically conceived in an explicitly critical and volitional mode. The priority which I propose to assign to institutional agency within the historical process is certainly not one that would require the historian to endorse this trend as though it were unambiguously desirable nor would it require him to turn a blind eye to the many occasions on which the institutional agency proves ineffective or redundant. It is rather a matter of attempting to set each element of human and social life that the historian studies within the widest possible framework of implication for the character of life within the society in question and at the same time within the widest framework of social authority and thus of collective agency to which that life can be realistically regarded as having been subject in that society. In this sense this priority is a matter of envisaging a human society as a moral unity and as a unity of action to the degree—usually quite low—to which its own internal articulation and its level of critical consciousness permitted it so to function.

In Chapter 5 an effort will be made to develop in a much more explicit and detailed way the import of the evaluative elements in this characterization of the agency of institutions. For present purposes, however, it may be useful to take note of an analogy between the appraisive relationship in which a society comes to stand to its own operating code and another form of second-order agency that develops concurrently in other areas. In what I have said about the critical and revisionary aspects of collective agency I have laid primary emphasis upon codes and norms of social conduct; but it needs to be added that a similar kind of critical and revisionary activity can be brought to bear upon *all* the beliefs that are accepted within a given society and in such a way as to give rise to systematic inquiry that supplies its own motivation and often retains only weak connections with the practical exigencies in which this new theoretical interest may have originated. The initiation of such a form of inquiry is an event of immense significance in the life of a society since it marks the legitimation of the critical and reconstructive impulse of the human mind in its most general form.[45] The most dramatic demonstration of how such inquiries, in spite of their abstract and theoretical character, can bring about major changes in the life of these societies are of course in the area of the natural sciences and the technologies that derive from them. But similar achievements have been realized in other areas such as law, the fine arts, and history itself; and here too there has been significant impact on the wider life of the society in question.

Two features, in particular, of this development are of special importance for the purposes of a theory of the historical process. One of these is the fact that the standard of truth by which such inquiries judge themselves supplies a standard by which progress in particular sectors of this second-order human activity can be judged. The way in which such a standard of progress can be employed for historical purposes will be discussed in Chapter 5. The second feature is that within the context of these critical inquiries that are carried out upon a preexisting body of beliefs and practices there are not only unique opportunities for individual human beings to make contributions of decisive importance but also the possibility of a new form of association among them that is based on this common pursuit. Because the development of the arts and sciences has typically taken place under the tutelage and at least partial control of other institutions—both religious and political—and many of these have been strongly inclined to suppose that they had a monopoly on such civilizing enterprises, a recognition that such undertakings had their analogues in other societies was slow to come. But when it did, it brought with it the idea and the ideal of a form of association and of cooperative work to which contributions could in principle be made by anyone. Even though the institutions that were formed to support and channel this work—the academies and professional associations and universities—remained for the most part local or national in character, they were imbued with a strongly universalistic ethos and have been typically allergic to any form of external direction or control. In this way the ideal of a noncoercive and potentially universal human community based on the exercise of creative and intellectual powers has gradually taken form; and it has frequently claimed to take precedence over the demands that are made upon its members (and human beings generally) by the practical and natural communities to which they also necessarily belong. The institutional structure supporting this claim has for the most part been very tenuous or altogether nonexistent and so it is hardly possible to speak of this ideal community of inquirers as an "action-community." Nevertheless, it has real importance for our interpretation of the historical process. History itself, understood as a discipline and a scholarly pursuit, has not remained untouched by the universalistic conception of inquiry I have been describing; and especially in its judgmental and interpetative dimension it has often been responsive to the stimulus it receives from that ethos. More specifically, it suggests itself that the development of a noncoercive and universal form of human association based on the exercise of those faculties which enable us to apprehend a common truth may serve as a model of the kind of human community that could serve as the *telos* in terms of which the dialectic of societies and institutions can be interpreted in a way that has a claim to universal acknowledgment.

V

In Chapter 1 the notion of a form of teleology that would be internal to the historical process was introduced and it was contrasted with other conceptions of teleology which, on the basis of various kinds of a priori considerations, postulate a goal or end-state toward which human history as a whole is held to be moving. It may be hoped that the line of argument developed in this chapter has substantially clarified this notion of an internal teleology of history. If the account that has been proposed here is correct, history owes its teleological character in the first instance to the central place of human action, especially in its collective forms, within it; and it is this element of agency that makes all of the distinctively teleological modes of conceptualization—those of ends and of means in particular—applicable to historical processes. It has also been argued that such agency has a dimension of historicity by virtue of which it defines its relationship to its own past. It does so selectively and often critically but always in such a way as to introduce an element of continuity and of cumulativeness into what would otherwise be the bare succession of events. In this sense, the "story" character of history is not something that is superadded to its constituent events by the historian but an essential ingredient in the process itself which these events compose whether they are ever rendered in the form of a history(n) or not. Nor is this a process that goes on only within particular societies. As these societies come into contact with one another, they also enter one another's actional fields and are assigned a certain place within the internal rationale of one another's life. Once again the movement of the historical process itself may be described as being integrative in the sense that it generates its own story character in this wider sphere of contacts just as it does in the narrower one. One may accordingly say that there is thus just as much and just as little unity in human history as a whole as is effected through the intentional relationships in which actual societies set up among one another. To use the language of Sartre, each society "totalizes" its own past and its present and future field of actions including the other totalizing societies which the latter comprises; and there is no antecedent logical form which these totalizations must assume in relation to one another.[46] Thus, there is no antecedent necessity that the Orient and the West must understand themselves and one another in a way that fits a cumulative schedule of development as Hegel hypothesized. These relationships can be nonexistent or they can be of trivial importance or they may be as important as the relationship between the Greco-Roman world and modern Europe or between Europe and America. In other words, although human history as such is to be sharply distinguished from any sense of the term "history" that applies to biological evolution or geological processes, it does not follow from this that mankind as such constitutes the proper unit in terms of which such a history would have to be constructed. It is in fact problematic whether human beings have always been able (or willing) to recognize one another's common humanity; and it is absolutely certain that even where it has been recognized, it has counted for little by comparison with the more restricted identities on which institutions have been based.[47] Nevertheless, the fact that such a universal human history has not in fact come into being does not mean that it cannot exist; and there are many signs that the actual movement of the histories of the various nonuniversal human communities has for some time now been manifestly in the direction of a community of fate if not of purpose. Whether this circumstance will lead to the emergence through internalization of a new and truly human—because universal—community is the great issue that we all face today.

It may seem that internal teleology as it has been construed here is just another expression for "subjective" teleology. This suggestion has already been considered and rejected in the form in which it implies that the intention associated with some sequence of action is merely the agent's "subjective" opinion as to what is going on—an opinion which may or may not stand the test of historical criticism. There is, however, another sense which the term "subjective" may carry and which has to do with the evaluative and moral issues which arise in connection with the concept of teleology. In this sense to say that all teleology is "subjective" would be to say that no end that a society sets for itself can claim any greater validity than any other end and that there is therefore no common principle of appraisal that would be applicable to the internal rationales in terms of which historical events are understood. The only standard that could be used for determining that a given sequence of events is to be regarded as a progress would be the order of priorities of some one or other of the parties who are affected by these events. A basis for an evaluative characterization that would be independent of such partisan involvement and yet carry an authority that reflects more than the historian's own preferences would be simply lacking. But it should be noted that this issue, that is, whether my rejection of all forms of external teleology carries with it a commitment to this kind of evaluative relativism in the domain of historical interpretation and judgment, is not one that has been dealt with in this chapter and it should accordingly be understood that it remains unresolved at this stage of my argument. It should not, in other words, be simply assumed that the pluralism that characterizes the forms of teleological organization that human agency contributes to the historical process and the unavailability of any single antecedent *telos* in terms of which all such agency could be interpreted compel the acceptance of a relativistic theory of historical judgment. Once again I must refer the reader to Chapter 5 for my attempt to confront this issue directly.

4. Historical Narrative

The last chapter dealt with history as a distinctive kind of sequence of events; and although the role of historicity in making possible such a sequence was emphasized, almost no attention was given to history in its second main sense of historiography. History as record and as text must therefore form the subject matter of this chapter; and an attempt will be made to build on the results achieved in the course of the preceding discussion of the historical process and to show their implications for the analysis of historiography. More specifically, attention will be concentrated on historical narrative as the form of historical writing which most directly reflects the features of the historical process that were distinguished in the last chapter. This characterization of historical narrative will have two principal aspects. First, since it is not my intention to claim that all historical writing must be narrative in character on pain of losing its status as historical, it will be necessary to clarify the position of narrative history vis-à-vis other forms of historical writing and historical inquiry, and to do so in a way that gives a clear sense to the notion of the centrality of narrative within history as a whole for which I will argue. The second part of the task of this chapter will be to propose a characterization of historical narrative itself and specifically of the mode of continuity it establishes among the temporally successive events it recounts. By contrast with the matters which were discussed in the last chapter, these topics relating to the status and nature of historical narrative have recently been the subject of active discussion; and it will therefore be useful to develop the theses which I am concerned to defend in much closer contact with opposing views than I have done hitherto. The interpretations of the nature of historical narrative which I will consider are for the most part theses about the logical structure of narrative. Although my own position is not conceived primarily in these terms, some of these views are deeply congenial to it while others, though often highly suggestive, appear to go in quite different directions. In both cases, my effort will be to show that what is missing is a satisfactory working conception of the wider context from which logical theses about historical narrative and explanation too often and too drastically abstract. As the preceding chapter indicates, I believe that context to be the dialectic of action which constitutes the historical process; and in this chapter I plan to develop the implications of this conception for our understanding of historical narrative.

I

The variety of forms which historical writing can assume is very great; and there can, as already indicated, be no question of trying to reduce them all to the narrative form, no matter how broad a definition of the latter we may eventually adopt. For one thing, the form of historical writing is often of the kind which Droysen described as "untersuchende" rather than "erzählende Geschichte" and relates to the order of the historian's inquiry much more directly than it does to the order of the events in the past with which he is concerned.[1] The presentation of evidence and the argumentation by which conclusions are drawn from this evidence are not usually cast in a narrative form. Ideally, one might argue, it should always be possible to effect a separation between the presentation and interpretation of evidence and whatever assertions about the past the historian is disposed to make on the basis of his scrutiny of that evidence. Even when this can be done, however, it would be a mistake to assume that the content of this assertion about the past must necessarily conform to the narrative mode. In a great many cases it might well do so or at any rate state some fact which would be readily incorporable into a narrative sequence as, for example, if the point to which the historical inquiry had been addressed were the date of a certain monarch's accession to power. But suppose that, instead, the concern of the historian were with the form of papal government in the Middle Ages and his conclusion were one that defined a certain relationship between ecclesiastical and secular authority.[2] Such an assertion on the part of the historian would not in any obvious way recount a series of events. Instead, it would attribute a certain structure to the institutional life of the Middle Ages; and it would typically do so in a form of statement which would normally be described as being "analytical" rather than as "narrative" in character.

This contrast of the narrative with the analytical mode is one which has achieved wide currency at the present time and its effect is to imply rather directly that the narrative mode in historiography is almost necessarily condemned to a certain shallowness and superficiality by comparison with the deeper insights that are accessible to the analytical mode.[3] The implication here is that the narrative historian is most often one who goes on using the familiar but crude descriptive apparatus of our commonsense understanding of actions and events and that as a result he is sharply limited with respect to the dimensions of these events which his account can capture. The analytical historian, by contrast, concentrates not on the sequential "...and then...and then..." in which narrative history too often exhausts itself but on the complex imbedding of each of the episodes of this narrative schema in wider patterns of culture or institutional life. These are in the current idiom "synchronic" with one another and with the episodes they determine; they are also typically of a degree of complexity and abstractness that suggests a substantial independence from the "subjective" rationales of the human agents who live and act under them. In any case, there has been a strong tendency for analytical history either to absorb the contrasting diachronic dimension of events into the synchronic altogether or, where it resists such absorption, to treat it as an unintelligible caesura between systems of synchronicity.[4] In either case, historical narrative with its commitment to the primacy of the diachronic mode and its traditional approach to the emergence of novelty through the schema of human agency must be sharply discounted.

If such views as these have become very influential among practicing historians, as they clearly have, that has been more a matter of the development of new research strategies than of philosophical argument designed to show the inadequacies of the narrative mode. Fortunately, however, the philosophical case against narrative has recently been made in a brief but powerful essay by Professor Maurice Mandelbaum, and it will be useful to review the main theses he propounds as a preliminary to the statement of my own view of the status of narrative within history as a whole.[5] In that essay Mandelbaum is concerned to call into question an interpretation of history "as a linear sequence of human actions" that is in fact very similar to the one that was put forward in the preceding chapter.[6] Against such an interpretation he argues that stories composed of successive episodes in this way require a good deal of initial analysis and explanation of "longer enduring factors which are not themselves links in the sequential chain of events which constitute the story."[7] Even in biography, which might seem to be the form of historical writing which most closely conforms to the narrative model, Mandelbaum argues that it is frequently necessary to "take into account not merely the situations by which [the] subject is confronted" but also "dispositional properties which are not themselves specific episodic events which form part of a sequential chain," that is, "factors of intelligence, temperament, and personality which often cannot be accounted for in terms of specific episodes which enter [the] narrative."[8] In other words, since stories are fully intelligible only if we know a good deal about relevant elements of structure and background and since the presentation of this information is not itself narrative in form and the factors so referred to are not themselves sequential episodes, historiography will necessarily have a nonnarrative component. But beyond that, Mandelbaum suggests that the whole conception of history as a series of antecedent-consequent relationships is misleading and should be replaced by a part-whole model of explanation in which the subject's "specific activities and decisions" will be made intelligible by being related to dispositions and traits of character which are not episodes at all and are instead stable features of that individual's makeup through most or all of his life. These linkages between the story of a person's life and his psychological and physical makeup are to be supplied by a deeper and more theoretical kind of inquiry which would be discouraged if emphasis were placed exclusively on historical narrative.

The crucial assertion that underlies this critique of history as narrative is the claim that the account a historian gives of structure and background is not itself narrative in character and deals not with episodes or actions but with stable environmental or dispositional facts which may not be at all obvious to common sense. So stated, this thesis has a solid core of truth. For example, when Henry Adams wrote his *History of the United States of America,* he devoted his first chapters to a masterly survey of the state of the country at the beginning of Jefferson's administration, in which he laid particular emphasis upon the undeveloped and relatively primitive conditions that prevailed, and he made no attempt to give this account a narrative form.[9] The features of the American scene he described were broadly synchronous rather than successive; and many of them related to permanent geographical features of the country. In a still more impressive example, Ferdinand Braudel's *Le Méditerranée et le monde méditerranéen dans l'âge de Philippe II,* the first two-thirds of that very long book are given over to an account of the structures—geographical, agricultural, economic, and so on—of the Mediterranean world before the "histoire événementielle"—in this case, the political and military history of the latter half of the sixteenth century—is reached.[10] Again, and in this case quite consciously and deliberately, the narrative form is abandoned; and it really seems that Braudel is describing the stable structures of life in the Mediterranean basin. These examples clearly give considerable plausibility to the claim that narrative history is not only not the substratum of all the other forms which historiography assumes but itself depends on a stratum of nonnarrative description and analysis.

One may wonder, however, whether such an objection would not rest on a conception of narrative history that is so restrictive as virtually to lack application. If narrative history must always proceed from one event to another and never interrupt the sequence of "and then's" with broader characterizations of one kind or another, then even the most famous exemplars of narrative history will not satisfy this requirement. From Thucydides to Macaulay the great narrative historians have felt quite free to interrupt the story they were telling for the purpose of describing the character of a statesman or the topography of a battlefield. In a book like Braudel's, of course, excursuses of this type have become so much larger and so much more important that it is the narrative sections that seem to be appendages of the main body rather than the reverse; but the older narrative historians were also trying to provide the sort of background that would make their narrative more intelligible than it would otherwise be. We might, of course, try to reinterpret the distinction between narrative and nonnarrative history by setting limits to these background characterizations and say that, when these limits are exceeded, the history in question is no longer of the narrative type. It is unlikely, however, that wide agreement could be achieved as to just how these limits should be defined; and in any case the deeper issue raised by Mandelbaum's objections would not be satisfactorily joined along such lines. That issue is not really whether narrative histories contain nonnarrative sections or, if they do, how extensive these may be. It concerns rather the nature of the structures which these nonnarrative sections reputedly deal with and the relationship of these structures to the events which make up the narrative portions of the history.

Although Mandelbaum does not discuss this issue in any detail, there are indications of the sort of view he is inclined to defend. Thus, he speaks disapprovingly of the widespread assumption "that what occurs in history is to be construed as if its occurrence were primarily, or even exclusively, due to intentional human actions" and that "history [is] a linear sequence of intelligible human actions" which it is the historian's job to trace.[11] This seems to indicate that his deeper objection is not to the literary form of narrative or to mistaken claims that this form is the universal form of historiography, but rather to the claim that history derives its characteristic mode of ordering its materials from the teleological organization of human action. If this conjecture is correct, then he would be saying not only that historians must abandon the narrative form on occasion but also that, when they do so, they must talk about something besides human actions and employ an explanatory mode quite different from that suggested by the "linear sequence of intelligible human actions." In its nonnarrative aspects, history will concern itself not with actions but with "traits," "dispositional properties," and "recurrent patterns (of) behavior" and these terms clearly designate, not episodes that occur at particular times, but stable and perduring features of the person or the situation which is under study.[12] It is these lasting characteristics that are to give unity and pattern to the lives of the individuals whose decisions and actions are to be related to them. Mandelbaum does not say that these traits incorporate lawlike regularities or that an action's being related to a permanent trait involves its subsumption under some such laws; but references to "recurrent patterns of behavior" strongly suggest that something of this kind is intended.

Now when one says as Mandelbaum does that the "background" against which we view human actions is not itself "a part of the story of [those] actions," this statement is susceptible of two interpretations.[13] It may mean that what is related by way of background is not part of the story because it is not an episode or event at all and therefore can find no place among the episodes which form the story; or it may mean that although the relevant background may consist of events, they are events of a kind which do not lend themselves to a narrative form of presentation. If one examines the examples which Mandelbaum offers, they seem to suggest now the one and now the other of these interpretations. Thus, when he states that "it would be a gross distortion of the events with which the historian is concerned if one were to regard the events which constitute an [election] campaign as a linear series...in which each event is causally related to a particular antecedent and itself leads to a particular consequent" and cites the need for attention to "such factors as the stable voting habits of some segments of the population and a recognition of the manner in which long-standing interests, disaffections and needs in various geographic, economic or ethnic groups will be relevant to eventual success or failure," he seems to be inclining to the second interpretation.[14] There is, moreover, much support for such a view in the actual practice of historians who in the course of their nonnarrative excursuses typically inform us as to patterns of life, whether in an individual or a society, that form a more or less uniform background against which the events of the story that is being told are thrown into sharp relief. These are, in other words, the things that people do over and over again— their habitual and familiar ways of making a living, worshipping, making war, or whatever. Precisely because there is little or nothing to differentiate one cycle in such routines from another and no clear sense in which the routine itself forms over time a dramatic unit with a beginning, a middle, and an end, it is scarcely surprising that background characterizations of recurrent patterns of action are usually given in nonnarrative terms and that those patterns are referred to by means of dispositional predicates. In fact, such terms normally serve simply as economical summarizations of patterns of action which are relevant to the understanding of the main story line but may not by themselves have any interesting dramatic structure.

But if such a characterization of what one would expect to find in the background of a narrative is unexceptionable, it remains unclear why such a conception must tell against the view of history as a "linear sequence of intelligible human actions." In speaking of "patterns of action" one is, after all, still speaking of actions, and of actions that follow one another in time and that are intelligible in the sense of being performed for a reason. It is not as though by introducing the notions of such patterns of actions into his narrative the historian had moved to entirely new ground or abandoned his interest in rational human agency. What he has done instead is to "thicken" his working conception of such agency by recognizing that it has distinguishable strata and that the episodes with which he deals in his narrative must be presented in such a way as to give a sense of the context in which they took place. To take the example of an election campaign which Mandelbaum himself proposes, the fact that the Southern states regularly voted Democratic in the post–Civil War period would presumably be the "whole" and the corresponding "part" would be their doing so in a particular election year. But in referring that part to a pattern of political behavior over many years as its proper whole the historian would not have enriched our understanding very greatly unless he also exhibited this pattern of political statistics as a pattern of agency based on certain attitudes toward the competing political parties and, most importantly, on the still-fresh memory of the Civil War. The only conception of narrative that could not admit this degree of complexity in the kind of agency with which it deals would be one so impoverished that it could hardly deserve to be taken seriously. Historical narrative is not, after all, a series of self-contained episodes, linked only to those that precede and follow it. Each episode of agency typically takes into account a great many features of the situation in which it occurs as well as of those that precede and that may follow upon it; and these features can include the very regularities themselves under which Mandelbaum wishes to subsume the episodes in a narrative. At one point in fact he seems to come close to acknowledging this fact when he says that "to understand the various strategems which each political party will employ, one must grasp their relationship to longer enduring factors which are not themselves links in the sequential chain of events." [15] It is unclear, however, whether Mandelbaum would agree that these "longer enduring factors" are recognized and taken into account not just by the historian but also by the designers of the strategems which the historian has to interpret and that the reason *why* the historian should pay attention to these regularities is precisely the fact that they characterize the patterns of agency of his subjects and thus may figure as premises in the counterstrategies of other such subjects. In any case, such patterns of action are typically so familiar to those who engage in them that among the latter there is no need to allude specifically to them for the purposes of making a story line intelligible. This need arises with increasing remoteness from this kind of familiarity with the context in which the actions of the story were performed; and the nonnarrative excursuses which the historian or novelist undertakes are often designed to help the reader to avoid confusing his own assumed contexts of action with those of the agents in the story. But the relationship in which these contextual elements of information stand to the actional developments of the story *sensu stricto* are not therefore different from those that obtain within the story itself; they are, in fact, included in the background of the story because they form a part of the background of the actions with which the story deals.

As I have already noted, Mandelbaum offers other examples of the part-whole relationship which seem to favor the first interpretation suggested above and which exclude events and thus actions from the background characterizations of the historian. These are the examples in which the relevant elements of information have to do with "dispositions" such as "factors of intelligence, temperament, and personality." One can certainly agree with Mandelbaum that such matters are indeed included in what we need to know in order to construct or understand a narrative, but here again it does not seem that the part-whole schema can do justice to the complexity of the relationship in which they stand to the events of the narrative proper. This can be shown best by means of an example which Mandelbaum does not use but which is unquestionably relevant to historical understanding and even more remote from the "linear sequence of intelligible human actions" than are the dispositional properties he does cite. I have in mind here the various features of the geographical setting in which the events of some narrative occur. Typically, the facts contained in a "geographical" preface to a historical account—distances, types of terrain, quality of soil, climate, and so on—do not describe human actions, and could not well be described in narrative form. Although these natural circumstances are not wholly unalterable by human action—the course of a river can be changed—they do constitute the more or less permanent nonhuman framework within which human history takes place; and while this environment may be very different in different places and times, its presence and its relevance to the understanding of human activities is a constant of human history. But if it would be impossible to give a historical account of human doings that abstracted altogether from this natural setting, it is equally clear that the geography in question is human geography, that is, those features of the natural setting that block or facilitate human effort in one or another of its major areas. These features of the natural setting have to be described because they stand in some relationship to human need and effort; and they assume their full significance in a historical account only when they are set in the context of a certain level of technology and technical capabilities. Thus, distances have a quite different meaning for purposes of sixteenth-century history than for twentieth-century history because the "coefficient of adversity" they present is specifiable only for a stipulated level of technology. All too often this interdependence of natural setting and human activity has been forgotten or left implicit in the geographical sections of history books; but in a work like Braudel's the topography, the climate, the resources of the Mediterranean area are described in a manner that makes their role within the human scene so clear that Braudel can truly speak of the "Mediterranean world" as an indissoluble unity of natural setting and human agency. The natural setting is thus the material precondition for those routines of action referred to above; and although mountain ranges and climates are certainly not actions, the context in which they become elements in the background of some historical narration is normally that of those purposive routines of action to which reference has been made.

Even if the dispositions referred to in the background characterization were the psychological ones which Mandelbaum himself proposes, the appropriateness of the part-whole schema would not be very much greater. There can, of course, be no doubt that "traits" or "dispositions" like those Mandelbaum cites do have their place within a historical account. A historian may tell his readers about such attributes of his subjects as, for example, their degree of intelligence, the state of their health, their capacity for enduring suffering or for sympathetic identification with others, or their physical strength. To these the historian of the future may wish, if he is able, to add disquisitions on the central nervous system of his subjects. The abilities and disabilities that are thus attributed to historical personages by way of explanatory preface to an account of something they did do seem to be somehow more permanent and more unalterable than the actions they help explain; and so they appear to satisfy the requirement of an explanatory structure that is antecedent to the episodic events of the narrative account itself. But in what sense can such attributions of dispositions be said to replace the "linear sequence" of human actions in the narrative? Suppose we take one of Mandelbaum's own examples and consider intelligence as a relatively stable attribute of the historical agents with whom we are concerned and attempt to see how this "background" feature of human personality might serve to explain human action. How, to cite a specific case, does the undoubted fact that General de Gaulle was a highly intelligent man help us to understand his career as a statesman? We might agree that his intelligence enabled de Gaulle to carry out policies in a way that would have been impossible for, say, a senile Hindenburg and that in this sense the possession of a certain level of intelligence may be a necessary condition for a given level of accomplishment. But it seems equally clear that just as the features of a natural setting have to be related to the kind of use that human beings want to make of them and can make of them before they will have much relevance to the concerns of history, so too a quality like intelligence has constantly to be situated within the properly actional context of the uses a given individual wishes to make of whatever natural endowments he may be supposed to possess. Intelligence in other words would be the necessary or supporting or facilitating condition for a form of activity which it does not by itself in any way dictate; and this does not seem to be a role that is very aptly described as that of whole to part.

This brief review of the case against narrative as Mandelbaum presents it strongly suggests that the distinction between historical narrative and its nonnarrative background can best be made *within* the domain of human agency that was marked out in the discussions of the last chapter and that the analytical functions of the historian can be adequately characterized without introducing a theory, like that of the part-whole relationships proposed by Mandelbaum, that breaks with the agency-based presuppositions of the narrative mode. The fundamental point here is that human agency has distinct strata. These were distinguished from one another as the "cyclical" and the "linear" and it was argued that a distinctively historical process is one that incorporates both kinds of agency: the kind that expresses itself in the more or less stable routines by which the business of life is regularly discharged and the distributive and collective actions that deviate from those routines or are addressed to situations that lie outside the prior organization of life within a given society. In an obvious sense, it is the latter that form the primary and most natural subject matter for narrative history since they mark the entrance of a society or an institution into an area of novelty and uncertainty that transcends the familiar domain of its established routines. What is done over and over again in pretty much the same circumstances and with pretty much the same kinds of results can be rendered in a typifying account in which primary emphasis is placed not on the temporal succession of actions as such but rather on the complex relationships among different human agents and between such agents and their natural environment upon which these stable routines are predicated. In such cases, although the element of novelty and uncertainty can never be wholly eliminated from any human action, enough stability and predictability is realized so that one can say that the element of temporality and succession that is inseparable from all human action is dominated by the organizing structures of social work; and although one can imagine a narrative that would faithfully reproduce each occasion on which these routines were deployed, it would be an incredibly redundant and boring narrative. It is just these cases in which the new action repeats the pattern of the prior ones and does not introduce any significant element of novelty that can be most readily accommodated to the part-whole schema; and it is this fact, more than anything else, which casts doubt on the suitability of that schema as a general interpretation of the way historical narrative proceeds. Narrative in the more usual and interesting sense is reserved for those singular events which do not form part of an established routine and for which there is not the alternative of a nonnarrative treatment because they create new situations in which the old routines on which a typifying account would rely may themselves be drawn into the process of change.

There is another important conclusion with respect to historical narrative that is suggested by the set of distinctions within the domain of human agency that were proposed in the last chapter. This is that the "regularities" with which the historian is typically concerned—the "stable factors of long-standing" of Mandelbaum's account—cannot claim the kind of unrestricted universality that would make them in principle independent of any spatial or temporal limits in the way that the regularities formulated in scientific laws are usually held to be. When a regularity is a pattern of action within some human community, there is not only no reason to suppose that that regularity must hold beyond the limits of that society; there is not even any reason to believe that it must always hold within that society. These are in other words "local" regularities which are themselves historical in the sense that they are in principle as subject to change as are the particular situations which they "govern." The spatio-temporal "locales" in which they obtain may be as extensive as mankind itself or as narrow as a single family. They may be passing fads or they may be so deeply ingrained in the life of a society that its members can hardly imagine what that life would be like if these regularities no longer held. But neither their actual scope, in space or in time, nor the degree of firmness with which they are established can affect their status as patterns of action; and it is because these regularities are patterns of action that they are inescapably subject to revision. Thus, if we say that the Greeks use oil instead of butter or that the Portuguese do not kill their bulls at the end of the corrida whereas the Spaniards do or that unlike the Germans the Russians tightly swaddle newborn infants, we are not stating a law; we are describing a shared pattern of action which belongs in the series of intelligible human actions although at a different stratum from particular episodes, and not in the domain of the nonhistorical regularities of natural science. The latter, of course, impinge in their own way on properly historical events whether as the necessity with which the victim of the assassin collapses or as the principle which a bit of technology turns to advantage. But this ever-present natural or cosmic background is of comparatively little relevance to the work of the historian. The proximate regularities under which the latter seeks to bring the events with which he deals are actional in character; and while those inevitably take the circumstances and limits posed by these natural regularities into account, there is no realistic prospect of our being able to extend the chain of derivation and establish a linkage between historical regularities and nonhistorical laws of unrestricted universality. When we try to ignore these discontinuities and assimilate the one kind of regularity to the other, we run into difficulties to which attention will be given in the course of this chapter.

It follows from what has been said that historical narrative constitutes the mode of understanding that is proper to events which for one reason or another are not just parts of wholes or new instances of a recurrent pattern and therefore require an individualizing rather than a typifying mode of treatment. It is important to understand, however, that this is not to deny that history incorporates forms of inquiry that address themselves to the past for the purpose of discovering those elements in the life of some human community which were for some period of time invariant. The results of such an inquiry which defines the life of the community under study in synchronic terms may be entirely adequate and satisfactory from the standpoint guiding the inquiry; and when this is so there is no need to ask whether they are obtained by means of a special abstraction from such forms of instability and change as may have been taking place within the community in question or whether the routines so uncovered in fact subsume the life of this community in a quite literal way. The point I am making is rather that this point of view is historical only in a limited sense and that historians are interested in *both* stability and change, in routines of life and in singular events that depart from those routines in such a way as to produce changes in them. There are also disciplines like anthropology that make use of historical methods of inquiry for the purpose of investigating a society in the past which in these aspects that are of interest to the anthropological inquirer may have been quite static.[16] A historian in the full sense, however, is, I am assuming, defined not just by the reference of his inquiries to the past but by the conception of the historical process within which he works; and this is a conception within which there are, in varying proportions, elements of both sameness and change, of routines and singular events. What is to count as a singular event will of course depend to some extent on the scope of the historical inquiry itself and on the way in which the routines themselves are understood. But the important point here is that a sequence of events that breaks up an established routine or gives rise to another one cannot be understood as simply an instance of either the prior or the later routine; and it is in this sense a singular event and one that requires an individuating form of representation. This form of representation, when applied to a number of events that succeed one another in time, is what I will refer to as historical narrative.[17]

II

Against the background of the conclusions reached in the course of the preceding section, it should now be possible to turn to the positive characterization of historical narrative. It is, to begin with, generally agreed that a narrative of whatever kind presents the events with which it is concerned in the temporal order in which they occurred. This does not mean that a narrative may never leap over events or return to an earlier point in the sequence; but rather that wherever it rejoins the movement of events it will proceed once more in a temporally sequential way. What is not so clear is whether a narrative must do more than report such events in their proper time order and whether it must exhibit them as being connected in ways that go beyond the relationship that derives from their position in that time order. Those philosophers of history who answer this question in the affirmative often use some such term as "chronicle" to designate a record of events which exhibits no supplementary form of continuity; and others who are not concerned to reserve the term "narrative" as such for a contrasting use make a distinction between "plain" and "significant" narrative.[18] This is a terminological issue on which nothing very momentous depends; but unless calendars and almanacs are to be included among narratives, it seems unlikely that very many "plain" narratives can be identified in which events are connected only by virtue of the temporal positions which they occupy in relation to one another. A narrative does not, after all, report just any events that happen to satisfy this condition of temporal order. Instead it limits itself to events which have something to do with the chosen theme or subject matter of the narrative; and when these events are human actions or utterances as they typically are, it becomes quite unlikely that the order in which they follow upon one another will be "nonsignificant" in the sense of contributing nothing to our understanding of why these events occurred. One may suspect that a narrative that really managed to report the sequence of events in such a way as to imply no further explanatory connection among them would also be one to which it would be hard to attribute any internal organizing structure—a beginning and an end, for example—in any sense that is not itself purely temporal in character. There is, of course, a difference between a narrative that does not go beyond the kind of commonsense connectedness that is virtually inseparable from anything we are likely to call a narrative and the narrative that stops to ask questions that cannot be answered without some sort of further inquiry; it may be that this is the distinction which those who have spoken of "plain" and "significant" narrative have had in mind. But even so it would still be the case that "plain" narratives suggest an explanation, however inadequate and superficial it may be, of the occurrence of the events they report; the criterion of significance, accordingly, would be one which all narratives would, however modestly, satisfy.

To assert that all narratives perform some explanatory function is to be brought face to face with issues relating to the nature of explanation and, more specifically, its logical structure. The most notable general conceptions of explanation are, as we have seen, the nomological-deductive theory and its teleological competitor; and the hypothesis upon which the philosophical analysis of historical narrative proceeds is that the logical structure of one of these will prove to be a reliable guide to the structure of narrative. I have examined elsewhere two current versions of the theory of narrative to which the nomological-deductive theory gives rise and have tried to identify its characteristic weaknesses.[19] The most conspicuous of these is the failure of such theories of narrative to give adequate attention to the kind of connectedness among events that characteristically arises in a context of human action; and as a result of this failure it has been necessary for the exponents of this view of narrative to seek the source of the connectedness of events in lawlike regularities that are wholly independent of the organization of events which action effects. In these circumstances, one would naturally expect that a teleological theory of explanation would be ideally well suited to the requirements of historical narrative and that, in view of the strong natural affinities between the two, a teleological theory of historical narrative would already have been fully elaborated. And yet surprisingly enough this proves to be not really the case. In the two most substantial explorations of the concept of historical explanation from a teleological standpoint—those of Professor William Dray and Professor G. H. von Wright—historical narrative as such has not been very extensively discussed, perhaps because the main concern of their accounts has been with the logical structure of such explanations as such rather than with its implications for the analysis of narrative.[20] As things stand, the closest thing we have to a teleological interpretation of narrative is the account presented by Professor W. B. Gallie; but in spite of its great suggestiveness the perspective from which it is constructed seems somewhat limiting.[21] Too often the focus of interest seems to be the process of following as a reader a historical narrative rather than of analyzing the teleological principle on which such a narrative is constructed, much less the historical process itself with which the historian deals. At the same time, however, the interpretation of narrative that will be presented here draws extensively on the pioneering work of these writers, and its main effort will be to connect these (not always identical) conceptions of teleology with the theory of the historical process that was developed in the last chapter and with a conception of historical narrative that corresponds with the latter.

It will be convenient to begin by locating a little more precisely the inadequacies of the presently available theories of teleological explanation as these relate to the analysis of historical narrative; and I will use Dray's theory of rational explanation as my example. This theory undertakes to show, against the claims made by the exponents of the covering-law theory, that human actions can be explained without recourse at any point to universal causal laws. As Dray puts it, rational explanations are the historian's reconstruction "of the agent's *calculation* of means to be adopted toward his chosen end in the light of the circumstances in which he found himself"; and "to explain the action we need to know what considerations convinced him that he should act as he did."[22] In this statement there is an explicit reference to the agent's future—"his chosen end"—which is said to govern his choice of means in the present; but otherwise there is no attention to the connections among events which might be implicit in the agent's "calculation." To be sure, the reference to "the circumstances in which he [the agent] found himself" does not exclude their being stated in a form which relates them to specific past events, but it does not require it either, and the whole bit of practical reasoning that is imputed to the agent might very well, for all Dray says here, be tied to actual events only through the one factual premise relating to circumstances at the time of the action. The point I am making is that with the exception of the reference to the end to be achieved there is little in such a conception of the explanation of human action that breaks out of the segmented conception of time discussed earlier and correspondingly little that suggests a mode of continuity among the events that compose a historical narrative.

What is most distinctive about the rational explanation theory, at least in Dray's version of it, is the emphasis it places on what it takes to be the *appraisive* character of the historian's judgment as to the reasons which led to the action he is trying to explain. The historian is trying to reach "a logical equilibrium at which point an action is matched with a calculation";[23] and when that point is reached the action is seen to be the appropriate one in the sense that "if the situation had been as the agent envisaged it (whether or not we from our point of vantage concur in his view of it) then what was done would have been the thing to do."[24] As Dray himself points out, however, this kind of appraisal does not imply any endorsement by the historian of the action under consideration and really reduces to the characterization of the action as "rationalizable" given a certain combination of beliefs about the agent's situation and certain goals to which he is committed. Once it is understood that the agent's calculations and preferences are such as to make the action in question a suitable one, that action has been satisfactorily explained at least for historical purposes; and there is no need, in Dray's view, to explain the fact that the agent had just these beliefs and these preferences and certainly no need to do so in a way that involves the use of general laws. This amounts to the view that it is legitimate in certain contexts of explanation to treat the rational agent as the final term of our explanation beyond which we do not seek further causes; and this is a view which has much to recommend it. But in the form in which Dray presents it, it may seem to require too sharp a rupture in the tissue of events to be acceptable. Unless an agent's having the beliefs and desires he has is a fit subject for historical analysis, the result may be that these beliefs and desires and the actions they motivate will lack any comprehensible relationship to prior events. In fact, this impression is due in large part, I believe, to Dray's rather abstract way of conceiving the agent's calculations and his tendency to emphasize the fact that they satisfy certain logical criteria of rationality rather than that they establish their own distinctive form of continuity with prior events. It is one thing to repudiate the claim that the continuity of historical events always requires that these events be subsumed under general laws, and this Dray has done with great skill and cogency. But if the competing model of rational explanation is construed in such a way that the policies of action by reference to which actions are to be explained stand in a "vertical" and abstract relationship to events and thus fail to establish any alternative form of continuity with prior events, then it will be difficult to translate this theory of historical explanation into a theory of historical narrative and of the continuity which is usually thought to be the distinctive mark of such narrative.

This criticism of the theory of rational explanation which has just been sketched is closely related to another one which is addressed to what might be called the individualistic bias of that theory. There has been a tendency on the part of philosophers of all persuasions to assume that the actions with which historians deal can be analyzed in much the same way as individual or personal decisions and to forget that these actions are in fact typically such as are taken in a public context and in behalf of some group or institution and that as such they are subject to multiple constraints beyond those that operate in the case of personal decisions. Whatever the balance of effective power within the group or society in question, it seems fair to say that significant actions must be in some comprehensible relationship to the traditions and established expectations of some substantial fraction of the membership of that group. It is, of course, possible for a minority and sometimes even for an individual to resolve upon a course of action on the basis of considerations that prescind from such traditions; but much the more common case is the one in which at least an effort is made to present what is to be done as reflecting shared understandings as to what the policies of the society are to be. Such understandings can be represented in the form of general principles from which an application to present circumstances is then deductively derived; but it is doubtful whether this is in fact the form in which the tradition would be understood by the people in question. The more plausible view is that this tradition is maintained in the more highly particularized and concrete form of an account of what that society has done and suffered over the period of its existence.[25] What I am suggesting then is not only that the "goals" which would figure in the major premise of a schematization of the rationale of a collective action are goals which command some degree of shared acceptance by the members of a single society, but also that such goals are not readily detachable from that society's understanding of what it has been doing over a longer period of time. If this is correct, then the statement of a policy of action for such a society would not involve a unilateral reference to a future change to be realized in a present situation. It would also and equally carry forward into its future a certain understanding of what that society has already done and suffered, and it would construe its present circumstances in terms of what they signify within the context of such a past. To the extent that schematizations of the rationale of historical action make it appear that having a goal on the part of some society or institution is simply a matter of deciding in the present to bring about some change in the future and to the extent that the reference these goals and these readings of present circumstances make to the past is thereby obscured, the illusion is created that all the operative reasons for such actions are located in the present and in the future.

The point I am making here is one that has to do with the comparative importance for historical purposes of different elements in the practical inference on the part of the historical agent which all these theories of teleological explanation in history postulate. It seems fair to say that the element in such practical inferences which has received least attention is the factual premise which describes the relevant features of the situation in which the agent finds himself (or supposes himself to be) and this neglect is doubtless explained by the fact that the function of this premise is simply to make the major premise dealing with goals or principles of action applicable to the given situation of the agent. Typical logical schematizations tend to suggest that the features of such situations to which reference is made in these "factual" premises are such as are readily describable in general terms and thus in terms that rather directly invoke the application of higher-order policies of the agent. It is the goals set by these policies that are controlling, and "situations" are simply classified according to the opportunities they present for the realization of these goals. But such a schema does not readily accommodate the case in which it may be something in the factual situation—an action by another party in that situation—which first creates the need for action and in which it may be another element in that situation—one's institutional affiliation and the traditions of that institution—that are centrally involved in the response that is forthcoming. Doubtless these cases could be accommodated to the schema of practical deliberation described above; but the fact remains that the tendency of that schema is to encourage a neglect by the philosophical analyst of the embeddedness of the agent himself and of his motives for action in the process which receives such scant recognition in the "factual" premise. The alternative would be to find ways of representing the practical inference of the historical agent that would not allow the relevant prior events which he is taking into account to disappear under descriptions cast in general terms. If that were done then the practical inference of the historical agent would not have the effect of sealing off his action within its own self-sufficient rationality, but would insure instead the continuity of that action with preceding events through the overlap between the practical inferences of different agents in which the conclusions of one such inference would provide the initial premise of that of another.

In this connection it may be worth noting that the usual counterpart to the neglect of continuity with prior events which I am attributing to the theory of rational explanation is a tendency to exaggerate the explicitness and degree of generality of the agent's calculations and to set impossibly high standards of rationality for these actions to meet.[26] In this connection it has been pointed out recently that there has been a tendency to make it a condition of an action's qualifying as rational that that action has been considered at a level of generality and in a context of alternatives which are in fact characteristic of only the most highly reflective decisions. These are extremely rare and yet we do not normally regard all other decisions as irrational whose ultimate justifying principles may never have been critically reviewed. Instead of enforcing such unrealistic conditions defining rationality upon actions that plainly cannot satisfy them, it seems more reasonable to interpret the rationality of action in terms of a congruence between one's goals and the predicted outcomes of actions taken on the occasion of opportunities that present themselves. For example, the rationality of Bismarck's action in revising the Ems dispatch would consist in the fact that the effect of the publication of the revised text upon the French public was to make the war Bismarck desired inevitable. To be sure, this goal formed part of a yet more comprehensive set of goals which Bismarck was trying to realize and so contributed to a systematic coherence within his policies. But this is quite different from saying that Bismarck methodically compared this course of action with others that may have been open to him and decided upon the action he took because he believed it would produce the optimal combination of benefits.

In more general terms the claim I am making is that human actions through their motivating reasons refer to a wide variety of events and circumstances in the past of the societies that undertake these actions. In some cases the feature of the past that is internalized in this way so as to become an element in the rationale of future action may be a specific event like the defeat of the Roman legions in the Teutoburger Forest by the Germanic tribes under Varus, an event which lived in the memory of both the Romans and the Germans and became a symbol of successful German resistance to Romanization. In other cases, the reference to the past would be more in the nature of a *reprise* as for example in the case of the reestablishment of the Roman Empire in 800 with the coronation of Charlemagne. In still other cases, a previous historical experience may serve as the model used by a society for interpreting a later one and for developing policies in the later situation; and here the case of the United States applying a concept of collective security based on the experience of Munich to Southeast Asia in the post–World War II world comes to mind. There is a host of other forms which this backward referencing of action can assume and in each of them a society may be said to act in a way which cannot be understood without a reference to its past because it makes that reference itself. In this way the action itself takes on a conceptual relationship to the past by which it is informed and it is by virtue of this relationship that events take on a retrospective as well as a prospective form of continuity. Whether this conceptual continuity should be understood as also a form of causal influence upon the present action is a question to which I will turn later, but it is already clear that the influence such events have on present action must be "routed through" the representations of them which human agents entertain. Events of various kinds can, of course, change the world in countless ways that are quite independent of our capacity to describe them. They cannot provide reasons for or against actions, however, otherwise than under a certain mode of conceptualization or description; and it is this same mode of conceptualization of them by the historical agents themselves which generates a form of meaningful connectedness among events over time and thus provides the basis for historical narrative. In other words, rational explanation, when freed from the model of individual decision and from the exclusive temporal orientation running from the present to the future—both stripped of descriptions that relate them to the past—reproduces the structure of action and the mode of temporal synthesis implicit in the latter; and in this temporal form the rational structure of action is the structure of narrative.

With regard to the structure or "logic" of historical narrative a number of general theses may now be enunciated. The first of these is fundamental to everything that has been said up to this point and it asserts that human actions are the primary events with which the historian deals and that historical narrative is to be understood as the reconstruction of a sequence of human actions within which one action and its consequences become the premise for a succeeding action and so on. The second thesis is that it is a condition of grasping this kind of action-based continuity of historical narrative that the actions themselves be identified by the historian under the descriptions which the agent may be supposed to have used as well as those used by those who were in some way affected by those actions. And finally I want to argue that the explanatory function of historical narrative is teleological in character in the sense that successive episodes are connected through the role assigned to them within the practical inferences of the agents involved in them. In fact, these theses are not as distinct from one another as this mode of statement may make it appear and are in fact successive restatements of a single thesis with the emphasis successively shifted from the priority of human actions within historical narrative to the centrality of the agent's description in the identification of actions and then to the teleological character of the continuity within a sequence of actions which take one another into account. Nevertheless, for the purpose of defending them, I will treat them as distinct theses and I will take them up in the same order in which I have introduced them. Wherever possible I will try to bring these theses into a realistic relationship to actual historical materials, but in the case of the third thesis, which is the most purely philosophical of the three, I will have to abandon historical ground almost entirely and argue the logical issues involved at their own quite abstract level.

III

The events that historians recount and seek to explain are extremely heterogeneous. They include wars and famines, rebellions and depressions, discoveries of continents and declines of empires. If one wishes to argue, as I do, that history has as its preferential subject matter human actions, this thesis can evidently draw no unambiguous support from the way in which historical events are—at least superficially and initially—named. Even in the short list above, there are designations of types of historical events which plainly refer to them as actions of some kind and there are others which just as plainly do not. Thus if a historian talks about the execution of Charles I, this very way of referring to that event implies that someone executed him and presumably also that someone ordered or authorized that execution, that is, that two distinct but related acts were performed by assignable persons or groups of persons. But if the historian's interest focuses on the depression of 1929 or the Irish famine of 1846–49 it is not at all obvious that these concepts of "depression" and "famine" are names of actions; nor is it clear what actions, if any, are necessarily included in what we mean when we speak of depressions and famines. We know of course that in the case of famine there is often, as there was in Ireland in 1846, a crop failure that reduces the food supply to the point where people go hungry and die. But a crop failure is a natural event, not an action; and its consequences—people going hungry and dying—are not actions either in the sense that is relevant here. It seems then that a history of the Irish famine would have to be an account of certain natural events—the successive crop failures in the 1846–49 period—and of the suffering and death they caused. How, it may be asked, can one claim that such a history of the Irish famine would be in any special sense an account of what men did, especially when the event itself is named after that element within it which is simply a natural event?

Considerations of this kind have led many philosophers to assume that history is not merely superficially heterogeneous but profoundly and unalterably so, and that it is a mixture of actions and nonactions in which the former enjoy at best a priority of interest and attention. In fact, however, even such examples as those given above do not, under closer inspection, really support these conclusions. For while the potato blight in Ireland certainly explains why the principal food supply of the Irish people was reduced to a small fraction of its normal quantity, that fact by itself does not explain the occurrence of a famine. If it did, the work of historians of the Irish famine would be easily done—much more easily and quickly than it in fact is. To be sure, historians take due note of the destruction of successive potato crops by the *philophthora infestans* fungus; but they are not satisfied to explain the famine—the suffering and death that followed upon the crop failures—simply by reference to the latter as their cause. As any reasonable person would, they ask, "What could have been done in the circumstances to prevent starvation?" If nothing could have been done by anyone at any time to prevent the deaths that occurred, then the famine would have to be regarded as an act of God or as an event similar to the collision of the earth with another planet. It is quite clear, however, that the famine was not uncontrollable or unpreventable in that sense. Various things could have been done by various persons and institutions; and the historian who wishes to explain the famine and not just a crop failure must ask whether any of these things were done and, if they were, why they failed to prevent large-scale starvation. If they were not even attempted, he must ask why this was so and whether they were considered and then rejected; and in the latter case why they were rejected. Accordingly Mrs. Cecil Woodham-Smith in her admirable book, *The Great Hunger,* pays only passing attention to the causes of the crop failures and a great deal of attention to the attitude of the British government, especially as formulated and expressed by the permanent undersecretary of the Treasury, Charles Edward Trevelyan.[27] Since that government was aware of the magnitude of the disaster and had direct responsibilities in the area, it was in the best position to take action if something was to be done. This fact explains and justifies Mrs. Woodham-Smith's close attention to the attitude of the British government in spite of the fact that the latter did not intervene in any significant way. At the same time, Mrs. Woodham-Smith shows why it would have been very difficult to distribute food on the required scale, even if a decision to make the effort had been made, by reason of the primitive system of communication and transportation in Ireland and the absence of a highly developed governmental apparatus for carrying out welfare functions. But she also shows why the British government was reluctant to make this effort at all and why in fact it did not. Now all of this is clearly in the nature of a consideration of the matter from the standpoint of a person—especially certain persons with the means to intervene—in the situation itself, and from this standpoint the Great Hunger cannot be explained until it has been shown what courses of action might have prevented starvation in spite of the crop failures, and also why they failed if they were undertaken and why they were or were not undertaken. Among these remedial courses of action are, of course, those that were open to the victims of the famine themselves, and Mrs. Woodham-Smith very properly raises such questions as why the Irish did not take to fishing when potatoes were unavailable, although it is not clear that she really explains this.

It would appear then that in these cases at least the historian shows a certain a priori selectivity in his analysis of the causes of such an event as the Great Hunger and that this selectivity is based upon a priority assigned to actions—possible and actual—over nonactions. In a period in which plant bacteriology and related prophylactic measures did not yet exist, a potato blight and the resultant crop failure were clearly nonactions, that is, they were not actions even in the marginal sense of being partially attributable to someone's negligence or folly. The potato blight was, moreover, a necessary condition of the famine since if it had not occurred there is no reason to think there would have been a famine. At the same time, this occurrence and its likely effects were known to many persons inside and outside Ireland; and so the possibility of doing something to prevent a famine unavoidably suggested itself to those persons at the time as it does to the historian of the event. A famine follows necessarily upon the destruction of the food supply only if nothing effective is done to provide food from other sources. In the Irish case nothing effective was done; and the decision of the British government not to attempt to supply food on a large scale can properly be regarded as a further and necessary condition for the famine's occurrence. But it was not just another condition, at least from the standpoint of the historian. It has already been noted that the historian pays some attention to the causes of the potato blight; but he draws his explanations of this event from other, non-historical sources and it is not his responsibility to discover its causes if they are not such as are already clear to the relevant branch of natural science. The specific scientific explanation which the historian borrows in this way will very likely have little or no connection with the rest of his narrative; and if it were to be revised by the plant bacteriologists, that change, too, would very likely have no impact on the historian's work. Certainly the fact that a potato blight had an identifiable natural cause is important if only as a means of warding off explanations that appeal immediately to the will of God and also as an indication of the area in which long-range solutions to the problem were to be sought. But in the main the occurrence of a potato blight is simply a fact that serves as an essential premise in the kind of explanation which the historian is really concerned to give. What has to be explained is what human beings did in the situation in which they were in their different ways confronted by this fact which was also a premise of their practical deliberations and of their actions. Those actions, as it turned out, were such as to make it inevitable that famine would follow upon the potato blight; and the historian's problem is to explain not that natural event itself but the course of action and inaction by virtue of which that event was permitted to lead to a famine. My point is that it is not the primary job of the historian to explain the natural events which provide the premises of human action but those actions themselves, unless of course these premises deal with events which are themselves in some measure, at least, the result of human action.

The thesis that human actions are the primary events with which the historian deals has now been interpreted to mean that human actions are treated as the decisive causes of the events the historian studies. The suggestion is thus that the historian has reasons for being interested in actions as actions and that this choice of a standpoint for interpreting events carries with it a mode of organization that is fundamental to an understanding of historical narrative. It is accordingly of considerable interest to note that the kind of organizing influence on the form of historical narrative that I am attributing to human action has an analogue in the field of law which may cast light on the parallel case of history. In the law, as in history, it is necessary to explain what caused certain events. While it is accepted that the events of the type to be explained may stand in invariant relationships of succession to some set of the conditions that obtained at the time of the event's occurrence, this fact is not of any special relevance for purposes of determining the cause of the event in legal contexts. Usually the sufficient conditions for producing the event are not known; even if they were, that would not permit us to make the all-important distinction between normal or usual conditions and the abnormal or unusual events which are typically regarded as intervening in the normal course of events and are therefore designated as *the* cause of the event to be explained. More importantly, since the purpose of legal inquiries into causes is to fix responsibility as a preliminary to reward or punishment, voluntary human actions have a special place among the conditions that produced a certain effect. Especially when these actions are intended to produce the effect in question, they are treated as the decisive cause of that event, and all of the other conditions necessary for the production of that event are reduced to the status of means or background conditions which are utilized by the action or on which the action supervenes, as it were, from outside. But even when the action is not intended to produce the effect, as in the case of a match dropped in a forest, it may well be treated as *the* cause of the forest fire since the latter was among the results of such an action that a normal person might reasonably be expected to bear in mind and seek to avoid. On the other hand, if the result was produced only because of certain exceptional conditions that could not be anticipated, then the action of dropping the match may no longer be ranked as a cause but be demoted instead to the status of a precondition. What is important in all these cases is the fact that a distinction is made among the conditions for the occurrence of an event—a distinction between cause and conditions—and it is made on the basis of an interest in the control of the outcome by human agency. As Professor H. L. A. Hart puts it, "a deliberate human act is . . . most often a barrier and a goal in tracing back causes . . . : it is something *through* which we do not trace the cause of a later event and something *to* which we do trace the cause through intervening events of other kinds."[28]

The reason for this priority of interest within the law in human agency is, as just indicated, quite clear and has to do with the directly practical concern of the law with determining who is to be held responsible and, if appropriate, punished. That motive cannot without further ado be assigned to the historian in order to explain why he evinces the same priority of interest in human agency as does the lawyer or the judge. In this connection it is interesting to note that Hart does discuss this parallelism between history and the law and makes the observation that "the narrative of history is scarcely ever a narrative of brute sequence, but is an account of the roles played by certain factors and especially by human agents. History is written to satisfy not only the need for explanation, but also the desire to identify and assess the contribution made by historical figures to changes of importance; to disasters and triumphs and to human happiness and suffering."[29] This has certainly been the case throughout most of the history of historiography, but it has the disadvantage of making it appear that this feature of his practice which the historian shares with the jurist is simply an "interest" and as such might or might not be shared by all historians. As Hart points out, even historians who share this interest need not be moralists; and it is not quite clear what answer Hart could give to those present-day historians who claim that their inquiries are motivated entirely by the "need for explanation" and therefore feel no reluctance to trace causes through and beyond deliberate human agency. The deeper question raised by this challenge must therefore be whether there is any obstacle stronger than a traditional orientation of the historian's interest that stands in the way of a form of historical inquiry that assigns no special or privileged position to human agency.

Let us return to the example of the Irish famine in order to answer this question. One can well imagine a historian who felt no interest in condemning or justifying the action or nonaction of Charles Edward Trevelyan and no disposition to treat his reaction to the famine as the final term in his explanatory account. What would such a historian's first step beyond the permanent under-secretary of the Treasury be? One can guess that his attention would be drawn either to the long-standing relationship between England and Ireland or to the prevailing assumptions as to the role of government in the economic sphere or to both and that in either case this historian's effort would be to represent Trevelyan's case as an instance of some much more widespread system of practice. But in what sense would such a procedure provide the basis for a distinction between the historian who is disposed to move through a deliberate human act in his search for causes and the one who is not? The latter after all is interested in the reasons why people act as they do and would certainly not neglect Trevelyan's own justification for his course of conduct which appealed to precisely the kind of laissez-faire principles on which the economic system of the day rested. In these circumstances it is a fair question whether in widening the inquiry so as to bring in such matters as the pattern of economic life one would really be moving beyond or through Trevelyan's action and not simply enlarging one's view of the system of practice within which his action could seem right and proper. This could be very useful particularly as a corrective for a view of Trevelyan's conduct as a purely individual act without any larger rationalizing context. But the fact remains that that larger context impinges upon a particular occasion of action only if it has been internalized by the prospective agent—in this case Trevelyan—so that it can inform his beliefs and intentions and through them find expression in action. The same observations apply in the case of the relationship between England and Ireland if that were to be the relevant larger context of explanation. Here again it is a question of certain beliefs or prevailing assumptions as to the way a subject people may be treated; and if one of those beliefs were, for example, that Irish lives do not count for very much, it would be less likely to be cited in justification of some action and might not even be acknowledged in this form by those who in fact hold it, but for all that it would be a belief and an implicit directive for action and as such it could be efficacious on a given occasion only if it were the belief of some person who had the opportunity or responsibility for the action that would bring it into play. One can of course imagine an official who unlike Trevelyan did not personally share either of these beliefs but who acted on them nevertheless on the grounds that he had no real alternative; and in such a case the "system" does take on an appearance of externality to the agent which might seem to justify the historian in holding that in citing that system as a cause he had moved beyond a deliberate human act to a larger and more impersonal cause. But there is not only no reason to view such a relationship between bodies of beliefs or rules and the persons through whose actions they find expression as typical; it is also quite clear that it is merely a special case of the relationship described above.[30] What is different is simply the fact that because the agent does not really accept the belief on which he acts another reason of a narrower and most probably prudential kind has to be inserted between that belief and his action in compliance with it. In other words, it is the agent's own beliefs which both resist the socially accepted belief on which he is to act and which provide him with a reason for compliance; and if he had the required information, it is in these terms that the historian would have to account for the action this person finally took. As Professor Hart points out in the course of his analysis of "interpersonal transactions" it is not usual to speak of one person "causing" another to do something even when threats are used or other means that satisfy the criterion of externality to the agent's beliefs that was cited above.[31] There seems even less justification for using such language in the case of compliance with a socially accepted belief for reasons other than those supplied by the belief itself.

These considerations provide the elements of a stronger argument for the centrality of human action within historical inquiry than did those predicated on a certain kind of interest on the historian's part. Such an argument would be designed to show that if a historian traces the events in which he is interested to human actions at all, he will not be able to move through them otherwise than for the purpose of more fully exploring the contexts of practice within which they find their place. Because these contexts are themselves defined in terms of a network of beliefs and policies and in terms of the relationships they establish among various potential agents, the historian may indeed move to higher levels of understanding than a (or perhaps any) individual agent could achieve; but he is moving within the same rationalizing medium as such agents do and he is under an obligation to show how these wider aspects of the actional context within which the latter function reach a particular agent or group of agents and inform the beliefs and purposes that find expression in their actions. No doubt such a story could be told about Charles Edward Trevelyan, although from Mrs. Woodham-Smith's account it appears that he was very much an agent in his own right. The main point, however, remains that there is no exit from the kinds of considerations that are generically the same as those involved in the initial agent's own action once the historian has entered upon an analysis of the role of the latter in some sequence of events. There is, moreover, strong reason to think that the supposition that there might be such an exit is due to an influence of a misleading model of the relationship in which agents stand to the wider institutional and social auspices under which they act.

The example that has been used here—the Irish famine of the 1840s—has one disadvantage in that it does not as clearly illustrate as some others might the full complexity of the exchanges that take place when *two* or more coherently organized societies or institutions are engaged with one another. It may be useful, therefore, to characterize such situations a little more fully and especially to draw attention to the way a society that is involved in such transactions has to make judgments of the nature and import of the actions in which the other society is engaged in its regard and to do so from the standpoint of the undertakings in which it is itself engaged. At the same time, the society so judged will be forming from its own standpoint *its* judgment as to what the first society is or is not doing; and in both cases some actions will be predicated upon the judgments so formed—actions for which the belief that the other society is acting in a certain way serves as an essential premise.[32] To these actions there will then correspond other actions that are similarly based on the part of the other society. A sequence of actions of this kind is one which may very appropriately be called a dialectic since in it each action responds to another which is imputed to the partner in the exchange, and it creates a new situation to which the latter then has to respond itself. As in conversation—the original model for the concept of dialectic—there is no guarantee that the partners involved in such a series of exchanges will understand one another correctly, but a response that is based on misunderstanding is no less a term in a dialectic than is one that is based on an accurate understanding. (Identification of such a move as one resting on a misunderstanding is, of course, itself a distinct matter and in relationships between institutions probably presents greater difficulties than in a conversation between individuals.) It should also be understood that a dialectic can be one of cooperation or of conflict or of some mixture of the two; and it may be one that is itself cyclical in nature, that is, is often repeated and thus familiar on both sides, or it may be one for which past experience offers no satisfactory model.

If one thinks of the history of a society as its sequence of movements through an option-tree, then the dialectical aspect of this movement would have to be represented by a kind of interlacing of the branches of two or more such trees.[33] This means that, if at any given point a society conceives itself to have a number of alternative courses of action before it, each of these will have to be understood and evaluated in terms of the possible responses it might call forth on the part of another society. The situation produced by a society's choice of a certain alternative course of action will in other words be itself modified in some more or less significant way by the choice made by another society in the new situation produced for it by the action of the first society. The latter will thus find itself in a situation involving a new set of alternatives—a situation which is the result of the sequence of its own action and the response which that action met on the part of another society; and in this way the two (or more) societies move one another forward through an option-tree that belongs wholly to neither of them and place themselves at choice-positions which they would not have chosen for themselves and which they could not have predicted with any very great degree of accuracy. Relationships of this kind have been intensively studied from a formal point of view within the theory of games; and the goal of these studies has been to construct a normative theory of rational choice under conditions of conflict and cooperation as well as under conditions of certainty and uncertainty.[34] My suggestion is that the concept of dialectic can be most profitably interpreted as a sequence of situations conceptualized in this way—situations which follow upon one another in time and which produce one another in such a way that neither party is in full control of the outcome at any given stage. I would also argue that the business of the historian involves in a quite central way the reconstruction of actual and particular sequences of this kind. If that is true, it is obvious that the concern of the historian is quite different from the normative intention of the games theorist and that he is making use of a conceptualization of historical situations which is very similar to that of the games theorist for purposes that are primarily descriptive and explanatory rather than normative. Whether *any* normative character at all attaches to the historian's use of such concepts is a question which must be deferred until Chapter 5.

These considerations offer an opportunity to correct a serious misconception to which my discussion of the historical process as a dialectic of action may give rise. This is the tendency to suppose that such a conception must have the effect of rationalizing the historical process to a quite unrealistic degree by representing human beings with their goals and beliefs as being somehow in the driver's seat and in control of their fate. Since such a picture would strike most people as quite unrealistic, the inference may be drawn that in order to do justice to the irrationality and lack of freedom that characterize our situation as historical beings we must give up the whole intentionalistic conception of history to which this erroneous picture is apparently due and adopt instead some theory of history in which impersonal laws and forces represent the severe constraints under which we actually live. In fact, however, the "unfreedom" of man as a historical being is something which the dialectical conception I have been proposing is uniquely well-suited to express and it does so in a way that avoids the semimythological tendency of many accounts of historical forces. It is a prime assumption of that dialectical approach that, while human beings are indeed the sources of the intentions by which their actions are identified, they have neither the knowledge nor the power that would enable them to control the consequences that are produced by these actions. Even actions that do not have a human vis-à-vis, as for example clearing the land to raise crops, may have unintended consequences such as erosion which human beings may be helpless to arrest but with which they have henceforth to contend. The consequence of an action can thus be to restrict or otherwise change the range of options which one would otherwise have had, and successive actions may modify the latter still further so as to produce a cycle of adjustments that moves farther and farther away from the goals one had originally set oneself. When there is a human vis-à-vis, his reactions are likely to be even more unpredictable and uncontrollable and their effect can be to compel me to choose between alternative courses of action, all of which are deeply unwelcome. In this way human beings can and do imprison one another; and it is not surprising that human history as a whole has often struck observers as a grandiose act of self-frustration on the part of mankind. But if we are thus coerced by history it is important to remember that this coercion has an intentional structure and that it is as the result of our actions and those of others in dialectical interplay with one another that the only alternatives we have are so often self-defeating. This kind of coercion with its complex intentional presuppositions is very different from the kind that is simply a function of the fact that we are finite and mortal beings; and it seems to me that it has a good title to be regarded as the historical, as distinct from the generically human, form of unfreedom.

I have been arguing that the *kind* of limit which human beings impose upon one another is comprehensible only within the intentional and dialectical framework that has been outlined above. At the same time, however, one must not forget that none of these limitations would be more significant in our lives than is a checkmate in a game of chess if it were not for the role that force and violence play in the real-life dialectic of societies.[35] When we speak of actions and counteractions and of the complex network of assumptions about the attendant circumstances of these actions and the possible responses with which they will meet, it must be remembered that the ultimate mode of contestation of our actions is that of force, which thus becomes a kind of implicit coefficient of every action that a society undertakes. Nor is it difficult to understand why this is so. Even when the firmest and most equitable understandings govern the allocation of whatever advantages may be pursued by various competing societies, the possibility always remains that one or more of these societies will not be prepared to live with its share; and the alternative of a resort to violence for the purpose of achieving its goals can never be finally foreclosed. In its collective form, such a resort to violence takes the form of war; and it is not just some misguided preference on the part of bellicose historians which has made so much of human history a history of war. Once the kind of social organization that makes war possible is in existence and the availability of war as the ultimate form of action is established in the human repertory of responses, it dominates all the relationships of societies with one another in a way which no one has as yet found a way of significantly modifying. For even if a given society is pacific and reasonable in its mode of life, it cannot simply ignore the fact that its neighbor may be very differently disposed so that a war may have to be fought in order to remove a threat to its existence. In such relationships as these the possibilities of misperception and misinterpretation by one society of the actions and intentions of another are almost infinite and the fact that such enormous issues are at stake is not likely to make the parties concerned more amenable to reconsideration or revision of their estimates. The dialectic among societies is thus one in which violence is always in the background and the survival and the well-being of each society is at stake. This is not to suggest that political and military aspects of the life of a society are more interesting or worthwhile than others but that they constitute the instrument of a kind of change of absolutely vital importance to all the interests of a society. To recur to the image of the life of a society as a combination of cyclical and linear forms of movement, a good argument can be made for the view that the new element in the situation of these societies—the element that requires a response and thus touches off a sequence of situations no one of which is stable—is typically the existence of another society that is at once a threat and an opportunity and that the nuclear history of these societies is the dialectic of violence in which they are involved. There may have been many things in both Rome and Carthage that were more admirable and more worthwhile than their capabilities in the area of national organization and political and military activity; but if, as seems evident, all of these depended upon the outcome of the struggle between the two "superpowers" of the Mediterranean basin, then the history of that struggle was indeed the central history of Rome and Carthage for almost two centuries.

The discussion up to this point might seem to suggest that the ingredients in a choice-situation for a society consist of certain fairly specific goals toward which it can move by one or more routes which then have to be evaluated in terms of likely responses which they may elicit from other societies. This is true as far as it goes, but it leaves out altogether a dimension of such situations that is of the greatest importance for a historian. This is the element of tradition understood as a corpus of norms, interpretative principles, and background beliefs of a great variety of kinds which any society builds up over time and which it brings to new situations that arise and which are interpreted for purposes of action in terms of the affinities they show to one or another of the categories that are the precipitate of past experience.[36] A tradition in this sense—a highly developed example would be that of the Roman curia—is presumably a set of formulae, some of which are general in form since they cover classes of cases and indicate how they are to be interpreted and what form the response to them should take, and of others that refer to particular historical events which are the paradigm cases or the precedents or the confirming instances for the general rule of judgment and action that is to control a given situation. Insofar as it embraces explicit references to past cases in this way a tradition represents a kind of extended historicity that goes back farther than the beginning of the particular episode in which a society may be involved at a given time. Thus, if the society in question were the Roman church and it were involved in a jurisdictional struggle with a particular Christian monarch, the relevant portion of the tradition would include past cases of such struggles together with whatever lessons of wider application had been learned from those cases. These past cases would thus have an important role in identifying the kind of contest in which the church was engaged at that time and in projecting certain ways of dealing with it. In this sense a tradition is, as H. G. Gadamer has pointed out, a body of "prejudices" or anticipatory judgments of an event or situation, and these judgments would encompass the nature and range of the alternative modes of response to a given type of situation.[37] It is quite possible that the range of responses so defined might not be the same as that embodied in the tradition of the society to which these responses are to be made; and it is also possible that this difference might be the source of serious misunderstanding between the two societies.

At the same time as tradition so conceived is an element within the dialectic of societies as described above, it is itself characterized by a form of change that is itself dialectical although in a somewhat different sense than that discussed previously. As a tradition is projected forward onto new cases which it assimilates to its available categories, it undergoes modifications which go beyond the mere addition of new confirming instances. If the new cases are very different from those that have arisen before, it will be possible to maintain a sense of continuity with the past only by modifying somewhat the respect in which this case and previous cases may be said to be "the same." This tendency will be reinforced by the attrition that a tradition undergoes in the course of its transmission from generation to generation. For a new generation that knows that more recent and (I am supposing) deviant cases well and the earlier "standard" cases only by report, this contrast of what is standard and what is nonstandard is likely to reverse itself with the result that the present case instead of being just barely incorporable into the tradition generates backward lines of continuity and sameness that capture the earlier cases or most of them but along a subtly different axis of identification. Since a premium is often set on the maintenance of continuity with the past as such, the fact that the mode of recapitulating the experience of a society has changed, and with it the respect in which continuity has been putatively maintained, will not normally be emphasized if indeed it is grasped at all. Such a process of change within a tradition is itself a kind of dialectic since in it a past understanding of past events is modified by an understanding that is, as I have said, projected backward out of a present that is importantly different. Of course, there is in this case the very important difference that his temporal location makes it impossible for one partner in such a dialectic to respond to this reinterpretation that supervenes on his original "statement"; and there is also the further difference that the fact of reinterpretation and change in the present is not objectified as such by those in the present who are in fact responsible for it.

At a later stage in the life of a society changes in a tradition become dialectical in a fuller sense. The temporally prior partner in the process of interpretation and reinterpretation cannot, of course, ever respond to the response that is made to him, much as we might like to know what Bach would have thought of Mozart and Shakespeare of Dickens. What can and does happen is that reinterpretation is eventually recognized for what it is and even assumes explicitly critical forms. In general, the relationship to tradition becomes much more self-consciously free and with this freedom comes a willingness to pick and choose and to appropriate elements in a tradition without any feeling of being obliged to reproduce it in its entirety. In its extreme forms this emancipated consciousness generates its own "tradition of the new" and often explicitly denies any meaningful continuity with the past; and in these circumstances it is the fact of residual continuity that becomes unconscious rather than that of change through implicit reinterpretation as previously. More generally, once tradition and departure from tradition become established as terms of thought that are available for self-understanding, a wide range of uses to which they can be put opens up; and, as Professor Pocock has shown, there are complex dialectical relationships among these.[38]

An example of the two kinds of dialectic—the dialectic among societies and the dialectic of a society with its own tradition—is offered by a recent book by William Bouwsma, *Venice and the Defense of Republican Liberty*.[39] The period under consideration in this study is the Italian Renaissance and the protagonists are in effect three cities, Florence, Rome, and Venice. Each of these is characterized by reference to the broad tradition of thought and practice relating to the conduct of civic affairs and these traditions are shown to reflect assumptions of quite different kinds about the nature of human society, the scope and proper function of human reason, and the locus of political and ecclesiastical authority. Rome is, of course, identified not only with the universalistic claims of the Catholic church which in turn go back to those of imperial Rome, but in the later sixteenth century it also represents the Counter-Reformation and the international effort to reestablish throughout Europe the authority of the *Respublica Christiana*. Florence, by contrast, is the city of the Renaissance par excellence in which a quite different conception—pluralistic and in important respects secularistic—of society and political authority had developed and been given effect in the institutions and political consciousness of the city. These two cities are thus presented by Bouwsma as defining themselves through their opposition to one another in a dialectic that is at once a matter of opposing beliefs and of very concrete political and military struggle. Venice, to which the central role in the book is assigned, is described as an independent republic without a strong tradition of political consciousness that would have committed it to one side or another of the struggle between Florence and Rome. But in the course of the mid-sixteenth century Venice is shown to have experienced a kind of awakening of political consciousness with the result that she took up the role of Florence within the Italian political world, after the latter's crushing defeat by imperial forces in 1529. As a result, Venice increasingly came into conflict with the claims of the papacy until the decisive struggle provoked by the interdict of 1609. This transformation of the political stance of Venice was at once a development in the domain of political thought and in the area of political action where a new party—the *giovani*—emerged as the bearers of this new orientation of Venetian policy. Bouwsma's claim is that in both areas the example of Florence was of great importance and that the result of this internal Venetian dialectic was to place Venice in a posture of opposition to Roman policy that was in its essence a continuation of the role Florence had played. The Italian political world of the sixteenth century is thus shown to be a field of force organized around three societies which define themselves both positively and negatively by reference to one another and which define themselves in terms of a tradition and a conception of their own past which they also, as in the case of Venice, are able to revise.

IV

The second thesis which I have undertaken to defend states that it is a condition of the kind of continuity I impute to historical narrative that the actions in question be identified under the descriptions which their agents and patients may be supposed to have used. Clearly this is a claim which flows quite directly from the conception itself of human action which has been set forth in the preceding discussion. In that conception the relationship of an action to its environment is in the first instance one which it stipulates itself through the organization of its situation which it effects. In other words it confers on some element in that situation the character of an "obstacle" or an "opportunity" in the light of the goal it proposes; and when this action is itself complete, the situation it will have produced becomes the occasion for another redescription in the light of the practical concerns of some other agent. The guiding assumption here is, thus, that the relationship between human agents and their environment and among such agents themselves is to be understood on the model of the practical inference; and from this it follows that the historian must be in a position to reconstruct these practical inferences if he is to understand the sequence of events in which they provide the principle of continuity or colligation.

There is a set of issues, much debated by philosophers of history, that have to do with the epistemological difficulties that are sometimes thought to be posed by this requirement; but these matters will be taken up in the next chapter. My concern here is with the role such descriptions and redescriptions play within a developing narrative and not with the mode of the historian's access to them. The nature of that role can perhaps be best suggested by drawing attention as Kenneth Burke has done to the "dramatic" character of history and to the "unending conversation" which it constitutes.[40] This analogy is one which should need no explanation after the discussion in the last two chapters that was intended to bring out the semantic character of the actional events with which history deals. The point of this discussion was not, of course, to remind the reader of how much of history literally consists in the talk of the agents involved nor was it to suggest that the historian's first obligation must be to reproduce that talk as though he were a glorified court reporter. The point was rather that all actional events, whether they are accompanied by any form of public discourse or not, must involve an element of implicit discourse in which the significance of relevant events and states of affairs is determined from the standpoint of certain predominant interests and concerns on the part of the agent, and various possible courses of action are evaluated in terms of their consequences as they bear on those interests. This process might be described as an encoding of the elements in an action situation in terms of their practical significance through the assignment to them of positive and negative values reflecting their eligibility in the light of the norms, interests, and knowledge which the agent brings to this situation. The claim that is made by my second thesis is that when a sequence of events is actional in the sense described and thus involves this kind of practical construal of events and circumstances on the part of the agent as a necessary preliminary to action, a historical narrative of those events must reconstruct the agent's descriptions wherever it is possible to do so or at the very least present the materials which enable the reader to do so. Otherwise the narrative will not be in a position to delineate the relationship in which these actions stand to one another and its continuity will be broken.

In defending this thesis I am not for a moment denying that there are other ways of describing such sequences of events which abstract from the contexts of practical concern reflected in what I have called the agent's description. It is always possible to describe any event and the changes which it brings about in an idiom which carries no implications (or at best very faint ones) that relate to any purposes that may be achieved or partially achieved or not achieved at all through the change which these events bring about. When the consequences of the action are thus described in a way that abstracts from any larger system of purposes within which it may be situated, they may be called the "natural consequences" of that action and in the simplest cases these will be physical changes. Even such actions as a political assassination can after all be described in terms of the movements of the bodies of the persons involved, the action of the pistol, the trajectory of the bullet, its impact, and so on, and generally in such a way as to abstract entirely from the purposive and actional character of the event and thus from its identity as an assassination. It is quite another matter to describe an action in a way that relates it, positively or negatively, to the achievement of some purpose. In the example just used, the initial description "political assassination" was clearly of this type since even this summary designation indicates the capacity in which the victim became the target of the bullets which struck him and also suggests the general area in which the more specific ulterior purposes of the assassins are to be sought. From another point of view this same act or its consequences might be described as a threat to constitutional government in a given country or in some other way, depending on the context of purposes and intention within which it is envisaged. No one would describe an action in this way unless either he or someone else had a practical stake in it one way or another and had projected further goals of action that would be influenced one way or another by it. A purely contemplative observer of such events and their consequences would lack the indispensable context of purposes and concern that is characteristic of human commentators on the consequences of action. Again, if human beings were solitary and isolated creatures and if the resources of the earth that supplied their needs were not in scarce supply so that competitive relationships became inevitable, there would be no reason for us to evaluate the consequences of the actions of others in terms of our own practical concerns since ex hypothesi they would be most unlikely to make any difference. But as things are, we are thrust into one another's company; and since we compete for so many of the same things, what one of us does has fateful consequences for the undertakings of others. The character and consequences of an action, considered from this standpoint, may be called "practical"; and the description they receive reflects the interests and thus in some sense the decisions and choices of the agent whose characterization it is. As has often been pointed out, the difference between these two modes of description—"practical" and "natural"—is closely comparable to the difference between, on the one hand, the accounts that would be given of the actions or moves of the players in some rule-governed game by persons who are familiar with these rules and can appreciate the point of a particular maneuver, relate it to a certain strategy for "winning," or detect the opportunity it creates for an opponent, and, on the other hand, accounts of those actions given by persons who are not familiar with the rules of the game, who do not know what constitutes winning or losing, and who must therefore describe what they observe simply in terms of the physical movements made by the players.

There is however another mode of characterization for human actions that goes beyond their "natural" description and treats actions as actions and yet appears to have almost as little to do with the agent's intention as those just discussed do. I have in mind here certain actions that are tightly circumscribed by social conventions and rules. If for example I buy an automobile or fire a subordinate or vote in an election, the nature of my action is defined by a multitude of socially accepted conventions and understandings; as a result, a characterization of my action as, e.g., a purchase can be taken as self-sufficient and as not standing in any further need of characterization in terms of my intentions. It may be acknowledged that I probably had such intentions—for example, a desire to impress my friends by a show of affluence—but these will be treated as being my business and the public meaning of my action will be regarded as the one given it in its legal definition as the purchase of an automobile. Of course, I can be assumed to have known what I was doing when I purchased the car and I could certainly be said to have intended to purchase a car; but just because this fact is taken to be so obvious as not to require notice except in some unusual case, as for example if I were to believe I was renting a car when I was really buying one, this kind of intention is, as it were, swallowed up in the public definition of my action. Certainly, if after buying a car without any apparent misunderstandings on either side I were to say that I had intended to rent the car and not buy it, the public definition of what I in fact did might very well take precedence over my claimed intention. All of these considerations thus seem to reduce the intentional aspect of my act to the status of something private and peripheral and thus to confirm the view that such intentions need not be centrally involved in the explanation of an action and to make the latter appear a more eligible candidate for a position in the kind of explanation that treats it as a compact unit without the complicating affiliations that belief and intention carry with them.

The important thing to notice in such cases as these is that the diminished importance of intention is brought about by elements within the action-situation itself taken in its full social context. For social purposes it is extremely important that it be possible to abstract on certain occasions from whatever intentions a person may have had and to be able to identify what he did as an action of a particular socially recognized type on the strength of certain public criteria of what counts as an action of this type. In these contexts the only relevant intention of the agent is the intention to perform an action of this publicly recognized type. Outside such well-defined situations, however, we may be much less certain how to describe what a person has done; and in such cases we will normally be much more willing to treat intentions as having the kind of constitutive role in the action in question that has been attributed to them in this book. It is also important to recognize that even the intention that we feel is too obvious to require mention because it is so firmly imbedded in a well-established social routine remains an intention nevertheless and that these very routines would not be possible if it were not the case that human beings can understand the conditions defining the actions of which they are composed and can perform them "intentionally." Beyond that, if history, as I have argued, is a mixture of actions that are incorporated into such social routines and those that in various ways break out of the latter, one would expect that the apparent importance of intention would vary a good deal within its domain. On some occasions, the only relevant intention may be the one that is implicit in the public description of the action itself; in others much more attention to the individual agent's beliefs and desires will be required. Neither kind of case should be treated as the model to which the other must be forcibly accommodated; nor should the "public" character that attaches to the former be misinterpreted in a way that removes it from the special context of shared understandings in which it comes into being. This "publicity" is in other words a very useful abbreviation or standardization of the intentional dimension of human action, not a substitute for it.

These observations must now be related to the thesis set forth above according to which narrative continuity is essentially dependent upon the descriptions agents use for the actions that they (and others) perform and upon the beliefs and intentions that are implicit in these descriptions. Once again it will be useful to take an example from an actual historical text that illustrates this principle of continuity. The example is drawn from Hubert Jedin's *History of the Council of Trent* and it has to do with the entente concluded in 1545 between Pope Paul III and the emperor, Charles V.[41] In essence this was an agreement between the two to wage war jointly against the Protestants in Germany. At the same time the pope announced the postponement of the opening of the Council of Trent, although he was very reluctant to take this action. Jedin explains that he took this step nevertheless because it was thought that the opening of the council might provoke a Protestant uprising in Germany before the emperor was in a position to deal with it; and he characterizes the pope's position more generally in the following terms:

> Paul III, on his part, concluded the alliance in the spirit in which every modern statesman enters upon similar compacts, viz. for one definite purpose, none other, in fact, than the overthrow of the Protestants. It was not his intention to issue a blank cheque out of sheer benevolence. The thought of yielding on any point in which the interests of the Papacy and his responsibility as head of the Church were at stake did not enter his mind for a moment. He never really trusted Charles V. He was prepared to do what he could in the hope that by means of the ultimate, bloody instrument of war the disrupted unity of the Church might yet be restored. It was this higher consideration that induced him to consent to the postponement of the opening of the Council. What a heavy burden he thus laid upon its presidents and its members was to be seen in the coming weeks and months.[42]

The emperor's view of the arrangement he had made with the pope was, as Jedin points out, quite different. In his estimation,

> The alliance did not do more than restore the normal conditions which corresponded to his wholly medieval conception of the Christian commonwealth of Western nations and of his own position as its secular head. He had always resented the Pope's policy of neutrality and his support of the "disturber of the peace" and "the friend of the Protestants and the Turks" as a violation of what he regarded as the normal political situation in the West. The feature of the alliance against the

German Protestants to which he attached perhaps the greatest importance was the resumption of close collaboration with the Pope. The
suggestion that what he proposed to the Pope implied nothing less than
the pontiff's subordination to his plans, hence the, sacrifice of his independence, would have appeared absurd to him. In his eyes victory over
the disturbers of the established order in Church and Empire was also a
triumph for the Church.[43]

This passage illustrates many of the features of historical narrative to
which attention has been drawn in the course of this chapter. It is clear,
for example, that neither Paul III nor Charles V is represented as acting in
his capacity as an individual human being but rather in his capacity as the
occupant of an office and the head of a vast institutional structure whose
interests he is concerned to defend. These institutional interests are themselves grasped by their representatives in historical terms and in terms of
the traditions established within each of these institutions that define its
proper relationship to the other. Each of the principals also has a view of
the intentions of the other which he substantiates by references to more
recent history and the policies followed by his vis-à-vis in the many-sided
struggles of sixteenth century Europe; and in both cases the predominant
feature of these reciprocating estimates is distrust and a sense of interests
that, although ideally harmonious, are in fact incompatible. But even
though their interests as leaders of two great institutions were indeed very
different, it is also clear from this passage that the conclusion of an
alliance was adequately motivated on each side by the short-run and
long-run goals in terms of which pope and emperor interpreted the practical import of events. Nevertheless, in the pope's case, the conclusion of
the entente involved a very real sacrifice in the form of a postponement of
the opening of the council and he had in effect to weigh the desirability of
a prompt opening of the council against the danger of a Protestant victory
in Germany with the unreliability of the emperor with his quite different
ideas about the proper position of the Church in relation to imperial authority always in the background of these deliberations. Finally, there is
an allusion at the end of the passage to the untoward consequences that
were to be produced by the delay in the opening of the council; and this
reference illustrates the constraining influence of past upon future action
that was discussed in the preceding chapter.

Now if we concentrate on the two events mentioned above—the pope's
forming an alliance with the emperor and his postponement of the opening
of the Council of Trent, is there any way in which someone who was not
in a position to reconstruct the "logic of the situation" as it emerges from
the foregoing characterizations of the intentions and beliefs of the pope
(or of "the papacy") could establish a connection between the one event
and the other?[44] According to Jedin, the pope agreed to postpone the

opening of the council because he was convinced that otherwise an uprising might occur which could frustrate the purpose for which he had entered into the alliance to begin with, that is, the purpose of defeating the
German Protestants. If he had not had the goal or if he had not held this
belief about the possible consequences of opening the council as scheduled, the second event—the postponement of the council—presumably
would not have occurred at all, and so it seems fair to conclude that the
postponement was decided upon precisely *as* a means to prevent an uprising. This is what is meant by saying that this belief was integral to the
agent's description of his own action and not that the description, "postponement of the opening of the Council of Trent," somehow magically
carries within it a conceptual linkage with the description, "means to
prevent an uprising of the German Protestants." Under the former description alone the action the pope took would have been unacceptable to
him since he had the strongest reasons for wishing to get the work of the
council underway. But under the second description which presents that
unwelcome action as being also a means to another goal of vital importance, the action was one that the pope saw he had to take. The net effect of
all this is a new practical encoding by the pope of several events in terms of
their means-end relationships to one another. The historian's narrative account of these events, moreover, is essentially borrowed from the terms in
which this encoding takes place and without the latter he would be left with
the blank fact of temporal sequence between the two events, that is, with
something much more like a chronicle than a narrative.

It is, of course, true that historical narratives contain a great many
events that are not related to one another within practical syllogisms like
the one I have implicitly attributed to Paul III; and not all of these are the
natural events whose status in historical narrative I discussed in the last
section. They are typically consequences of the actions that have been
decided upon through such practical reasoning. Sometimes these are at
least partially foreseen as were the negative consequences of the postponement of the opening of the council which, in the pope's mind, presumably centered on the continuing weakness of the Roman communion
in the face of theological attack as long as its own dogmatic position had
not been authoritatively redefined. In the account Jedin gives, this certainly very unwelcome consequence of the postponement is represented
as being in effect accepted by the pope as an unavoidable cost associated
with a decision which on other grounds he felt obliged to take; and to the
extent that this was the case one can say that these consequences were
drawn into the perimeter of his practical deliberations. But the more
common case is that in which consequences are produced that no one may
have envisaged in advance or assigned a place to within their way of
setting up their own action-situation. Nevertheless, if these consequences
are significant enough to merit inclusion in a historical narrative at all, one

must assume it will be because they were to have a place within the practical construal of the situation on which subsequent actions, whether by the same agent or by another, were based. They will in other words provide the reason or part of the reason why such a subsequent action took the form it did. Such an unintended and unforeseen consequence of an action will, moreover, have to be taken into account by the historian in just that aspect in which it assumes this practical significance. The point is thus not that the practical calculations of human agents set the limits to the domain of fact with which the historian must deal, but rather that what escapes even such putative control by human agency—and a very great deal does—is reintegrated into that domain of agency whenever it has the kind of significance that qualifies it for inclusion in a historical narrative at all.

It was noted above that in the case of the pope's action in postponing the council there were two descriptions of his action, the one simply as a postponement and the other as a means to another end. It would be misleading to leave the impression that since narrative is dependent for its continuity upon descriptions like the latter, the former are somehow ideally eliminable from it. Not only is this not the case but action-descriptions like the former play an essential and often predominant role in such narrative. This is in the first instance due to the obvious fact that unless such descriptions were included one would not know *what* action had been performed. But the point here is a little more interesting than its obviousness suggests. It is that we would not know what had been done unless the action were described in a manner that conveys its public or socially identifiable character. I have commented above on the way certain rule-governed action-descriptions appear to abstract from whatever intentions their agent may be supposed to have had in performing them; and while my point in so doing was to argue that this elimination of intention is not to be taken at face value, it is also worth noting that this public or neutral mode of characterizing actions can also be found in historical narrative. Contrary to a good deal of what has been said on this subject and often from a standpoint congenial to that of the present study, the historian's description of actions does not normally require any form of impersonation of or identification with the agent in question. There is, in other words, not a full stop in the narrative while the historian as it were slips into the situation and into the intentions and beliefs of some historical agent; if this were the normal procedure it would constantly generate difficulties of the kind that are encountered by the reader of *Mrs. Dalloway,* who must search for events that figure in the conscious life of distinct characters and are yet, like the tolling of Big Ben, unmistakably the same event. Instead, the historian for the most part takes up his position in a zone which is coextensive with the territory mapped by the knowledge, interests, or descriptive vocabulary of the agents concerned, but he has to survey it in a quite different manner. There is in fact a prima facie obligation for the historian not to accept any agent's description of his own action just as it stands since these descriptions often conflict and the espousal of one of them would make it impossible for him to accept and thus do comparable justice to the descriptions of the same events offered by other agents. The sheer plurality of agency makes any simple strategy of associating himself with an agent's system of descriptions impracticable for the historian. Where the same event can be set within more than one context of practical interest and is thus a candidate for sharply contrasting descriptions, the conscientious historian will typically try to cast his own initial description of the event in question into an idiom in which it would be at least recognizable to all the agents involved. For example, if he were describing the event in recent American history known as the Saturday Night Massacre, he would presumably not begin by saying either that Nixon was attacking the principle that the president is subject to the law of the land or that he acted to frustrate the schemes of a Kennedy-inspired clique in the special prosecutor's office, even though one of these statements might be true. Rather, he would say something to the effect that the president ordered one attorney general and then another to fire Archibald Cox, the special prosecutor, and that he was finally dismissed.

All of this may make it sound now as though the hallmark of the historian's mode of description were precisely an avoidance of the agent's description rather than the positive concern to reconstruct that description which was imputed to the historian in the preceding discussion. It might almost seem in fact that on the view I am proposing now the historian must pitch his description to the highest common denominator of description he can find among parties in conflict and that in some cases this requirement might have the effect of actually pushing his description down into the domain of the natural as distinct from the practical consequences of an action. That, however, is not what happens. Normally there will have been a prior account of the interests and goals and character of the agents in question which enables the reader to carry out a practical encoding of the elements in the action-situation and thus to place the action taken in an intelligible relationship to those goals. Sometimes the task of reconstructing such a practical inference will not be as straightforward as it sometimes is and the historian then intervenes directly to supply the missing steps. In both cases, however, the result is that the narrative moves back and forth between levels of description of a given event, one of which is concerned with what might be called the "brute facts" of the matter and the other with the same event under the descriptions that express its practical significance for the agents involved. It is of course by no means certain that the first kind of description can always be found without dropping below the level of descriptions that have any real relevance to a historical understanding of what occurred. It can happen that the disagreements between two parties are so profound that they extend to almost every description that might be offered of an event that involves both of them. But fortunately this does not always happen and when it does not, the historian is in a position to move in the manner described from a relatively neutral description of an event to the descriptions expressing the various forms of practical significance it has for the parties concerned. These descriptions are not thereby espoused or endorsed by the historian himself; they are rather imputed to their sponsors in the historical situation itself. But this does not mean that they are presented simply as opinions about an event which is objectively described only in the neutral language of the historian. As has been emphasized repeatedly, these practical descriptions are themselves part and parcel of the event with which the historian is concerned and they supply the essential element of colligation without which the event would stand isolated and unexplained. The objectivity of the historian's initial description is not the result of abstracting from the agents' descriptions as such but rather of fixing on elements that are common to all these descriptions and that can thus serve as a public term of reference to these events for those—the historian and his reader among them—who at least at this stage are concerned to learn what happened without thereby necessarily committing themselves to a particular partisan view of that event. Whether it is proper for the historian to assume any other more directly evaluative posture toward the events he recounts is a matter that will be taken up in the next chapter.

One other source of resistance to the role assigned here to the agent's description in the constitution of a narrative deserves at least passing attention. This is the strong feeling of suspicion that is often directed at "official" declarations of the reasons for some action that has been taken and at the "ideological" considerations to which these often appeal. To some extent this feeling may spring from an unwillingness to believe that the representatives of institutions ever really believe what they say, even when they say it in private. Such a view is naive to the extent that it rests on the assumption that unless such official persons "mean" what they say in some subjectively sincere way what they say does not mean what it seems to mean; and this is surely a mistake that is due to a failure to understand the independence of an institutional role from the personality of its incumbent. Misguided though it is, moreover, even this view of the public world would not license the historian to abstract altogether from the way an agent fits his actions into some larger practical design. If it were inspired by such a view as I have just outlined, the belief that there is a very different sort of alternative to such explorations as Jedin's of the actional logic of a situation is likely to be at bottom a belief that the strategies which the historian discovers when he penetrates behind the screen of ideology conform to some basically very simple and universal logic of self-interest and that this is so powerful an explanatory tool that it dispenses the historian from the necessity to occupy himself for very long with the rhetorical dress which self-interest puts on for its public appearances. But whatever the degree of plausibility of this view—in my opinion not very great—it should be obvious that even the narrowest kind of self-interest has a means-end form of organization and that when one seeks to reconstruct a sequence of action that is assumed to be motivated in this way one can hardly afford to disregard information that casts light on the way the agent conceives the self-interest he pursues and how he perceives the means by which such ends can best be achieved.

V

The third thesis with respect to historical narrative set forth above was the claim that the explanatory function of narrative is discharged through a teleological ordering of the historical materials which is modeled on the practical inferences of the historical agent. Since the import of this claim has already been very extensively developed in the course of preceding discussions, it seems unnecessary at this stage to add to what has already been said by way of further characterization of what this teleological ordering involves. The underlying thought is simply that human action sets up its own form of continuity over time which it is the responsibility of the historian to retrace and that this continuity has a logical character that accrues to it through the agent's description of the goals and circumstances of his action. The real question that arises with respect to such a claim as this is whether such an ordering of historical narrative really can claim to satisfy whatever criteria may be appropriate for establishing its explanatory character. I will try to deal with this question in two stages. First, I will review a number of philosophical criticisms that have been directed against the "logical connection" thesis that is associated with the claim in behalf of teleological forms of explanation. Then I will examine the principal alternative that has been proposed to the kind of historical explanation that takes its principal regularities from the systems of human practice it studies and I will try to show that the attempt to replace these with laws of unrestricted generality is in fact visibly parasitic on the teleological explanation it claims to replace.

Among the criticisms to which the "logical connection" argument has been subjected perhaps the greatest interest attaches to the argument advanced by J. L. Mackie which purports to show that such a conception of teleology gives us "nothing but a set of interlocking concepts, with no shadow of an account or explanation of how A *came to* do B."[45] According to Mackie, "our natural way of speaking of conscious purposive human action treats intendings, desirings, believings, and so on as elements in accounts of how actions come about" and this view entails that "these intendings must be, as occurrences, logically distinct from any related actions."[46] "There is no more logical connection here than there is between someone's hoping that Leeds will win the Cup Final and Leed's winning the Cup Final."[47] Mackie agrees that there is a logical connection between the *content* of the intention and some true description of the effect of the action to which it leads; and he acknowledges that even a physicalistic theory would have to incorporate some counterpart "for the agent's *seeing his action as* of a certain kind, for his intending a certain event *under a certain description*, and for his believing that a certain *kind* of action would lead to a certain *kind* of outcome."[48] But he concedes this much to the "logical connection" argument only on the condition that these believings and intendings be treated as the "joint efficient causes" of the action in question and that as such they be recognized as logically distinct occurrences from that action itself. Otherwise, the action would be "explained" by reference to two occurrences which turn out not to be logically distinguishable from it and thus the whole interlocking triad of intention, belief, and action would not have been explained at all in the sense of being related to something other than itself.

One way to approach this argument is to consider Mackie's claim that there are "preformed intentions, intentions which exist before any behavior manifests them."[49] This claim is in keeping with the commonsense assumption that we can often say truly of someone that from a certain time onward he intends to bring about G at time t and that he believes that unless he does B by time t he will not be able to bring about G at time t. The *content* of this intention, Mackie tells us, is such as to include a reference to G as the effect of B; but this logical connection between the content of the intention and the effect of the action in no way affects the logical independence of the intention as an occurrence. In other words, once that intention has established itself within a certain slot in our mental history, no subsequent event can dislodge it; and this is to say that its occurrence is logically independent of the occurrence of the action that it refers to. But is this really the whole story? Suppose that time t arrives and the agent does not do B and takes no other measure that might be calculated to bring about G. It seems to me that in these circumstances we would have to choose between saying that the agent had changed his mind and given up his intention or that he never *really* intended to bring about G at t. Otherwise we would find ourselves with an inconsistent triad of propositions to the effect that the agent intends to bring about G, believes he must do B in order to bring about G, and does not do B. Perhaps Mackie does not regard these propositions as being inconsistent with one another. He says, for example, that "intendings must be, as occurrences, logically distinct from any related actions" and that "if there can be preformed intentions, it cannot then be impossible that exactly similar items should continue to exist and so be concurrent with, but logically distinct from, the actions that fulfill them.''[50] Why, it might be asked, would not this line of argument justify our saying that ''it cannot then be impossible that exactly similar items should continue to exist and so be concurrent but logically distinct from the nonperformance of the actions that would have fulfilled them''? Conceivably he would say that this is impossible because one cannot intend to perform an action at a given time when that time has passed; but this would merely be to avoid the difficulty of giving a sense to the notion of the fulfillment of an intention by an action when the strong thesis of logical independence is espoused. That difficulty is to see how the intention as such can be ''fulfilled'' if nothing that happens subsequently in the way of performance or nonperformance of the intended action can affect the character of that intention as an intention to perform a particular action. It is not a question here of maintaining that an intention's carrying a reference to a future action magically insures the occurrence of that action. It is rather a matter of insisting that the nonperformance of the action which had been described as being intended must react upon that description itself. This in fact often happens as for example when we say on the occasion of some nonperformance of this kind that the person in question was ''only talking'' or that he was deceiving himself. More frequently, however, we explain the nonperformance by concluding that the person in question *must* have changed his mind. The intention is thereby sealed off from the action to which it referred in such a way that the logical independence of its occurrence no longer creates any difficulties. We could accordingly agree with Mackie that there will always be *some* description of what occurred in the period leading up to the moment of performance/nonperformance which will not be affected by the fact of nonperformance; but it will typically be a description of that occurrence as a defunct intention or as a specious intention. If, on the other hand, the prima facie intention is not to undergo this kind of redescription, then it cannot come up to the moment of action to which it carries a reference without passing over into action. In this sense there is something prospective and provisional about our ascriptions of intentions, to which Mackie's way of speaking of ''exactly similar items'' that precede the moment of performance and are concurrent with the performance hardly does justice since it suggests that intentions possess their character as intentions in such a stable and unalterable way that they are proof against this kind of redescription.

These considerations appear to show that Mackie was in error when he argued that a logical connection between the occurrence of an intention and the performance of the corresponding action would cancel the explanatory character of a teleological argument. It would certainly be unhelpful if one were always to respond to requests for explanations of why a person acted as he did simply by saying that he did so because he intended to; and in such a case Mackie's charge that we would have given "no shadow of an account of how A came to do B" would be justified.[51] But if our answer takes the form of a reference to A's intention to bring about G and to his belief that he must do B in order to bring about G, we will have supplied information that goes beyond the fact that A did B in a way in which, for example, the statement that the baby Edward Heath was a future prime minister does not go beyond the statement that Edward Heath became prime minister. But if so, why should the fact that this intention and this belief jointly imply that A will do B destroy their explanatory function? The belief that this must be the result seems to me to stem from a fear that some necessary connection between matters of fact is being introduced so that once an intention is in existence it will be impossible for the action not to follow. But these fears are groundless. The action *can* fail to follow if the intention is changed or abandoned and the prospective agent has thereby broken the connection between himself and the action in question. With this possibility in mind one can always say "A intends to do B but he may not do it," just as one says "A hopes that B will occur but B may very well not occur." But in the case of hoping, no special explanation is required if B does not occur although A has gone right on hoping that it will; and in the case of intending, it *is* required. In the absence of such a special explanation we will have to adjust our description of A's intentions in the light of what he has failed to do just as on other occasions we adjust our description of someone's actions in the light of his intentions and his knowledge, and say that A was testing his scientific apparatus and not that he was electrocuting the neighbor's cat although that was an accidental result of the test. The point at issue is thus not one that turns on a necessary connection among matters of fact but on a conceptual linkage between two—when beliefs are included, three—kinds of description when they are applied to the same person on the same occasion; and this linkage is such that we cannot apply two of these descriptions and withhold the third (in the absence of further explanation) without doing violence to the concept of intention. Mackie denies that this is so, but he does not provide any alternative analysis of that concept which would resolve the anomalies produced by the strong independence thesis and simply assumes that the logic of intending and of hoping is the same.

Mackie's attack on the "logical connection" argument is not of course the only one in the armory of the philosophical critic of teleology. Another strategy is to attempt to show that our ordinary explanations of human actions prove to have presuppositions which, when fully developed, bring these explanations into conformity with a nonteleological model of explanation that is substantially identical with the one employed in the natural sciences. One such presupposition to which attention has been drawn by

Professor C. G. Hempel is that the agent whose actions are to be explained is a rational being, that is, one whose actions are controlled to a significant degree by rational considerations.[52] This presupposition is an assumption of fact which has to be added to the premises of a rational explanation if the latter is to provide adequate grounds for believing not just that it would have been rational for the agent to do x but also that he in fact did x for certain stated reasons. The rationality that is thus imputed to x also has to be susceptible of interpretation in light of specific features of the situation in which x acts and when so interpreted will yield "descriptive generalizations telling us how a rational agent will act in situations of that kind."[53] In other words, the concept of rationality in this use becomes a "descriptive-psychological concept governed by objective criteria of application; any normative or evaluative connotations it may carry with it are inessential for the explanatory force of the argument."[54] Since the attribution of rationality now involves verifiable empirical claims, it is subject to disconfirmation; but even when it is borne out by the facts, the explanation in which it finds its place will have a nomological character. In Hempel's words, the added premise concerning the rationality of the agent and what it implies in the way of behavior in the given situation "restores the covering-law form to the explanation."[55]

It is very doubtful, however, whether this last claim can in fact be sustained. Certainly one can agree that teleological explanations of human actions have as a material premise that the agents in question are rational; but it would also appear that this assumption is a good deal weaker and therefore harder to refute than Hempel seems to believe. Its force is primarily to deny that the agent's behavior is so incoherent and lacking in continuity of purpose that one can't make any sense of it or understand what the agent is about. What is thus excluded by the premise of the agent's rationality is a condition in which the agent's intentions are either unrelated to what we take to be his real environment or so fragmentary and unstable as to be virtually unconstruable. But if the premise of the agent's rationality serves principally to negate any possible belief that he may be irrational in any of the above senses, then it becomes much less plausible to suggest that, when taken together with various features of the situation, it will generate "descriptive psychological generalizations" about the way a rational agent will act. It is true that if we have detailed and accurate information about a man's beliefs and attitudes, we will often be able to construct fairly accurate projections of the way he will behave. But if such predictions were to be falsified, we would not normally conclude that our assumption of rationality on the part of the agent was false. Instead, we would very likely conclude that his information was defective in some respect that we had not taken into account or that his attitudes were not quite what we had assumed them to be, or perhaps even that they were in the process of change. As long as we can reconstruct a picture of what the agent was trying to do that is consistent with all that we now know about him—including this last and unpredicted action—we are not likely to conclude that he is irrational. The point is that what he does now has a bearing on the truth or falsity of our antecedent characterization of his attitudes and beliefs; and there is no point in his career at which we can say with absolute definiteness that he believes so-and-so and must therefore act in a certain way on pain of being judged irrational if he does not. Unless there occur breakdowns or discontinuities of a pathological order, we reinterpret the sense of an agent's conduct continually in the light of what he does and says. Each time we do so, we can, of course, reorganize what we know about him in the form of a deductive syllogism in which his performance of some future action becomes predictable on the premises as as we now state them; but this recurring formalism can be seriously misleading if it obscures the continuing hermeneutic character of our understanding of other human beings.

A more serious confusion results if we insist on interpreting such explanatory syllogisms on causal, nomological lines, as Hempel does. This requirement entails that the explanation include not only a singular judgment to the effect that the agent is rational but a universal premise stating that in a situation of a certain kind the rational thing to do is y, the action to be explained. Since the "descriptive-empirical content" of the concept of rationality does not by itself give the goals of rational action, these will, as I have pointed out, have to be provided by the desires and priorities of the agent, and the "rational thing to do" will then be stipulated in the light of what the agent knows or believes about his situation. But if the notion of rationality is relativized in this way to the beliefs and desires of the agent in question, does it yield anything that could be described as a universally valid causal law? This is apparently what Hempel is claiming when he says that "a covering-law form is restored to the explanation" when the factual premise relating to the agent's rationality is acknowledged. But this would be a very strange covering law. It would say in effect that everyone who is rational, that is, capable of determining his actions on the basis of a logical relationship between his intentions and his beliefs, will perform the action which his beliefs declare to be the best way of achieving his intention. The peculiarity of this "covering law" is that the wider regularities under which it subsumes such a person's action in so explaining it turn out to be just the ones that are contained in the policy of action he is in fact following, as this would be expressed in the form of a practical syllogism. Since the effective import of the statement that an agent is rational is simply that he is following more or less coherent policies of some kind, and that his behavior is therefore interpretable by subsumption under these policies and the related beliefs, it would seem that all the work in this explanation is really being done by its teleological component, that is, the practical syllogism that is imputed to the agent. The "logical connection" therefore turns out to play just the role in the explanation of action that the proponents of teleological explanation assign to it. It would thus appear that the only sense in which "the nomological form has been restored to the explanation" is one that makes it parasitic on the regularities inherent in the policies of the agent, and these are certainly not lawlike regularities in any ordinary interpretation of this notion. If the nomological theory of explanation is satisfied with such a dependency, it will of course be trivially true that whenever a teleological explanation is applicable to human action a nomological explanation (in this weak sense) will be too. But whether such a result could plausibly be regarded as a vindication of the claims originally made by the covering-law theory is at least open to serious question.

That not all adherents of the nomological view of explanation are prepared to accept this outcome is clearly indicated by a recently developed line of argument which purports to show that we are compelled to go beyond the kind of explanatory syllogism that preserves its teleological character and to postulate regularities that are independent of those implicit in the beliefs and attitudes of those whose actions are to be explained. Such an argument has been advanced by Professor Donald Davidson and it sets out from the observation that, for purposes of explaining *why* an action occurred, it is not enough to establish that a person had beliefs and attitudes which would justify the action by showing that it was the rational thing to do for a person with these beliefs and attitudes.[56] It is not enough because, although this person may in fact have had these beliefs, they need not have been the operative reasons for his acting as he did on the occasion in question. If they are to *explain* his action, these reasons must be shown to have been what brought about his action; this becomes especially important when there are several different sets of reasons under which an action might be "rationalized" by a particular person. To treat a certain belief or attitude as the *cause* of some action is, then, just to make this distinction between the rationalizing or justifying force of a reference to beliefs and attitudes held by the agent and its explanatory force, which on this view must depend on a belief's being what accounts for the action having been performed on this occasion. Stated in a somewhat different way, this view holds that the "because" in such statements as "He did *x* because . . ." is a causal "because" which introduces the beliefs and attitudes which jointly account for the occurrence of the action, which they, of course, justify as well, at least from the point of view of the agent.

The most striking feature of the view under consideration is that while it adopts a causal interpretation of the "because" in such statements as the one above, it does not require that the connection it signalizes between reasons and action be interpreted as an instance of a specific causal law. In other words, it is not required that in explanations of human actions some universal law be cited to the effect that persons who hold such and such beliefs and attitudes always act in a certain way. Indeed, it is conceded that in most cases there will be no such laws linking events under the descriptions in which they interest us. What *is* required by the causal "because" is that there be *some* law that is instantiated by *some* true description of the events in question, but not necessarily or normally by a description of them as reasons or as actions. These laws may in fact be formulated by concepts that are only very remotely connected with our initial description of events as reasons and action—as remote, for example, as a description in terms of neurological concepts. At the same time, it is asserted that the superficial connectedness of events under their initial descriptions supplies evidence for the existence of the genuine causal law; and it is the existence of such an unspecified causal law that is, allegedly, asserted by the explanatory "because" although an explanation can be given without actually producing or citing this law.

Underlying this whole line of argument there is an assumption to the effect that the distinction between the reasons a person might have for acting in a certain way and *the* reason or reasons why he so acted on a particular occasion can be made only when the notion of a causal law is introduced. At the same time, however, it is clear that this assumption that a causal law exists will not put us in a position to make this very distinction between determining and nondetermining reasons since such a law will not, in all likelihood, deal with events considered under their description as reasons at all and, therefore, cannot indicate which of them was *the* reason for acting and which not. Such laws will, in fact, bypass reasons as such altogether; and when and if they are discovered they will presumably state that, when a person is in a certain condition (this is to be described by means of concepts that involve no reference to reasons), behavior of a certain kind will regularly ensue. Since for purposes of explaining it this behavior will typically have been conceptualized otherwise than as action or a purposive, reason-based doing, it remains unclear how an explanation at such a level will cast any light on the determining reasons for this behavior under its description as an action. There seems, in fact, to be a prima facie contradiction between an insistence on making a distinction among the reasons a person has for acting in a certain way and a conception of causal law that substitutes a whole new classification of events that had previously been viewed as reasons and as actions. Conceivably, proponents of this view believe that there are further laws that link these events under their new descriptions with the human tendency to conceptualize them as "reasons" and as "actions"; and if so, they could say that *the* reason why a person acted as he did is that event or state which, under a nonrationalizing description, is regularly associated with the action and which, in accordance with the secondary law, is conceptualized in the form of a reason. But in that event the argument under review would imply that the distinction between determining and nondetermining reasons could be made only if we were in possession of two different kinds of causal laws, one of which abstracts altogether from classifications of events as reasons and actions. This seems strange because distinctions of this kind are not normally made in this way at all, but rather in terms of considerations that are internal to the purposive economy of the individual in question, that is, on the basis of what he knew and did not know, the degree of importance to him of various outcomes, the inhibitions and restraints under which he operated, the nature of the action and its consequences as he envisaged them, and so on. Sometimes the outcome of such analyses is inconclusive; but they can also achieve a high degree of reliability, and, whatever their defects, those are not likely to be compensated for by a form of analysis that is pursued in different terms altogether.

Although it appears that these criticisms do not successfully impugn the role of teleological explanation in history, the fact remains that there is a strongly established body of opinion holding that this form of explanation is not adequate to all the requirements of a theory of explanation in history and that some alternative form of explanation that is at least much closer to the nomological type is therefore required. Such a view as this typically rejects what has been called the "stage-setting" argument that distinguishes between conditions and causes and identifies the latter with human actions while the former comprise all the circumstances that make up the situation upon which these actions supervene.[57] As a result, that supervening action is not seen, as it has been here, as itself stipulating what is to be its relationship to the various elements—both natural and social—in the practical field it undertakes to change in some way or other. Instead, actions are taken "neat," that is, simply as occurrences among other occurrences and with minimal attention to the beliefs and intentions of which they are the vehicles. When they are so treated, the "logical connection" that derives from this intentional dimension of the action gets short shrift; and the only question of moment is taken to be the one that concerns the relationships of necessary or sufficient conditionship in which certain other events stand to the action in question. Since these events often include not only other human actions but natural events and states of affairs as well, and since some of these are undoubtedly necessary conditions for the occurrence of the actions that are to be explained, it can appear on this form of analysis that human actions are "caused" by a great variety of natural and social events in a sense that is allegedly independent of any supplementary logical bond which may be thought to hold between the events in question. Usually, of course, it is not feasible to expand the list of necessary conditions for the occurrence of an action to the point where it might be said to constitute a set of sufficient conditions for the latter, and in this sense the goal of nomological explanation is rarely, if ever, achieved in history. Nevertheless, similar difficulties are encountered by causal explanations in the natural sciences and, even if they are more pervasive in history, it can be claimed on this view that the kind of explanation that is being—less successfully—sought by the historian is nomological in nature.

If we look to history itself to determine in what measure this model of explanation might be said to apply to the explanatory procedures actually used there, at least some apparently supporting evidence can be found. It is by no means uncommon for historians to identify an event as a necessary condition for a human action and even to characterize that event as the cause of that action; and they may do so without apparently paying any attention to the beliefs and intentions of the agents in question. For example, a flood can cause the inhabitants of an area to flee to higher ground; and a crop failure can cause riots. Certainly if the flood had not occurred, it is reasonable to assume that the inhabitants would not have fled; and if the crops had not failed, the riots would presumably not have broken out. But if in such cases as these the historian does not mention beliefs and intentions, it is not because these have somehow been eliminated from the explanation he is offering but because they are taken to be either so obvious as not to require special mention or derivable from the wider context of the account that has been given. In the flood example the action of fleeing to higher ground would typically reflect the belief that a flood is about to occur, that, if one stays where one is, one is very likely to drown, and that one's safety is dependent on reaching higher ground. The relevant intention is, of course, the intention of avoiding death. But if one explicitly incorporates these beliefs and intentions into the explanation in which the flood is designated as the cause of the flight to higher ground, the results will be rather incongruous. For the factual premises of the explanation, and thus the antecedent of any nomological regularity that may emerge, now include both the statement that a flood was occurring or about to occur and the statement that the inhabitants of the region believed that a flood was occurring or about to occur. If the latter were not true, it is not apparent how the flood could have caused them to move to higher ground. But if it is the case that the inhabitants believed that a flood was about to occur, what work does the *occurrence* of the flood do in this explanation that is not done by the belief that a flood was about to occur?[58] It seems in other words as though the flood cannot make people flee unless their beliefs and intentions are included in the explanation; but if they are, the causative role of the flood is preempted by the corresponding belief. But if the mention of the flood itself is redundant in the explanation, it follows that what we are left with in the explanation are statements of belief held by the agents which may or may not be accurate; and it will be through these beliefs and the related intentions that a natural event like a flood "causes" action. Of course, it can cause death and destruction quite independently of such forms of representation within the mental life of prospective agents; and if in fact the beliefs held by agents are not correct, natural events as such may also explain why the actions predicated upon these false beliefs fail to achieve their objectives.

A similar line of argument might be constructed to meet other efforts that have been made to "peel off" elements of the practical syllogism and represent them as independent elements in a nomological regularity. Thus, instead of treating a natural event like a flood as a cause, we might cite some social fact like the existence of a code of honor as the cause of a death in a duel.[59] But once again it is impenetrably obscure how a code of honor can cause a death (or a duel) unless it has been internalized by the agents in question so that it becomes an element in their decisions about the actions they perform; and once this is the case, it is these internalized rules of conduct that carry the burden of explaining how a person acts. Indeed, it seems correct to say that the *existence* of such a code of honor as distinct from whatever status it can claim as an abstract set of prescriptions depends precisely on its being accepted and used in the context of decision in this way. In any case it is not clear how an appeal to the existence of a code of honor in an explanation could be taken as referring to anything outside or independent of the set of beliefs which the agent himself regards as relevant to his own deliberations as to how he is to act.

It is, of course, arguable that even when this reduction of the explanation to its intentional elements (beliefs and intentions in the antecedent and an action in the consequent) is accomplished, they will nevertheless compose a statement that can be taken as expressing a (tentative) nomological regularity without any reliance on a logical connection of the kind that teleological explanation requires. This may in fact be true in the sense that if one simply treats having a belief and having an intention as distinct events in the career of the subject of the inquiry and abstracts from any logical connection in which they might jointly stand to the consequent in this explanatory syllogism, these distinct terms might be found to compose a regular succession and to satisfy the other Millian canons of induction so as to qualify as a nomological regularity or law. But even if the historical inquirer is successful in persuading himself that he has not relied on his intuitive sense that there *is* a logical connection involved in such a regularity, he certainly cannot offer such assurances as regards the agent himself; and one suspects that it would in fact be necessary to include among the factual premises of this explanation a statement to the effect that that agent holds these beliefs and intentions in a way that includes an awareness of their logical relationship to one another and to the action that is reported in the consequent. But in that case the "nomological" character of the explanation begins to look rather queer and more than a little problematic. The reason is the same one that was noted briefly in connection with the examination of Hempel's argument about rationality above and it is simply the fact that the nomological regularity has turned out to be dependent upon the agent's acting on a teleological principle in which a logical connection *is* acknowledged between these same beliefs and intentions which the historical inquirer is determined to treat as discrete episodes. The latter's protestations that these connections count for nothing in his formulation of the nomological regularity which alone is of interest to him may well be sincere; but that will not make such a regularity any less parasitic upon the one that is implicit in the agent's action and that *does* involve just the logical connection that is bracketed in the explanation the historian has given. The situation thus appears to be one in which a nomological regularity will be discoverable just in case a teleological explanation is constructible; and the difference between the two is due to the sanitizing transposition of the elements of the latter into the logical *form* of a nomological explanation.

It would require a great deal more analysis of a wide variety of examples of historical explanation to show how widespread the inversion of the relationship between teleological and nomological forms of explanation as described above really is. Even among those who are prepared to accept the claims of teleological explanation in wide areas of social and historical inquiry, there is a disposition to conclude much too hastily that, whenever a difficulty appears in the way of a teleological mode of analysis, a jump must be made to "causal," that is, nomological, forms of explanation.[60] The picture thus evoked is one of successive strata of human agency of which those located near the top are characterized by more explicit consciousness and by "rational," teleological forms of order while the "deeper" ones are typically "unconscious" and *therefore* require causal analysis in a sense of "causal" that is opposed to "teleological" and thus presumably implies regularities that have nothing to do with purpose. This transition to a radically different form of analysis is most often held to be necessary at points where it is no longer individual policies of action that guide the conduct to be explained but social and institutional policies which, as has been pointed out, can *appear* to be independent of the agent whose conduct they "determine" and to constrain rather than guide his choices. The other occasion that is often judged to require a resort to these alternative methods of explanation is the kind of case in which the agent is apparently unconscious of the motives which the inquirer has reason to believe are influencing his conduct or at any rate is unable to raise these to the level of explicit recognition and critical evaluation. In earlier chapters an effort has been made to show how both these cases can be dealt with satisfactorily within the resources of a teleological theory of human action and I will not restate the arguments presented there. In the light of the observations that have just been made with regard to nomological regularities in human action, however, it does seem clear that if the partisans of a shift to causal analysis in such cases as these are not convinced by the line of thought developed in these earlier discussions they face very great difficulties of their own. For if they have really discovered forms of behavior that are not steered by policies that are in turn "routed through" the beliefs and intentions of their agents, what will the units be in terms of which the governing nomological regularities these inquirers seek will be formulated?[61] The only units that fit this description are purely physical or physiological changes in or movements of the bodies of the human beings in question; these are not actional units at all, and the regularities expressible in terms of such units are those developed within the natural sciences. But such processes as these are *presupposed* by history and only occasionally have to be cited by way of explanation of occurrences involving human beings that lie outside the sphere of purposive conduct. It thus appears that in descending to a stratum of behavior characterized by nomological regularities of this sort the historian would either have left behind altogether the domain into which his inquiries properly fall or he would be attempting some implausible fusion of his discipline with that of physics or physiology. But if he wisely draws back from such an attempt, he will once again face the problem of making clear how the regularities in which his causal mode of analysis deals can govern human action from without, that is, without taking the form of regularities that are internal to the understanding that agent has of his situation and his purposes; and that, if it is not impossible, will not be easy.[62]

A final observation is suggested by the contrast between "deep" causal determinants of human action and the kind that are accessible to the agents themselves and readily formulable in teleological terms. It is that there is a strong tendency on the part of many students of these matters to suppose that, when any branch of knowledge achieves a high degree of theoretical development, this very fact is evidence that it conforms to the nomological model of explanation. This supposition is natural enough in the light of the prior achievements of the natural sciences in which genuine nomological regularities loom so large. Nevertheless, it is damaging since it prejudges so drastically the possibility of achieving a comparable degree of theoretical development within a basically teleological framework of analysis. There is, however, at the present time a growing recognition of the distinct character and status of what are sometimes called the "praxeological" sciences which, like economics, take as their point of departure some form of rational human action as defined in terms of certain axioms about goals and the means of achieving them and proceed to construct, often by purely deductive means, a theoretical account of the immensely complex structures of interlocking agency that can develop out of this simple paradigm of action.[63] A comparison of the historical enterprise with the infinitely more formal and normative undertakings of these sciences has already been suggested, and the point I am concerned with here is a somewhat different one. It is that in spite of its "rational" and praxeological character a science like economics does not always or necessarily "expose" this aspect of its mode of conceptualization. Thus, the rational human action of buying or selling may be quite adequately symbolized by a number in an index of economic activity in a certain period; and that number may play a part in establishing a regularity in the market that conforms to a theory-based prediction and thus may seem indistinguishable, from a conceptual point of view, from regularities that are predicted and confirmed in the natural sciences. But the difference that is made by beginning with a situation defined in terms of rational purposive action remains; it sometimes finds dramatic expression even within the economic domain itself when other forms of "rationality" interfere with the kinds of decisions that would be made on the basis of the considerations taken into account by economics alone. The moral I would propose is that it is important to bear in mind that there are forms of conceptualization that are praxeological in the sense that they take their rise from an analysis of purposive human action but that are situated at such a high level of abstraction that this fact may no longer be readily evident and may even seem implausible in the light of the formal similarities which the theoretical apparatus in which these concepts are imbedded may bear to structures of theory in the nonpraxeological sciences. If this injunction were taken seriously, the impulse to jump to "causal" forms of analysis would be restrained and the result might well be to expose the immense and instructive complexity to which the simple paradigms of action that have been described here can give rise.

5. Understanding and Interpretation

In the preceding two chapters I have discussed history as process and history as narrative, but up to this point very little if anything has been said about the historian himself. In this chapter that deficiency will be partially corrected. More specifically, I want to consider two functions—those of understanding and of interpretation—which the historian must discharge and to determine whether these functions can be satisfactorily described within the framework of the general approach to history which hae been developed in the course of the preceding chapters. For purposes of this discussion "understanding" will have much the same meaning as *Verstehen*—that is, the kind of knowledge we claim to have of the intentional life of other human subjects—and one main task of this chapter will be to examine the claim that *Verstehen* is a certral element in the methodology of history and the humanistic disciplines generally as well as some of the objections that have been made against this claim. Even if this claim can be sustained, however, it seems clear that historians often impute forms of significance to events which are not derivable simply from the intentional life of the human beings who were involved in those events and which therefore imply a standpoint and a context that transcend the latter. The term "interpretation" will be used here as a broad term of reference to such judgments of historical significance. The question that is always asked about them is whether they do not inevitably introduce a normative or evaluative element into the historian's account of the past and whether the effect of such implicit evaluative judgments must not be to limit the validity of the account of the past in which they figure to those who share the standpoint from which they were made. One major effort of this chapter will be to deal with the issues raised by this question.

It may be useful to draw attention to the fact that these two notions—"understanding" and "interpretation"—correspond at least roughly to the two forms of intentionality which were distinguished from one another in the earlier discussion of fiction.[1] "Understanding" is the effort on the part of the historian to describe accurately the intentional life of the agents with whom he is concerned; but with this difference from the case of imaginative literature that these agents have had a real, independent existence of their own which the historian must reconstruct as best he can instead of "constituting" it as in the case of fiction. This difference is what makes it possible for the historian to be mistaken with respect to his dramatis personae in a way the novelist hardly could be; more generally it is what accounts for the opacity of the independent intentional life which the historian often finds it so difficult to penetrate. At the same time, since the historian not only does not create the persons whose actions he describes but also stands within the same temporal process in which they occupied earlier positions, difficulties arise with respect to the role within history of the other kind of intentionality that was distinguished in the case of fiction. This was the ordering of the events of a fiction which is effected through generic plot-structures. When that ordering becomes "interpretation," as it does in history, and generates evaluative and moral implications that relate to these events, it may well seem to tell us more about the historian than it does about the historical agents that are the subjects of such interpretation. Unlike the creator of a fiction, the historian is not in a position to shape the lives of his "characters" into the kind of congruence with his evaluative framework that is required if the authority of the latter within its fictional world is to be sustained. Instead, the interpretation of the historian tends to take on the character of a further incremental "event" within the same series of events to which the event it interprets belongs; and once this happens any more general authority it may claim becomes thoroughly problematic.[2] Since neither his attempt to understand nor his attempt to interpret an independent intentional life can claim to issue from a consciousness enjoying any special or transcendental status, both these functions of the historian may come under suspicion as fraudulent claims to such status or as an aggressive design of subjecting other lives to a set of evaluative standards that may be quite alien to them.

These doubts about understanding and interpretation set the task of this chapter. It will already be apparent that one familiar way of resolving these doubts is not compatible with the account of history that has been given thus far. I have in mind the view that proposes not of course to excise both understanding and interpretation from history but rather, more plausibly, to admit them only on the condition that their "subjective" character is openly acknowledged.[3] This is the course that has been taken by many contemporary historians, who recognize that it is psychologically impossible to compose a history that really excludes both interpretation and understanding but who also feel that they have an obligation to their readers to put them on guard against the special bias or principle of partisanship which in their view these forms of judgment necessarily involve. If these strategies were taken literally, the result would be to establish a distinction between the cognitively valid core of history on the one hand and on the other both the language of action—as incorporating an element of teleology that implies an understanding of the agent's intention—and the structure of narrative insofar as such structure rests upon judgments of significance that are ultimately evaluative in character. History conceived as the residuum of these two exclusionary operations would be so strange and incoherent a remnant that one cannot help wondering whether the status of the excluded elements within history as we know it is not much more deeply grounded than any psychological conception of the historian's "bias" would allow. Such, at any rate, is the working hypothesis on which this chapter will proceed; and it will undertake to show that to a considerable extent the difficulties associated with understanding and interpretation are due to faulty philosophical formulations of the nature of these functions themselves. When these formulations are corrected, it will be argued, there will no longer be any good reason to view understanding and interpretation as being "subjective" in some sense that would require that the historian hold them at arm's length even though he cannot give them up altogether.

There are, of course, forms of skepticism about historical knowledge which do not address themselves in the first instance to understanding and interpretation as special judgmental operations within history but raise instead questions about the possibility in principle of any knowledge of the past. Skeptical views of this more general kind will not be considered here. This is partly because they have been effectively dealt with by other writers on the philosophy of history and partly because the discussion of historicity in Chapter 2 made it clear that our referential commerce with the past is far too fundamental to our understanding of both self and world for the revisionary implications of such skeptical views to have any practical import for us.[4] We are, in other words, so irreversibly committed to the claim that we have knowledge of the past that if we were to contemplate giving it up there would be no more secure island of certitude to which we could withdraw. In this sense, at least, the conception of historical knowledge that is presupposed here is indefeasibly realistic. Such a conception does not, however, entail any simplistic view of the mode in which the past is accessible to us and, in particular, not any strained analogy between historical and perceptual knowledge; and it acknowledges fully the essential role of the evidentiary and inferential procedures of the professional historian in the constitution of what is to count as historical fact.[5] Historicity establishes our access to the domain within which these more exact determinations can be made, but this is emphatically not to say that our first surmise with respect to the nature and circumstances of some object of reference in the past is automatically validated. The significance of our historicity lies rather in the fact that it transforms any skeptical thesis about historical knowledge like Russell's into a thesis—a very peculiar one—about the past, that is, into the claim that a certain people who have memory beliefs about a certain period in their past did not in fact exist at that time.[6] In other words, skepticism about the past can express itself only by using the same referential framework as the beliefs it wants to call into question and by putting forward what amounts to a competing claim about the past. It seems clear that the most such arguments could establish is that the past was extra-ordinarily different from what we usually suppose it to have been and not that there can be no such thing as historical knowledge.

I

Some of the reasons why the concept of understanding (or *Verstehen*) strikes many as problematic have already been suggested. The goal of understanding is an accurate apprehension of the intentional life of other human beings or of certain elements within that life; and we all know that it is possible and indeed common to be quite seriously mistaken in our beliefs about what other people desire, what they know, why they acted as they did, and even what they are doing. We also know that the likeli-hood of error in such matters increases when the individuals concerned stand on opposite sides of some conflict or antagonistic relationship. It seems realistic, therefore, to expect that when the persons whose lives we seek to understand are remote from us in time and when there is not even the possibility in principle of the kind of direct exchange with them that might correct some of our misapprehensions, there must be even more doubt as to our ability to understand what they did and why they did it. Finally, there is the difficulty which was noted in the preceding chapter and which has to do with the distinction between determining and justify-ing rationales for action. It was pointed out that for any given action it is possible to construct an indefinitely large number of justificatory argu-ments, all of which lead up to the conclusion that that action was the right or proper or rational thing to do in the situation in question. This is a technique of argument with which we are all made familiar by those disingenuous casuists who can always find a description that is applicable to some action of theirs and that gives it at least a semblance of justifica-tion. How, it is asked, can one determine which set of reasons among all these possible justifying rationales that can be proposed for an action was the really operative one, the one that really accounts for the fact that this person on this occasion acted in this way? The implied answer is that we cannot and that, if we are concerned for the epistemic standing of history, we would be wise to avoid assigning any very prominent place within it to the kind of judgment that understanding typically involves.

Serious as these difficulties may on occasion become, they do not seem to account for the intensity of the skeptical reaction which the claims of understanding typically arouse.[7] After all, similar difficulties can be shown to exist in other areas of knowledge—perception, for example, where the likelihood of error increases dramatically under certain assign-able conditions, both physical and psychological—and yet no one suggests that we ought to reject such knowledge-claims in principle. There is, moreover, something artificial about the way in which the "problem" of understanding is typically presented. The suggestion seems to be that we have, on the one hand, a description of an action and on the other an indefinitely large set of practical syllogisms, each of which would justify the action in question but without our being in a position to determine which one actually caused the agent to act as he did. But in any actual situation the difficulty is unlikely to arise in this radical form. If we are able to provide an action-description for the case in hand at all, we would probably be in possession of some knowledge about the agent and the circumstances of his action or we might well be able to acquire such knowledge. Such knowledge would almost certainly eliminate from consideration a great many of the *possible* explanations of his action by reference to different sets of reasons. Some of the latter might be eliminated on the grounds that they would involve the possession of knowledge which the agent was not in a position to have. Others which he might indeed have been in a position to formulate could be shown to be irrelevant to any purposes and concerns which he in fact had; and we might also be in a position to show that his having been decisively influenced by certain sets of considerations would be inconsistent with other information that we have about him. With any luck and with any familiarity with the history of the agent and the nature of the situation in which his action took place it should be possible to situate his action within a reasonably well-defined practical field; and although some ambiguities may remain as to the precise character of his intention the radical indeterminacy of the situation envisaged at the outset will usually have disappeared.

These remarks are, of course, entirely preliminary in character and are designed merely to put in question the assumption that understanding is a wholly arbitrary and capricious form of judgment. In other words, that assumption which so often dominates philosophical discussions of understanding does not appear to be especially warranted simply on the basis of our actual experience of the practical difficulties we encounter in connection with understanding. In these circumstances it seems reasonable to wonder whether some of the resistance to the notion of understanding may not stem from further assumptions which tend to be associated—perhaps improperly—with understanding. One such assumption, for example, is reflected in the persistent use of the term "subjective" to characterize virtually everything that has to do with the agent's intention and his beliefs about the situation in which he acts. There is, of course, a proper sense in which this term can be applied to the point of view of both the historian and the historical agent. Since the sources on which the former draws to compose his description of the latter's intention are not some privileged divination of the inner life of the agent but evidence of various kinds that is open to scrutiny and appraisal by an open class of inquirers, it must always be in order to raise a question as to whether a given attribution of an action has been properly derived from all the available˚ evidence. Similarly, one must always be able to challenge a statement by the agent himself in which he imputes an action-description of a certain kind to his own action and to claim that the agent is either not telling the truth or that his memory is faulty. But it would be something quite different to agree that a given attribution of beliefs and intentions to an agent is correct—that is, not to propose any substitute for it as the agent's description of his own action—and yet to go on to suggest that as such it represents merely the agent's opinion as to the nature of his action and therefore not something which the historian must feel any obligation not to override or correct. This would be to treat the agent as though he were simply another person engaged like the historian in the business of trying to understand an event although from a vantage point much closer to the latter and with all the advantages and disadvantages which such proximity entails. Against such a symmetrical treatment of the historian and his subject it needs to be pointed out that as forming part of the rationale of the agent's actions the beliefs of that agent form part of the historical reality with which the historian deals; and that, as such, they make that action the kind of action it is, whether they are right or wrong. They may in fact be mistaken and it may also be that the historian will be in a position to show that they were wrong. But that fact does not detract from the constitutive role of these beliefs within the action of some agent, and in that constitutive role there is nothing "subjective" about them and nothing that entitles the historian to treat them as though they were mere opinions about a matter of which he knows the truth. The difference which such a mode of treatment would obscure resides in the fact that historians are trying to understand historical agents but historical agents are not for the most part trying to understand themselves. Because the historian is trying to understand a past agent and his actions, the beliefs that are elements in the rationale of such actions are to be treated as constituting the setting within which the action was undertaken and they will continue to be so even if it develops that they were in fact mistaken. The beliefs of the historian, by contrast, stand or fall with their truth or falsity and if they prove false there is no alternative role in which they could figure within a historical account.[8] To speak of the action-description imputed to an agent as merely his subjective view of his situation runs the risk of obscuring this vital difference between the situation of the agent and that of the historian; and once that difference is obscured the historian may begin to think that he is not under any obligation at all to pay attention to the internal rationale of action since its ingredient beliefs so often prove to be erroneous by his standards. Instead he will undertake to display the agent's action, shorn of its internal rationale, within the true situation of the agent as he—the historian—defines it with only a remark here and there on the surprising misapprehension of the nature of this situation of which this or that agent or perhaps the society to which they belonged was apparently guilty. Such a form of historiography would be the antithesis of the whole conception of the historical process that has been built up in the course of this study.

If the kind of difficulty I have just been discussing really rests on a confusion of the situation of the historical agent with that of the historian, much more serious issues are raised by some of the ways in which the notion of understanding has been interpreted by philosophers who argue in its behalf. Here too the emphasis is typically on the "subjective" character of understanding both as regards the locus of the object to which it is directed and the nature of the operations which it necessitates on the part of those who perform it; but no prejudicial implication is associated with the mentalistic character thus imputed to understanding. Nevertheless, the effect of such an interpretation is often to introduce complications into our conception of understanding which render its status—in my view quite needlessly—problematic; and these complications play into the hands of critics who are all too ready to read the philosophical presuppositions which these interpretations entail into any and all theories of understanding. One such interpretation is that proposed by R. G. Collingwood, and it will be useful to examine with some care the view he defends with respect to the nature of both the object to which understanding addresses itself and the operations it requires.[9]

In the first case—that of the object of understanding—it is Collingwood's view that the special concern of history has to be defined in terms of a contrast between the "inside" and the "outside" of an event and that, whereas the natural sciences are concerned with the "outside" or physical aspect of the event, the historian directs his inquiries to its "inside." Only some events have an "inside" at all, namely, events involving sentient organisms; and among these Collingwood declares the object of history to be confined to those which involve an element of thought as well as of feeling. The general effect of this account and especially of its somewhat simplistic contrast of the "inside" with the "outside" is to suggest that the ultimate object of understanding lies on the other side of a kind of physical screen that is interposed between it and the human consciousness that is seeking to apprehend it; and this at least sounds like the kind of mysterious transition in terms of which traditional dualism conceived the relationship between mind and body. In any case, it makes access to the object of understanding sound forbiddingly difficult and uncertain at best. At the same time, moreover, Collingwood lays down the further requirement that in order for true understanding to occur this very thought that was in the mind of a human being at some time in the past must be revived in the mind of the historian. The historian must, in other words, "reenact" the very same thought which his subject thought at some time in the past; and of course the historian must also be aware that the thought he is presently thinking *is* a reenactment of that earlier thought. But to many the possibility of such reenactment has seemed even more problematic than the prior task of gaining access to the thought of the original agent in its domicile within the arcana of mind. Altogether Collingwood's account of understanding appears to associate it with a theory of mind that raises at least as many questions as does the original notion of understanding itself; and it may well be the case that the difficulties associated with this wider theory have contributed to the discrediting of understanding itself. There is admittedly another, sounder aspect of Collingwood's theory of history which emphasizes the connection of thought with action and the status of action as the "unity of the outside and the inside of an event"; but it is to be feared that the gap which this metaphor suggests is more easily opened up than it is closed. [10]

The discussion of Cartesian dualism in Chapter 1 has already made clear why the hypothesis of an inner state raises difficulties and how these can be avoided by an intentionalistic construal of mental acts. These same considerations also suggest what is wrong with the Collingwoodian contrast between the "inside" and the "outside" of an event. It is noticeable to begin with that this contrast has not been made in such a way as to effect a clean distinction between the one term of the contrast and the other. Although Collingwood says that "by the outside of an event I mean everything belonging to it that can be described in terms of bodies and their movements," the examples he gives of the sort of thing that would constitute this outer aspect of an event are "the passage of Caesar, accompanied by certain men across a river called the Rubicon at one date, or the spilling of his blood on the floor of the Senate-house at another." [11] What strikes one about these examples is the fact that they are not pure physical descriptions—not, in other words, the kinds of descriptions which a physicist might be expected to give of the same events—but rather ambiguous action-descriptions in which the words "passage" and "spilling" strongly suggest that someone has *done* something in the one case and in the other has done it very likely in the context of some undertaking for which a rationale could be found. When Collingwood goes on to say that "by the inside of the event I mean that in it which can only be described in terms of thought: Caesar's defiance of Republican law, or the clash of constitutional policy between him and his assassins," what he has provided is a fuller action description than he gave when he was concerned with the "outside" of the event, and strong, though incomplete, indications of the reasons for these actions. [12] The contrast is thus one between a more and a less complete action-description and not really one between thought and movement as Collingwood appears to suggest. This is important because it means that the historian's concern with actions is even more comprehensive than Collingwood's account seems to imply. If that account were taken literally, Collingwood's statement that the historian's "work may begin with the outside but ... can never end there'' and that his main task is ''to think himself into [the] action, to discern the thought of [the] agent'' would mean that in such a case the historian would be moving from a physical, nonactional description of an event to an action-description which incorporates the thought of the agent, whereas what his own example suggests is rather a movement from a less to a more highly developed action-description.[13] There are, of course, some cases in which the historian's starting point will indeed be the outside in the sense of some purely physical description of an event or, more likely, an object—the discovery of some unidentified object at a cult site, for example—but any general picture of the historian as not reaching the level of action-descriptions until he has somehow breached the wall of purely physical descriptions and reached the thought of the agent on the farther side would surely be a misrepresentation.

Similar observations apply to what Collingwood has to say about the inner or thought side of the events with which the historian is concerned. Collingwood says that ''at bottom'' the historian ''is concerned with thoughts alone'' and ''not with events as such at all'' or only insofar as they express thoughts and ''reveal to him the thoughts of which he is in search.''[14] This way of putting things seems to confine the historian's interest to mental events in a fairly restricted sense of that term, but just as the ''outside'' turned out to be already contaminated by the ''inside'' in the description of it which the historian is likely to use, so the ''inside'' turns out not to be as rigidly distinct from outer events as Collingwood's formulation would seem to imply it is. For what are these thoughts which the historian imputes to the agent thoughts *of*? In Caesar's case they were undoubtedly thoughts of such matters as the Republican constitution and of his sentatorial opposition, but they were also thoughts of his armies and the movements they would have to make and the battles they would have to fight. They were thus thoughts of events which, though not themselves physical in any strict sense, could not be described without reference to movements and other physical changes. Typically the fruit of such a process of thought would be a plan of action which would take into account a whole host of ''outer'' circumstances and assign them a place in the realization of a certain intention. As I have already indicated, such a plan would include references to other potential agents and to their intentions and actions and thus at least implicitly to their knowledge of and reactions to the first agent's intentions. In this kind of complex dialectic of action and reaction, it will remain true that every thought and every intention is someone's thought or intention, but it is hard to see what value the distinction between ''inside'' and ''outside,'' understood as a contrast between thought and movement, would have for purposes of characterizing the historian's mode of understanding of such events. The reason is simply that such a distinction misrepresents the conceptual level at which these events must be understood as taking place—a level at which physical events such as movements are *already* understood as expressions of thought and intention and thoughts are understood as thoughts of, among other things, the events which are in the process of taking place in the public space that is shared by the various interacting agents. Collingwood's account has the disadvantage of seeming to imply that the historian's interest is limited to one aspect of this process—the thought side—and that the level of action-concepts is reached only by uniting a thought which has first been isolated in its pure state with an "outside" that consists of pure movement.

These observations on the disadvantages of relying on the "inside-outside" contrast in the analysis of understanding receive support from the use that is made of that same contrast in philosophical arguments which, unlike Collingwood's, are motivated by a desire to show the limits of *Verstehen* as a method of inquiry in history or elsewhere. One well-known example of such arguments is Theodore Abel's claim that the method of understanding or *Verstehen* has at best a heuristic value in that it suggests possible explanations for some human action while lacking any means for the critical evaluation or verification of these hypotheses which it generates.[15] Abel's argument is of particular interest because it illustrates very clearly the way in which certain important aspects of understanding tend to be bypassed when it is conceived in terms of contrasts like those noted above. One of his examples will serve to show how this happens. It concerns an observer who notes that on the occasion of a sharp drop in the temperature his neighbor goes outside his house, chops some wood, and takes it into the house where he places it in the fireplace and proceeds to light a fire. The observer concludes that his neighbor "began to feel chilly and in order to get warm lighted a fire."[16] In this explicitly teleological form the explanation is said to be inconclusive because the neighbor may very well have had another motive than a desire to get warm; even if he were to declare that this was his motive, he might not be telling the truth or might even have been acting out of some unconscious motive. What the observer has done in this case, according to Abel, is simply to project a sequence that he has experienced himself—the sequence of "feeling cold" and "seeking warmth"—upon the observed behavior of his neighbor. Understanding thus typically involves a translation of items of observed behavior into internal "feeling-states" which have accompanied such behavior in one's own case; and we generalize this experienced sequence into a "behavior maxim" which we then apply to another case like that of the neighbor who builds a fire. The inference we thereby make is causal in character but is very likely to be faulty since it may be based only on an association in our own experience for which no wider statistical warrant has been established. Understanding as such provides no "verification" or "objective validity" for the "behavior maxim" it generates; in fact it may do no more than to "relieve us of a sense of apprehension which would undoubtedly haunt us" if we were unable to find an analogy in our own experience to the observed sequence of behavior on the part of some other person.[17]

What is most strange about Abel's way of treating this example is his insistence upon substituting a sequence of internal "feeling-states" for the sequence of actions which the neighbor is seen to perform. The effect of that translation is to produce precisely the kind of arbitrariness in the association of the two items in the "behavior maxim" for which Abel then proceeds to censure the method of understanding. This results because these "feeling-states" lack the kind of context which their objective counterparts have and which permits the observer (and for that matter the neighbor himself) to connect them in a way that involves a means-end relationship and not just sequence as such. What the observer surmised was that his neighbor had chopped the wood in order to be able to start a fire and thus to keep the temperature inside his house from dropping as it was doing outside. Incidentally, the concern of his neighbor may have been to keep his pipes from bursting and not a desire to "seek warmth," but in any case the explanation is a perfectly good one as it stands. If it were to be challenged, it would be necessary to point to something in the conduct of the neighbor or in the relevant circumstances that suggests an alternative interpretation of his conduct, and interestingly enough this is what Abel in fact does when he suggests that visitors may be coming and the neighbor may want to show off his fireplace. But then this explanation is apparently dismissed as being as footless as its predecessor and everything is made to depend upon some statistically established concomitance between "feeling cold" and "seeking warmth." The whole strategy of the argument thus appears to consist in first refusing to follow out the logic of the original explanation which the observer offers and then "translating" that explanation into a psychological idiom of internal states in which it would be virtually impossible to supply the kind of context for these "feeling-states" that would enable one to do more than note their sequence in time. Within the wider context of public actions and events in which the original explanation situated itself it *is* possible to point to features of the situation which corroborate or disconfirm the kind of account that understanding offers of such episodes as the one in Abel's example, and often the degree of certitude that can be achieved is adequate for all practical purposes and certainly as good as anything that could be achieved by counting feelings or fires in some wider population than this example affords.

Difficulties of a somewhat different kind are associated with the second reuqirement contained in Collingwood's theory of understanding. This requirement has to do with the nature of the mental act that has to be performed by the historian; and it is to the effect that unless a kind of identity is achieved between the thought of the historian and the thought of a human agent in the past, there can be no understanding by the former of the latter. The historian must, in other words, think exactly the same thought that Julius Caesar or Thomas à Becket thought on the occasion of whatever action of the one or the other the historian seeks to understand, and in addition the historian must know that he is thinking such a thought. As Collingwood puts it, the historian may be said to become the person in the past whom he understands, in the sense that "to know that I am my own present self re-enacting Becket's thought" is "to know that I am Becket."[18] This is a form of identity which is possible only in the case of those beings who are endowed with a capacity for thought; and a good deal of what Collingwood has to say on the subject has to do with the peculiar power of thought for not only "occurring here and now in this context" but also for "sustain[ing] itself through a change of context and reviv[ing] in another one."[19] For reasons which are not altogether clear, Collingwood felt that it was necessary to interpret the kind of identity that is so achieved between the thought of the historian and the thought of the past agent in the strongest possible terms and in this way he was led to reject the suggestion that a distinction between specific identity or identity of content and numerical identity could be applied to these acts of thought. As a result he found himself in the very strange position of asserting not only that the thought of the historian and the thought of, say, Euclid are identical in point of content, that is, of *what* is thought by the one and the other, but also that the historian's act of thinking this is itself identical with the act of thought of Euclid. Collingwood appears to have believed that, if one were to treat these acts of thought as being discrete even though their content was the same, it would necessarily follow that the connection between the present and the past upon which historical knowledge depends would be broken. This is interesting since Collingwood seems to be coming close to an explicit conception of historicity in his denial that "consciousness [is] a mere succession of states" and in his insistence on the ability of thought to maintain contact with its own past episodes.[20] But what never does become clear is why this important principle of the temporal integration of experience should be interpreted in such a way that it is not only the content or object of a past thought that can be revived but the act itself. The argument he in fact gives on this point is that in order "to know what someone else is thinking" it is not enough to know "the same object which he knows"; one must also know "the act by which he knows it."[21] But once again it is plain that such knowledge does not require that the very same act be occurring now but at most that an act of the same kind be occurring now and that it have the same content as the original act. If the distinction between specific and numerical identity is not applied in this way to acts of thought that are separated in time and performed, as we would normally say, by different persons, we will be forced to conclude that when I as a historian am thinking the same thought as Euclid then Euclid is also thinking it; and this could be the case only if both the historian and Euclid were understood to be capable of "standing outside time," at least in their capacity as thinkers though not in their capacity as spatio-temporally situated beings. But if such an assumption can be entertained, a theory of historicity is really not necessary since such a theory is designed as an account of how beings who are in time and whose thoughts pass away quite as irrevocably as do their bodily states can nevertheless maintain a continuity with their own past. If in one aspect of their being—that of thought—the condition of temporality is simply suspended, then of course everything that is assignable to that aspect of their being is not transient but permanently and timelessly available *in propria persona*. But the problem we will have to face will then be to explain how beings that are capable of this kind of transtemporal identity can also be distinct and separate from one another in time; and that will not be easy.

These are not, however, the features of Collingwood's account of understanding to which I want to devote my attention. Let us suppose that an emendation of that theory were to be carried out and all of its major theses were to be interpreted in such a way as to incorporate a distinction between the specific and the numerical identity of acts of thoughts and between the content of an act of thought and that act itself. If this were done one set of difficulties would have been removed and with them the peculiar conception of identity discussed above, but another more serious difficulty would remain. The theory would still require that the historian be able to think the same thought as Plato; and this means not only that the object of the one thought and the other will be the same but also that the act of thought performed by the historian will be specifically (though not numerically) the same as that of Plato. The new issue is whether this is possible even with the relaxation of the terms defining identity for these purposes; and it arises because such a reenactment of Plato's thought by the historian involves a transplantation of that thought from one mental context to another. These are both "contexts of discussion and theory" and comprise all the background beliefs with which the thought in question was associated in the mind of Plato and with which it is now to be associated in the mind of the historian who reenacts the latter's thought. How, it may be asked, can the historian reenact Plato's thought if this means, as it presumably must, believing what Plato believed when the mental context of the historian may already include beliefs that are incompatible with Plato's beliefs? Collingwood appears to recognize that there is a difficulty here when he says that "part of the context in which [Plato's thought] exists in my mind might, if it was a fallacious argument, be other activities of thought consisting in knowing how to refute it"; but his way of dealing with this possibility is scarcely convincing.[22] All he says is that "even if I refuted it, it would still be the

same act.''[23] How "the act of following the logical structure" of an argument of Plato's could be specifically the same act as Plato's when in the
historian's case it exposes a fallacy which Plato may never have seen
remains quite unclear. There are, moreover, other cases in which the
conflict between the historian's mental context and that of the past agent
will be immediate and insurmountable as in the case in which the historian
has a bit of knowledge about that agent's situation which the agent himself
did not possess; and in such circumstances the historian cannot possibly
share the uncertainty in which the agent's deliberations were conducted.
More generally, these differences of context entail that what was a question for someone in the past may no longer be a question for the historian; and conversely what was a certainty may now be a question in the
mind of the historian. In both cases the reason is that "thought" has
moved on since the time at which the past agent lived and the historian
inescapably has undergone the influence of those changes. How then can
he possibly understand the "thought" of some past human agent if such
understanding is defined in a way that makes it necessary for him to
assume a mental posture which is incompatible with his own? He cannot
after all suspend his own beliefs at will although he can of course attempt
to imagine what it would be like to have beliefs very different from his
own. Such attempts may have very considerable value but they just as
clearly do not satisfy Collingwood's criterion, since to imagine that one
believes something is not either specifically or numerically the same act as
believing it, whatever "it" may be.

These considerations are hard to dismiss and they clearly raise grave
difficulties even for the less stringent interpretation of what Collingwood
means by the identity that is to obtain between the historian's thought and
that of some past agent. Indeed, these difficulties are so serious that the
conception of historical understanding as reenactment in any sense
closely resembling the one Collingwood gave to it seems doomed. The
real question is not so much whether the conception of reenactment can
be saved as in what form if any the whole conception of understanding
itself can survive the abandonment of what has traditionally been one of
its central components. In connection with the effort to answer that question it will be useful to draw upon the work of H.-G. Gadamer, who in his
Wahrheit und Methode has attempted to reconstruct a general hermeneutic theory—a theory of what is involved when human beings try to make
sense of or interpret what other human beings have said or done—
on a philosophical foundation that is quite different from, and at some
points in explicit conflict with, the presuppositions of traditional conceptions of understanding as reenactment. His position is one that
may be said to generalize the kind of point that was made above against
Collingwood's theory of understanding on the basis of considerations that
relate to the differing temporal positions of the historian and his subject;

but in certain respects the final implications that Gadamer draws with respect to the validity of the truth-claims which understanding makes remain somewhat ambiguous. The view which I wish to defend in this connection will be developed out of a critical examination of Gadamer's theory and of the ambiguities in which it appears to issue.

The root idea from which Gadamer's theory of interpretation derives is that of exploring a number of alternative cases in which something like reenactment may be said to occur and then, in the light of these cases, to reexamine the one which has traditionally been thought to exemplify most perfectly the operation of historical understanding: the interpretation of a text. The alternative cases of reenactment which Gadamer emphasizes are those in which the changes that have taken place since the original creation of the object of interpretation are not only manifest but also undeniably relevant to the task of interpretation itself. Thus the interpretation of a judicial statute often obliges the judge to apply it to situations that were not contemplated by the original legislator because they had not yet come into being. In such cases there is no possibility of somehow extracting the judicial decision from the original intention of the legislator who ex hypothesi did not consider the kind of case that now faces the judge and therefore could not have given a sense to the statute that would determine its mode of application to the present anomalous case. In such cases, it is interesting to note, we speak of the judge as exercising quasi-legislative functions and this is to say that we describe what he does in interpreting the statute and applying it in a certain way to this new case by means of an analogy to the original act to which the statute owes its existence. Viewed in this light, judicial interpretation is a continuation or amplification of an original act of creation which has proved to be incomplete by reason of what has occurred between that act and the present in which the statute is to be applied. As a result, a judicial decision can itself constitute an important episode in legal or constitutional history and no one really tries to pretend that this importance is ascribable to its being a new "discovery" of what was ideally implicit in the original meaning of the statute. Precisely in the judicial case the sense that the judge is not bound by his cognitive relationship to something that was given in an original, authoritative, and in principle wholly determinate form sometimes arouses anxiety since it is associated with a picture of the interpretation of the law as an arbitrary exercise of personal will. It is clear, however, that the kind of "concretization" or specification of the law that Gadamer imputes to judicial interpretation can be just as scrupulous in the attention it gives to the original statute and to the more general norms of the legal order as any juristic purist could require; and it will still inescapably involve a carrying forward of the sense of the original statute into a domain of application within which new distinctions have emerged and old ones may have disappeared. In this sense the problem of interpretation becomes a problem of translation and of the accommodation of a prior meaning within a partially modified semantic field. Such an adaptation will itself count as an event or *Geschehen;* and it will as a consequence become more difficult, at least within the law, to draw a definite boundary line between what counts as an event and what as an interpretation of an event.

There are other examples that Gadamer draws from areas as diverse as theology and dramatic production to make the same general point about "application" as the rendering of some original statement within the context of a new situation in which equivalences must be found for the operative terms of the original. But the point of all these examples is to make it possible to demonstrate that the features they exhibit are also present in the case of historical interpretation as well. Prima facie, it would appear that the kind of interpretation which the legal historian carries out in the case of a given statute must be very different from the kind that a judge does who has to apply that statute to a present-day situation. Gadamer's way of rebutting this negative presumption as regards the historical case is first to point out that the historian stands in a present that is in some degree, however remotely, continuous with the period in the history of the law which he is seeking to interpret. In this same present a certain ordering of the domain of law and of the relationship of that domain to others has been realized; and to the extent that this is true the legal historian himself will be drawn into the substantive issues in the law which are raised by the ancient statute, when he undertakes to understand the latter in its relationship to the disposition of such matters in the law of his own day. The suggestion is not so much that the historian can only see an ancient statute or legal system through the lens of the law as it exists in his own time, but rather that his special task as a historian—the task of characterizing some past episode or period in the history of the law—can be performed only through a process of interpretation in which one important element is the prior understanding which he has, and presumably shares with his readers, of the legal ordering of the world in which he lives.[24] If, as Neurath suggested, human language is like a ship in mid-ocean which can be repaired or rebuilt only out of the materials of which it presently consists, then the same might be said of interpretation as the effort, not to substitute a new language for the one we now use, but to work back from the language we now use to the language which was used in a time prior to our own and which we must reconstruct if we are to understand the distinctive cultural productions of the period in which that language was spoken. In both cases, if Gadamer is right, the outcome of these efforts of reconstruction will be a "fusion of horizons" (*Horizontverschmelzung*) such that the original work is enabled to speak within a world that may be very different in its semantic ordering from the one in which it came into being.

It will be apparent that there are strong elements of affinity between the view of interpretation which Gadamer has developed and the account of the historical process which was presented in an earlier chapter of this book. In that account emphasis was repeatedly placed on the intentional character of the continuity between historical events; and it is clear that such a principle of continuity involves interpretation in Gadamer's sense. At the same time, one cannot help wondering what the implications may be if a model of interpretation which works well at the level of historical events themselves is made to serve the purpose of illuminating the practice of the historian as well. It is one thing to speak of the creative misinterpretations of which history offers so many examples—French revolutionaries modeling themselves on Roman patriots and English Puritans thinking of themselves as Hebrew prophets—and it would obviously be foolish to censure the historical errors and misapprehensions that such modes of self-identification may have involved. At the same time, one wants to retain the possibility of declaring that these were indeed errors and of doing so on some basis that is stronger than that of simply another temporally situated *prise de position;* and it needs to be made clear whether Gadamer can make a place for this kind of disallowing of interpretations on the ground that they misrepresent their objects. More generally, there may be some justified anxiety that in such a theory of understanding as this the distinction between what belongs to the historical process and what belongs to the sphere of interpretation of that process will have become so indistinct that the element of interpretation will be absorbed into the process itself. If that were to happen, the notion of historical truth would be in difficult straits, to say the least, since every attempt to state retrospectively what the character of the historical process has been would slip into the status of another increment to that process itself and as such would elude appraisal in terms of its truth-value in much the same way as do the kinds of historical repetition that are the work not of historical thought but of the more intuitive and less critical forms of historicity. If this were to happen, the whole historical process would have taken on the character of an interpretation of itself but in circumstances that insulated that interpretation and its component elements against epistemic appraisal. The historian would become, in this view, just another historical agent of a rather special kind whose function it is to express in the form of an account of the past the time-bound perspective of his own age.

What is not really clear in Gadamer's theory is the way he conceives the conflict between the existential status of history—history(n) as part of history(e)—and its properly epistemic aspect—history(n) as defining what history(e) has been. That there can be conflicts arising out of these complex relationships of history to history is not something that needs much proof. What is not so clear is whether this conflict is one of principle. The

title of Gadamer's book—*Wahrheit und Methode*—clearly suggests that
truth in the domain of the *Geisteswissenschaften* is not to be achieved by
means of method—that is, by the institutionalized exclusion of the historian's own situation from the process of inquiry. It is argued that truth is
more likely to be achieved through a kind of interaction with the past in
which the historian does not try to suppress his own time-bound standpoint and thus does not approach the past in the character of one to whom
the past can have nothing to say because the features of the historian's
own situation which would be relevant to such an exchange have been
denied expression within the framework of his historical inquiries. This
sounds as though some redefinition of truth were being proposed that is
essentially independent of the epistemic controls that are associated with
the concept of method; and as though the main criticism to be made of the
kind of truth that *is* associated with "method" was the indifference it breeds
to the value of the new denotatum of "truth." This may turn out to be an
important point; but one may still feel that the nature of the conflict
between the two conceptions needs further definition. In particular, are
there not considerations which speak strongly in favor of a compatibility
of "truth" and "method" and perhaps even of "method" as a necessary
condition for the kind of "truth" in which Gadamer is interested, once
certain limiting prepossessions that may not be essential to "method"
have been dropped? For example, when some episode in the historical
process carries with it an interpretation of a portion of its own historical
past, we may not be very interested in the truth or falsity of that interpretation but, if we are, there is no obstacle in the way of our approaching
it from an epistemic standpoint and attempting to determine what its
truth-value is. Similarly, as Gadamer has pointed out, there is the possibility that an expressly historical interpretation may be treated as itself a bit
of history(e). In neither case is it clear why the fact that our interest in the
episode in question tends to be predominantly of one kind rather than the
other—an interest in its role in the historical process or in its truth-
value—should lead us to suppose that the one approach excludes the
other. Moreover, if Gadamer is making the stronger claim that an expressly historical interpretation is always and necessarily an episode in
the historical process, this will be true whether that interpretation proceeds under the directives of "method" or not. But if that is so, then
Gadamer's polemic against method seems somewhat overstated because
it sounds at times as though "method" were responsible not so much for a
false meta-theory of history(n) but for a less satisfactory practice of his-
tory(n) itself than we might otherwise have. This would be a valid claim
only if it could be shown either that a superior form of history(n) can be
produced if there is an acceptance by historians of their own historical
situatedness and its implications for their relationship to the past or that
history(n) would be improved if it were to declare its independence of the

constraints of "method" altogether. Gadamer is presumably not making the latter claim; and he has not made any real case for the former. What remains therefore is a second-level thesis characterizing history(n), but doing so in a way that has no clear implications for a judgment on "method" insofar as its positive achievements are concerned.[25] Perhaps one could say that what is wrong with the general approach to history(n) that proceeds under the slogans of "method" is its insensitivity to historicity in its most general and widely shared forms as well as to the kind of stake in the past which such historicity typically involves. With this goes a belief that history(n) can not only emancipate itself from such an "existential" mode of relationship to the past as historicity involves but that it will positively benefit from doing so. Against such a view Gadamer's position would be that history(n) not only cannot divest itself of its own historicity in this manner but that at least certain of its functions will suffer if it tries to abstract entirely from every mode of involvement in the past that cannot be defined in purely cognitive terms. But one could accept the case he makes on these terms and yet continue to believe that "method" has an essential contribution to make to historical understanding.

Not only is it arguable that the notion of method would retain this measure of justification but it rather clearly appears that Gadamer's own argument tacitly assumes that it will. In that argument the notion of *Wirkungsgeschichte* has a very important place. As a concept of the historical process or of history(e), *Wirkungsgeschichte* presents no special problems; but this is not the case if it is understood as a history(n) that recognizes that the events it relates are such as to incorporate an important element of interpretation and of interpretation that reflects the situatedness and temporal distance of the interpreter from the object of his interpretation. For the question immediately arises: can such a *Wirkungsgeschichte* actually be constructed? Here Gadamer seems to avoid a direct answer and tends to speak instead of a *wirkungsgeschichtliches Bewusstsein* and of the impossibility of the kind of *complete* objectification of our situation which an actual *Wirkungsgeschichte* would require.[26] The point is clearly a difficult one for his kind of theory since an actual *Wirkungsgeschichte*(n) would embrace a series of episodes in which a different kind of sense is successively made of, for example, some single text by different interpreters; and this is to say that the historian would have to be able to characterize the mode of understanding of a given thinker or of a given period and contrast it with another such mode of understanding and so on. What Gadamer does not like about such a procedure as this is that these successive ways of making sense of something are being treated by the historian in a way that neutralizes the truth- or validity-claim that they made for themselves; and the historian has, by treating them in this way, implicitly withdrawn his own antecedent assumptions—his

Vorhabe—from any significant contact with those possibly conflicting claims. At the same time, the perspective of the historian is tacitly allowed to determine what is true or real without qualification or possibility of contestation. But manifestly Gadamer cannot have it both ways. The notion of *Wirkungsgeschichte* is either a genuine vision of the way in which the historical process moves forward or it is simply a new name for a skeptical relativism. If it is the former, than one must be able to proceed to the construction of a corresponding history(n), whether or not it is possible for such a history to be completed, whatever that would mean. That task in turn will require that the kind of *Horizontverschmelzung* that takes place when a work is assimilated to a mode of interest and a system of distinctions that may be quite different from those used by its creator must be susceptible of being reversed and a distinction must be made between the intentional life of the creator and of the interpreter. It is on just this point, however, that Gadamer's intention is rather unclear and one is left with a sense of uncertainty as to whether it is possible to isolate the meaning of the "other," that is, of an author or a prior interpreter, as such within the *Wirkungsgeschichte*(e) that connects us with it. One might well concede to Gadamer that even when this interest in the meaning of the other as such arises, there is no way in which the inquiry it motivates can go forward otherwise than in terms of the criteria of reality of the historian himself, and in this sense Gadamer's major thesis that interpretation always proceeds via a truth-claim with respect to the object to which the interpretandum refers would be safeguarded. This means that even attempts to identify the meaning of a text or the intention of an agent would not be able to disavow the temporal locus from which they originate and also that the idiom of reenactment would be quite inappropriate to the task of identifying that meaning. But it is extremely important that the possibility of such an interest as this be acknowledged and that it be recognized that, although it proceeds under criteria of reality which the interpreter can acknowledge, this interest does not require that some degree of convergence between these criteria and those implicit in the work to be interpreted must take place. In this sense truth with respect to the object that is addressed in the work under study and truth with respect to the character of the beliefs and intentions reflected in that work are distinct and independent of one another. If they were not, then by definition interpretation would be possible only in those cases where a fusion of horizons takes place and the criteria of reality of the interpreter are modified through contact with those of the work he studies. In such cases the truth of an interpretation would reflect a shared truth in respect of the object addressed in the work. But if as Gadamer says all understanding is interpretation, it would follow that one can understand only what one can somehow manage to agree with and this is manifestly not the case. The role of truth in interpretation and understanding thus appears to be different in quite significant ways from the account Gadamer gives of it.

It is now beginning to appear that these ostensibly antithetical theories of understanding—Collingwood's and Gadamer's—may have more in common than one would have supposed. Each of them holds that one can understand only what one can in some sense espouse on one's own, although of course there are great differences between the conditions that define the character of this espousal in the one case and the other. In Collingwood's case the thought that is to be understood is thought again by the historian but this reenactment is only provisional since the historian is not required to embrace whatever belief it is that this thought expresses, except on the occasion of his effort to understand it. Gadamer, who does not believe that such reenactment is possible at all, allows the interpreter a correspondingly greater freedom, as his concept of a fusion of horizons implies. But at the same time as Gadamer allows interpretation to bring out possibilities of meaning that were latent in the work it addresses instead of confining itself to those that were realized in the thought of its original creator, his conception of understanding makes it a carrying forward into a new set of circumstances of a work that is capable of maintaining its identity through these changes. Within that identity as it successively reconstitutes itself in interpretation there is thus a kind of complexly mediated agreement between the interpreter and his subject; and this agreement, unlike the one of which Collingwood speaks, is not merely provisional in the sense of being a tool of method but represents the position which the interpreter now occupies and has nothing hypothetical or provisional about it. Both Collingwood and Gadamer thus reject the view of understanding according to which the proper form for the propositions which the historian has to formulate in dealing with the intentional life of past human agents is something like "x believed so and so." They insist that it is a necessary condition for understanding that the historian drop the modal prefix "x believes" and, subject to the different sets of conditions described above, entertain as a belief of his own the proposition previously imbedded within the longer belief-sentence.

It is, however, just this view of understanding as involving the essential use of a belief-operator which seems to be the correct one; and I would therefore endorse the view of understanding which has recently been put forward by Arthur Danto and which declares that "understanding entails nothing so far as concerns the truth or falsity of what is understood."[27] It may well be that the kind of case in which there is no overlap between the beliefs of the interpreter and those of his subject is merely a limiting case since if this disagreement extended to a whole variety of background beliefs that are usually not the focus of interpretation the possibility of understanding would presumably break down in a quite radical way. It is also very likely that the subjects *chosen* for interpretation are generally those that are believed to have something to say to us which we will be able to accept and indeed benefit from. Indeed, one may suspect that if it were not for the existence of the kind of interpretation that generates "tradition" through preserving in the cumulative manner that Gadamer describes the truth-value of what has been handed down within a society, there would be no occasion for the kind of understanding that is *not* held to the maintenance of such continuity. But none of these facts implies that understanding necessarily involves a ratification of the truth-claims made by the person or work that is under consideration.

It should be made clear at this point that a great deal of what Gadamer has to say about understanding can be retained even though his skeptical attitude toward the possibility of separating understanding from truth-claims is rejected. The goal of such understanding is to make something that was said or done in the past intelligible in circumstances in which the background beliefs and more generally the semantic ordering of experience have undergone significant changes. It will accordingly be necessary to approach such understanding through a series of steps that make explicit the relevant differences between the semantic field within which something was said in the past and our own semantic field; and this is to say that temporal distance will have much the same kind of significance for an investigation that is concerned with meaning as it does, in Gadamer's view, within an investigation concerned with truth. Not only will the interpretative routes by which we reach an accurate understanding of what was said be such as to show unmistakably what the starting point of this effort of understanding has been; a great many of the secondary characterizations that we offer of the meaning we have managed to understand will continue to reflect contrasts that can be made within *our* way of ordering the elements of experience and that might well have been unintelligible or pointless within the semantic ordering of the author of the statement under study. A good example of the way such analyses might proceed is a study like Lucien Febvre's of Rabelais's religious beliefs in which the problem of understanding certain prima facie blasphemous statements by that author is approached through a careful exploration of the very extensive differences between the semantic domain within which they were made and our own.[28] Quite obviously, no such preliminaries to understanding were necessary in Rabelais's own day; and, however successful they prove to be, there will always be differences between an understanding like Rabelais's own that does not have to proceed in this way and one that remains dependent upon a complex form of semantic triangulation that uses reference points that were unknown to Rabelais. It would seem, therefore, that "reconstruction" must always be a more satisfactory description of what this process involves than "reenactment" can be; and that the meaning we seek to grasp can be reached only as the final term, with a series of semantic adjustments that bear witness to the temporal and semantic distance at which we stand from it. But this very important fact would be itself misunderstood if it were assumed that it implies an inevitable failure of the effort to understand. The only effort that must inevitably fail here is the effort to be Rabelais or a member of his audience and thereby to understand what one or the other said exclusively within *their* horizon. But the fact that this is impossible does not in any way compel us to give up the effort to characterize that horizon as one that differs from our own nor does it mean that such an effort must take the form of the kind of "fusion of horizons" that Gadamer describes. The difference between them is that for Gadamer such a fusion must apparently always involve some sort of reconciliation of the conflicting truth-claims that are made by the work that is to be understood and by the interpreter. To sum up, one might say that the distance at which the interpreter always stands from the person he seeks to understand is symbolized by the belief-operator he must use and that that operator itself introduces a statement which, though it may be cast in the words of the original text or utterance, is understood through adjustments effected within a semantic field that is different from the one in which it was made.

It is time now to ask what remains, after these philosophical excursions, of the doubts about understanding with which this chapter began. These doubts had a predominantly epistemological character and had to do with the possibility of access to the object of understanding when this is a belief or intention of some past human agent. Whatever complexities this access may involve, it is now clear that they need not be compounded by reading a requirement of reenactment into the concept of understanding as Collingwood did. At the same time, however, we have seen that a complete bypassing of epistemological issues in the ontological manner of a theory of understanding like Gadamer's, which rejects reenactment, generates a new set of difficulties when it denies meaning a status as an object of understanding that is independent of truth-value and treats the "owner" of that meaning as vanishing into the *Geschehen* in the course of which what he said or did is successively reinterpreted. The upshot of this critical review of theories of understanding thus appears to be a position that acknowledges meaning as such as an object of understanding and approaches the question of truth as one that arises in the first instance in connection with the attribution of such a meaning—typically a belief or an intention—to a particular human subject rather than with respect to the content of the assertion which that meaning may serve to make. The question to be examined now is what residual difficulties, if any, may still be connected with the notion of understanding, so construed. Quite obviously, this question will be philosophically interesting only if it concerns difficulties that are inseparable from understanding as such and not failures of understanding that are chargeable to the contingent unavailability of some of the evidentiary materials that it requires.

The chief difficulty that is attributed to theories of understanding has to do with the alleged arbitrariness of the associations they establish between "inner" or "subjective" states of mind and the forms of conduct which they are supposed to explain. In the course of the examination of the variant of this objection proposed by Theodore Abel, it became evident that this "arbitrariness" is in large part an artifact of the procedures used in giving an account of what understanding consists in and that it results, more specifically, from the way our perceptions of intentions, by being treated as "feeling-states," are isolated from the larger context of actions and events to which they stand in multiple relationships that would surely be of decisive importance in connection with the verification of the knowledge-claims they make. The alternative to this unsatisfactory way of dealing with our knowledge of intentions is clearly to avoid severing its connection with that context of action by transferring it to a mental or psychological domain whose relationship to public events of whatever kind must remain both contingent and problematic. In other words, intentions as objects of knowledge are to be left, to the extent possible, "in the world" and this means that they are to be considered primarily in the medium of those descriptions of their actions that are used by the responsible agents themselves or that are realistically attributable to them. The vice of many discussions of understanding that issue in skeptical conclusions is their tendency to reverse this procedure and to trace actions back to dispositions like "jealousy" and "ambition" whose relationship to specific features of the situation in question and of the actions being taken within it is left both sketchy and vague. Since dispositions or motives like these can be applied to a great variety of quite different ways of behaving and can hardly by themselves provide a guide to the relevant features of any particular situation, an explanation couched in these terms is often felt—and quite justifiably—to be uninformative and unhelpful. At best it serves to summarize some aspect of a situation or a sequence of action that has previously been laid before the observer in the kind of detail that gives a definite sense of these more general modes of description. In this role such descriptions of the motives and attitudes of human agents doubtless retain their usefulness; but to invoke them otherwise than in the closest possible association with specific actions that are imputable to the person so described can only produce the sort of uninformative hypostasis that is then denounced as a pseudo-explanation. My contention is thus that, if this is avoided and the problem of understanding is approached *in situ* and in its native context of action-descriptions, the kind of philosophical perplexity to which understanding is commonly supposed to lead need not arise. In what follows I want to defend this thesis with specific reference to the conceptual features that have been attributed to actions and action-descriptions in the preceding discussions.[29]

The problem of understanding in history may be described, consistently with the view of the historical process and of historical narrative that has been developed in preceding chapters, as the problem of how the historian can justify the movement he makes from the various kinds of evidence with which he has to work to the kind of statement in which the characteristic form of teleological connectedness among historical events is fully displayed. That form is one in which an action is described in such a way as to exhibit it at once as a response to some prior event—itself typically an action—and as an attempt to bring about a result that is appropriate in the light of the agent's goals and situation as determined by preceding events. There are some action verbs like "to retaliate" that perform both these functions at once and thus convey the fact that the action carries these retrospective and prospective references. Even in cases where verbs like this are explicitly used, however, the more specific character of these references must be filled in by further information supplied in other sentences; and in many other cases the dual-reference character of the action will be conveyed primarily in these more roundabout ways and without the use of verbs which in and of themselves carry this implication. Even when this convenient grammatical device is not available, however, the problem remains much the same as when it is available, that is, to fit an event into a teleologically organized sequence of actions; and this means under a description which directly or indirectly imputes to it the kind of response-character and attempt-character that have been delineated in the preceding discussions. And so if there is an epistemological difficulty about understanding, it must arise with respect to the way the use of such descriptions can be justified.

Let us use an example drawn from contemporary history for the purpose of exploring this question. Shortly after the outbreak of the Arab-Israeli war in 1973 the United States government began large-scale air shipments of weapons and ammunitions to Israel. This is a fact which was openly acknowledged by the U.S. government in public statements at the time and presumably no historical controversy could arise about it. Enough was also said at the time to make it clear *why* this action was taken, that is, in response to what events and with a view to what outcomes, but let us for the moment disregard the availability of such self-describing statements by those responsible for the action in question. How might we proceed to justify the amplification by a historian of this fact into a statement that the United States in shipping these arms was helping the Israelis against the Arabs?—a statement which at least begins to place this action in the kind of connected sequence of actions and events that has been declared to be typical of historical narrative. There are presumably no grounds—least of all philosophical—for doubting that an Arab-Israeli war had in fact broken out just before these shipments began or that the shipments had not been planned independently of the outbreak of the war or that the Israelis were suffering heavy material losses and were in danger of running short of tanks and airplanes. Neither can there be any sensible doubt that these facts were known to the U.S. government or that the Israelis had asked for the weapons which were in fact shipped. But if the situation is determined in all these respects, the question becomes not so much how one could *justify* the statement that the United States was helping the Israelis against the Arabs as how one could *avoid* characterizing the action it took in such terms. Unless the factual premises on which this account of what the American government did can be overturned or unless other matters of fact can be established that suggest a quite different intention, the presumption in favor of the account given must be overwhelmingly strong. But if that is the case, then we have justified a statement about this historical event which exhibits it as a response to the outbreak of the war and more specifically to the initial setbacks of the Israeli army and as an attempt to insure that Israel would not be defeated and occupied by the Arab forces. This is not to say that the relationship between the United States and Israel was governed— even on this occasion taken by itself—by altruistic motives or that other intentions and *arrière-pensées* on the part of the United States may not have been involved such as the desire to demonstrate American solidarity with a de facto ally to other American client-states around the world. Clearly, however, such ancillary characterizations themselves presuppose the truth of the account of the American action under consideration here or at least must be consistent with it.

It may be replied that I have made things too easy for myself by choosing an example that is relatively free of the kinds of ambiguity that dog the historian's inquiries in less well-documented contexts. A more difficult example, itself drawn from contemporary history, would have been the delay of the Russian army east of the Vistula in September 1944, when the Polish resistance rose against the Germans in Warsaw. Here the "fact" would presumably be that the Russians did not attempt to advance from their positions east of Warsaw during the period of the uprising and the issue would be whether this statement is to be amplified into a statement that they were thereby allowing the Polish resistance movement to be destroyed or into a statement that they were regrouping their forces after the vigorous advances of the preceding months and in preparation for the fall invasion of Germany. Both of these amplifications might well be true and either might have constituted sufficient reason for the Russian delay, so there is an inherent ambiguity here that is not present in the earlier example. Nevertheless, one can readily imagine further "facts" that inquiry into this matter might turn up which would have the effect of resolving or at least reducing this ambiguity, for example, of exhibiting the situation of the Russian forces as having been such that failure to advance could only be understood as an expression of—at least—indifference to the fate of the Polish resistance. In other words, even if in a given case the state of the available evidence is such that it is much more difficult or even impossible to approach the point at which the possible wider construals of an action are as firmly circumscribed as they are in the U.S.-Israeli case, this does not demonstrate any vice in the procedures that were outlined in our examination of that case. There is doubtless a danger that the historian may rely incautiously on presumptions governing how an action (or lack of action) in a certain set of circumstances is to be construed—presumptions that are in fact applicable only within his own culture. But once again this presumption, if it is fallacious, can be discovered to be so and replaced by another with which the historian may not feel quite as much at home as he did with its predecessor but which will lend itself to comparable uses in determining what amplified narrative characterizations of a particular, more neutrally characterized action are justifiable.

Let us now lift the interdict on the use of the agent's own statements about his action and see what further complications of the task of understanding may arise when these are included within the evidence which the historian may use. Such statements themselves quite regularly situate the action being described within a sequence of events in the characteristic narrative manner; and it is not surprising, therefore, that they constitute one of the principal sources from which the historian seeks to gather knowledge of the agent's intentions and beliefs. It would, however, be very naive to suppose that the historian can take such declarations at face value and base his knowledge-claim with respect to the intentions of these agents solely on their own statements. Such statements may very well be deliberate falsehoods which it is in the interest of the agent to spread because he has reasons for not wanting anyone to know what his real intention is. Alternatively, a statement by an agent characterizing his own intentions may in certain circumstances be partially or wholly mistaken, especially when there has been a lapse of time between the action itself and the agent's account of it. More generally, it is apparent that all utterances including those that describe one's own actions are themselves actions and as such must finally be governed by whatever master-intention it is that informs the system of actions to which they belong. There are circumstances in which any acknowledgment of what one is doing will stand in the way of the achievement of one's objective and there are others in which it may be necessary to misdescribe one's action, that is, to misrepresent one's intention, in order to assure success. It might conceivably be the case that the agent is committed to a policy of a still higher order which requires that he be ready to describe his actions truthfully on any and all occasions; but such beings are presumably rare. Typically, it will be an overall objective of a less Kantian kind that dictates what one says, and to whom, about what one is doing; and there need be nothing discreditable about the imposition of such controls over what one says or makes public. There are, of course, also agents whose overriding objective is always defined in such narrow first-person terms that they are inhibited from acknowledging anything that would come into conflict with their amour-propre.

These observations might seem to introduce new and grave complications into our analysis of understanding since they represent the utterances of the agent as being interpretable only in the context of the very intention which the historian is seeking to identify, and it may therefore appear as though the whole system of actions-cum-utterances of a given agent might be impenetrably closed to the external observer. But in fact this possibility is an extremely remote one. There are, first of all, many cases in which the agent's description of his action is broadly consistent with the other indications we have of the intention of that action; in such cases no special problem arises. Indeed, these two sources of evidence—discursive and nondiscursive—will in such cases lend one another support. The difficulty, if there is one, will therefore arise only in the case where what the agent says about his own action and about his intention in performing it is irreconcilable with what we know about the action from other sources. In such cases the historian may discount the agent's statement altogether, on grounds like those cited above, as mendacious or insincere and as motivated by a desire to conceal his true intention. When, for example, a powerful country like Nazi Germany describes its attack against a smaller and weaker country like Poland as a response to provocations by the latter and the historian is in a position to show that invasion plans and troop movements preceded the occurrence of the supposedly provocative incident, he will not hesitate to attribute the invasion to an aggressive intention on the part of the invading country. In another case, however, in which the agent's description of his own action seems glaringly at odds with what the historian knows about the action itself, it may turn out that the disparity can be best accounted for by reference to certain mistaken beliefs which the agent held at the time of the action and which led him to believe that that action would have a quite different set of consequences from those that were actually produced. In such a case, the historian could honor the agent's description of his own action while at the same time explaining why things worked out so differently. In order to maintain his claim that the intention based on false beliefs was genuine, however, the historian would have to pay close attention to the way the agent reacted when the fact of his error was brought to his attention, if in fact it ever was. If there was then some attempt to rectify the situation produced by the misconceived action, that would argue, ceteris paribus, in favor of the genuineness of the error while a refusal to accept even the strongest evidence that things were otherwise than the original intention assumed them to be or a persistence in the original line of action in spite of these counterindications would inevitably raise questions about the sincerity of the agent's professions. The American intervention in Vietnam with the vicissitudes through which it passed comes to mind in this connection as a good example of the kind of historical event about which questions like this would have to be raised.

What I have been trying to show is that if the historian is in a position to apply action-descriptions to *any* of the events with which he is concerned and to make plausible assumptions with regard to what the historical agents he is dealing with may have known or not known about the various elements of their situations, he will also be in a position to begin construing the teleological ordering of the events in question. Of course, if for whatever reason someone were to be unwilling to allow the historian's treatment of the American-Israeli episode mentioned above to begin with the statement that the U.S. shipped arms to Israel, then it would not be possible to advance from that statement and from the other statements of fact with respect to what was taking place at the time and what the U.S. government knew of those events, to the statement that the U.S. was helping Israel against the Arabs. In such a case, it would be fair to ask the objector what description he would be willing to apply to the event which he is unwilling to call a "shipment of arms" or why he believes no such event took place. But even if he were able to show that another description would be more appropriate and accurate or that the U.S. in fact did nothing at all, then *that* description or that fact would serve as the beginning of *another* story about the American part in the Arab-Israeli War; and narrative continuity would again be established although along different lines from those proposed above. Where the evidence available to the historian is much more exiguous than it is in the case of a contemporaneous event like this one, it is likely that there will be severe restraints upon what the historian can achieve in the way of narrative continuity; but, as has already been pointed out, this is not the kind of difficulty about understanding that requires philosophical attention. By contrast, where the relevant action-descriptions are available, together with other contextual information relating to the circumstances of action and the information base upon which it proceeded, there does not appear to be any difficulty of principle associated with the movement of inference leading to a fully realized form of narrative continuity. In other words where the existence of an actional context is established, the use of the action-description that has been conceded will, together with other circumstances and especially those that relate to what the agents knew and did not know, authorize the use of additional action-descriptions; and these will, with luck, generate teleological continuity in terms of which historical narrative has been characterized.

The premise upon which the above argument rests is, of course, that some suitable action-description of the events in question will be available to the historian, where "suitable" means that it expresses the character of the action in a form in which the agent could in principle have acknowledged it. This is to say that what is being excluded is the case in which the terms in which the intention of the agent is cast are wholly discontinuous with those with which the historian would himself be familiar and would use for the formation of his own intentions. In such a case, even though these intentions were intentions that found expression in action and thus made some describable difference in the world that is common to such an agent and the imagined observer, there would be no correspondence between the "reading" of those effects that the historian would propose on the basis of his own ways of constructing a system of ends and the actual intention of the agent. Whether in such circumstances it would even be possible for the historian to become aware of the fact that a system of intentions was finding expression in the changes he notes as having taken place in the world is a real question, but one which need not be pursued here. The real value of such an imagined case as this is rather to bring out the presuppositions on which the construals of intention like those above rest and to enable us to judge how justified these are.

Those presuppositions may for present purposes be reduced to one: if understanding is to be possible, the agent and the historian must share a language. "Language" here does not mean something as specific as German or French, or if it does it must be such natural languages understood as lending themselves to a system of equivalences among them of the kind that make translation possible. When understanding takes place as it typically does within a society in which people communicate with one another in connection with undertakings that can succeed only if there is cooperation and thus a shared understanding of what is being done, this condition is secured in advance. Without a common vocabulary containing the concepts of the goals of social work and of the actions by which it could be accomplished, a society would be impossible. When a historian addresses himself to the past of his own society or of one which has stood in some communicative relationship with the latter, the guiding assumption is that here too a common language—a shared vocabulary of action-descriptions—exists, or that it can be brought into being through a process of semantic adjustments within the language the historian himself uses. In general, the hypothesis of connaturality which is often said to underlie the whole enterprise of understanding may be said to have a semantic character in the sense that it requires some degree of overlap between the units of meaning that are utilized on the one side and the other in the definition of actions. It is not necessary of course to think of such meanings as composing a permanent repertory of *voci mentali* to which we have access simply by virtue of the structure of the human mind, as Vico seems to have thought.[30] But in another sense Vico was profoundly right when he identified the *verum* of cultural and historical studies with the *factum*—surely the quintessentially human *factum*—that is constituted by the semantic organization of our experience of the world in our capacity as active and social beings. His claim is thus that our own status as beings who live and work within an inherited and shared language gives us access in principle to an indefinitely extensive domain of language-mediated human reality. One can hardly imagine another hypothesis under which the "human sciences" could go forward; and if it is correct then the answer to the kind of skepticism that raises the possibility of forms of intentional organization that would be radically unintelligible to us seems clear. The answer is that, whatever ultimate limits may be set to this form of intelligibility, by reason of modes of intentional life that are radically discontinuous with our own, there is no reason to suppose that these coincide with any of the barriers to understanding which we encounter and surmount as we move outward in time and in space toward other societies and cultures in our own historical world. We are, in other words, already "inside" these great amalgams of utterance and action by virtue of our own status as agents and language-users to whom both intersubjectivity and the teleological structure of action are already familiar and because we ourselves live within societies that are in a line of semantic descent and of communicative contact with the intentional life we seek as historians to understand.[31]

II

At the beginning of this chapter I proposed a distinction between "understanding" and "interpretation" which was designed to reflect the prior distinction between the intentional life of the human subjects of a narrative, whether fictional or factual, and that of the author of that narrative. In the account that has just been given of understanding, it was argued that the historian must concern himself with what I have called the agent's description of his situation and his action and that it is the historian's responsibility to determine as accurately as he can and on the basis of all available evidence just what the intentions and beliefs of such agents in the past really were. It was recognized that this is often an extremely difficult task and also that one principal source of these difficulties lies in the fact that the life-situation of the historian is so often profoundly different from that of the human agents in the past with whom he is concerned and yet it is only with the instruments of understanding that are drawn from that life that it is possible for the historian to approach the past at all. Among the writers whose views were considered in the preceding section there were those who take a positive view of this involvement of the historian's own perspective in the delineation of historical fact and regard it not only as being unavoidable but also as constituting the key to a proper understanding of his function. The more usual view among historians, however, has been that an understanding of a person in the past requires a rigorous distinction between intentions and beliefs that are properly attributable to that person and those that are attributable to the inquirer. For those who belong to the former group it is almost axiomatic that any attempt to understand the past will be an interpretation as well if only by virtue of the role which they assign to the present in such understanding. But for those who hold that it is the special responsibility of the historian to resist *Horizontverschmelzung,* understanding and interpretation must remain at least in principle distinct from one another. If interpretation proves to be a valid mode of judgment for the historian at all, it will be one which he must exercise *in propria persona* and this is to say in full consciousness of the distinction between his own position within the historical process and that of the subjects of his inquiry. The authority of such an interpretation, if it can claim one, will on this view have to be quite different from that of understanding since understanding rests on the rationale which it imputes to the agent and interpretation takes the further step of determining the significance of the actions that issue from that rationale and of doing so from a standpoint which may be different from and quite possibly in conflict with that of the agents whose actions are being judged. To put the same point somewhat differently, if understanding situates the actions of historical agents within the context of the beliefs and goals that were peculiar to those agents and to their time, interpretation subjects those actions to a further scrutiny in the light of standards or norms which may be very different from the agent's and which even if they coincide with the latter do not owe their authority for purposes of historical judgment to that fact. In this section the topic of interpretation in this sense as a distinct mode of historical judgment will be taken up and examined with a view to determining what kind and what degree of validity it can claim.

The use of the term "interpretation" which I am adopting here is somewhat unconventional so a few clarifications at the outset will not be amiss. It is important first of all to understand that although attention has been drawn to the temporal distance between the historian/interpreter and the subject of his interpretation, that distance is not the sole or even the primary distinguishing feature of the historical judgments which I propose to group together under the rubric of interpretation. For example, the great-uncle of the last man to speak Cornish could not have so described himself; and so it follows that a description of that person in those terms by a historian would qualify as an interpretation in my sense. But because the great-uncle of the last man to speak Cornish would presumably have had no grounds for dissenting from this historical description, if *per impossibile* he could have known of it, this is not a particularly good example of interpretation in my sense. Of course, he might not think that it expressed any very important fact about him or that it was worth including in his biography; if so, the interpretative character of the description would become somewhat more marked. As things are, we simply have no way of knowing what his views might have been; and so the issue of the interpretative character of such a description really does not arise in any pressing form. When it *is* possible to bring a historian's description into some definite relationship of comparison with the beliefs of a subject of a history, however, the historian cannot allow the validity of his interpretation to depend upon its being confirmed by the agent's description. An interpretation is in other words a judgment which the historian must be prepared to defend even though it is not the kind of statement which the subject of the interpretation would have made about himself whether because he thought it was false or because he thought it was unimportant by comparison with other true statements about himself. The point here is that interpretation in my sense *may* involve a substantive difference of belief between the historian and the subject of the interpretation and not just the formal difference occasioned by the circumstance that the subject could not, by reason of his temporal position, have described himself in the way that the historian does. Since the difference is of this kind, it is clear that the authority with which this contravening judgment is made by the historian will be a matter of much greater importance than it would if the difference were a purely formal one of temporal perspective.

A relatively simple case of historical interpretation that has a critical or judgmental function of this kind is the one which has to do with a determination by the historian that some one or other of the beliefs—usually these would be factual beliefs—upon which historical agents relied for the purposes of action was in fact false. There is, I take it, nothing especially mysterious in the fact that historians are on occasion able to achieve better knowledge of a given situation in the past than some person living in that situation or perhaps than any one of those persons. Sometimes the historian's advantage is limited to a particular period of time in the life of his subject and it may in fact be owed to a discovery which the latter himself made at a later date—too late, perhaps, to be of any use to him. But there are other cases in which the historian knows something which no one in the past situation knew, for example, that ancient mathematicians would not be able to square the circle. In either case knowledge of this kind will enable the historian to explain certain mistakes or failures on the part of his subjects in a way that ex hypothesi would not have been possible for them. Such determinations as these are relatively unproblematic because the epistemic procedures they involve are such as would presumably have been recognized as valid by the agent. It is just a fact that he did not or could not employ them on the occasion in question; but he is assumed to have been perfectly conversant with the kind of fact they ascertain and on other occasions probably used such procedures to make similar findings of fact.

If the case in which the historian is better informed with respect to a specific matter of fact than were the subjects of his history does not present any special difficulties, it does suggest some interesting wider possibilities. A great many human activities are after all concerned directly or indirectly with the discovery of truth; and in fact the "arts and sciences"—both practical and theoretical—may be regarded as so many departments of human effort in which mankind has been trying to discover "truths" that are useful in the conduct of life. The invention of the wheel can, for example, be described as the discovery of the truth that loads can be moved more easily in a certain way; and we know that there have been whole civilizations—some of them with major achievements to their credit—that never made this discovery, just as there are others at the present time which have not yet made other comparable discoveries. These observations suggest a picture of the historian as occupying a standpoint from which he can plot the "learning processes" of various societies and establish the degree of progress they achieve. If it is assumed that the historian is cognizant of the most advanced achievements that have been realized anywhere in the area of effort with which he is concerned, then he will clearly be in a position to place a given system of technology or of scientific knowledge on an axis of development in a way that would have been impossible for its exponents. In other words, because he can view all the historical phenomena that fall within the category of efforts to control natural processes for certain definite purposes, he can situate them within a progressive development that is ordered by the degree of success that has been achieved in attaining a goal that is set by the nature of the activity itself, whether it be military science or agriculture or theoretical physics. Such a view will be at once an interpretation in the sense of that term that has been adopted here since it goes beyond the description that would have been available in principle to contemporaries of the events in question; and it does so on the strength of an authoritative criterion of scientific progress that overrides any self-characterizations with which it may come into conflict.

There have, of course, been challenges to the assumptions on which this conception of the self-ordering character of those human activities which are concerned with the discovery of truth rests.[32] It has been argued that we cannot simply assume that these activities are homogeneous in the sense that they all place themselves under the authority of a single set of standards for determining what is to count as a question and what as an answer in some domain of inquiry. If these objections are valid, then it would be illegitimate to compare, for example, Greek science with modern science and to make judgments of the relatively more advanced character of the latter over the former since it would just not be the case that both were really trying to do the same thing. But even if one concedes that the nature of inquiry itself may shift in ways that make valid comparative judgments more difficult, it does not seem reasonable to conclude that these shifts are so numerous or so radical as to negate entirely the "naive" assumption we make of the progressive character of the human activities in question. At any rate, as long as the chief sponsor of the relativistic interpretation of the history of science can declare that "scientific development is fundamentally evolutionary" and as such "unidirectional and irreversible," it would seem that even he still views the process of scientific change from a standpoint that is neutral in the sense that what counts as a loss and as a gain is determined by criteria that are not under the exclusive control of either of the paradigms that succeed one another.[33] To the extent that he continues to make such judgments he is evidently still operating within the old "naive" assumptions about the univocal character of progress within specified areas of inquiry, and the possibility of the kind of special history that takes this kind of progress as the organizing interpretative principle for a certain department of human activity must still be intact.

When it comes to raising these suppositions to the level of an explicit criterion for determining what constitutes progress in human history, however, difficulties quickly appear. Some of these can be identified if we examine R. G. Collingwood's attempt to work out a satisfactory statement of just such a criterion.[34] His treatment of the matter takes the form of an effort to specify the circumstances in which it is legitimate for the historian to regard a novelty that appears in a society's repertory of methods or techniques of action as an improvement over what preceded it. Collingwood argues that a historian can make such a judgment on a change that occurs in the life of a society only if he can understand both stages in that life—the stage that precedes the change and the one that follows it—"with enough sympathy and insight to reconstruct their experience for himself."[35] But even when these conditions are met, it will be meaningful to speak of this change as an improvement only if a further condition is met. An improvement can be said to have taken place only if it can be shown that before this change a society was attempting unsuccessfully to solve a problem to which the change that takes place provides a satisfactory solution. In recognizing a problem and attempting to solve it, a society is acknowledging an inadequacy in its own mode of life and thus accepts in advance the possibility that some other society or some later stage in its own evolution will, by achieving the solution to that problem, bring about an improvement in its way of life. In the absence of such a recognition the historian might very well have to regard the two periods as being simply different from one another with no way of weighing the various points of difference in such a way as to arrive at an overall judgment of the one as an improvement over the other.

There can be no doubt that the conception outlined by Collingwood would apply satisfactorily to a certain range of cases in which we interpret a change as constituting an improvement. These are the areas of social activity in which a society comes to think of itself as being confronted with problems to which its "solutions" may or may not be adequate. Such a view of one's own level of performance as a society is by no means universal and it is in fact most highly developed where something like a scientific tradition—a tradition of systematic inquiry—has come into being and where the practical arts have come to be conceived in terms that imply the possibility of a continuing advance beyond the stage they have presently reached. In societies in which this kind of critical consciousness has not emerged there may be real improvements but because they are not understood as forming part of a continuing and indefinite process of improvement the procedures of the society in the relevant area will very likely restabilize themselves at a new level without anything that could plausibly be interpreted as an acknowledgment of a possible inadequacy for which some further improvement would be the remedy. The question thus becomes one of determining what degree of freedom the historian is to have in identifying that Collingwood calls the "attempts" that a society is making to "solve" its problems. Just how explicit do these attempts have to be and how clearly does the society need to identify the area in which its "problems" exist? Depending on the way this question is answered, the scope of Collingwood's conception of progress in history will be either quite narrow or quite broad; but unfortunately it is not possible to determine on the basis of the brief sketch he gives us of his theory how he would have resolved this ambiguity. What he does tell us about the role of the historian in this connection tends rather to add another dimension of uncertainty to his treatment of the matter. He tells us that "progress is not a mere fact to be discovered by historical thinking; it is only through historical thinking that it comes about at all."[36] One might well agree with Collingwood that "historical thinking" is a necessary condition for the occurrence of progress in the sense that Einstein could not be said to have advanced beyond Newton unless he knew of Newton's prior existence or at least of the prior existence of his theory; but this hardly justifies one in claiming that historical thinking "creates" progress.

It is significant I think that almost all of Collingwood's examples of historical episodes to which his conception of progress applies are drawn from intellectual history or the history of science where, as has already been pointed out, it is relatively easy to identify an "attempt" to solve a problem and the success or failure in which that attempt issues. At the same time, however, he recognizes that there may be progress in other areas which are not ordinarily thought to have the characteristic form of a mode of inquiry. Among these is morality, and Collingwood tells us that "part of our moral life consists of our coping with problems arising not out of our animal nature but out of our social institutions . . . which create moral problems only insofar as they are already themselves the expression of moral ideals."[37] "A man who asks himself whether he should take voluntary part in his country's war...is involved in a conflict between the moral forces embodied in the institution of the state, and those embodied not merely in the ideal but in the equally actual reality of international peace and intercourse."[38] "To solve the problem of war...is only possible by devising new institutions which shall recognize in full the moral claims made by the state without leaving unsatisfied the further claims to which in historical fact the old institutions have given rise."[39] He then suggests that a similar mode of treatment is applicable to economics as well as to politics and to law but the further development of this idea is not carried out. It is thus left unclear whether the "problems" which are said to arise in these different areas are supposed to have any common character and in particular whether that common character, if there is one, could be plausibly regarded, as some of Collingwood's remarks suggest, as being a moral or an ethical one.

This possibility is not developed by Collingwood, however, and one may wonder whether, if it had been, he would have been able to adhere to the conditions he had laid down for determining the progressive character of new developments in more restricted areas of human achievement. As it stands, his theory seems primarily concerned with these areas which, as was noted earlier, incorporate standards of reference by which they can be judged, that is, by reference to the which achievements in this area can be compared with one another and placed on an axis of progress in a way that in principle transcends the point of view of the individual agents who are involved in this form of activity. It seems obvious, however, that even if the various special histories of the arts and sciences can be dealt with on these principles, there can be no question of reducing human history as a whole to the history of science and technology or all other forms of interpretative judgment in history to the kind that equates progress with the growth of knowledge.[40] Even within the limits of the kind of special history that accepts such an equation, issues of interpretation arise that resist treatment in such terms and that compel the historian to approach a domain of human activity not just in terms of the adequacy or inadequacy of the factual beliefs on which this activity was predicated but also in terms of the goals and the standards it reflects. After all, as historians we are interested not only in the levels of competence that were achieved by a given society but also in the uses that were made of that competence and the ends to which it was directed. But when we attempt this form of judgment we may well be obliged to take issue with the view—whether implicit or explicit—of the society in question itself, as to what its real "problems" are; and it is this fact that makes it seem so problematic whether we would be able to abide by Collingwood's condition requiring us to base our own judgment on just that view.

It would be less than candid, however, not to acknowledge that we typically feel much less sure of what the basis of a contravening interpretation would be in such a case than we do in the case where the disagreement is factual in character. When, as can easily happen, the interpretation which we are called upon to make is directly evaluative and adequately expressible only in moral terms, the reluctance we feel is intensified and often passes over into a principled skepticism with respect to the possibility of rationally defensible judgments on the desirability of what was done in the past. This skepticism typically has a predominantly psychological cast and bases itself in the first instance on the observation that at bottom historians are just as partisan in their attitudes and judgments as were the direct participants in the events of which they are ostensibly the impartial reporters. This observation which undeniably registers an important fact about historiography then comes to be associated with a skeptical attitude with respect to the very possibility of an evaluative judgment that is more than the expression of a personal preference; and the inference is then drawn that the epistemic legitimization of history requires that the role of such evaluative judgments in history be either eliminated altogether or reduced to an absolute minimum. It is now widely accepted among historians that the former goal is not really feasible although this is usually argued on the basis of psychological rather than logical considerations. But the real issue underlying this whole controversy is not the psychological one which has to do with whether the historian can in practice abstain from evaluative judgments on the events he reports or whether he will inevitably "give himself away." The question is rather whether quite apart from any overt or covert signaling of his attitude the historian is not *obliged* to make use of certain evaluative assumptions simply for the purpose of bringing about a narrative ordering of the events he is concerned to present. In a sense, this is the old problem of "selection" which arises out of the circumstance that there is an indefinitely large number of "facts" in any possible area of inquiry, however restricted, so that it must always be in order to ask the historian *why* certain of these facts were included in his account and certain others were not. But this problem arises in a special way for a theory of history like the one that has been presented in the preceding chapters. That theory rests on the postulate that whatever selection the historian makes has to recognize and shape itself around a prior selection which has been effected by the human beings who in their capacity as agents are the subjects of his history. To them certain of the features of their situation were important or interesting and certain others were not; and to them certain of the consequences of their actions were significant and others were not. This kind of selectiveness is obviously inseparable from human agency as such and from the intentional life of which it forms a part; and I have argued repeatedly that such agency plays a constitutive role in the historical process and that it is the historian's responsibility to reconstruct that process as a dialectic of agency. But if all this is accepted, then it might be asked what further kind of selection the historian will have to make that goes beyond the one that has antecedently been effected by his subjects. Has not the earlier discussion of selection supplied the only answer we need to the question that has been raised about the evaluative role of the historian?

The answer I would give to this question might be either "yes" or "no." "No" if the question implies that an answer is already available; "yes" if the question were taken as suggesting that the prior discussion of agency supplies the elements out of which an answer to the problem of selection could be constructed although in a way that goes substantially beyond anything that has been said so far. As a preliminary to an argument showing that it is not possible for the historian to rely *exclusively* upon the kind of selectivity that is implicit in the intentional life of his subjects, I have already tried to show how in the area of factual beliefs the historian may come to know something that was unknown to his subjects and that may help to explain the outcome of their undertakings. When this happens the historian is no longer merely reporting what others believed but is drawn, precisely in his work as a historian, into a substantive claim or assertion that may well run counter to some belief held by his subjects. Similarly, I now propose to argue, the historian cannot simply take his evaluative standards from his principals and abstain entirely from any judgment in his own right on the issues with which these historical agents themselves had to deal. Here, too, he must envisage the situation with which he has to deal in a way that remains in principle independent of the criteria of significance that were used by one or another of the parties involved in it and thereby enables him to raise questions about the kind of justification that was claimed for their actions by these parties. There is, moreover, as I will argue, something about human action as there is something about belief that invites this kind of independent appraisal or at least cannot take refuge from it in a claim to be wholly sovereign and self-justifying within a domain of discourse which it completely controls.[41]

The situation out of which the unavoidability of evaluative judgments on the part of the historian can best be understood may be described as follows. The historian is primarily concerned with actions which human beings have performed in the past and with actions which have had some significant effect upon other human beings as well as upon the agents themselves. Typically, these human beings who act and undergo the effects of action are involved in some form of conflict with one another and so the consequences of these actions are characteristically experienced by those who suffer them as being adverse to their own interests. In many situations these "patients" are also agents, and the actions they perform are similarly unwelcome to the other party. To this one must add that in such situations of conflict each side usually feels the need to justify the stand it takes and the actions it performs; and these justifications in effect reproduce the primary conflict at the level of claims about rights and duties and so on. There may be a good deal of hypocrisy and window-dressing in such justifications; but they also serve a serious purpose which is that of claiming some measure of public validity for the description which some agent or patient gives of what he has done or suffered. In that sense it can be said that both agents attempt to situate the transactions in which they are involved in a public moral space and, however inept or disingenuous their mode of presentation may be in a given case, it does entail an acknowledgment that some general evaluative criteria are relevant to the determination of what has been done and what has been suffered.

Up to this point the activity of the historian in dealing with human transactions of this kind has been described mainly in terms of his inquiry into the context of belief and purpose out of which human actions issue. It has also been emphasized that the historian must understand a given sequence of action from both sides and that he must show a special sensitivity to the kinds of misunderstandings and misinterpretations that are a characteristic feature of the relationship between such parties in conflict with one another. At the same time, this emphasis upon the differing contexts out of which action issues was not intended as a requirement that the historian impersonate his protagonists and, as it were, write his history of their doings now from the one side and now from the other. The effect of such a procedure would be to produce not one history but two, and two histories that would be irreconcilable with one another at many points. In the end the historian must come up against the obligation to make these stories *one* story so that what the agent does is what the patient suffers and the other way around as well. And since the descriptions that are used by the agent and the patient for expressing what they have done and suffered are unavoidably evaluative in nature, the historian finds himself in the position of having to mediate between those disparate descriptions in order to arrive at some unified account of what actually happened. The only alternative to such mediation would be a decision to abstract completely for historical purposes from the whole dimension of the events in question to which these partisan descriptions relate and to do so in favor of a form of interest in them that would be wholly independent of the rights and wrongs of the matter as the parties involved perceived them. Such an alternative may indeed be available to the author of a special history; a military historian, for example, can concentrate entirely on Napoleon's conduct of the wars he fought and ignore what his victories (and defeats) meant to the history of Europe. But if the step beyond special histories that was described above has been taken and the interest of the historian is addressed precisely to the larger human significance of great historical undertakings or of the institutional design of the life of a given society, then matters stand very differently and the likelihood that the historian's judgments can be isolated from any logical relationship to those of the agents themselves is greatly reduced.[42]

Unfortunately the strategies that are most often adopted by historians for the purpose of dealing with this problem are hardly adequate to it. Perhaps the most popular of these consists in simply identifying oneself with the perspective on events of *one* of the parties in conflict and espousing more or less uncritically the case that was made at the time for the actions that were undertaken by those who represented that side in the conflict. This is the course followed by most of the authors of national histories, who are typically themselves members of the same national communities whose history they have undertaken to write. The appeal of this method consists in the fact that it relieves the historian of the necessity of dealing critically with two sets of descriptions since it is determined from the outset that an absolute priority for purposes of evaluation and judgment attaches to the descriptions of events that issue from the background or presuppositions associated with one side. But, of course, just to the degree that this priority is made automatic and thus removed from the sphere in which it would be subject to challenge and qualification the task of mediation itself has been avoided through what amounts to a suppression of the moral existence of one of the participants in the situation. When he writes entirely for an internal constituency and thus for one that is already just as convinced as he is (and with as little critical basis) of the unique and privileged position of their country in any relationship it may enter with another, a historian can often get away with this kind of high-handed burking of the issue; but once the procedure is detected he can hardly claim to have a *right* to make these assumptions that so drastically simplify his task. He must then attempt to put on at least a show of impartiality and to justify his nation, and himself in his capacity as the advocate of that nation, by an appeal to criteria other than the irresistible plausibility of the view of events which he has espoused. But once again, in making this wider kind of claim, he will himself have entered an area of evaluative judgment for which a stronger authority is claimed, and he will have no reason to suppose that the conclusion he had previously embraced will have any special standing or authority here.

At a much higher level of reflection on the problem of selection in history one encounters a view of the role played by the subjective interest of the historian which is scarcely more satisfactory as an account of the evaluative element in the latter's judgment than the wholly uncritical procedure just described. I have in mind the view proposed by Professor Morton White which takes the form of an interpretation of what is meant by *the* cause, that is, the decisive cause of a historical event, and of the notion of "what happened" or of what consequences of a given event are to be included in the historian's narrative, and makes both a function of the kind of interest that the historian happens to take in the events in question.[43] In his analysis of the concept of the decisive cause White argues that it is plausibly treated as being the "abnormal" cause or that one among the contributory causes of an event that is unusual in relation to some background of expectation and some conception of what constitutes the normal mode of existence of whatever kind of thing this case may concern. Thus, either the fact that a man has an ulcerated stomach or the fact that he has just eaten parsnips might be treated by observers with different interests and different backgrounds of knowledge as *the* cause of his indisposition provided that these two causes are so associated with one another that the one can figure as an abnormal event against the background of the other. In the case of a determination by the historian of "what happened" the historian's subjective interest plays an even more important role since, in the case of effects, not even the requirement of abnormality that defines the decisive cause constrains the historian's choice. It follows that the principles by which the "chronicle" underlying a historical narrative is constituted are radically dependent upon the subjective interests of the historian and that there is no basis for regarding one string of events that may be picked out by such an interest as having a higher claim to inclusion within a narrative than any other. White acknowledges that the historian's choice of a particular cause or effect of an event for inclusion in his narrative may derive from a value-judgment on his part; but he insists that there is no logical connection between such a value-judgment and the designation of something as the cause or the effect of a given event. Beyond that White tells us very little about such value-judgments except that they may be "inarbitrable" and not subject to any further debate. It is in any case clear that we are not to look to such judgments or to whatever justification they may claim for themselves as the source of an order of priority by which the conflict among different forms of subject interest on the part of the historian might be even partially resolved.

This position may fairly be described as an extreme example of the absolutization of subjective interest as the sole principle of selection in history. It is extreme because it does not even require that such value-judgments by the historian be subject to some form of justification addressed to other historians. The result is that so long as causal relationships are respected any string of events will constitute a history even if the only person to whom the story so constructed seems significant is the historian himself who constructs it. One immediate difficulty arising out of such a view is that if the historian makes use of a nondebatable and possibly quite eccentric norm of significance in selecting the aspects of some event for inclusion in his narrative, one might be hard put to say *what* the resulting account would be a history of. Usually when the historian identifies the event of which he proposes to write a history, for example, the French Revolution, this very choice is understood to impose certain limits on what he might include in or exclude from his history; and the same would be true if he were to choose some special aspect of such an event, for example, the military or the religious or the diplomatic aspect of the French Revolution. There can be no doubt that the historian of almost any event retains a wide range of options, but these remain options within a domain demarcated by such generally understood rubrics as "the French Revolution" and that fact imposes definite constraints, though certainly not onerous ones, on what can count as a form of interest in the event so designated. To ignore these constraints is of course possible; but if one does so one runs the risk of producing something unintelligible to one's professional colleagues since it has no points of contact with their work.

Even if one corrects White's position by interpreting what he says about the subjective interest of the historian in a way that acknowledges the necessity of making this interest intelligible at least to his professional colleagues, other difficulties remain. Most notable among these is the absence of any account of the wider context within which these interests—now to be understood as shared (or at least in principle shareable) research priorities within the professional community of historians—find their place. A great many of these have a purely technical character and are justifiable by reference to the contribution a particular line of investigation can make to the understanding of some larger topic which is judged to be quite unchallengeably worthy of study. But the interest historians take in these larger topics themselves is not one that can be plausibly justified on such technical grounds; and the determination of "what happened" in such great episodes of American national history as the Civil War is accordingly not a matter that can be resolved by reference to norms that are peculiar to the community of historians, much less to an individual historian. The history of the Civil War is important to historians for the same reasons it is important to all the citizens of this country; and those reasons have to do with the fact that the Civil War determined whether the Union would be preserved and whether slavery would be abolished. To be sure, when the history under study is not that of one's own society but of one that may be remote in time and space, judgments of importance may seem to be less obviously connected with concerns which the historian shares with nonhistorians. Nevertheless the continuity is still there as anyone knows who reads modern histories of Greece and Rome in which the foci of interest are chosen on the basis of the historian's judgments—sometimes anachronistic and sometimes not—as to what is of paramount human importance in that time and in his own. There are, of course, historians who profess to regard all such "existential" dimensions of their métier as being beneath their dignity but they typically maintain this posture of mind only by treating history as though it were some permanently established bureaucratic entity that is far too majestic to have to justify itself by demonstrating its continuity with wider human interests. But even when such an attitude is adopted, it does not really insure that the historian will in fact operate in a sphere that is independent of any wider evaluative assumptions. It insures only that his adherence to the standards that define what is important in his domain of inquiry will be uncritical and perhaps even largely unconscious.

These observations can be developed further in a way that bears on the relationship in which the historian's judgments of importance stand to the concerns of the historical agents with whom he deals. I have been arguing that the standards of significance and of interest which the historian employs are finally derivative from evaluative judgments which he makes in his capacity as a human being and which he presumably shares with at least some nonhistorians. It is moreover by reference to such evaluative assumptions—assumptions that pick out certain kinds of events as having a special significance, whether positive or negative—that determinations of "what happened" or of what strings of events are worthy of inclusion in a narrative are derived. But if this is so, then the historian's judgment of "what happened" and of the kind of significance that qualifies an event for inclusion in a historical narrative is one which inevitably comes to stand in certain relationships to judgments that were made—implicitly or explicitly—by the historical agents themselves who were the contemporaries of and even participants in the event in question. If for example the historian regards the First World War as a European civil war and the destruction of "the concert of Europe" as the significant issue of that war, that is, as what in a preeminent sense "happened" in that war, it will be impossible for him not to view the nationalistic attitudes which the several European nations manifested both before and during the war in a certain (negative) light. This does not mean that the historian must therefore distribute praise and blame to historical agents according to his judgment of the tendency of the actions they performed, although on occasion it may be appropriate for him to do so. What is more important than such direct expressions of the historian's judgment on individuals and groups is the ordering function within the narrative itself of the historian's judgment of the significant outcome of these events and its influence upon the way in which the roles of the historical agents are construed and the significance that is to be imputed to their actions by virtue of the points at which they intersect the line of events picked out by a given judgment of "what happened." It is this orientation of the narrative that is the vital function of the evaluative assumptions that the historian makes; and just as there could be no story of the agents with whom he deals unless they were beings who themselves establish criteria of importance and thereby select certain features of their situation as having a special significance, so there could be no story *for* the historian unless he were a being of the same kind and could establish priorities by which some things in the past stand out as having greater importance than do others.

But if the historian is not to be just another partisan in the same contest of which he is the historian, incongruously intervening across the centuries to lend aid to this one or that one among the original contestants, it is also clear that he must not be simply a representative of interests that are characteristic of his own time and freely appropriate from the life of the past as its true significance whatever is related to contemporary interests without concern for the internal criteria of significance of the life from which these elements are abstracted. The only way in which he can satisfy all these requirements and limitations on his role is by employing a framework of interpretation within which significance is defined in terms that are in principle applicable to *both* the present and the past. If such a framework of interpretation is indeed available, then the result of superimposing it upon episodes in the past within which no one can be said to have used it as *his* standard of significance will inevitably be to produce a version of their story rather different from any that could have been provided by a contemporary. The difference will consist in the fact that, in addition to the kind of significance that human actions take on through the relationship in which they stand to the purposes for which they are designed and to the purposes which they oppose and perhaps frustrate, a further dimension of significance will have been added through the relationship in which these actions stand to an end for which a wider and perhaps universal validity is claimed. It is in any case this last possibility that needs to be explored further, however unlikely such a conception may be judged to be at the present time. The issue it poses is simply whether we have any right to assume that we now have enough in common with the inhabitants of the past so as to be able to sustain an evaluative judgment like those described above. After all, there is always the danger that whatever standards we bring to this task may themselves be culture-bound and parochial and even unintelligible or repugnant to those on whose lives and institutions they would be brought to bear by such a moral history as I am undertaking to define here. These are serious objections and yet they cannot be taken as absolutely conclusive. There are after all weighty considerations on the other side of this issue. I have in mind in particular the universal interest which must attach to the moral dimension of social and institutional practice by contrast with the more limited domains of activity to which reference has been made. By this I mean that while an individual may be quite genuinely indifferent to what goes on in some special department of human culture like military science or agriculture and consequently declare the "progress" achieved in that domain to have no claim on his interest, no one can honestly remain indifferent to the way in which the fundamental claims and needs of human beings are treated within the society in which he lives. It is, of course, possible not to think about such matters in general terms at all and simply to feel satisfied or dissatisfied with one's own lot in life; but the fact remains that to the extent to which a person becomes capable of a more general view of the human scene the set of practices and laws that determine how his interests will be interpreted must engage his concern. If they did not do so, we would be inclined to say not that such a person is merely lacking in curiosity or breadth of mind as we might if such a lack of interest were expressed in some more restricted domain of human activity; but rather that he does not understand his own interests and is perhaps either deficient in intelligence or positively irrational. Clearly, too, since the arrangements by which these fundamental human relationships receive a particular complexion within a given society are subject to change, the same kind of interest which requires continuing attention to those arrangements also dictates that any human undertakings or actions that seem likely to modify the latter should also be the subject of scrutiny by all the members of that society.[44]

How does all of this apply to history? What I am looking for is an aspect of the historical process in which human beings might take an interest which is not itself contingent upon further interests which they might or might not share with one another; and my suggestion has been that anything that determines the state of moral equilibrium or disequilibrium between the groups that make up a society and the interests they represent meets this requirement. What I want to suggest now is that a history that takes this set of relationships and the ways in which they change as the result of human actions as its focus would have a very strong claim to being regarded as a nuclear element in human history as a whole and as the logical locus for a more comprehensive form of evaluative judgment on the part of the historian than seems to be allowed for by either of the two views that were just surveyed. By contrast with Collingwood's view which requires that if a subsequent society is to be said to have improved on the performance of a predecessor the latter must in some sense have recognized that it was dealing with a problem which it did not know how to solve, the view I am proposing holds that human societies are *always* dealing with a fundamental and universal problem, whether they recognize this fact or not, and this is the moral problem of defining the relationships in which their members are to stand to one another. In a sense, one might be justified in arguing that all societies do in fact recognize the existence of this problem because they all treat their way of interpreting these relationships as requiring justification of one kind or another. Such justifications can be plausibly viewed as standing answers to questions and even challenges that might be raised to the way in which certain groups of interests or of persons or of both are treated; but such implicit recognition of the possibility of contestation is very far from constituting an admission that such relationships are in principle prob-

lematic and as such remain permanently open to questioning and modification. In that sense the existence of moral problems of this fundamental kind is more often denied or even hidden than it is recognized in the
way that Collingwood appears to require; and it follows that a view of the
life of a society that is informed by the assumption that moral problems
always exist cannot rest its authority on anything like the fact that the
problems which one society fails to solve and which another at least
partially solves have been recognized as the "same" problems by these
very societies much as they might be by two physicists, one of whom
succeeds where the other tried but failed. Instead the credentials of such a
mode of historical analysis and evaluation derive from an interpretation of
the reciprocity underlying human action and choice and from a line of
argument showing that this conception of reciprocity is applicable even to
societies which at least ostensibly repudiate the metaethical presuppositions on which it rests. The societies I have in mind here are most
notably those which declare the sanctions for their most fundamental
codes of practice to be religious or metaphysical in nature and thus
essentially independent of the preferences and choices of the human beings who compose these societies.[45]

It would not be very sensible to argue that a history which takes as its
central theme the transactions from which a particular form of moral life
emerges must be an object of interest to every human being in just the
same way in which the comparable events of his own time must be. The
important issue is not whether it is possible to motivate such an interest
on the part of every human being capable of pursuing it but rather whether
there is in principle a form of historical interest in which everyone *could*
share because it presupposes no special practical or prudential interest on
their part other than the fact of being human. It is, of course, true that
each of us is most interested in his own fate as a human being and in the
movement of events in his own time as they determine what that fate may
be. But this inevitable parochiality need not prevent us from coming to
see how the same great options of slavery and freedom, poverty and
security, peace and war have shaped the experience of men in other
periods and it may even help us in achieving such an imaginative extension of our interests. The deep thematic unity of such a vision of the
historical process can be defined as an interest in what human beings have
done to (and for) one another and what they have made themselves as a
result of the way they have shaped their relationships to others. A history
organized around such an interest is not disqualified thereby from entering
any or all of the various special domains of human activity in which
historians have traditionally interested themselves; but it does so on its
own terms and these are such as to require a constant and vigilant consciousness that the significance of a technology or a military or an economic accomplishment lies in the human lives on which it impinges and

more specifically in the impact it has on the relationships in which these lives stand to one another. Although statements by individual human beings—*témoignages*—can make an especially valuable contribution to such a history, its focus must not be conceived in biographical terms. Its fundamental concern is with groups of people who are bound together by some community of fate; and it conceives that fate primarily in terms of the kinds of collective actions of which they were the objects or the agents or, as is most often the case, both at once. But at the same time as it considers human beings in terms of their group membership and their participation in a shared fate, it also remembers that all groups are composed of individuals and it does not allow the espousal by such individuals of the collective interests of their communities—perfectly sincere as it may be—to obscure the fact that these interests have their costs and their benefits to individual human beings. To bear this fact in mind is not to recur to some egoistic theory of human motivation or of human happiness. It is rather to refuse to allow these individual human beings to be so completely absorbed within the collectivities to which they belong that it becomes impossible to appraise the quality of their lives by any standards other than those of that collectivity. And it is at the same time to insist that all of these individual human beings, whatever they may be in the eyes of the dominant institutions under which they live, are persons and that as such—that is, in their capacity as agents and patients—they are participants in the fundamental relationship of reciprocity upon which morality and moral appraisals finally rest.

No argument of the kind suggested above in behalf of a nuclear human history that is moral in character will have much chance of acceptance unless it can be made philosophically persuasive enough to prevail against the overwhelming skepticism which any such idea is certain to encounter. One way of setting about that task is to point out the affinities between this conception of an evaluative perspective on human history and Kant's "Idea for a Universal History from a Cosmopolitan Point of View."[46] Brief as it is, the work that bears that name has a special significance within the corpus of Kant's writings since it constitutes his principal attempt to deal with conceptual problems that arise in the area of history—problems which are distinct from both those that arise in the natural sciences and in the domain of morality. Kant had dealt with both of these sets of philosophical problems in his first two critiques, and in the third critique he had analyzed the kind of teleological judgment that is involved in the explanation of biological processes; but in none of these works did he take up the special problem of history—the problem of achieving a satisfactory conception of the process that is generated by beings—human beings—who straddle the two realms of nature and freedom scrutinized in the two first critiques. In some ways the treatment Kant gave this problem when he finally turned to it in his works on history retained traces of the older kind of teleological thought with many references to the goal that "Nature" had in mind for man and the various artifices by which she was moving toward the realization of that goal. In the main, however, Kant's conception of the teleological ordering of history that was to guide the "universal history from a cosmopolitan point of view" for which he was calling was profoundly original in a number of ways that make it highly relevant to the present discussion of evaluation in history.

The special interest that attaches to Kant's theory of history is most evident if one understands it as a series of proposals concerning the kind of movement that must take place in human affairs if the historian is to be justified in speaking of progress. Kant, in other words, does not claim to have achieved a speculative insight into the nature of the historical process by virtue of which he is enabled to issue assurances as to what the terminal state of that process will be. Instead, he appears to be laying down a set of conditions that define the kind of change that would have to take place if it is to be possible for us to regard history as the realization of some end or purpose of universal significance. What he is offering is thus a framework for ordering the materials which the empirical historian alone can provide and which may or may not be of such a nature as to show that the process which the framework stipulates is in fact taking place in the real world. Kant himself was optimistic on this point; but his conviction that empirical realization was already well under way is less interesting than the design of the framework itself. The latter incorporates the fairly traditional assumption that the "natural end" of man is the development of all his "natural capacities"; but Kant's two further assumptions are more interesting. These are that it is man's distinctive trait—his rationality—which makes it possible for him to have capacities which can be fully developed in the race rather than in the individual; and, secondly, that precisely because man alone is endowed with reason he must "by himself, produce everything that goes beyond the mechanical ordering of his animal existence and . . . he should partake of no happiness or perfection than what he himself, independently of instinct, has created by his own reason."[47] The implication of this last proviso is quite unmistakably that the human achievements with which the historian is to be concerned are those that partake of the nature of decision and action and are thus in principle subject to the kind of appraisal and justification that makes use of shared rational standards.

The multiplicity of human potentialities that require the exercise of reason is such that even if he were to accept Kant's argument thus far, the historian would still be in the position of having to choose one or more of these to serve as the axis of development for his history; and it is not apparent what title one such potentiality would have to rank before others in the constitution of a nuclear human history. It is just this question of precedence and priority which Kant proceeds to address when he declares that "the development of all the capacities that can be achieved by mankind is attainable only in society and more specifically in the society with the greatest freedom."[48] What this amounts to is the claim that all the human achievements that might be used as the normative goals of human history have a common condition and that this condition is the creation of a form of social life in which "freedom under external laws is associated in the highest degree with irresistible power."[49] Whatever interest one takes as defining the good toward which human history is to be shown as moving, it will turn out to require a corresponding form of social life; and it would follow, therefore, that if it is possible to determine what the form of that social order should ideally be then the movement of mankind toward such an order would have a unique claim to be regarded as the central event of human history. As Kant says, "the achievement of a universal civic society that administers law among men" is "the greatest problem for the human race to the solution of which Nature drives man."[50] "The problem," he adds, "is the most difficult and the last to be solved by mankind." It is of course also quite insoluble as long as one approaches it with only the empirical concept of man as the subject of a variety of different and quite possibly conflicting desires, since these desires can only lead each of us to attempt to shape the social order in such a way as to be onesidedly favorable to our preferences. A solution will be possible only when attention is shifted from this multiplicity of goals and interests to the common rational nature of man and when the standard of adequacy for the social and political order is its conformity with the requirements of what Kant calls the rational will.

Kant's conception of the rational will is closely bound up with his distinction between the phenomenal and the noumenal aspects of selfhood and with his doctrine of freedom; and this association is inevitably prejudicial, given the unfavorable estimate of these elements in his system that generally prevails at the present time. And yet the fundamental intuitions on which the Kantian concept of rationality rests are as simple as they are powerful. At bottom, rationality is a capacity for formulating the "maxim" of one's action and for making one's actual performance of that action conditional upon its passing certain critical tests. These tests are designed to determine the consistency of such an action not only with other actions which one is oneself inclined to perform on prudential grounds but also with the wider system of cooperation with other human beings to which we belong.[51] The underlying assumption here is that the other members of this association are also capable of bringing their actions under maxims and of raising the same question of consistency as we do; and therefore there can be no such thing as an action which it would be right for me to perform without its being entailed that the same action would be equally right for another person to perform if relevantly similar circumstances were to arise. The only freedom I can allow myself is thus the freedom which I am prepared to recognize equally in the case of others; and the only obligations I can impose on others are those which I must accept for myself when I find myself in the same kind of situation. In this sense the rational will is the same in all of us, however different the content of the empirical will may be; and "all of us" here means all human beings. In practice, of course, the notion of being bound only by rules that are equally binding on others has been given effect only within the various natural communities that human beings form, and even there its realization has been very imperfect. But Kant is convinced not only that this de facto limitation which human rationality suffers is surmountable but also that the nature of our rational powers is in fact such as to demand that this same mode of coordination of our actions under common rules be extended to govern our relationships with all human beings. In their purest and original form these capacities of the rational will give rise to moral obligations; and in Kant's view the satisfaction of a moral obligation is closely dependent upon the intention with which we choose and act and in particular upon the avoidance of any admixture of interested motives, that is, motives other than pure respect for obligation as such. But in the domain of law this condition is wisely dropped and the universal "civic union" among men of which Kant speaks is defined in terms that abstract from the motives its members have for compliance and focus instead upon the commitment to a process of validation of actions through reference to a common body of laws.[52]

As has already been indicated, Kant's way for formulating all these claims associated them with metaphysical doctrines of various kinds, and the fact that Kant himself understood the perils of metaphysics and sought to guard against them by attributing a special kind of postulational status to such features of human nature as its noumenal freedom is not likely to make them much more attractive to contemporary philosophical tastes. Then too there can be no doubt that "material" elements need to be brought into the process of rational evaluation in ways far more extensive than Kant was willing to allow; and the logical requirement of universalizability seems more appropriately regarded as a necessary than as a sufficient condition for the moral rightness of a maxim of action. Nevertheless, in spite of these difficulties, there is no reason to doubt that Kant's analysis identifies an absolutely fundamental feature of the relationship that is set up between human beings when they become users of language. In at least one respect, however, Kant's way of conceiving this social dimension of rationality is ill-adapted to the use for which he intends it—that is, as the basis for a philosophical or normative view of human history. This is so because it rests on an absolute contrast between the noumenal nature of man as a moral being endowed with freedom and entitled to respect and his phenomenal nature as a being subject to causal law and to the "pathological" urgings of his animal nature. It is simply very difficult to see how such a contrast as this between a nature that stands outside history and change altogether and one that undergoes change in time but in a manner to which moral distinctions are utterly irrelevant can ever help us to understand the changes that take place in historical time and to do so in a way that exhibits these changes as a moral progress. If, as Kant claims, the contrast between man's true moral nature and his actual "empirical" motivation is *always* given and, though not exactly a universal datum of consciousness, at least forms part of the background of our unavoidable consciousness of the rightness and wrongness of our own actions, how are we to account for the indisputable fact of imperfect moral knowledge and downright moral error in human history? And why is it that the moral progress of mankind—such as it is—takes place by incremental steps that are themselves very different from the absolute contrast Kant draws and also takes place within a domain that, unlike either of the two recognized within that Kantian contrast, is both "empirical" and "moral." It is empirical because it is composed of the desires and ambitions which are the driving motor of all social institutions; and it is moral because a certain legitimacy is claimed for existing social arrangements and this legitimacy is conceived in such a way as to involve some recognition, however inadequate and inconsistent it may be, of the moral personalities and moral entitlements of the human beings upon whose lives those arrangements have an influence. Although Kant's conception of man's "unsocial sociability" as the factor that leads men both to violate and to observe in some measure the limits set by the moral personalities of other human beings is an ingenious one, it does not seem that that conception by itself is adequate to focus his attention on the primary locus of moral contestation within human societies in a context of partial understanding and partial acknowledgment of the kind of legitimacy that attaches to the demands other human beings make upon us. The difficulty, in other words, is that of understanding how mankind can be "in the dark" as to its true moral situation when each one of us is conceived by Kant to be, in the noumenal dimension of his personality, a fully realized moral being whose inner freedom and understanding of the moral law need only find the appropriate institutional equivalents in the public and historical world.

It may be somewhat surprising that Hegel should be proposed as a philosopher who can offer a corrective for some of these weaknesses in the Kantian conception of human history as moral progress.[53] Hegel, after all, is principally known as a harsh critic of both the overall Kantian system of contrasts between phenomena and noumena and of the abstract moralizing approach to the understanding of society and history which he believed they encourage. It is not possible (or necessary) to raise here the larger question of the relationship between the Kantian and the Hegelian philosophies. It is evident, however, that in at least one respect Hegel can be seen as offering a way of formulating some of Kant's central ideas so as to make their use as the central principle of interpretation and evaluation of actual human histories a good deal more plausible. Very roughly, what Hegel contributes to the kind of theory that was outlined above is a account of just that obscurity and fragmentariness that characterize our moral understanding of other human beings and that proved so difficult to reconcile with the underlying presuppositions of the Kantian scheme. The obstacle that stands in the way of moral progress, according to Hegel, is not one that can be captured within the typical "fools or knaves" alternatives of so much Enlightenment historiography with its implication that moral failure is typically the result of moral ignorance on the part of the many which is artificially maintained by the intelligent but selfishly motivated few. The net result of such a contrast is the implication that the true state of the moral world is always in principle known at least to some influential minority within society and that it is only as a result of a deliberate policy of obscuring that truth through the devices of superstition and fear that general moral enlightenment is prevented and the selfish interests of the few are served. Hegel's view of the matter is very different; it may be described as attributing a conceptual basis to the failures of moral understanding that violate the fundamental condition of reciprocity which, in Hegel's view quite as much as in Kant's, governs the relationship of one human consciousness to another. The difficulty which mankind experiences and which it is able to solve only very gradually and very slowly is one of achieving a conceptualization of the self that will permit that reciprocity to emerge as something more than a kind of appendage to an already fully constituted self. The crucial insight on which Hegel's position rests has to do with the interdependence of our concept of the self and our concept of the other and it involves the claim that these conceptions move forward pari passu until they reach a point at which the underlying identity of the one with the other is grasped. Hegel is scornful of the belief that morality can rest on feeling alone and that it can therefore dispense with the hard labor of the concept. That labor is not, however, as we might be tempted to suppose, simply the cerebral activity of some individual thinker. It is equally the penetration of a society's institutions and practices by a conception that reconstrues the relationships between the human beings who live under them and it is thus a modification of the conditions defining public discourse and communication as much as it is the solution of a problem by an individual thinker. Clearly, too, such a conception of selfhood is not one that can be formulated primarily in psychological terms, and indeed one of the distortions to which the concept of selfhood is subject is precisely a tendency to treat it as a collection of inner states which can be described in abstraction from the social and historical milieu of the person in question. The evolution through which the concept of the self must pass if the nature of the mutuality that binds finite individual persons together is to be understood either in theory or in practice is thus one that comprehends virtually the whole of what is sometimes called the "form of life" of a human community, that is, the whole system of ordering the business of that community as it relates to the purposes and interests of its members.

The suggestion is thus that there is a significant conceptual aspect to the moral development of mankind and that the full recognition of the self in the other must wait upon a mode of conceptualization that is capable of expressing that identity. When the matter is posed in this way, it is clear that the next step must be some further explanation of why the concept of person—for it is this concept in its full range of moral implication that is in question here—should be so difficult to achieve and to institutionalize. The answer that Hegel gives to this question and that in one form or another has been restated by almost all the principal thinkers in the idealistic tradition has been subject to multiple and serious misunderstandings; but its essential import is not really so difficult to state. Freely expressed, what Hegel is saying is that the difficulty is one that is inseparably connected with what he takes to be the externalizing, self-objectifying activity of human consciousness. That activity can of course be understood in more or less mythic terms as the production or creation of the world which consciousness inhabits; but it is clear that, whatever Hegel's own confusions may have been in this respect, his fundamental point survives even when it is understood that this activity is conceptual and classificatory in nature rather than productive in any literal sense. In any case, authentic self-understanding on the part of the conscious beings who perform these constitutive functions from which a certain conceptual ordering of the world emerges is blocked as long as the model for that self-understanding is sought within the constituted domain itself. This is most especially so when that domain undergoes the final measure of objectification that occurs when the object is declared to be fully independent of the constituting activity in the sense of wearing the character in which it is experienced simply because that is what it is. What is apprehended under the auspices of this false objectification that detaches the object of knowledge from the act of knowing can hardly serve as an adequate model for the understanding of selfhood. As a result the various attempts which have been made to interpret the nature of human subjectivity are doomed to failure which typically takes the form of a mismatch between the self and its object. What is most relevant to the matter under consideration, however, is the fact that as long as this relationship between the self and its object is misconceived, it will remain impossible for the self to recognize what it has in common with the other, and in place of the co-constitutive functions which the latter exercises within an intersubjective community of selves it will be envisaged only in some mode of objectification that incorporates it into the thing-world of the self. In short, because the self is unable to conceptualize its own functions and status satisfactorily it is shut off from a recognition of the complementarity inherent in its relationship to the other and can understand that relationship only at the level of a conflict between being animated by competing desires and lacking any principle of rational mediation.

The dialectic of the master and the slave in the *Phenomenology of Mind* is a brilliant account of the playing out of this conflict which, it must be remembered, is fully reciprocal in the sense that recognition is being denied from both sides.[54] The upshot of that conflict is in fact an internalization of that reciprocity arising out of a perception of the valuelessness of a recognition of one's status as superior by a consciousness that is denied coordinate status. This is, of course, only one step, although a crucially important one, along the route which leads to a full understanding of the principle of intersubjectivity. Hegel's rendering of that principle has sometimes been made to sound as though what it involves must be some implausible fusion of previously distinct egos; but this is to substitute a material image of doubtful suitability for the much subtler point which Hegel is making. That point is that as rational beings these egos meet within a milieu which is neutral with respect to the distinctions between particular egos—between what is mine and what is yours—and that within that milieu communication is bound by the rational norms that impose this neutrality. This is, of course, not to say that distinctions among persons are never rationally justifiable or that my case may not be validly distinguishable from yours. It is, however, to say that such distinctions must be *rationally* justifiable and thus susceptible of being derived from prior assumptions or goals that are themselves in no sense under the unique control of one of the parties in question. The outcome of the dialectic of self-consciousness, as Hegel calls it, is precisely a recognition that one can no longer play the egocentric game and this recognition comes because it turns out that the attempt to play that game invariably ensnares itself in the apparatus of justification which it seeks to exploit for its own particularistic ends. The "identity" of the self and the other that thus emerges is not one that can be grasped in the material mode as though it were merely the breaking down of the walls by which each ego had felt itself to be securely separated from its congeners. It is rather the discovery that as a rational being one was already operating in a way to which the existence of such walls is irrelevant and that efforts to create a self-contained and independent moral economy must work against the grain of the very rationality which they seek to harness for this purpose.

It may be possible to generalize the point that Hegel is making in a way that makes its relevance to the task of historical evaluation somewhat more apparent. For a long time now the chief obstacle in the way of such evaluations has been the presumption that particular historical societies can constitute by themselves complete moral worlds which shape the consciousnesses of their members so thoroughly that they offer no principle of resistance to the code imposed upon them. Such "worlds" are also held to be characterized by a logical integrity that enables them to provide an answer that is satisfactory by their own internal standards to any challenge that is addressed to them from without. This presumption appears to correspond to the observable discontinuities that characterize the moral codes of distinct historical societies; and the effect of the presumption is to ratify and indeed to absolutize this appearance. The parallel between the case of two individual human beings who confront one another as in the dialectic of the master and the slave and the case of two or more societies which deny any principle of mutuality between them seems quite clear; in the latter case as in the former the question that needs to be raised is whether the "fit" between the egocentric mode of functioning of the individual or of the society and the structure of norms that are applied to the justification of such behavior is as close as it is claimed to be or whether there is not in addition to the tension amounting to overt conflict *between* the two parties—individual or social—an internal tension within each of them between what is done and the implicit premises on which the very attempt at justification itself must rest. That natural human societies are as internally repressive and externally aggressive as the most "realistic" social theory portrays them as being need not be doubted. It is something else, however, to claim that they comport themselves in these ways without undergoing any internal strain and most particularly with a consciousness that is free from any sense of responsibility to satisfy some more comprehensive standard of right. Indeed it seems a good deal more plausible to suggest that in spite of the most emphatic "will to egocentricity," as it might be called, such societies (and such individuals) are constantly subverted though not necessarily overthrown by the very justificatory instrument of which they avail themselves for the purpose of obtaining a "voluntary" acceptance of their form of life.

Profound as Hegel's insight into these matters was, there is as already noted much in his general mode of thought that tends to suggest that the movement toward a full internalization of the principle of reciprocity is going on in the third person in the sense that the controls over the transition from stage to stage in this movement are logical in nature and operate on a schedule laid down in the "idea" itself. And although Hegel certainly understood that language as the instrument of thought is a primary locus of that element of universality within human experience and social existence by which every particular is ultimately subverted, it can hardly be said that he gives us a clear idea of how language performs this function. Strangely enough, it was not until the emergence of linguistic philosophy in the mid-twentieth century and more specifically of the so-called "good reasons" approach to questions of ethical theory that it became possible to show in convincing illustrative detail just how the dialectic of justification proceeds and how anyone who enters upon that process is confronted with progressively less attractive options if he persists in an egocentric course while ostensibly accepting the conventions on which the justificatory process itself rests.[55] Unfortunately, the philosophical self-consciousness of this largely neo-Wittgensteinian movement of thought was such as to set its face rigidly against any idea of an affinity with such an apparently uncommonsensical philosopher as Hegel. In any case, perhaps at least partly as a result of its lack of a wider philosophical perspective, the neo-Wittgensteinian movement proved to be of rather brief duration. It is a matter of considerable interest, therefore, that some of the principal themes of that movement of thought have now been reformulated by a philosopher in the Continental tradition and in such a way as to throw into sharp relief just the kinds of affinity with wider philosophical options to which reference has been made.

In Jürgen Habermas's theory of the "ideal speech situation" we have an explicit statement of the presuppositions on which communication between human beings rests and, what is perhaps even more important, of the ways in which these conditions can be violated.[56] His analysis takes the form of a theory of "communicative competence" as a necessary adjunct to the "linguistic competence" that is evidenced in the "mastery of an abstract system of rules, based on an innate language apparatus, regardless of how the latter is in fact used in actual speech."[57] Like linguistic competence, communicative competence can be described only in terms of a set of abstract rules; but instead of being rules stipulating what will count as a well-formed sentence in a given natural language the rules on which communicative competence rests are pragmatic in character and define the relationship in which the users of language must stand to one another if communication is to be possible. Habermas calls these rules "dialogue-constitutive universals" and they jointly determine an "ideal speech situation" although in actual practice it may not be fully realized or may be violated or subverted in various ways. Perhaps the most important point is that this ideal speech situation retains its authority in spite of such violations and is indeed involved in our being able to say that a given practice is a violation. Thus, it is certainly possible to make use of speech for the purpose of intentionally misinforming one's interlocutor, that is, lying; but there is an internal incoherence in such a practice because the liar must implicitly accept the norm governing all such situations which is that both sides are entitled to assume that the other is conscientiously stating what he believes to be the truth as best he can. In other words, if a person participates in a social transaction which would have no sense if certain norms were not assumed to be accepted on both sides, that person can violate such norms but he cannot repudiate their authority. Habermas also claims that another such norm defining the ideal speech situation is a requirement that neither speaker be subject to a unilateral constraint on his self-representation, that is, on his free expression of his opinion on the matter under discussion. This is not to deny that there may be differential constraints on this self-representation that lie outside the communicative situation itself, and it is obvious that there will normally be such. What it does mean is that ideally the speech situation must not itself be so designed as to involve the imposition of such a constraint as it would be, for example, if one partner to the discussion were to threaten the other with unpleasant consequences if he did not agree with him. The self-defeating feature of such a procedure would of course be that the partner who was placed under this special constraint would in fact not be agreeing in the sense of expressing a like opinion independently arrived at, but rather saying what he had been compelled o say; and the very nature of the threat is such as to recognize this distinction.

There is a good deal more to the theory than can be presented here; but in general one can say that it gives an account of the dimension of "pure intersubjectivity" in the speech situation, an intersubjectivity that is "determined by a symmetrical relationship between I and You (We and You), I and He (We and They) . . . and a complete symmetry in the distribution of assertion and dispute, revelation and concealment, prescription and conformity among the partners of communication."[58] Such a set of relationships attaching to participation in the speech situation amounts in fact to a kind of mini-ethic of communication in the sense that it constitutes a set of norms that apply equally to all who so participate, norms that can be repudiated by none because they are implicitly relied upon for the purpose of performing the acts in which communication consists as well as the various deformations of these acts which exploit the presuppositions of the communicatory relationship. It is this mini-ethic which Habermas proposes to use for the purpose of social analysis. That use appears to have two complementary forms. On the one hand, the ideal speech situation serves as a model of a perfected general form of intersubjectivity in "which the motivational base of all actions [can be assumed to be] organized linguistically, i.e. within the structure of potential speech . . . [and] the actual motivations of the actor [are] identical with the linguistically apprehensible motivations of the speaker."[59] At the same time, however, it is recognzied that such a pure form of intersubjectivity does not exist in actual social relationships and the model is accordingly to be used as the standard of comparison in identifying the actual constraints that distort communication and human reciprocity generally. As Habermas observes, "the greater the share of . . . motivations that cannot be freely converted in public communication, the greater the deviance from the model of pure communicative action."[60] With this model of society based on the communicative relationship, Habermas further associates two empirical hypotheses: "first, that these deviations increase in proportion to the degree of repression which characterizes the institutional system within a given society; and secondly that the degree of repression depends in turn on the developmental stage of the productive forces and on the organization of authority, that is of the institutionalization of political and economic power."[61]

The three views that have been presented—those of Kant, Hegel, and Habermas—suggest in different but complementary ways what the basis for an evaluative judgment in historical contexts might be. If they are persuasive where so many other efforts have apparently failed, it is, I think, because of a distinctive feature which they share and which has to do with the level at which they engage the problem of achieving evaluative objectivity in history. The classic move on the part of the philosophical historian has been to cast his version of the telos by reference to which progress and regression in history should be judged in the form of a value-judgment to the effect that the supremely worthwhile goal which alone qualifies for this status is such-and-such. The equally classic riposte has been that in the judgment of others there are other goals that rank as high or higher than the one thus established; and in the absence of any generally accepted decision-procedure for determining which of these goals is the truly authoritative one the whole matter of the teleological ordering of history is consigned to the status of a matter of unarbitrable opinion. If I read them correctly, however, it is just this sequence of moves that is avoided by the writers discussed above and it is avoided because it has been internalized and the proper conclusions drawn which in effect lift the whole discussion to a new level. This is achieved by reinterpreting the conflicts among human beings that fill the historical scene in such a way as to include among them the very judgmental conflicts that relate to such matters as the true goal of human history and to redefine that goal itself in such a way as to make the resolution of these conflicts a necessary condition for qualifying some postulated goal as the common telos of mankind's development. One might say that the novel feature of this procedure is that the answer to the question, "Does human history have a goal?" is being modeled on the question itself or rather on our sense of the conditions that would have to be met by any valid answer to this question. Necessarily, the positive answer that can be given under these circumstances has more the form of a Kantian Idea than that of a fully determinate conception of a particular end-state; and the Idea will itself also be strongly formalistic in character since it will emphasize the collective method of judgment from which any definition of an end will have to emerge more than the determinate detailed "substantive" character of that end. Furthermore, an Idea, in the Kantian sense, does not guarantee or even predict its own realization and so in this case the conception of mutuality which is proposed as satisfying the requirements implicit in the question about the goal of history may well turn out to be one which human beings fail to realize although in order to be taken seriously at all it presumably has to have some reasonable chance of being realized. It is, of course, true that the eyes of many who raise this question about the goal or meaning of human history an answer that does not claim to be based on any independent insight into the historical process or into the "true" nature of the good will not be likely to appear very satisfactory; and such persons are likely to go on asking their question as though it were a request for a particularly momentous bit of information which they just happen not to have. Their chances of obtaining the kind of answer they claim to want do not seem to be very good, however, and the more realistic choice seems to be between abandoning the question altogether and interpreting it as has been done here as carrying a set of implicit criteria defining what would count as a satisfactory answer to it. It is perhaps worth adding also that even if those criteria are discoverable and do prove sound, there will always be a negative side to the goal they define since it can hardly be a compendium of all human perfections. There will, in particular, be some highly desirable states which may be possible only in a context that is less than optimal as, for example, certain kinds of heroism or altruistic conduct presuppose the prior existence of some misfortune; and there are others, like certain forms of personal attachment in a nonegalitarian social order, which can hardly be reconciled with the broadly egalitarian requirements of a Kantian "kingdom of ends." But to those who are disposed to challenge the latter conception on the grounds that it involves a sacrifice of these good things, the only answer can be that the same objection could be made to every such conception of the goal of history since all of them necessarily entail certain losses as the condition of certain gains and that the only issue therefore must be whether the conception of the goal which requires *these* losses in order to achieve *these* gains is a uniquely valid one.

Since the feasibility of such a principle of interpretation and implicit evaluation will very likely seem deeply problematic to most historians and philosophers today, it may be useful to spell out what it does and does not entail in terms of a concrete example. That example will be the institution of slavery.[63] In spite of all the differences which set apart, for example, black slavery in the United States in the nineteenth century from *douleia* in ancient Greece, it seems possible to winnow out a central meaning of "slavery" as the involuntary subjection of one human being to the will and purposes of another in the form of legal ownership. As such, slavery is the institution which most directly and most fundamentally violates the condition of human reciprocity which was discussed above. It follows that for purposes of a history of a society that practices slavery the amelioration or abolition of slavery must figure as an ideal end in the light of which the significance of various human actions within that society are appraised. It may of course be the case that at a given time there was simply no prospect of any action being taken to abolish slavery and in such circumstances it would be radically anachronistic for the historian to sit continually in judgment on such a society for its failure to eliminate that institution. But an acceptance of this fact does not render the ideal end referred to above irrelevant to the history of a slave society. If, for example, there are trends within such a society that tend, perhaps quite independently of any intention to achieve this end, to make the expansion of the slave population more or less likely, then these must have a special interest for the historian. So must any testimony available to him that casts a light on the actual condition of life of the slave populations and especially whatever has a bearing upon the way they envisage their condition and the efforts they make to overcome it. In all of this, the historian would not be particularly concerned with the implications of the institution of slavery for the moral worth of those who impose it although it would be appropriate to give attention to those isolated individuals who may have been able to perceive the moral quality of slavery more accurately than their contemporaries. It does not follow either that the historian will be unable to recognize any benefits that may be attributable to the institution of slavery or that he must regard whatever system of labor it is replaced by as necessarily superior in every respect. Finally, although the historian should normally be interested in the way such an institution as slavery colors the whole life of the society in which it exists, he is not compelled to conclude that the presence of slavery in a society negates the value of all its accomplishments and that nothing sound can be built upon such corrupt foundations. What the critical historian must try to show is the tension existing between such an institution of slavery and such sound perceptions of fundamental human powers as a society may have achieved whether in the medium of its art, its philosophy, or its political institutions; and, wherever possible, he will seek to show how such strains arise in the life of the society itself although he must also recognize the possibility that there may have been no developed sense in the society in question of the kind of contradiction that slavery involves and that on both sides—the slaves and the slaveholders—the institution was viewed as perfectly "natural." To sum up, then, what the historian cannot do is to accede to that assumption of naturalness himself, and he must remain permanently alert for whatever developments within a society give promise of challenging that sense and of calling into question the institution of slavery itself since it is not a place where humanity can rest.

The point has already been made that the position of the interpretative historian which I have been discussing is not one that can be understood in terms of his temporal distance from the historical agent. Rather it is one that must be understood in terms of the moral distance between the one and the other; and if this is to some degree a function of temporal distance, the relationship is at best a loose one. What I have been suggesting is that this moral difference consists in the fact that, if the historian is to be more than just another partisan, he must attempt to envisage the human actions with which he deals as taking place within an ideal framework of human reciprocity in which the egocentricity of the moral perspective of the agents is, to the extent possible, discounted and replaced by a fairer and broader description of what was done and thus·of "what happened." A narrative constructed from such a point of view will still take human agency and the intentions by which it is animated as the source of the distinctive teleological organization of the events it relates; but it will situate that agency in its irreducible plurality within a domain in which it is understood that the relationships of one human being to another are to be governed by the rationality which they have in common rather than by the particular desires that set them against one another. What this means in practice is that such a narrative will not necessarily break off where the interest of the agents in the train of events breaks off but may instead pursue it further for the purpose of reaching some morally relevant consequence that lay outside the vision of the protagonists and, in its wider implications, quite possibly beyond what anyone at the time was able to appreciate and not just by virtue of their temporal position. Such a narrative will differ, too, in that it will not construe a historical episode solely in terms of the alternative possibilities of resolution that were envisaged by the agents themselves; thus in examining the events leading to the outbreak of the First World War it will bear in mind the common interests that were being sacrificed on the altar of national egoism and the ways in which these might have found an efficacious form of expression and of influence upon events. In a certain sense such a narrative might be said to be as much concerned with what did not happen as with what did; it is therefore important that in order to avoid passing off into the empyrean of abstract moral possibilities it accommodate its sense of what might have been done to some estimate of the resources of the time in imagination and moral understanding. The locus of possibility will after all be different from one society and one time to another; and that is a fact to which the historian must try to remain sensitive. He must also be guided by such signals as he can receive from within a given society at a given time of its susceptibility for entertaining alternative possibilities of action. But if such a narrative must not exaggerate the degree of tension between such alternative possibilities of action that characterize a society neither must it allow its portrayal of the latter to suggest a condition of absolute and tensionless coincidence with itself and with some one ineluctable course of action. It is that mode of misrepresentation which the narrative perspective I have been describing is primarily designed to block.

It will be replied to the case that has been made so far that there is no more reason to suppose that the historian's access to a universal mode of moral perception is any more assured than that of the historical agents themselves and that in the one case as in the other the claim to such universality will typically be found associated with a quite substantial degree of parochialism so that in actuality, if not in intention, the historian is doomed to resume the very character of a partisan of which the view set forth above would in principle divest him. It follows that for all its proud pretenses historiography is really just as much a way of pursuing nonuniversal and thus partisan ends as are the admittedly parochial human undertakings it records. It may well be this perception which has encouraged Gadamerian efforts to treat historiography not as a reflexive movement of mind with a methodology and set of critical norms of its own but rather as being itself the expression of a newly emergent and inevitably time-bound and finite perspective that is more properly thought of as itself constituting a *Geschehen* than as the enunciation of a timeless truth about earlier postures of spirit. This is not, however, the only conclusion that can be drawn from the admitted fact that all efforts to apprehend the truth of the past in moral terms are infected by parochialism and accordingly subject to continuing revision. The fact that any branch of inquiry itself has a history and in that sense forms a part of a more inclusive human *Geschehen* does not oblige us to conclude that it cannot also be viewed in a different way as the cumulative emergence of a form of judgment that is both stable and intersubjectively valid. It may, of course, be that the conception of such a form of historiography is itself an Idea in the Kantian sense and that, just as the ideal of mutuality and reciprocity which it utilizes as a standard for the appraisal of human actions is one whose applicability to human affairs remains permanently problematic, so the corresponding form of historiography should be regarded primarily as an ideal standard for use in appraising the kind of understanding that historiography actually affords us. If, as some think, mankind is permanently imprisoned in its own egocentric systems of praxis, then the idea of holding events up to a standard like that proposed by Kant's kingdom of ends is an absurdity, and the form of historiography that is premised on this conception will have to be regarded as a chimera. But if the jury is still out on that issue, then the false starts and misguided inspirations that have marked the effort to practice history in this mode need not tell against the conception itself more damagingly than comparable failures and shifts of direction do against any other rational effort. As long as there has not been shown to be some fundamental vice in the presuppositions of such a form of historiography, either because the idea of a common basis for moral distinctions is a delusion or because human beings are psychologically incapable of a form of motivation predicated on those distinctions, it will be justifiable to attribute such failures as we experience to our own incapacity and to go on believing that the ordering of human events which such a form of historiography would effect is in principle sound. And even if our worst fears were to prove true and humanity were to show itself to have too weak a hold on its moral vocation for the latter to have a serious chance of prevailing, the history of this failure could be written only from a standpoint defined in terms of the very ideal that fails of realization. The most momentous fact of universal significance about human history would thus still be a moral one.

It is often observed by way of response to a line of argument like the one I have developed here that such a view will inevitably lead to an a priori and finally ideological approach to the materials of historical inquiry and to a disposition to force them into conformity with some presiding conception of moral progress. History, it is suggested, has everything to lose from the imposition of such a set of assumptions and it stands to benefit correspondingly when its inquiries proceed in full independence from every presuppositional scheme or at any rate treats no such scheme as being uniquely privileged and not susceptible of relativization to some optional point of view. The danger doubtless exists, but there is no reason to think that it is unavoidable. After all, what has been proposed is an idea of the values that the historical process might realize and not an ideology that declares that these values are gradually but surely being realized; and this same idea is equally well suited for determinations that the movement has been in the other direction during some period of time or that no significant change has taken place at all. Then, too, it should be recalled that the kind of interest which this way of looking at history has been said to hold for all human beings is not put forward as the only valid reason that we have for being interested in the past at all nor has it been argued that historical inquiry should be confined to those topics that directly contribute to our understanding of the fundamental human relationships on which this conception turns. Not only do all the multiple points of view from which it is possible to take an interest in history retain their validity; there is also no question of limiting the freedom of the individual historian to initiate inquiries of whatever kind he judges to be profitable. If the moral idea that has been proposed had to be protected by some implicit limitation on the scope of historical inquiry or by some obligatory line of interpretation for the findings of such inquiry, its claim to acceptance would certainly be very weak. The intention by which this essentially Kantian idea is inspired is not that of restricting what the historian may do but the quite different one of suggesting a framework within which the findings of these multiple and distinct historical inquiries may find a measure of coordination. For that framework of interpretation, it is true, a special authority has been claimed which rests upon a conception of moral personality; and this conception, it has been argued, is foundational for historical inquiry in a way that makes it impossible to treat it as depending finally upon an arbitrary and "subjective" choice. It is not clear, however, why that claim to a special authority should be unwelcome to the historian unless he has adopted some one or another of the forms of moral skepticism which have been noted in this chapter or thinks that he has reasons for asserting that it is impossible in principle to bring moral ideas into any secure relationship to the empirical materials of historical inquiry. In either case, however, such a historian seems to be left with very serious questions about the character of the unity that can be claimed by the historical enterprise; and it is not clear how he will be able either to answer these questions or to dismiss them.

6. Conclusion
The Humanities Again

The preceding discussion of the evaluative dimension of historical interpretation can, it is hoped, stand on its own legs. At the same time, however, it is not hard to see that even though, as I have repeatedly emphasized, the concerns by which inquiry in the historical and humanistic
disciplines is motivated are broad human concerns which humanists share
with their fellow human beings, there are features of our present cultural
situation that tend to empty any such characterization of humanistic
inquiry of much of its significance. I have in mind in particular the institutional matrix in which the humanities exist and in which their component disciplines appear as simply so many scholarly fiefs among all the
others into which the *totum scibile* has been carved up. Under these
conditions, which are imposed by the overwhelmingly academic character
of the humanities in our day and by the way in which academic work
is—for perfectly understandable reasons—organized, it becomes increasingly difficult to gain comprehension for the claim that the central
concerns of the humanities are not to be understood in terms that relate
them to self-sufficient forms of scholarly specialization. More specifically,
these circumstances can make it seem quite implausible that the form of
interest that the humanities take in the human actuality they study and
that finds expression in judgments of significance like those described in
the last chapter is really human and not merely disciplinary or discipline-
bound. Even when the special character of the humanistic disciplines is
characterized as it usually is in terms of their concern with "values,"
there seems to be something ritualistic and unconvincing about such declarations, as though everyone involved really knew that "humanistic"
and "human" don't mean the same thing. And in truth they do not; but
the humanistic form of interest is nevertheless not one that is confined to
the domain of scholarship, and in favorable circumstances it develops out
of generically human forms of interest. More importantly, when it does, it
supplies the indispensable motivating condition for the pursuit of inquiries
in which evaluative interpretations play the role described in the preceding chapter. In what follows I want to explore at least briefly the relationship in which the "humanistic" stands to the "human" with the
purpose of defining the kind of human community that *needs* to understand itself and its past in evaluative and moral terms and thus supplies
the social context within which history and the humanities have a place
and a vitally important function.

The premise on which this discussion of the broader social context of the humanities rests is of course the one that was laid down at the beginning of this book and that relates to man's possession of certain capacities like those for language, action, and moral judgment. These together with some others constitute the relevant sense of the term "human"; and they make possible a form of social existence that is itself distinctively human. The question I am concerned with here is, "When does 'human' become 'humanistic'?" and more specifically, "Under what conditions can a human group or society be properly described as 'humanistic'?" The locution, "a humanistic society," is admittedly not a familiar one or one for which a perfectly definite sense is already at hand, but I propose it nevertheless because it seems to express as well as any available locution an important distinction that needs to be made between different societies and also between different stages in the life of a single society. This is a distinction that relates to the place that is accorded to these capabilities in the picture that different societies form of man and his place in the cosmos. As a first approximation, one might say that a society is on the way to becoming "humanistic" when it achieves a widely shared recognition that human beings possess these powers and that they are significant and valuable by reason of the role they play in distinctively human activities. To this it should be added that in other respects the world view of such a society must be at least roughly compatible with its belief that the human powers it has identified have the significance it attributes to them. Or if there are elements in the society's belief system that tend to call that significance into question or perhaps deny the efficacy of any human power in favor of some other superior form of nonhuman agency, then it would be a condition of qualifying as "humanistic" that the society in question find ways, even quite devious ones, of reasserting its judgment of the significance of these human powers in the face of whatever superhuman powers may be held to threaten them.[1]

The relationship between humanism and religious belief is one that has given difficulties for centuries and has caused a good deal of personal anguish to those humanists like St. Jerome and Petrarch who have aspired to be sincere Christians. That there is some deep source of conflict here seems undeniable; but it would just as certainly be mistaken to define humanism as atheistic or even antireligious. There have been forms of religious belief that are radically incompatible with humanism because they proclaim the nothingness of man and transfer to their gods every possible form of agency or achievement with which man might otherwise be tempted to credit himself. Then, too, there are forms of religious belief in which natural forces have not yet reached the degree of personification that would permit human beings to understand themselves as persons through their relationship to their superhuman counterparts. But there are also religions that teach that there is something, however limited, that human beings as individuals and as societies can do and that thus concede a measure of significance and value to the achievements of human culture and even allow a modicum of human pride, as well as of shame, stemming from the contemplation of what has been done. It even seems plausible to argue that some measure of human self-assertion has maintained itself, however covertly, even within the most inhospitable and man-denying systems of belief.[2] Nevertheless, it seems proper to speak of a humanistic disposition on the part of a society only when it has become possible to assert openly that these human powers are real and that what can be achieved by means of them is significant and valuable.

At this point, a second element in the notion of a humanistic society needs to be added. Let us suppose that a society has distinguished as characteristically human the powers to which I have been referring and that it regards them, with whatever qualifications it may wish to retain, as worthy of further development. If such development occurs, it will take many forms but among these will typically be representations—literary, historical, and artistic—of human beings engaged in the significant exercise of these same powers. Many—perhaps most—of the figures so represented may at first be mythical in character, and the predicaments in which they find themselves as well as their successes and failures in dealing with them may seem to have more to do with certain universal features of the human situation than with local circumstances or with the situation of the society in which these representations come into being. But if we consider the Greek example for a moment, whether it be the Homeric poems or the tragic drama of the fifth century B.C., it is clear that the very stories which reflect constants of human character and human fate also had for their time and their society another kind of reality as well. Together they composed the past of Athens and more broadly of Greece; and with the dramas of Euripides and the history of Thucydides this world of representation was expanded to include the present-day scene of fifth-century Athens as well. What this amounts to is the emergence of a relationship of a society to itself—a relationship that is essentially mediated by the images of self that literature and history create and that come to constitute a common fund of reference for the members of a society and for many successive generations within that society.

The themes with which such representations dealt are typically those that concern human beings most deeply: birth and death, good and evil, knowledge and illusion. The individuals portrayed are for the most part those on whom the fate of the community in some way depends, and they are shown in those postures of action and feeling that represent the most significant possibilities of the human condition. However remote in time and archaic in quality the figures of epic and tragedy may have seemed to a fifth-century Athenian, he could hardly have avoided a sense of implication in the events that were related, a sense of what one or another outcome or the equivalents he could imagine for his own day would mean to him.[3] Thus the figures of Creon and Antigone, representing as they do such radically different conceptions of social duty, project quite different futures for their city; and even if a Greek had felt as Hegel did that the conflict between Creon and Antigone was one between two rights rather than between a right and a wrong, the effect of the drama on him could hardly have been anything but profoundly disturbing and of a character to modify significantly his perception of the state. Similar observations would apply to comedy as well as to tragedy and while the import of the representation of the comic in human life—the absurd rigidities and ob-sessions which give so much delight in their portrayals by Aristophanes and Molière—is not the grim shaking of the foundations of tragedy, it is rarely without its underlying social point which turns, as was pointed out earlier, on a movement of estrangement and reconciliation within a human group. All of these genres together compose a grammar of character types to which certain implicit judgments and evaluations are attached; and even when the conventions of realistic mise-en-scène are drastically mod-ified, as they were later, the reference such works make to a model of social relatedness, however ambiguous and complex it may be, remains of central importance.

When characters and actions are represented that are laden with pas-sion and with passionate belief and when these events are of a kind that visibly take place in one's own world or in a world that is in one way or another continuous with one's own, it is quite impossible to suppose that such a representation could simply serve the neutral purpose of bringing such events to the attention of the audience. It is true that we very often feel that a great part of the achievement of a work of representation is that it gives us an insight into aspects of a situation which we might very well have missed or failed to understand if it had occurred in real life. Some-times, too, we feel that the only response that is appropriate to a drama or a story is something like "Life is like that." But even this is after all a response; and it is a response, not just from the author but from the audience as well. The term "response" is subject to many interpretations, ranging from the attempt of a spectator at a play to intervene in the action on the stage—a real intervention in an unreal action—to the applause that conveys the audience's satisfaction with a performance as a performance or with the play as a play. The kind of response I have in mind is certainly not a real action of any kind nor even a real feeling of sorrow or of joy such as we might experience in real life at the outcome of some series of events; but it is a response to the events represented themselves. It might be described as the sense we make of the represented events as this would be conveyed by the description we would give of the quality of the charac-ters and their actions and the appropriateness of the outcome of the story in the light of this estimate. These judgments are made in the first instance by the author himself and it is these judgments which we as readers are in a position of having to endorse, as we typically do in *Tom Jones,* or to reject, as many readers do the apparent satisfaction which Henry James felt with the Ververs, father and daughter, when they celebrate their equivocal victory at the end of *The Golden Bowl.*

Although it is clear that such responses as these have an unmistakably moral character, it is equally important to recognize how different that character may be, as it is encountered in the medium of a literary or historical representation, from what it would be in its treatment by a moralist or moral philosopher. Quite simply, the moralist tends to conceive the individuals and groups whose rights and duties in relation to one another he seeks to determine, in abstraction from any determinate past, whether personal or collective. Through a form of conceptual simplification that is undoubtedly quite legitimate for the moralist's purposes, the persons involved in the kind of case he considers are defined as human beings, as having certain needs and abilities, as able to understand certain moral concepts, and perhaps as having bound themselves to one another in some form of common undertaking. What they do not often have is histories that extend back from the moment under consideration— histories that fuse with the histories of their communities and that may comprise matters that have an important bearing on the way these persons now perceive and respond to one another. It may be for example that they belong to different groups—whether families or states—whose relationships in the past have been marked by violence or injustice or exploitation; such past events can render the moral relationship in which they stand to one another now very much more complex and resistant to univocal interpretation than they would be in a more abstract schematization. This *is* the moral world of history and of literature and it is a world in which typically something has *already* happened that makes the abstract moral paradigm, not inapplicable, but at least a great deal more problematic in its relevance than it would be in a case that is postulated in abstraction from such a background. Because literary and historical representations include this past and because it is often the past of those who are making an effort of self-understanding through these images, it seems appropriate to say that these modes of representation have an existential character that is often lacking in moral philosophy. The point here is, of course, not to justify the humanist in turning aside from the abstract moral issue but to note that in cases considered in this way the judgment that is reached may be at once more painful and more tentative.

In any case the main claim I want to make is that the appraisive function of the works in which human lives are lifted to the level of an explicit scrutiny informed by interests like the ones I have described presupposes and itself helps to bring into being a distinctive form of human community. This is not achieved by the imposition of some massive uniformity of belief or a comprehensive Weltanschauung from which answers to all questions that face a society could be derived. What humanism as the acceptance within a society of what I have called the humanistic priorities of interest does is rather to modify subtly the nature of these problems themselves by altering the ways in which they are defined and, in some measure, the human beings who raise them. It does so by focusing on the fundamental communicative transaction among human beings which is always central to such "problems" and upon the reciprocating functions of expression and understanding which that transaction incorporates. In so doing it stimulates the emergence of a kind of human self-knowledge that is not merely personal or psychological but bound up with the whole body of presuppositions that underlie our relationships to one another and our role as beings capable of reasoned knowledge and choice. And in the representations of human character and action that are the supreme expression of this kind of interest on the part of human beings this consciousness of self is brought to bear upon the actuality of moral experience within some real human community. When that happens and when such a community maintains in a serious and sustained way this kind of relationship to itself and to its past in a degree of critical freedom that insures that its fictions will not become myths, it begins to exemplify the main features of that "community of interpretation" which Josiah Royce so insightfully described.[4] Not surprisingly, the knowledge of itself and its past that such a community aspires to achieve will have a pervasively teleological character and will interpret the significance of events and actions in the light of the presiding conceptions of the good whose authority it acknowledges. It is within such a community, moreover, that an interest is formed in an account of the past in which human actions and their consequences assume the special importance attributed to them in earlier chapters. Without such a principle of congruence between the interest in the present by which historical inquiry is ultimately motivated and the mode of conceptualization in terms of which the past is understood, it is hard to see what the adequate motive for such inquiry could be, at least if it is to command the attention of any general audience.[5]

It will of course be pointed out that a great deal of what we know about the past, whether of our own society or others, is not cast in such an evaluative form at all; and the same could be said with equal justification of the great fund of nonhistorical information about the natural world or about the working of social institutions or the incidents of individual human lives. All of this is true; but the fact remains that when we draw on this stock of evaluatively neutral knowledge for the purposes of action, and especially action in which we are to be collectively implicated, we must have a way of bringing those portions of it with which we are concerned into some definite relation to the kind of interpretation of our situation that *is* informed by a sense of moral priorities. There is, one may say, a kind of matrix within which "facts" and "information" are received and take on an evaluative valence through the relationship in which they come to stand to the governing imperatives of the life, whether individual or social, on which they bear. In some considerable measure that "matrix" will be formed by beliefs about the nature of things that at least claim to be perfectly general in their import; but it will also incorporate a set of ideas that relate specifically to the situation and prospects of a given society and that express its sense of what and where it is. Such a sense of its own identity on the part of a society can hardly be imagined in any form other than the historical, or at any rate this seems to be the case for any society that has moved beyond a static condition and not only has become what it is through a process of historical change but also acknowledges that this is the case. It may be that in spite of the historical character of this consciousness that a society has of itself it will claim to have achieved a state in which change can only be deterioration; but no such conviction can in fact arrest the process of dialectical interaction with its past that the changing circumstances of its life bring with them. It is true that the professional and scholarly forms assumed by this historical consciousness will justifiably wish to distance themselves in various ways from those that are more generally shared within the societies in which the former develop. But if they were to detach themselves so definitively that the criteria of interest and relevance they employed were entirely internal and overlapped only incidentally with those that express the character of the "stake" their society has in its past, they would lack even that relationship to the general historical consciousness of their time that would permit them to correct the errors in which the latter may have involved itself.

The community which progressively works out a measure of consensus through the medium of such representations of human character and action has often been referred to as a "republic of letters." A republic of letters is not of course a society in the full sense but rather a tiny, though potentially influential, fragment of a larger society in which the great majority may remain quite untouched by the activities of the literate minority. Very often, indeed, the fact that membership in or sponsorship by a privileged stratum within a society has been the enabling condition for the pursuit of humanistic interests has caused the latter to be regarded as the special preserve of the elite few rather than as the matters of universal human import they claim to be. The dialectic of claimed universality and imputed particularity that arises out of the social locus of the humanities is one that dogs them to this day and is well worthy of more detailed study than it has received. Nevertheless, in spite of these paradoxes, it is a fact that in both the ancient world and in the modern European world approximations to a community of this kind have come into being for significant periods of time and under circumstances that enabled them to exert a considerable degree of influence, especially in the educational and cultural domain.[6] It is also true that this conception of a republic of letters made a substantial contribution to the emergence of a "critical public" in the eighteenth century and thus to a vitally important element in the theory and practice of liberal democracy.[7] In an age of mass democracy with its strong tendency to cultural *Gleichschaltung* a good deal may depend upon our ability to maintain the posture of mind of which that critical and ethical interest in social life is an expression and which the humanities have traditionally done so much to shape.[8]

Notes

Chapter 1

1. A bibliography of the history of philosophy in which the earlier phases of the analytical movement are well represented can be found in P. Gardiner, ed., *Theories of History* (The Free Press, Glencoe, Ill., 1959). A number of the most important discussions of history and historical knowledge by Ernest Nagel, Karl Popper, and Carl G. Hempel (notably Hempel's "The Function of General Laws in History") are also reprinted here. Another shorter collection of such essays in which the anticovering-law position tends to predominate is William Dray, ed., *Philosophical Analysis and History* (Harper and Row, New York, 1960). A bibliography that lists many of the more recent works in the field is included in K. Acham, *Analytische Geschichtsphilosophie* (Verlag Karl Alber: Friburg/Munich, 1974).

2. The pioneering work in this new period in the analytical philosophy of history was clearly William Dray, *Laws and Explanation in History* (Oxford University Press, Oxford and London, 1957), which has had almost as wide an influence as Hempel's original article with which it takes issue.

3. This classic statement of the covering-law theory is Hempel's article, "The Function of General Laws in History," *Journal of Philosophy* 39 (1942): 35–48. Subsequent restatements by Hempel of his position can be found in "Rational Action," *Proceedings and Addresses of the American Philosophical Association* 35 (1961–62): 5–22; "Explanation in Science and History," in Dray, *Philosophical Analysis and History*, pp. 95–126; and "Reasons and Covering-Law Explanations," in Sidney Hook, ed., *Philosophy and History. A Symposium* (New York University Press, New York, 1963), pp. 143–63.

4. Arthur Danto, *Analytical Philosophy of History* (Cambridge University Press: Cambridge, 1964), and Morton G. White, *Foundations of Historical Knowledge* (Harper and Row, New York, 1965).

5. A discussion of many of the problems with which analytical philosophy of history deals by a practicing historian is Robert F. Berkhofer, Jr., *A Behavioral Approach to Historical Analysis* (The Free Press, New York, 1969). The historian who has perhaps expressed himself most extensively (and most negatively) as to what analytical philosophy of history has to offer history is J. H. Hexter, whose review of the White and Danto books in *The New York Review of Books* 8, no. 2 (1967): 24–28, illustrates the acrimony that can characterize these cross-disciplinary exchanges. For White's and Danto's replies, see *NYRB* 8, no. 5 (1967): pp. 28f., and ibid., no. 9, pp. 41–42. Hexter has stated his own views on history and its methodology at much greater length in *The History Primer* (Basic Books, New York, 1971) and in a collection of his essays, *Doing History* (Indiana University Press, Bloomington, Ind., 1971).

6. For an impressive demonstration of just how weak the claims to have achieved this really are, see Alan Donagan, "The Popper-Hempel Theory Reconsidered," *History and Theory* 4, no. 1 (1964): 3–26, reprinted in Dray, *Philosophical Analysis and History*, pp. 127–59.

7. As, for example, by Morton White in his *Foundations of Historical Knowledge*, pp. 85ff. See my discussion of White's position in chap. 4.

8. For such a use of the term, see William Dray, "The Historical Explanation of Actions Reconsidered," in Hook, *Philosophy and History*, pp. 132–33.

9. Wilfred Sellars, "Philosophy and the Scientific Image of Man," in *Science, Perception and Reality* (Routledge and Kegan Paul, London, 1963), pp. 1–40.

10. See the critical discussion of this tendency in Ernest Gombrich, *In Search of Cultural History* (Clarendon Press, Oxford, 1967), pp. 6ff.

11. This point has been noted by John Plamenatz in *Man and Society* (Longmans: London, 1963), 2:214–15.

12. On this point see Marx's closely similar criticism of Hegel in his *Critique of Hegel's Philosophy of the State,* ed. and trans. J. O'Malley and A. Jolia (Cambridge University Press, Cambridge, 1970), pp. 12f.

13. My discussion of teleological explanation both here and throughout the book has benefited greatly from the treatment of that topic in Charles Taylor, *The Explanation of Behavior* (Routledge and Kegan Paul, London, 1967), especially chap. 1. See also his article, "Relations between Cause and Action," *Proceedings of the 7th Inter-American Congress of Philosophy* (Les Presses de l'Université Laval, Quebec, 1967), 1:243–55.

14. These requirements are discussed in Taylor, *Explanation of Behavior,* p. 10ff., where they are illustrated by references to an essay by Ernest Nagel, "Teleological Explanations and Teleological Systems," in H. Feigl and M. Brodbeck, eds., *Readings in the Philosophy of Science* (Appleton-Century-Crofts, New York, 1953), pp. 537–38. In showing how a teleological explanation can be accommodated to the standard form of scientific explanation Nagel lays special emphasis on the elimination from the description of the components in a "teleological" system of any reference to the state they maintain by the way a change in one compensates for a change in another. For more general discussions of teleological explanations in the light of a broadly positivistic conception of scientific explanation and method, see C. G. Hempel, *Aspects of Scientific Explanation* (The Free Press, New York, 1965), pp. 325–29; and W. Stegmuller, *Probleme und Resultate der Wissenschaftstheorie und analytischen Philosophie* (Springer Verlag, Heidelberg and New York, 1969), vol. 1, chap. 8.

15. See for example I. Scheffler, *Anatomy of Inquiry: Philosophical Studies in the Theory of Science* (Alfred Knopf, New York, 1963), pt. I, pp. 76–123.

16. The philosophical import of the logical issues raised by the distinction of "extensional" and "intensional" is discussed in many of the essays collected in A. Marras, ed., *Intentionality, Mind, and Language* (University of Illinois Press: Urbana, Ill, 1972). See especially the essay by R. Chisholm, "Sentences about Believing" and the exchange of letters between Chisholm and Sellars on the subject of intentionality.

17. See Brentano's *Psychology from an Empirical Standpoint,* ed. O. Kraus and L. McAlister (Routledge and Kegan Paul, London, 1973), pp. 88–94. Brentano later abandoned the term "intentional" and as far as one can tell the concept as well.

18. Husserl's principal exposition of his interpretation of the concept of intentionality is in the *Logical Investigations,* trans. J. Findlay (Routledge and Kegan Paul, London, 1970), especially the *Fifth Investigation,* 2:533–659. For a recent collection of contemporary essays on this and other aspects of Husserl's philosophy see F. Elliston and P. McCormick, eds., *Husserl: Expositions and Appraisals* (University of Notre Dame Press, Notre Dame, Ind., 1977). Important essays on Husserl's concept of the noema are A. Gurvitch, "Husserl's Theory of the Intentionality of Consciousness in Historical Perspective," in E. Lee and M. Mandelbaum, eds., *Phenomenology and Existentialism* (Johns Hopkins University Press, Baltimore, 1967), pp. 25–58; and D. Follesdal, "Husserl's Concept of the Noema," *Journal of Philosophy,* 66 (1969): 680–87.

19. These are roughly the views as I understand them of W. V. Quine, as expounded for example in *Word and Object* (Technology Press and John Wiley and Sons, New York, 1960), chap. 6; and of R. Chisholm, whose most important statement on the subject, apart from the essays in the Marras collection, can be found in his *Perception: A Philosophical Study* (Cornell University Press, Ithaca, N.Y., 1957), chap. 11.

20. This aspect of Husserl's philosophy becomes explicit in his late, unfinished work, *The Crisis of European Sciences and Transcendental Phenomenology,* trans. David Carr

(Northwestern University Press, Evanston, Illinois, 1970). A valuable study of this work and especially of the relationship between phenomenology and history, which Husserl had come ·to interpret in increasingly positive terms, is David Carr, *Phenomenology and the Problem of History* (Northwestern University Press, Evanston, Illinois, 1974).

21. Husserl's *Logical Invstigations,* 1:279. For a study of the treatment of language and subjectivity in the First Investigation, from which this passage is taken, see Jacques Derrida, *Speech and Phenomena and Other Essays in Husserl's Theory of Signs,* trans. D. Allison (Northwestern University Press, Evanston, Illinois, 1973), especially pp. 32–47.

22. Heidegger's account of this central concept of his philosophy is given in *Being and Time,* trans. E. Robinson and J. Macquarrie (Harper and Row, New York, 1962), especially in pt. I, chaps. 2 and 4.

23. A good statement of this view of time, especially with reference to its role in the representation of human experience, can be found in H. Meyerhoff, *Time In Literature* (University of California Press, Berkeley, 1955), especially chap. 2.

24. For an interesting treatment of the implications of the now all-too-current conception of "values," see Martin Heidegger, "Nietzsche's Wort, 'Gott Ist Tot,' " in *Holzwege* (V. Klostermann, Frankfort on Main, 1950), pp. 193–247. I have tried to interpret Heidegger's philosophy as a whole as being importantly influenced by this rejection of the concept of a value-property in my *Principles and Persons: A Philosophical Interpretation of Existentialism* (Johns Hopkins University Press, Baltimore, 1967), pp. 114ff.

25. A valuable beginning has, however, been made in an essay by K. O. Apel, "Das Apriori der Kommunikationsgemeinschaft und die Grundlagen der Ethic" in *Transformation der Philosophie* (Suhr Kamp Verlag, Frankfort on Main, 1973), 2:358–435, to which I am indebted in what follows. Apel's position has clear affinities with that of Jürgen Habermas which is discussed in chap. 5.

26. The notion of such a partnership is proposed by K. O. Apel, *Transformation der Philosophie,* 2:400.

27. The classical exposition of this notion is Husserl's treatment of intersubjectivity in *Cartesian Meditations,* trans. D. Cairns (M. Nijhoff, The Hague, 1960), the Fifth Meditation.

28. The notion of an "unendliche Aufgabe" is taken from Kant's discussion in the *Critique of Pure Reason* of the "regulative" function of metaphysical conceptions that transcend experience; and it has to be emphasized that the central proposition of ethics, the categorical imperative, is *not* assigned this kind of conditional status by Kant. Nevertheless, as my discussion of his ethical views in their bearing on history in Chapter 5 suggests, there is a broader sense in which an approach to ethical issues like the one sketched here and in Chapter 5 is clearly of Kantian derivation.

29. It should be noted that the contrast of levels noted here in connection with philosophy gives rise to a more serious ambiguity relating to the status of literature among the humanities. In one aspect—usually regarded as the properly creative one—literature is the actual production of poems or novels or dramas by the authors of these works; in another, it is the study by the scholar and the critic of such works which have been produced by others. The resulting question is, of course, whether the adjective "humanistic" applies with equal propriety to literature in both these senses. Historically, it has probably been the second level—the level of literary study as contrasted with literary creation—that has typically been thought of as humanistic; and even now it seems more natural to describe a Kittredge or a Bradley as a humanist than Shakespeare himself. Nevertheless, the authority of these linguistic intuitions is not absolute. There are writers like Montaigne and Erasmus who were unquestionably humanists but do not seem to fit very comfortably at either the "creative" or the "critical" level because their thought fuses commentary on a text with fresh insights of their own. There are others like a Thomas Mann or a Matthew Arnold who function both as poets or novelists and as critics without any visible discontinuity in the kind of interest by which their work is informed at the one level or the other. But what counts most heavily

against a construal of what is humanistic and what is not in terms of the level at which work is done is simply the fact that such a construal would automatically make all critical or second-level work "humanistic" and thus obscure important distinctions that need to be made at this level. A great deal of work that is critical in the sense that it presupposes the existence of a text composed by someone else has no transparently valid title to be considered as humanistic, for example, the vast labors that go into the establishment of an authoritative text for some classical work or the kind of exegesis that confines itself, as was so often the custom among classical scholars, to points of grammar and stylistics and perhaps deliberately never reaches the themes with which the author himself was concerned. There is no need to deny the value of such work; but there is reason to question its priority of title to being described as "humanistic." What seems more important than the level at which the work is done is the character of the interest by which it is informed; and what I am suggesting is that that interest is best interpreted as one which both the creator and the critic can in their different ways share. That would be true of an interest in human beings of the kind that derives very naturally and directly from the "manifest image of man" as further specified by the two additional conditions relating specifically to literary representations of human beings that were introduced above.

In history, there really is no distinction to be made between a primary and creative activity and a secondary study of the products of such activity. What is primary for the historian is *any* kind of evidence that he can use for the purpose of reconstructing the past events with which he is concerned; and the text he himself produces is "creative" in the only sense that is at all proper within the discipline of history. It is true that the materials which the historian utilizes as evidence are predominantly written sources of various kinds; and so it might be thought that the historian's work is after all a kind of critical activity carried out upon a preexistent text and thus, by reason of its level, "humanistic" in the sense I am rejecting here. But this would be to strain the contrast of the "creative" and the "critical" to the breaking point. The historian approaches a written source primarily with a view to the indications it may contain relating to the events he wishes to reconstruct; and although such a source may also be a literary creation in its own right, it too will typically be utilized by the historian for the purpose of the account which he is trying to construct. He is thus concerned not to characterize or to estimate the creative achievement of the primary author but to glean from it whatever relates to the events he is studying. There is, of course, the special case of the history of literature (and indeed of historiography itself) and here the original text itself *is* the primary object of interest and not merely an avenue of access to an event or state of affairs that is distinct from it. Such histories, which are concerned with the products of human thought in its several domains, represent an important subvariety of historical work about which there will be more to say later; but they are hardly a suitable model for the understanding of history generally.

30. There are many general accounts of the structuralist movement but perhaps Jean Piaget, *Structuralism,* trans. C. Maschler (Basic Books, New York, 1970), is as helpful as any. For the more specifically literary aspects of the movement, see J. Culler, *Structuralist Poetics: Structuralism, Linguistics, and the Study of Literature* (Cornell University Press, Ithaca, N.Y., 1975), and R. Macksey and E. Donato, eds., *The Structuralist Controversy: The Language of Criticism and the Sciences of Man* (The Johns Hopkins University Press, Baltimore, 1970).

31. For a particularly forceful, if not lucid, statement of this thesis, see Michel Foucault, *The Order of Things: An Archaeology of the Human Sciences* (Pantheon Books, New York, 1970) especially chapts. 9 and 10.

32. One cannot help reflecting that these two forms of interest are more compatible than the structuralists appear to suppose. Chess, for example, is a human activity that is tightly circumscribed by its own code, but that fact in no way reduces the interest we feel in a particular match which may be the supreme realization of the possibilities of a certain style of play of which there are many other, far more hum-drum examples. Why should not a

particular literary work claim the same kind of interest at the same time as it is acknowledged that it both draws on and exemplifies multiple codes, conventions, and so on?

33. For a discussion of some of the differences between the situation of the ancient historian and his modern counterpart, see Raymond Aron, "Thucydide et le récit des événements," *History and Theory* 1, no. 2 (1961): 103–28. Reprinted as chap. 5 of the author's *Dimensions de la conscience historique* (Plon, Paris, 1961).

34. For an energetic defense of the new history associated with the *Annales* school in France, see L. Febvre, *Combats pour l'histoire,* 2d ed. (A. Colin, Paris, 1965). A much more detailed account of various aspects of this historiographical movement can be found in J. Le Goff and P. Nora, eds., *Faire de l'histoire* (Gallimard, Paris, 1974).

Chapter 2

1. The use of the term "literature" for purposes of the comparison and contrast I want to make with history might be questioned. "Literature," after all, in its larger sense includes history as well as philosophical and essayistic forms of discourse; and in any case to describe something as "literature" seems to have more to do with the way it is written, that is, the care and attention shown to the writing as such and to its aesthetic quality, than it does with its subject matter. In some ways, the term "fiction" serves the purposes of the comparison I want to make in a more exact way, and I have accordingly also made some use of it. But in spite of its currently extended use as a kind of synonym for "imaginative literature," it still seems to me to retain for most ears its limiting associations with one type of imaginative literature. I have, therefore, gone on using the term "literature" as well, and I have added the qualifier "imaginative" from time to time to make the relevant sense as clear as possible.

Two recent articles that treat the concept of "fiction" or "literature" from a philosophical point of view and attempt to define its relationship to history are Louis Mink, "History and Fiction as Modes of Comprehension," *New Literary History* 1 (Spring 1971): 541–58; and N. M. L. Nathan, "History, Literature and the Classification of Knowledge," *Australasian Journal of Philosophy* 48, no. 2 (1970): 213–33.

2. Hayden White, *Metahistory: The Historical Imagination in Nineteenth Century Europe* (The Johns Hopkins University Press, Baltimore, 1973).

3. *Poetics* 9. 51b. 1–12, trans. Gerald F. Else, in his *Aristotle's Poetics: The Argument* (Harvard University Press: Cambridge, Mass., 1967), pp. 301–2.

4. In Else, *Aristotle's Poetics,* p. 305.

5. An account of some of the later phases of this evolution is given in M. H. Abrams, *The Mirror and the Lamp: Romantic Theory and the Critical Tradition* (Oxford University Press, New York, 1953).

6. For an excellent discussion of ostensibly nonmimetic literary forms and the sense in which they may be in fact regarded as having a mimetic character by virtue of the mimesis of speech they involve, see Barbara Herrnstein Smith, "Poetry As Fiction," *New Literary History* 2 (Winter 1971): 259–81.

7. Apparently this example has been often used. My association of it is with Evelyn Waugh; but in his *The Actor and the Spectator* (Yale University Press, New Haven, Conn., 1975), pp. 93–94, Lewis White Beck attributes it to Anthony Trollope although he says he is unable to find it in Trollope's *Autobiography.*

8. In saying this I do not wish to be understood as claiming that there is no way at all in which an author can be mistaken about features of the world he creates. There can, after all, be internal inconsistencies in a work of fiction, and in such cases, barring special explanations, one of the assertions the author has made about a character or a situation must be false. There is also the case in which the author has situated his fictional events in a "real" place and in the course of a description of the latter, which he is evidently trying to make as accurate as possible, simply makes a mistake. It may on occasion be difficult to distinguish such cases of genuine error from those in which the author has deliberately provided one of

his characters with a nonexistent address on a real street; but it is not impossible and the distinction in any case is clear enough. For a more detailed discussion of some of these problems relating to the relationship between fiction and the real world, see sec. 3, chap. 2.

9. Philosophical discussions of reference in fictional contexts can be found in John Searle, "The Logical Status of Fictional Discourse," *New Literary History* 6 (Winter 1975): 319–32; and Avrum Stroll, "Presupposing, Existence, and 'The Language of Fiction'," *Studi Internazionali di Filosofia* 4 (Fall 1972): 51–66.

10. There are some philosophers to whom the whole notion of reference to entities which are acknowledged not to exist is unwelcome; and to them especially the account presented here might be more acceptable if I were to speak instead of "quasi-reference" or "pseudo-reference." In *Languages of Art* (Bobbs-Merrill, Indianapolis and New York, 1968), pp. 21–22, Nelson Goodman appears to lean toward this view when he lays it down that a picture of Mr. Pickwick (and presumably this would hold for a book about him as well) should be referred to via an "unbreakable one-place predicate"—"Pickwick-picture" into which "we cannot reach . . . and quantify over [its] parts," that is, Mr. Pickwick. But since, as he says, this requirement is not intended as "a reform of everyday usage," all it really amounts to is a formal way of acknowledging what is independently clear enough, namely, that Mr. Pickwick is a fictional character and not to be sought in the real world. In any case, we are free to go on talking about Mr. Pickwick just as we always have and there seems to be no good reason not to speak of this "talking-about" as "referring." For a useful discussion of the technical and nontechnical senses of "reference," see Richard Rorty, "Realism and Reference," *The Monist* 59 (1976): 321–40.

11. As far as I have been able to determine, the principal study of literature from a phenomenological standpoint, Roman Ingarden's *The Literary Work of Art,* trans. G. Grabowitz (Northwestern University Press, Evanston, Ill., 1973), contains no discussion of this kind of internal intentionality in works of fiction.

12. It seems clear that in addition to the "truths" about fictional characters and situations that are generated by the author's explicit statements there are many others that are inferrable from the latter. For example, although an author may make no reference to the birth of a character, one can assume in the absence of stipulations to the contrary that he was in fact born; and a host of other statements about him are similarly inferrable. Such inferences usually reflect the same presumptions that would be operative in real-life situations; but if the characters were Olympian gods, another set of presumptions would justify a quite different set of inferences that would go beyond the author's explicit descriptive statements.

13. See for example Morton White, *Foundations of Historical Knowledge,* chap. 4; and H. L. A. Hart and A. M. Honoré, *Causation in the Law* (Oxford University Press, London, 1959), chap. 2. For a critique of the distinction between condition and cause, see Maurice Mandelbaum, *The Anatomy of Historical Knowledge* (The Johns Hopkins University Press, Baltimore, 1977), whose argument, however, seems to fail to take into account the role that *interest* in a certain aspect of a phenomenon plays in its designation as a decisive cause.

14. The role of the practical syllogism in teleological explanation is discussed by G. H. von Wright in his *Explanation and Understanding* (Cornell University Press, Ithaca, N.Y., 1971), chap. 3. A particularly interesting account of action-chains can be found in chap. 4, pp. 135–45.

15. Frank Kermode, *The Sense of an Ending: Studies in the Theory of Fiction* (Oxford University Press, London, 1967). A contrasting view of the relationships to one another of fiction, history, and myth is presented in Warner Berthoff, "Fiction, History, and Myth: Notes toward the Discrimination of Narrative Forms," in M. Bloomfield, ed., *The Interpretation of Narrative* (Harvard University Press, Cambridge, Mass., 1970), pp. 263–87. I have also attempted to understand the argument of Edward Said, *Beginnings* (Basic Books, New York, 1976), in the hope that it might form a helpful pendant to Kermode's treatment of "endings," but unfortunately this attempt has failed.

16. Arthur Danto, *Analytical Philosophy of History,* chap. 8.

17. See the discussion of this point in Cedric Whitman, *Sophocles: A Study of Heroic Humanism* (Harvard University Press, Cambridge, Mass., 1951).

18. The difficulties in the way of any such relationship among irrational persons is aptly illustrated by the conversations among three mental patients, each of whom believed he was Christ, which are reported in M. Rokeach, *The Three Christs of Ypsilanti: A Psychological Study* (Alfred Knopf, New York, 1964).

19. A treatment of these matters that appears to be very close to my own has been developed by Herbert Fingarette in *Self-Deception* (Routledge and Kegan Paul, London, 1969), chaps. 3 and 4. The common ancestor of Fingarette's view and my own is, I suspect, Sartre's distinction between thetic and nonthetic modes of consciousness as developed in *Being and Nothingness*, trans. Hazel Barnes (Philosophical Library, New York, 1956), pt. II, chap. 1. I have also found Alasdair MacIntyre's *The Unconscious: A Conceptual Study* (Routledge and Kegan Paul, London, 1958), very helpful in connection with these matters.

20. The most radical critique known to me of a conception of imaginative literature like the one presented here is that of Alain Robbe-Grillet in his *For A New Novel,* trans. Richard Howard (Grove Press, New York, 1965), especially the essay, "Nature, Humanism, Tragedy." Robbe-Grillet's main thesis, which is developed in the form of a critique of Camus and Sartre, is a repudiation of the use of metaphorical language for purposes of describing "nature" and more generally the objects that confront human beings. He argues that the function of these metaphors is to anthropomophize these objects and thus finally to set the stamp of the human upon them in a way that subtly reestablishes the subterranean identity of man with his world which Sartre and Camus were ostensibly rejecting. There is a real insight here into the tendency of a great deal of imaginative literature to draw "nature" into the story and the teleological order it is constructing and into the way this tendency can persevere even when it has been rejected in principle. But why should a recognition of the independent status of objects require that the temporal dimension of the experience of the human characters be truncated in the way it is in Robbe-Grillet's novels or that persons be described entirely in the present tense and then mainly in terms of the objects that form their perceptual field? What Robbe-Grillet seems to have tried to do is not only to sever the metaphysical bond between man and the world—the bond which metaphor establishes—but also to assimilate to the degree that this is possible the description of persons to the description of things. As a consequence of this strategy of overkill, the relationship in which a human being stands to himself in the mode of introspection and most especially of temporal continuity with his own past is declared suspect and relationships *among* human beings are denied the kind of moral and psychological reality which literature has traditionally imputed to them.

Clearly, however, if the only sure way of blocking the tendency of the human imagination to postulate a form of communication between itself and the world is to take such drastic measures as these, the prospects for telling a story can hardly be very bright; and in fact the notion of "story" is itself quite understandably suspect in Robbe-Grillet's eyes. But even if one were to agree that he has succeeded in not telling a "story," it seems quite clear that the heroic precautions he has taken in order to avoid doing so have not been sufficient to keep him from violating many of his own prescriptions. To begin with, Robbe-Grillet refers to objects by their familiar names—"pipes," "pictures," "doors"—which identify them in terms of their contexts of use and this means in terms of the relationship in which they stand to human beings. But surely this is an anthropomorphic illusion, and a more consistent objectivism would have required the abandonment of the symbols that effect this false incorporation of these spatio-temporal occupants into the life-world of human beings. Even if Robbe-Grillet were to comply and attempt to reach a more authentic level of brute fact, however, the results would be the same as long as he continued to express the content of his perceptual experience in words and thereby tied them to that same context of human meaningfulness which he tells us is in principle alien to them. Once that step has been taken, it will hardly aggravate the offense against the independence of objects if metaphorical descriptions of these same objects supervene upon the basic classificatory and functional descriptions we have already applied to them.

Nor do the prospects for Robbe-Grillet's undertaking seem any better when one examines the treatment he has accorded to temporal continuity and to relations between persons in his own novels. It is true that he has done all he could to eliminate any use of verbs like "to remember" that directly acknowledge an intentional commerce with a person's past, and the imaginings of his characters are also usually described in the same present tense that is used for perceptual experience although they may implicitly refer to some occasion in the past. But these abstentions hardly make much difference since they do not and cannot eliminate the references to the past which are a necessary condition of the comprehensibility of the events in these novels. Unless the reader assumes that Wallas, the detective in *Les Gommes,* knows what happened at the beginning of the novel—namely, that a shot was fired in the house of Dr. Juard—and that he is investigating that incident, nothing in the novel makes sense. But if at least that much in the way of access to the past is required in order to set the novel in movement, why should references to this past incident *as past* be under an interdict and why should Wallas not be allowed a capacity for reference to other past events that may be more remote in time? Similarly in the case of interpersonal relationships it is evident that there is a constant stratum of presupposition that underlies the presentation of the characters in these novels. Among these is the unavoidable presumption that certain of these characters are aware of one another's existence, that they are able to distinguish one person from another, although not necessarily with perfect accuracy, and that when they speak they are addressing another person or replying to something that person has said. Without these elementary forms of the internal intentionality that establishes relationships between the characters themselves within the novel, no one could orient himself within the world of the novel. But, if so, why should there be no direct acknowledgment by the author or by the characters of such facts as these? One can imagine a preference for a style of narration in which such matters are left implicit, but they are presupposed and there is no basis for the claim that a fictional representation that dispenses with them is somehow closer to the way things really are than the one that directly acknowledges their presence.

21. The two statements of this position with which I will be concerned are Hans Meyerhoff, *Time In Literature,* chap. 2; and Monroe Beardsley, "The Humanities and Human Understanding," in T. B. Stroup, ed., *The Humanities and the Understanding of Reality* (University of Kentucky Press, Lexington, Ky., 1966), pp. 1–31.

22. A good example of the work along these lines that is being done in France is C. Bremond, *Logique du récit* (Éditions du Seuil, Paris, 1973) while good examples of recent American work on narrative are available in the special number of *New Literary History* 6 (1974–75), "On Narrative and Narratives."

23. See especially *The Philosophy of Literary Form: Studies in Symbolic Action* (Random House, Vintage Books: New York, 1957), in which the title-essay contains a number of interesting observations on the way Burke conceives history within the framework of his general theory. That theory is presented in *A Grammar of Motives* (World Publishing Company, Meridian Books, Cleveland and New York, 1962).

24. Frye's theory received its major statement in *The Anatomy of Criticism: Four Essays* (Princeton University Press, Princeton, N.J., 1957). His contribution to a special number of *Daedalus* on "Theory in Humanistic Studies"—"The Critical Path: An Essay on the Social Context of Literary Criticism"—is also full of interest and is now available as a book, *The Critical Path* (Indiana University Press, Bloomington, Ind., 1971).

25. Frye, *The Anatomy of Criticism,* p. 141.

26. Ibid., p. 147.

27. Ibid., p. 162.

28. There is an important question here to which I have not attempted to provide an answer. How is it that a story that is set in a world that may be very different from our own can nevertheless not only interest us deeply but also seem to afford insights into life as we

know it under the very different circumstances of our own world? The answer that immediately suggests itself is that the respects in which these worlds differ from one another are not as important as they may seem and that those elements in the fictional world that function as the vehicles of insight into our own lives actually represent, though perhaps under unfamiliar descriptions, counterparts in our own world. If one were to take this line, one would in effect be accepting the principle that the cognitive function of works of fiction presupposes their relevance to the one "real" world; and while this principle seems plausible to me, I have not tried to construct a supporting argument for it.

29. See n.21 above for the relevant works of these two authors.

30. I am assuming here that the nomological regularities at issue here are not the trivial ones I discuss in Chapter 4.

31. I take the phrase "the language of concern" from Northrop Frye, *The Critical Path.*

32. Matters grow still more complicated when real historical individuals become central characters in works of fiction in which all sorts of wildly false accounts are given of their activities, as for example in E. M. Doctorow's *Ragtime.* Fictions of this kind seem to owe whatever effect they hope to achieve to their deliberate violation of the distinction between history and fiction; but the result is that one does not know what to make of or how to classify the strange amalgam they produce.

Chapter 3

1. For a statement of a view condemning such a "false" universality and its antihistorical implications, see G. Lukács, *The Historical Novel* (Merlin Press, London, 1962), especially Chapters 1 and 2. An interesting study of Soviet literature and of the way such an insistence upon a positive identification on the part of fictional heroes with the "progressive" tendencies of their time has worked itself out there is Rufus Mathewson, *The Positive Hero in Russian Literature,* 2d ed. (Stanford University Press, Stanford, Ca., 1975).

2. A recent work in the theory of history that conspicuously fails to take into account the erosion that generic plot-structures undergo when they are transferred to the real historical events is Hayden White, *Metahistory.*

3. The conception of time which I am contending against here is the one that Heidegger characterizes in *Being and Time,* II, 6, as the "ordinary representation of time" in which "the basic phenomenon of time is seen in the 'now', and indeed in that pure 'now' which has been shorn of its full structure—that which they call the 'Present'" (pp. 478–79). He also characterizes this idea of time as "a theoretical 'representation' of a continuous stream of 'nows'" and asserts that "when *Dasein* is 'living along' in an everyday concernful manner it just never understands itself as running along in a continuously enduring sequence of pure 'nows'" (p. 462) but rather "always temporalizes itself in a unity with an awaiting and a retaining" (p. 459). To understand how Heidegger can describe such a representation of time as being both "ordinary" and "theoretical" I think we must interpret him as meaning not that the "theoretical" construal of time is an arbitrary creation of the philosopher or the scientist to which common sense is a stranger, but rather that it is the representation of time that "common sense" itself produces (and for reasons that Heidegger analyzes) while at the same time relying upon a quite different understanding of its own temporality in which the present, the past, and the future are not logically segmented in the way its "theoretical representation" requires. This (mistaken) proto-theory of time is then taken over by philosophy and science and mightily reinforced. In the literature of twentieth-century philosophy perhaps the purest instance of a theory of time as a sequence of "nows" is to be found in Bertrand Russell's account of memory in *The Analysis of Mind* (Macmillan, New York, 1921), pp. 159f., where he offers his famous example of a world that comes into existence with a population that has full-blown memories of a past it never had. This example is designed to throw into sharp relief the absolute logical distinction between what is the case

now—such as people's having the memory beliefs just described—and what was the case at the time to which these beliefs ostensibly refer. For an insightful critical discussion of Russell's treatment of memory and the role he assigns to the notion of the present, see N. Malcolm, *Memory and Mind* (Cornell University Press, Ithaca, N.Y., 1977), pp. 80ff.

4. Arthur Danto, "Complex Events," in P. Kurtz, ed., *Language and Human Nature: A French-American Philosopers' Dialogue* (Warren H. Green, St. Louis, Mo., 1971), pp. 225–36.

5. Ibid., p. 228.

6. I have in mind here primarily the position of W. V. Quine as expounded in *World and Object*. See especially the discussion of "referential opacity," pp. 141–56, and chap. 6, "The Flight from Intension."

7. The "non-tensed" character of such images is noted by N. Malcolm in *Mind and Memory,* pp. 82f.

8. I will also on occasion use the term "history" without any notation when the context is such as to make a greater degree of precision inappropriate.

9. This question, or rather the implied negative answer to it, is my version of the point I take Heidegger to be making when he says that "proximally and for the most part even *history* gets understood *publicly* as happening *within-time*" (*Being and Time*, p. 478). What Heidegger calls "the 'time' of within-timeness," that is, "time as an endless irreversible sequence of nows" (p. 478), is substantially identical with the kind of time that is governed by the restrictions of the model I have been discussing. It is one of his most important theses that "time as within-timeness . . . stems from the temporality of *Dasein*" (p. 429), that is, from a mode of temporality in which, for example, transtemporal reference is not "levelled off" by being accommodated to a conception of *Dasein* "as the sum of the momentary actualities of Experiences which come along successively and disappear" (p. 426). In these passages Heidegger evidently has history in the sense of history(e) primarily in mind; but it is clear that since "Historie"—Heidegger's term for historiography or history(n)—is itself essentially bound up with and dependent upon the temporality of *Dasein,* that is, the temporality that is free of the restrictions laid down in the model, it could not be adequately conceptualized as coming into being within the domain governed by the latter.

10. An attempt to do just this has in fact been made by Jack W. Meiland in his *Scepticism and Historical Knowledge* (Random House, New York, 1965). Meiland argues in favor of a "construction" theory of history which is to replace the "discovery" theory and represents the historian not as "trying to discover facts about an independently existing realm of past events" but rather as dealing "with a certain class of present entities (which we call 'documents' and which includes artifacts, memoirs, records, and memory beliefs) in a certain way" (p. 192). The "discovery" theory by contrast describes the historian as attempting to do something that is in fact impossible, since to know a past fact would require that one have a concept of the past and this, Meiland argues, is a concept which we only *think* we have and for which we are unable to specify any way in which it could be acquired.

The extraordinary peculiarity of this theory is its failure to explain in what sense "documents" are "present entities." Unless such documents were themselves assumed to have a history and a history that sets them into some relevant relationship to the past events that are the object of the historian's inquiry, they would be of no interest or use to the historian; and so the concept of the past comes in again through the concept of a historical document. It also comes back in Meiland's own statement that, according to the "constructionist," "the past (or at least the historical past) *is* what is made of it by the historian in the present" (p. 141). This is one of those identity statements that would lose any appearance of significance if the central term—in this case, "the past"—were not at the same time understood as being something different from what it is declared to be in the statement itself. But of course once this residual sense of the term on which the statement relies for its point is acknowledged, the latter cannot any longer claim to be straightforwardly true; and this residual sense must also make nonsense of such locutions as "creating a part of the past" (p. 193) which Meiland wants to use in describing the historian's function.

11. For a discussion of this issue see P. T. Geach, "Intentional Identity," *Journal of Philosophy* 64 (1967): 627–32. For one of the very few discussions I have been able to find of the extensionality/intensionality issue in connection with temporal relations, see G. E. M. Anscombe, "Causality and Extensionality," *Journal of Philosophy* 66, no. 6 (1969): 156–59.

12. For an example of such a use of "belief" and "knowledge," see Danto, *Analytical Philosophy of Action*, pp. 18–19.

13. This statement may appear to make much too strong a claim but a judgment on its merits should be deferred until the concept of history(e) has been more fully elaborated in the later portions of this chapter. If what I say there about the dialectical aspects of history(e) is correct, then it will follow that a great many historical actions cannot be described otherwise than in a way that implies such an overlap among the intentional fields of other agents, whether individuals or institutions. Thus, to give an example, Polybius described the decision of the Romans to intervene in Sicily in support of the city of Messina, at the beginning of what was to be the First Punic War, as having been taken on the basis of their belief that that city would be viewed by the Carthaginians as a valuable base in a movement of expansion that would eventually threaten Rome itself. Here one intention is clearly "stacked" upon another intention that is imputed to the Carthaginians. In other cases it might be the historian who establishes this identity of an object or situation under the two (or more) descriptions that accrue to it within distinct systems of agency; but in all cases this is a relationship that is integral to the concept of history(e) as I construe it. See Polybius, *Histories*, trans. W. Paton (Harvard University Press, Cambridge, Mass., 1922), 1:25–27 (Book I, 10).

14. For a defense of the view that a philosophical understanding of language is incomplete unless it incorporates a phenomenological account of the noetic conditions that must be satisfied by the beings who use language, see E. Pivcevic, *Husserl and Phenomenology* (Hutchinson, London, 1970).

15. For an illuminating discussion of this aspect of contemporary philosophy see K. O. Apel, "Die Entfaltung der sprachanalytischen Philosophie und das Problem der Geisteswissenschaften," in *Transformation der Philosophie*, vol. 1, pp. 28–95. This essay has been translated by H. Hostellilie as *Analytical Philosophy of Language and the Geisteswissenschaften* (D. Reidel, Dordrecht, 1967).

16. The classical exposition of the concept of historicity is Heidegger's, in *Being and Time*, pp. 424–55; but in spite of the currency the term has achieved since, it does not appear to be used very often in the special ontological sense that Heidegger gave to the term, most probably because the distinction he makes between the historicity of *Dasein* and the derivative historicity of things is not fully understood. For a good discussion of Heidegger's treatment of history, see T. Wren, "Heidegger's Philosophy of History," *Journal of the British Society for Phenomenology* 3, no. 2 (May 1972): 111–25, and D. C. Hoy, "History, Historicity, and Historiography," in M. Murray, ed., *Heidegger and Modern Philosophy* (Yale University Press, New Haven, Conn., 1978), pp. 329–53. For an account of the history of the concept of historicity, see G. Bauer, *Geschichtlichkeit: Wege und Irrwege eines Begriffs* (de Gruyter, Berlin, 1963).

17. This point is effectively made in J. Habermas, "Analytische Wissenschaftstheorie und Dialektik," in T. Adorno, ed., *Der Positivismusstreit in der deutschen Soziologie* (Neuwied, Berlin, 1969), pp. 159–91. An earlier development of the same idea can be found in A. Schutz, "Common Sense and Scientific Interpretation of Action," in M. Natanson, ed., *Collected Papers, I: The Problem of Social Reality* (Martinus Nijhoff, The Hague, 1962), pp. 1–37.

18. Heidegger, *Being and Time*, p. 426. The indispensable background for this locution is Heidegger's theory of temporal *ecstasis* in its several forms, which is developed on pp.

377–81. Also of great interest in this connection is his conception of the "world" as a "referential totality," (*Verweisungszusammenhang*) which is discussed on pp. 99, 103–5, and elsewhere.

19. An effective attack on the idea of a conceptual continuity between cosmic and human history is mounted in F. Gottl, *Die Grenzen der Geschichte* (Duncker und Humblot, Leipzig, 1904). This book remains, it appears, largely unnoticed, in spite of Heidegger's comment on its merits, and certainly deserves to be better known. For a study by a distinguished scientist that explores some of the senses in which nature may be said to have a "history," see C. F. von Weizsacker, *The History of Nature*, trans. F. D. Wieck (University of Chicago Press, Chicago, Ill., 1949).

20. For Heidegger's treatment of this distinction, see *Being and Time*, pp. 431–34. A strikingly similar account of the historicity of "things" is given by A. Danto, in "Historical Language and Historical Reality," *The Review of Metaphysics* 27, no. 2 (December 1973): 253ff.; but Danto makes no explicit attempt to subordinate the historicity of things to that of persons in the way that Heidegger does.

21. It is for this ontologically distinctive form of process that Heidegger employs the term *Geschehen* which has the ancillary advantage of its etymological ties to *Geschichte* on which Heidegger plays. See *Being and Time*, pp. 41, 427, 431.

22. This point is very emphatically made in Heidegger's *Hölderlin und das Wesen der Dichtung*, trans. by D. Scott as "Hölderlin and the Essence of Poetry" in W. Brock, ed., *Existence and Being* (Regnery, Chicago, 1949). It is in this work that the famous statement—adapted from Hölderlin—"wir sind ein Gesprach" occurs. See pp. 300–301.

23. The implications of this fact for the philosophy of social science have been powerfully stated by P. Winch in *The Idea of a Social Science* (Routledge and Kegan Paul, London, 1958).

24. The role of futurity in the constitution of historicity is more fully described by Heidegger in *Being and Time*, pp. 437–39, 446–49. The implications for historiography that Heidegger draws from this essential future-reference that is involved in "having a past" are by no means clear but sound distinctly voluntaristic, and their long-run compatibility with the traditional requirements of impartiality and objectivity is at least doubtful. It is these implications that are developed very much further in H.-G. Gadamer, *Truth and Method* (Seabury Press: New York, 1975), trans. from *Wahrheit und Methode*, 2d ed. (J. C. B. Mohn/Paul Siebeck, Tübingen, 1965) but without resolving the disturbing questions raised by Heidegger's own statements on this subject. For my discussion of Gadamer's position, see chapter 5.

25. In spite of the pervasively individualistic cast of much of Heidegger's treatment of *Dasein*, there can be no doubt that his conception of historicity acknowledges, although it does not elaborate on, its social and shared character. This is most evident in his insistence that the generation is the primary unit that is to be understood as the vehicle of tradition and that, as Heidegger puts it, "hands itself down to itself in a possibility which it has inherited and yet has chosen" (*Being and Time*, p. 435; for the reference to the role of generations, see pp. 436f.). The degree of passivity or of revisionary activity that characterizes *Dasein's* reception of its "heritage" has been the subject of some discussion, but it seems clear that tradition is not conceived by Heidegger as having any mandatory normative status, as for example when he declares that "the repeating of that which is possible does not bring back again something that is 'past', nor does it bind the 'Present' back to that which has already been 'outstripped'. Arising, as it does, from a resolute projection of oneself, repetition does not let itself be persuaded of something by what is 'past', just in order that this, as something which was formerly actual, may recur. Rather, the repetition makes a *reciprocative rejoinder* to the possibility of existence which has-been-there" (*Being and Time*, p. 438).

26. The literature dealing with methodological individualism and alternatives to it is now very extensive. A good review of the state of the question as well as a short bibliography can be found in Steven Lukes, "Methodological Individualism Reconsidered," in A. Ryan, ed.,

The Philosophy of Social Explanation (Oxford University Press, London, 1973), pp. 119–29. The position I outline below is close to the one Lukes defends although developed in a different way.

27. It appears that skeptical doubts about the existence of social entities that maintain their identity through time are still being expressed, as for example by J. Passmore in "Objectivity in History," in Dray, *Philosophical Analysis and History*, pp. 75–94, where it is the existence of "England" as a continuous entity that could be the subject or protagonist of a narrative history is called into question. For a helpful discussion of this kind of skepticism, which seems to me to reflect a misunderstanding of the claims that are involved in such a postulation, see H. Fain, *Between Philosophy and History: The Resurrection of Speculative Philosophy of History within the Analytical Tradition* (Princeton University Press, Princeton, N.J., 1970), chap. 12.

28. It may be that the term "economic" would be even better suited than "psychological" to designate the conception of rationality that I am arguing against here. At any rate, it is a conception that frequently surfaces in analyses of social behavior that utilize the tools of economic science for this purpose, as for example in A. Downs, *An Economic Theory of Democracy* (Harper, New York, 1957), chap. 2. A critical discussion of Downs's views and others like it can be found in S. Benn, "Rationality and Political Behaviour," in S. I. Benn and G. W. Mortimore, eds., *Rationality and the Social Sciences* (Routledge and Kegan Paul, London, 1976), pp. 246–67.

29. I have in mind here not only some of the classical philosophical interpretations of social life, like Plato's, but more recent positions in social science itself, like functionalism. For a critique of the functionalist way of conceptualizing the relationship of individual human beings to the institutional auspices under which they live, see Robert Murphy, *The Dialectic of Social Life* (Basic Books, New York, 1971).

30. A conception of this general kind was apparently worked out in nonphilosophical terms by Rudolf Smend, whose conception of "self-integration" is briefly discussed by W. Schieder in his *Geschichte als Wissenschaft* (Oldenbourg, Munich, 1965), p. 91.

31. An interesting example of such an application of the predicate "intentional" to societies with a view of calling their existence into question can be found in J. Margolies, "War and Ideology," in V. Held et al., ed., *Philosophy, Morality, and International Affairs* (Oxford University Press, New York, 1974), pp. 254f.

32. The "ahistorical" character of contemporary society and of the forms of consciousness that are currently in the ascendant is discussed in a variety of studies, among them R. Wittram, *Das Interesse an der Geschichte*, 3d ed. (Vandenhoeck and Ruprecht, Göttingen, 1968); J. Lukacs, *Historical Consciousness* (Harper and Row, New York, 1968); and J. H. Plumb, *The Death of the Past* (Houghton Mifflin, Boston, 1969). The Plumb book is an extreme statement of the view that history as science requires the severing of all "existential" forms of involvement in the past and seems to regard historicity as more or less pernicious in all its forms except those that manifest themselves in a deep suspicion of the version of events that comes down to us from our predecessors.

33. One of the few historians who have taken an active interest in the forms assumed by the construals of *their* pasts espoused by the subjects of a history is J. G. A. Pocock, whose essays on these themes have been collected in *Politics, Language, and Time* (Atheneum, New York, 1971). His more recent *The Machiavellian Moment* (Princeton University Press, Princeton, 1975), contains some fascinating discussions of the special kind of temporality and historicity that characterizes a certain kind of political society that does not claim to have its source of legitimacy in the eternal.

34. My discussion here is heavily indebted to J. Bennett, *Rationality* (Routledge and Kegan Paul, London, 1964), especially chap. 9; and I must hope that Bennett knows more about bees than I do. My sense of my own ignorance in these matters has, however, led me to consult two recent authoritative works on bees, K. von Frisch, *Bees: Their Vision, Chemical Senses and Language* (Cornell University Press, Ithaca, N.Y., 1950), and M.

Lindauer, *Communication among Social Bees* (Harvard University Press, Cambridge, Mass., 1961); the remarkable feats of communication by bees that are reported in these books notwithstanding, I find no indication in them of anything like a capacity for temporal reference, much less for cross-generational "cultural" continuity.

35. See J. Gunnell, *Time and Political Philosophy* (Wesleyan University Press, Middletown, Conn., 1968), pp. 34ff.

36. See C. Lévi-Strauss, *The Savage Mind* (University of Chicago Press, Chicago, Ill., 1962), especially chap. 8. The last chapter of this book is a defense of ahistorical societies against the treatment of them in Sartre's *Critique de la raison dialectique* (Gallimard, Paris, 1960).

37. Mircea Eliade, *The Myth of the Eternal Return; or Cosmos and History,* trans. W. Trask (Princeton University Press, Princeton, N.J., 1954), especially chap. 4. An interesting discussion of the role within political philosophy of the longing for the stability of the society of the mythic age is J. Gunnell, *Time and Political Philosophy*.

38. For Heidegger's use of this notion, see *Being and Time,* pp. 42, 83, 88.

39. An individual action in this context would be one that is not part of a trend and therefore does not contribute to any pattern of group action. Thus, if one member of a family were to take swimming lessons, that would not make it the case that the family was taking swimming lessons. But if other members of the family were to follow suit, influenced perhaps by the example of the first but still independently of one another and not as the result of any family decision, then one could say that the family was taking swimming lessons and this would be a case of distributive group agency of a (modestly) linear kind. It is, of course, not necessary that the units of distributive agency be individual human beings. For example, within some larger institutional complex like a school system individual units which in such a case would be schools and not individual human beings might act independently of one another in some way that would form a pattern attributable to the system as a whole. Normally, such actions would be taken in areas that are left to the discretion of the component units by the higher institutional authority; but one can easily imagine cases of distributive agency which would take the form of a common failure to observe some centrally imposed rule. In such cases distributive agency would contribute to a measure of disintegration of the authority of the superordinate institution but in others it might have the effect of establishing new uniformities within the system to which express collective authority would later accrue. Finally, within the "international system," where there is no real collective authority, the units are nation states and these by their at best loosely coordinated actions bring into being patterns of distributive agency.

40. I hope this brief characterization of collective agency will not mislead the reader into supposing that I am assuming an overly simplistic model of decision-making within institutions. It is clear that even when institutions are governed by constitutions that lay down as precisely as possible what the procedures of collective decision and action are to be, that fact does not guarantee that the actions taken by these institutions will not be the result of constraints that operate outside the formal decision-making routines. A study of how, in a specific case (the Cuban missile crisis of 1962), the established bureaucratic procedures of the governmental apparatus can influence and constrain the decision-making powers of the executive has been made by Graham Allison in his *Essence of Decision* (Little, Brown, Boston, 1971); and I would certainly want to acknowledge the fact he emphasizes so strongly, namely, that in order for collective decision-making and action to be feasible at all a more or less permanent set of institutional routines has to be in existence which can constrain at the same time as they make possible the exercise of power at the summit.

41. A strong indictment of the historiographical tradition from a point of view generally quite similar to that described here is Phillip Bagby, *Culture and History* (University of California Press, Berkeley, 1963). Bagby looks to anthropology as a way of studying human culture from which the historian must learn if he is to correct his ways; but it is interesting to note that in the latter part of the book when he begins to define the focus of specifically

historical inquiry it is political societies and states that suddenly dominate the discussion and not the "cultures" that up to that point had appeared to be the proper units of historical inquiry. The same observation might also be made with respect to W. McNeil, *The Shape of European History* (Oxford University Press, New York, 1974).

42. The great sponsor of the state as the primary unit in terms of which historical analysis is to proceed is, of course, Hegel but the influence of his view of the state penetrates the whole modern historiographical tradition. For a study of—among other things—its influence on German historiography, see G. Iggers, *The German Conception of History* (Wesleyn University Press, Middletown, Conn., 1968). Outside Germany the importance of the contribution of J. G. Droysen to this tradition is not widely appreciated; and a full translation into English of his *Historik,* ed. R. Hübner (Oldenbourg, Munich, 1943) would perform a real service to students of the theory of history.

43. I take the phrase, "the generative order" of society from George Santayana, *Dominations and Powers* (Scribner's, New York, 1951), pp. 23–24.

44. For a discussion of the transparency of language, see H. G. Gadamer, *Truth and Method,* p. 363ff.

45. For a study of some of the organizational and institutional aspects of the growth of science, see S. Toulmin, *Human Understanding,* vol. 1, *The Collective Use and Evolution of Concepts* (Princeton University Press, Princeton, N.J., 1972).

46. For Sartre's use of the concept of totalization, see *Critique de la raison dialectical* (Gallimard, Paris, 1960), Introduction. This work has been translated by A. M. Sheridan-Smith as *Critique of Dialectical Reason* (Humanities Press, Atlantic Highlands, N.J., 1976).

47. In this connection the difficulties experienced by Europeans in the Age of Exploration in recognizing as human the inhabitants of nonwhite and non-European countries are of considerable interest. See for example L. Hanke, *Aristotle and the American Indians* (Regnery, Chicago, Ill., 1959).

Chapter 4

1. Droysen, *Historik,* pp. 276–99.

2. For example, a book like W. Ullman, *The Growth of Papal Government in the Middle Ages* (Methuen, London, 1962).

3. The comments of R. Berkhofer in his *A Behavioral Approach to Historical Analysis,* p. 27, may be taken as typical of this view of narrative history.

4. As for example in M. Foucault, *The Archaeology of Knowledge,* trans. A. M. Sheridan Smith ((Harper and Row, New York, 1972), especially pt. IV, chap. 5. In contemporary French discussions of the theory of history only P. Veyne's *Comment on écrit l'histoire: Essai d'épistémologie* (Editions du Seuil, Paris, 1971) seems to make a larger place for narrative continuity than those of the structuralist persuasion typically do; but his otherwise excellent book suffers from a failure to define the concept of "une intrigue" in a philosophically interesting way.

5. "A Note on History as Narrative," *History and Theory* 6, no. 3 (1967): 413–19. It should not, of course, be supposed that by introducing his treatment of narrative at this point I am assimilating Mandelbaum to the structuralist point of view, whether on history or anything else. It is just that the case he makes against narrative is one that at least many structuralists could subscribe to although they have not formulated it with Mandelbaum's clarity or concision. See also the replies to this essay by R. Ely, R. Gruner, and W. Dray that appeared in *History and Theory* 8, no. 2 (1969).

6. Mandelbaum, "History as Narrative," p. 416.

7. Ibid., p. 417.

8. Ibid.

9. Henry Adams, *History of the United States of America during the Administrations of Jefferson and Madison* (University of Chicago Press, Chicago, Ill., 1967).

10. Fernand Braudel, *The Mediterranean and the Mediterranean World in the Age of Phillippe II,* trans. S. Reynolds ((Harper and Row, New York, 1972).

11. Mandelbaum, "History as Narrative," pp. 415–16.

12. Ibid., pp. 417–18.

13. Ibid., p. 418.

14. Ibid., p. 416.

15. Ibid., p. 417.

16. For a discussion of the role of history in anthropology, see E. Evans-Pritchard, *Anthropology and History* (Manchester University Press, Manchester, 1961). An interesting example of the way in which an anthropologist may approach specifically historical materials is offered by V. Turner, *Dramas, Fields, and Metaphors: Symbolic Action in Human Society* (Cornell University Press, Ithaca, N.Y., 1974). For an argument designed to show that anthropology provides a model for inquiry from which historians should learn, see P. Bagby, *Culture and History.*

17. The view proposed here in effect assigns to social science the domain of what the older sociology called "social statics," that is, the analysis of the relatively stable synchronic patterns of institutional life; and in this respect it is very similar to the one put forward by N. Rotenstreich in his *Between Past and Present: An Essay on History* (Yale University Press, New Haven, Conn., 1958) and most particularly in Chapter 4, "History and Social Science." Against such claims it would doubtless be argued by many social scientists that their domain of inquiry also includes "social dynamics," or the study of transitions from one state of relative social equilibrium to another, and that its goal is the discovery of the laws governing these movements. The prospects of actually discovering such laws is discussed in the later sections of this chapter; and the conclusion drawn there is that, if these laws are supposed to be true nomological universals, the prospects are not at all good. What is of greater relevance at this point in the argument is to point out that the way I propose to delimit the domains of history and the social sciences rests on the still more fundamental claim that *both* deal with human action and thus with a domain that is itself historical in the sense that its governing regularities are in principle "local" in character. Such an underlying assumption might be expressed by saying that the social sciences are themselves "historical" and, properly interpreted, this claim is indeed one that I would endorse. At the same time, however, it seems important to acknowledge that history in this very broad and fundamental sense also has its (relatively) nonhistorical sectors or aspects; and it seems sensible to use this distinction as a clue to the way the main disciplinary responsibilities of history and the social sciences are to be defined in relation to one another. Actually, of course, it is easy to overestimate the importance of establishing such lines of demarcation and there is nothing in my position that militates against the establishment of an intimate commerce between history and the social sciences. Indeed, I hope I have shown how their common concern with actional and thus ultimately teleological forms of order can serve as the basis for such a collaborative relationship. It is only when such a rapprochement proceeds under the auspices of a false and "scientistic" theory of the conceptual structure of the social sciences that it becomes a damaging form of *Gleichschaltung* for history.

18. For a good statement of the view I am rejecting, see W. H. Walsh, "'Plain' and 'Significant' Narrative in History," *Journal of Philosophy* 55 (1958): 479–84.

19. "Narrative History and the Concept of Action," *History and Theory* 9 (1970): 265–89. The theories of narrative discussed here are those of Arthur Danto as stated in his *Analytical Philosophy of History* and of Morton G. White as stated in *Foundations of Historical Knowledge.* In his more recent article, "Historical Language and Historical Reality," pp. 219–59, Danto has evidently attempted to make up for this deficiency in the way history was conceived in *Analytical Philosophy of History;* but the way in which he does so leaves many doubts as to just how significant a revision this is intended to represent. He is now willing to speak, as he was not earlier, of "history as *internal* to history" and what he means by this is that "historical reality is composed in relevant part of the *representations* of historical

reality on the part of men who live their lives in terms of these." But at the same time as he recognizes this history-within-history, he also calls it "history-as-reality" and then rather perplexingly counterposes it to "history-as-science." It gradually becomes evident from the examples he uses that "history-as-reality" is very far from being the full set of events to which I have referred as history(e) and which it would be the business of history(n) to recount correctly. It is conceived rather as the set of beliefs that people have and have had about the same events to which history-as-science addresses its attention; thus it is a kind of competitor of the latter with the resulting opposition of the two to one another noted above. Such beliefs or, as Danto calls them, "representations" are, of course, themselves "part of historical reality"; but Danto lays it down quite emphatically that "to treat representations as part of reality is not to be interested in questions of truth or falsity." This is true as far as it goes, but it applies only to the truth and falsity of the representations themselves and it quite leaves out of the picture the whole topic of truth and falsity *with respect to* these representations as well as the place of such truth (and falsity) in the effort of history-as-science to state the truth about the past. It thus seems to be the case that, although the modifications Danto has undertaken of his original position could be taken as pointing in the direction of a much larger role for beliefs and intentions in the explanation of events, their implications have in fact been contained within a much narrower compass and are there made to serve the purpose of exposing alleged errors due to the "crossing of externality with intentionality" rather than of showing how fundamental "internality" really is to the understanding of "externality" by (precisely) history-as-science.

20. Unlike von Wright, Dray has written on historical narrative, notably, in "Mandelbaum on Historical Narrative," *History and Theory* 8, no. 2 (1969): 287–94; and in "On the Nature and Role of Narrative in Historiography," *History and Theory* 10 (1971): 153–71.

21. W. B. Gallie, *Philosophy and the Historical Understanding* (Chatto and Windus, London, 1964).

22. Dray, *Laws and Explanation in History,* p. 122.

23. Ibid., p. 125.

24. Ibid., p. 124.

25. The claim that people make sense of their lives more through the stories they tell themselves than through rules under which they subsume particular episodes was argued by R. Hepburn in an important article, "Vision and Choice in Morality," in *Proceedings of the Aristotelian Society,* suppl. vol. 30 (1956): 14–31. Hepburn's claim relates to individual lives, and the suggestion I am making is that much the same holds true for the way we make sense of the life we have in common with other members of the society to which we belong.

26. I am indebted in what follows to Howard Adelman, "Rational Explanation Reconsidered: Case Studies and the Hempel-Dray Model," *History and Theory* 13, no. 3 (1974): 208–24.

27. Cecil Woodham-Smith, *The Great Hunger* (Harper and Row, New York, 1962).

28. H. L. A. Hart and A. M. Honoré, *Causation in the Law,* p. 41.

29. Ibid., p. 59.

30. This view of the relationship between rules and the persons who act under them is not only misconceived; it is also, unfortunately, very widespread and influential, among both social scientists and philosophers. Perhaps the most direct statement of this view is E. Durkheim's in *Les regles de la methode sociologique* (Alcan, Paris, 1927), where he says of "social facts" that "since their essential characteristic consists in the power they possess of exerting, from outside, a pressure on individual consciousness, they do not derive from individual consciousness, and in consequence sociology is not a corollary of psychology" (translation taken from G. Homans, "Bringing Men Back In," in A. Ryan, *The Philosophy of Social Explanation,* p. 52). A similar statement by a philosopher is K. Tranoy's in his "Historical Explanation: Causes and Conditions," *Theoria* 38 (1962): 234–49, where in the course of an analysis of the abdication of Queen Kristina of Sweden he speaks of "conditioning events which lie outside the agents in [this historical event]" (p. 239) and includes among

these the "social, economic, physical and *mental* events which affect...the motives, purposes, needs, fears, hopes, plans, etc. of Kristina...and others involved in the event, e.g. ...political institutions, etc." The vice of these ways of conceiving such situations is not that they introdue an element of "externality" that is wholly absent; it is rather that they elide the condition under which alone these "external" elements in the social situation of an agent can influence the latter's actions and that is through their being adopted as policies of action by the agent himself, whether straightforwardly or via some prudential calculation like the one I have described. In either case the effect of such an espousal is to incorporate the "external" condition into the "internal" rationale of the action taken.

31. Hart and Honoré, *Causation in the Law*, pp. 48–55.

32. M. Merleau-Ponty's *Humanism and Terror*, trans. J. O'Neill (Beacon Press, Boston, 1969), contains some valuable discussions of such decisions as this and of their implications as well.

33. Although it does not take in the specifically plural character of such option-trees to which I am drawing attention, G. H. von Wright's essay, "The Logic of Action: A Sketch," in N. Rescher, ed., *The Logic of Decision and Action* (University of Pittsburgh Press, Pittsburgh, Pa., 1966), is an important contribution to the understanding of the logic of action that is involved in all such processes.

34. "The prisoner's dilemma," to which so much attention is currently being given, is an example of the way a quasi-mathematical form of analysis can be brought to bear upon a type of situation that is also central to the analysis of the historical process. On terror as an instrument for maintaining solidarity of purpose within an institution under conditions in which it is endangered, see J.-P. Sartre, *Critique de la raison dialectique*, 1:447ff.

35. Here again both Sartre's *Critique de la raison dialectique* and Aron's well-justified censure of Sartre's own unnecessarily sanguinary attitude in *Histoire et dialectique de la violence*, trans. by B. Cooper as *History and the Dialectic of Violence* (Harper and Row, New York, 1975), make very pertinent reading.

36. One of the most interesting recent studies of the concept of tradition is H.-G. Gadamer's *Truth and Method*, in which however the impersonal character of tradition is so strongly emphasized that Gadamer is prepared to impute agency to the texts that are handed down and even to the language in which they are written rather than to their authors—a view that can hardly lead to anything but mystification, as E. Hirsch has ably shown in his *Validity in Interpretation* (Yale University Press, New Haven, Conn., 1967), pp. 245–64.

37. *Truth and Method*, p. 268.

38. See above, n.33, chapter 3.

39. William Bouwsma, *Venice and the Defense of Republican Liberty* (University of California Press, Berkeley, 1968).

40. K. Burke, *The Philosophy of Literary Form*, p. 94.

41. Hubert Jedin, *A History of the Council of Trent*, trans. E. Graf (B. Herder, St. Louis, Mo., 1957).

42. Ibid., 1:525–26.

43. Ibid., 1:525.

44. For K. Popper's tantalizingly brief account of situational logic, see his *The Poverty of Historicism* (Beacon Press, Boston, 1957), pp. 147–52. There appears to be an unresolved problem concerning the relationship in which Popper's conception of situational logic stands to his equally emphatic sponsorship of the covering-law theory of explanation. The puzzle is simply that his account of situational logic seems so clearly to be appealing to some notion of rational explanation; and yet the place of such a mode of explanation within a nomological theory remains unexplained. That Popper's commitment to the use of the postulate of rationality in explanations of human actions was not a passing one is made clear by his (again very brief) article, "La rationalité et le statut du principe de rationalité", in E. Claasen, ed., *Les fondements philosophiques des systèmes économiques* (Payot, Paris, 1967), pp. 142–50.

45. J. L. Mackie, *The Cement of the Universe: A Study of Causation* (Oxford University Press, London, 1974), p. 292.

46. Ibid., p. 293 and p. 291.

47. Ibid., p. 288.

48. Ibid., p. 295.

49. Ibid., p. 291.

50. Ibid., pp. 291–92.

51. Ibid., p. 292.

52. C. G. Hempel, "Rational Action," pp. 5–22.

53. Ibid., p. 13.

54. Ibid.

55. Ibid.

56. D. Davidson, "Actions, Reasons, and Causes," *Journal of Philosophy* 60 (1963): 685–700.

57. For one such argument, see J. Feinberg, "Causing Voluntary Actions," in *Doing and Deserving: Essays in the Theory of Responsibility* (Princeton University Press, Princeton, N.J., 1970). A broader attack on the same position is mounted in M. Mandelbaum's recent *The Anatomy of Historical Knowledge,* especially pt. II, chap. 4.

58. It would perhaps be more normal to use the word "know" rather than "believe" in such contexts as these, thereby committing oneself to an acceptance of the fact that the flood was occurring or about to occur. For my purposes, however, this would make no difference since I am contending that even if it is true, as the people in question believe, that a flood is occurring, it is not the occurrence of the flood as such that explains their behavior but rather their apprehension of this fact. It is this "apprehension" that is referred to by my use of "believe"; and although that term may have connotations that are inappropriate in this context, there are plenty of others in which "know" would be equally inappropriate since the "fact" would be in doubt. Perhaps what is needed is a verb that would carry the special connotations of neither "know" nor "believe" and yet draw attention to the mental or intentional dimension of an action-situation.

59. A suggestion of this type is made by M. Mandelbaum in his "Psychology and Societal Facts," in R. G. Colodny, ed., *Logic, Laws, and Life: Some Philosophical Complications* (University of Pittsburgh Press, Pittsburgh, Pa., 1977), pp. 235–53.

60. My argument here could be further developed along the same general lines so as to generate significant implications for the analysis of social-scientific laws. Although it is clear that genuine regularities relating to human action *may* be discoverable and stateable in the form of nomological universals without necessarily conforming to the requirements of a teleological or rational explanation, there would be a very strong presumption that this regularity as so stated would be derivative from one that *does* have a teleological or rational character and that, if the inquiry were pressed into the situational logic of the action-situation in question, the "rational" character of the regularity would emerge and, when disengaged from its presuppositional status within the nonrational explanation, would yield something very like a rational explanation. For an example of such a transition from one kind of explanation to another, see n.61 below.

61. By way of explanation of this notion of "routing through" which I utilize here and elsewhere, I would cite the very interesting observations made by the psychologist Roger Brown on a theory of collective movements developed by N. Smelser. In commenting on the "six determinants of collective behavior" which Smelser had proposed as the "multiple determinants of some single outcome," Brown notes that the principle of "continuity involved is perhaps better described as a continuity of locus rather than of substance and the locus is simply the relevant social unit." But he then goes on to say that "the social unit will not do the job. The locus involved (perhaps it is a substance) must really be the human mind . . . . Smelser's six determinants will only generate collective behavior if they are at

work in the same mind. It is continuity of mind that fills the role of continuity of substance." And to this he adds that "even as conditions apprehended by the same mind the determinants are not sufficient. The way in which they are apprehended or combined is critical" (*Social Psychology* [The Free Press, New York, 1965], pp. 732–33).

62. Such a shift from "rational" to "causal" explanations of human action is declared to be legitimate in principle and in fact often to be necessary by R. Bernstein in his recent book. *The Restructuring of Social and Political Theory* (Harcourt Brace Jovanovich, New York, 1976), pp. 63–74. In the article by A. MacIntyre to which he refers—"The Idea of a Social Science," in *Against the Self-Images of the Age: Essays of Ideology and Philosophy* (Schocken Books, New York, 1971), pp. 211–29—MacIntyre in the course of a critique of Peter Winch's views claims as Bernstein does that social science cannot limit itself as Winch would have it do to "intelligible" or rule-governed forms of conduct. His example of a regularity that requires a causal form of analysis is that of "the high correlation between agnatic segmentary kinship systems and nomadic pastoralism as a form of economy" (p. 222). (This form of "societal law" appears to be of the "abstractive-functional" type described by M. Mandelbaum in "Societal Laws," *British Journal for the Philosophy of Science* 8 [1957]: 211–24.) Since this correlation is to be interpreted as reflecting "adaptations, in this case of kinship patterns, of which the agents themselves are not aware, to the environment and to the level of technology prevailing," "it would in principle be possible to formulate causal laws governing such adaptations." But if this correlation is a fit subject for causal analysis, then so must be the correlation between industrialization and a kinship system based on the nuclear family. Now on just this subject George Homans has argued that "the job of a science does not end with pointing out inter-relations" such as this, as the functionalists are too prone to assume, and proceeds to sketch an explanation that goes beyond the fact of correlation and does so moreover in terms which he describes as "psychological" but which are also quite clearly "rational" in the sense I have been using. This is not to imply that the industrial workers of the nineteenth century *decided* to concentrate on the nuclear family or even that they understood that such would be the result of the new organization of their working time that was entailed by industrialization. It is unlikely that they did and so their "adaptation," like that of the pastoral nomads of MacIntyre's example, was presumably one of which they were largely unaware. But the emergence of the nuclear family was a *consequence* of the new work-regime inasmuch as these workers "had to forgo, if only for lack of time, the cultivation of the extended kinship ties" ("Bringing Men Back In," [p. 58]). The decision to go to work in the factories was a rational one, although taken often under severe constraints and with many misgivings; and so the shift in the effective kinship system has to be viewed as an (unintended) consequence of a rational decision. But it would be an odd "causal" law that did no more than formulate a regularity involving an action (entry into factory work) and its unintended consequence (emergence of the nuclear family). The reason is simply that given certain plausible auxiliary assumptions about the circumstances of life of those involved, the effects of factory work, and time available, it can be shown that the decision to enter factory work *entails*—whether those making it understand this fact or not—that there will not be time or energy left for a variety of other activities. So in some sense the decision to enter upon factory work was a decision to live in a way that excluded the possibility of "cultivating extended kinship ties"; or if this way of putting the matter is unacceptable, one could say that the decision to remain in such work when the character of this consequence it carries has become inescapably evident would be implicitly a decision to adopt new priorities as far as kinship relations are concerned. But this restores the form of rational explanation by exposing the elements of decision, belief, attitude, and so on that were not allowed to show in the purely correlational "causal" law; and it is the presumption that there is such an intentional infrastructure in all cases of human action that I have been arguing for. It seems plausible that unwillingness to accept this conclusion is due as much to the difference in the language that would typically be used, for example, by the industrial worker for describing his family life and explaining why he

doesn't see more of his third cousins and the language of the anthropologist with its very much higher level of abstraction. But clearly such differences do not exclude the possibility that the correlation between the functional subsystems that the anthropologist describes in his characteristically abstract language is traceable to connections made and consequences accepted within the life of the subject of the inquiry and thus within the very different modes of formulation and description that are available to him.

63. The concept of praxeology apparently still awaits a reasonably exact circumscription. It is discussed in R. von Mises, *History and Theory* (Yale University Press, New Haven, Conn., 1957), pp. 271ff.; and more fully in S. I. Benn and G. W. Mortimore, eds., *Rationality and the Social Sciences,* especially chap. 7. Interesting comments on the role of praxeology in history can be found in P. Veyne, *Comment on écrit l'histoire,* pp. 290ff.; and the discussion of the social sciences in J. Habermas, *Zur Logik der Sozialwissenschaften* (Suhrkamp: Frankfort on Main, 1970) chap. II, while it does not invoke the concept of praxeology itself has a clear bearing on the whole topic of the rational character of the social sciences.

Chapter 5

1. See Chapter 2, sec. 1.

2. A view of this kind seems to be presented in N. Rotenstreich, *Between Past and Present: An Essay on History,* pp. 38ff., but it is not clear that Rotenstreich would be willing to accept the full relativistic conclusions of such a view.

3. I have in mind here the kind of position that has been stated by historians like Carl Becker in his *Every Man His Own Historian* (Appleton-Century-Crofts, New York, 1935).

4. For an extended and insightful critique of the various forms of skepticism about historical knowledge, see A. Danto, *Analytical Philosophy of History,* chaps. 3–6.

5. The arguments against such "realism" that have been propounded by L. Goldstein in his recent *Historical Knowing* (University of Texas Press, Austin, Texas, 1976) all seem to rest on the assumption that the realist must treat historical knowledge as though it were perceptual or quasi-perceptual in nature; and this supposition seems to me to have been decisively refuted by P. Nowell-Smith in his "The Constructionist Theory of History," *History and Theory,* Beiheft (1977), pp. 1–28. Another sense of the term "realism" has been introduced into philosophical discussions of history by Michael Dummett, "The Reality of the Past," *Proceedings of the Aristotelian Society,* vol. 69 (1968–9), pp. 239–58; and this sense has to do with applying the law of the excluded middle to statements about the past even though there is no evidence available that would enable us to evaluate the truth-value that we thus declare them to have. Dummett appears to have some reservations about "realism" in this sense, but it would surely be a very strange ontology which allowed some statements about the past to have truth-values and not others. It would seem that in order to "have a past" at all one must treat the whole domain as determinate in respect to truth-value since it would not make much sense to inquire, for example, into some period about which little or nothing is known unless it were assumed in advance that there are determinate states of affairs to be discovered and not just generated in some paradoxical way by the inquiry itself.

6. Russell's use of this example is in *The Analysis of Mind,* pp. 159f. For a detailed examination of his argument, see A. Danto, *Analytical Philosophy of History,* pp. 78ff.

7. A recent book that avoids this tendentious approach is T. Mischel, ed., *Understanding Other Persons* (Rowman and Littlefield, Totowa, N.J., 1974).

8. This point is made in my "Interpretation and the Dialectic of Action," Symposium on Interpretation, Eastern Division Meeting of the American Philosopical Association, 1972, which is printed in *Journal of Philosophy* 69, no. 20 (1972): 718–34.

9. R. G. Collingwood, *The Idea of History* (Oxford University Press, Oxford, 1946), pp. 321–34. Critical discussions of Collingwood's position on this and other matters can be found in A. Donagan, *The Later Philosophy of R. G. Collingwood* (Clarendon Press, Oxford,

1962), chap. 8. I must confess that I am unable to accept Donagan's claim (p. 221) that Collingwood is mistaken in supposing that a distinction can be made between numerical and specific difference. In my view his error was rather to insist that the identity of the historian's thought with that of his subject had to be of *both* kinds.

10. Collingwood, *The Idea of History*, p. 213.

11. Ibid.

12. Ibid.

13. Ibid.

14. Ibid., p. 217.

15. T. Abel, "The Operation Called 'Verstehen'," in H. Feigl and M. Brodbeck, *Readings in the Philosophy of Science*, pp. 677–87. Another critique of Abel's argument can be found in J. Habermas, *Zur Logik der Sozialwissenschaften*, pp. 61–64.

16. Abel, "The Operation Called 'Verstehen'," p. 679.

17. Ibid., pp. 686–87.

18. Collingwood, *The Idea of History*, p. 297.

19. Ibid.

20. Ibid., p. 287.

21. Ibid., p. 288.

22. Ibid., p. 301.

23. Ibid., pp. 301–2.

24. Gadamer, *Truth and Method;* see pp. 389ff.

25. In the appendix on "Hermeneutics and Historicism" that he added to the second edition of *Truth and Method,* Gadamer explicitly declares that "fundamentally I am not proposing a method but...am describing what is the case.... I am trying to go beyond the concept of method held by modern science...to envisage in a fundamentally universal way what always happens" (pp. 465–66). This statement seems to imply that since the hermeneutical phenomena to which Gadamer wants to draw attention are constant, whatever pains may have been taken by the author of the text to remove every trace of himself and of his time from the interpretation he is constructing, the theory of hermeneutics will be itself neutral with respect to the distinction between cases in which "method" as been employed and those in which it has not. But if this is really Gadamer's view, then the implied opposition between "truth" and "method" becomes hard to understand.

26. Gadamer, *Truth and Method*, p. 268.

27. Danto, "Historical Language and Historical Reality," p. 258.

28. Lucien Febvre, *Le problème de l'incroyance au xvie siècle: la religion de Rabelais* (Editions Albin Michel, Paris, 1942).

29. A very interesting article that has an important bearing on my argument here is S. Paulson, "Two Types of Motive Explanation," *American Philosophical Quarterly* 9, no.2 (1972): 193–99.

30. For a discussion of these aspects of Vico's position, see Isaiah Berlin, *Vico and Herder: Two Studies in the History of Ideas* (The Hogarth Press, London, 1976), pp. 41, 64f.

31. I cannot explore here the bearings of the conception of understanding outlined above on current work in psychohistory; but an observation on one central difficulty confronting the latter may be in order. This arises out of the fact that the account which the agent himself gives of his intentions is normally couched in terms of some publicly intelligible goal and in this way his action is situated within a socially recognizable context to which it is represented as responding in some "realistic," that is, intersubjectively plausible way. In contrast to this, the psychologist's description of the agent's intentions tends to be constructed in terms of goals that are depicted as states of satisfaction or gratification on the part of the agent and thus in a large measure of abstraction from the public and social milieu within which such actions take place. One way of dealing with this disparity is to treat it as a case of appearance and reality with the result that the agent's description is simply discounted as being erroneous and as serving the purpose of insulating him against a recognition of the true

character of his motivation. Another would be to try to find a way of integrating these two descriptions and thus of explaining why a person whose "real" goal is the one stipulated in the psychological construal of his intention would be led by *that* intention so described to perform an action which bears the particular set of social characteristics which the agent's description assigns to it. Otherwise, if this linkage between descriptions is not effected, the tendency of psychological analysis will be to shut the agent up within his own internal economy of feeling-states; and it is a real question in what sense the resultant analysis could count as "historical" at all. If as I have argued the primary orientation of the historian's interest is toward what the agent does as distinct from what goes on in his psyche, it follows that he must not only situate his agents in a public world but also treat their thoughts and intentions as relating themselves to that public milieu. Above all he must treat them in terms of the active relationship in which they stand to the events and institutional arrangements of that world.

There is a special reason why this requirement has to be taken with great seriousness when a psychological interpretation is intended as a contribution to history. That reason is that the actions with which history is primarily concerned are actions which depend for their effect upon their being perceived by others and perhaps by quite large numbers of people as having a certain public or socially defined character. It may be that the agent himself will not be able to work out in advance just how his action will be perceived or what its social consequences will be, but unless he is to be thought of as a kind of sleepwalker it can hardly be doubted that these public descriptions of his action—whether in the language of politics or law or religion or whatever—will be reflected in the terms in which the agent himself envisages that action. In these circumstances one might be tempted to argue that even if it were conceded that this same action bears, as it were, another description within the private psychic economy of its individual agent, the historian might still be right to concentrate his attention upon the public and social description of the action as defining *what* the agent should be said to have done for the purposes of history. More generally, however, one might wonder whether, even in cases where the focus of interest is upon the agent's own rationale of action, the weight of the social description would not be at least as great as that of the psychological description. Instead of thinking of this action as being, so to speak, over-determined by two disparate sets of supporting reasons, one psychological and the other social, we might find that a psychological vocabulary for describing an agent's intentions proves inadequate to the task unless it in effect incorporates many of the norms governing the social situation within which that agent lives and works. In that case, we would be moving away from the picture of two sets of reasons—one operative and the other specious—for one action and toward a conception of these two sets of reasons as interpreting one another, the social ones giving the psychological ones a more definite set of implications for intersubjective contexts than they could have provided for themselves and the psychological ones explicating, when the need arises, the attachment of a given individual to the social roles and functions that are assigned to him. This is a significantly different picture from the one suggested by the flat distinction between the psychological and the social since it does not imply any element of unreality or speciousness on the one side or another and, instead, treats the "psychological" and the "social" as representing different forms of abstraction from a common matrix of human persons living in association with one another. If either of these forms of abstraction were to proceed so far in its own direction as effectively to lose contact with the unitary life-context that is being abstracted from and we were thus to arrive at a conception of the inner emotional economy that was so fully integrated that the question of an individual's stake in it could no longer be meaningfully raised, we would in effect have abandoned the conceptual terrain on which history is most likely to be at home.

32. T. Kuhn, *The Structure of Scientific Revolutions* (University of Chicago Press, Chicago, Ill., 1970).

33. T. Kuhn, "Reflections on My Critics," in I. Lakatos and A. Musgrave, eds., *Criticism*

and the Growth of Knowledge (Cambridge University Press, Cambridge, 1970), pp. 231–78.

34. Collingwood, *The Idea of History*, pp. 321ff.

35. Ibid., p. 329.

36. Ibid., p. 333.

37. Ibid., pp. 330–31.

38. Ibid., p. 331.

39. Ibid.

40. It sometimes seems to be assumed that value-differences within the historical domain can be accounted for and thus in principle reconciled by relating them to the differences in the "information base" on which attitudes and policies are founded. See for example K. Acham, *Analytische Geschichtsphilosophie*, pp. 290–91. This assumption seems to a very optimistic one and may spring from an overly simplistic conception of the "information" that is relevant to the formation of such attitudes and policies. Unless the further assumption is made that religious and ethical beliefs, for example, are rather straightforwardly dependent upon the state of scientific knowledge, it seems clear that conflicts in which they are involved will hardly admit the resolution by appeal to a neutral scientific "information base."

41. The general spirit of the parallelism I am proposing here between the teleological ordering of inquiry and that of social life is perhaps best conveyed by Johns Rawls's statement in his *A Theory of Justice* (Harvard University Press, Cambridge, Mass., 1971) that "justice is the first virtue of social institutions, as truth is of systems of thought" (p. 3).

42. This is not to say that the historian will necessarily be "taking sides" in the account he gives of some conflict between individuals or institutions. It may quite often be the case that the observation he has to make on the "merits" of the issue between the two parties is one that has to do with the sterility or destructiveness of the system of conventions within which *both* are acting.

43. M. White, *Foundations of Historical Knowledge*, pp. 128ff. and pp. 225ff.

44. It may seem that I am simply reviving here something like the view that was so effectively criticized by H. Butterfield in *The Whig Interpretation of History* (Bell, London, 1941); this is not the case. The continuity postulated by the Whig historian was a continuity of *intention;* and Butterfield has little difficulty showing that Martin Luther, for example, not only did not intend to further the cause of liberty as it was understood by nineteenth-century liberals but was in fact actively opposed to the initiatives in his own time that *were* "liberal" in the later sense of the term. This is an important point but it is no less important to see that there is a story in which Luther and his actions play a significant role and which traces the consequences of these actions and relates them to the movement toward a greater degree of social freedom. No matter what continuities the historian decides to use as the thread on which he orders the episodes with which he deals, it will prove necessary to piece it out in good part in terms of such unintended consequences since it obviously cannot be the continuity of a single purpose that maintains its identity in spite of such differences in circumstances as those in the Luther case. The real question is rather *what* terminal state could be used as the reference point in terms of which a line of continuity through events could be followed and followed in the justified belief that that state has a valid claim on the interest of every human being. This, however, is a question that Butterfield does not raise and his case against the "Whig interpretation of history" thus leaves open the possibility that in some other version that avoided an attribution of an identity of purpose and that presumably would also be construed in a less narrowly political and less specifically "Western" way would retain its claim to serious consideration.

45. Even in the case of such societies in which the "metaethical" premises of the argument I am constructing would presumably be unacceptable, a very considerable degree of agreement with much of the resulting set of evaluative principles would still be possible.

46. The relevant writings of Kant have been collected in L. W. Beck, ed., *On History* (Bobbs-Merrill, Indianapolis, Ind., 1963) and include, in addition to the essay mentioned,

Kant's "Eternal Peace" and a number of other shorter but important pieces. Kant's philosophy of history has recently been the object of increasing interest, and among the works devoted to it in whole or in part W. Galston, *Kant and the Problem of History* (University of Chicago Press, Chicago, Ill., 1975), and G. A. Kelly, *Idealism, Politics and History* (Cambridge University Press, Cambridge, 1964) may be mentioned. The idea of history as being somehow in principle "cosmopolitan" is developed interestingly by W. B. Gallie, *Philosophy and the Historical Understanding,* chap. 3.

47. Kant, *On History,* p. 13.

48. Ibid., p. 16.

49. Ibid.

50. Ibid., pp. 16–17.

51. The prevailing interpretation of Kant's moral philosophy views his theory of justice as being purely formal in character and as being related only in an external and contingent manner to the substantial interest—other than the moral interest itself—of the persons who are to judge and act under the guidance of that principle. I would concede that this is true at least in the sense that Kant's theory requires considerable amplification if it is to encompass such interests in a way that assigns them a genuine place within its version of the moral life; but I disagree with the prevailing interpretation in believing that there is a great deal more than is commonly supposed in Kant's own formulation of his position on which such an amplification could build. Kant's strictures against assigning self-interest a role in the concept of morality were so severe that it comes as rather a surprise to discover that he himself in fact treats self-interest as the base from which the test for the morality of a maxim of action is made; and in the *Critique of Practical Reason,* trans. L. W. Beck (Bobbs-Merrill, Indianapolis, Ind., 1956) he goes so far as to speak of "the concept of obligation" as "extend[ing] the maxim of self-love also to the happiness of others" (p. 35). This way of speaking is very different from the grim suppression of all considerations of self-interest that the standard interpretation attributes to Kant.

52. It should be noted however that Kant on occasion described this civic union as an "ethical commonwealth" (and indeed as an "invisible church") in a way that makes unmistakably clear that its members have to be conceived as motivated by directly moral considerations. See his *Religion within the Limits of Reason Alone,* trans. T. Greene and H. Hudson (Harper and Row, New York, 1970), pp. 90ff.

53. The aspect of Hegel's philosophy of history to which I am drawing attention here emerges with greatest clarity in his *Phenomenology of Mind,* trans. J. Baillie (Allen and Unwin, London, 1931). An excellent study of these aspects of Hegel's view of history that appeared recently is G. O'Brien, *Hegel on Reason and History: A Contemporary Interpretation* (University of Chicago Press, Chicago, Ill., 1975); and the chapters on history and society in Charles Taylor, *Hegel* (Cambridge University Press, 1975), pt. 4, are also extremely relevant to my discussion of Hegel. Also of interest in this connection are H.-G. Gadamer, *Hegel's Dialectic: Five Hermeneutical Studies,* trans. P. Christoper (Yale University Press, New Haven, Conn., 1976); and J. Shklar, *Freedom and Independence: A Study of the Political Ideas of Hegel's 'Phenomenology of Mind'* (Cambridge University Press, 1976). The dialectic of subject and object is treated as the key to the understanding of Hegel's philosophy as a whole in E. Bloch, *Subject-Object: Erläuterungen zu Hegel* (Suhrkamp, Frankfort on Main, 1962).

54. Hegel, *Phenomenology of Mind,* pp. 228–40.

55. For a recent account of how this line of argument works, see B. Williams, *Morality: An Introduction to Ethics* (Harper and Row, New York, 1972), chap. 2. It should be understood that in signalizing this achievement of the "Oxford" approach to ethics of the fifties, I am by no means endorsing that movement as a whole or accepting the claims that it made in its own behalf. For a critique of some of those claims, see my *Principles and Persons,* pp. 130–32.

56. Habermas's most explicit statements of this theory can be found in two articles in

Inquiry, "On Systematically Distorted Communication" 13, no. 3 (1970): 205–18; and "Towards a Theory of Communicative Competence" 13, no. 4 (1970): 360–75. A similar view is developed by K. O. Apel in *Transformation der Philosophie*, 2:358–435.

57. Habermas, "Toward a Theory of Communicative Competence," p. 361.

58. Ibid., p. 371.

59. Ibid., p. 373.

60. Ibid., pp. 373–74.

61. Ibid., p. 374. For a critique of the conception of emancipatory reflection that Habermas bases on his view of the constraints on "self-representation" that are inherent in the social order, see H.-G. Gadamer's essays in the exchange between (mainly) Habermas and Gadamer in *Hermeneutik und Ideologiekritik* (Suhrkamp, Frankfort on Main, 1971). The relevant essays are "Rhetorik, Hermeneutik, und Ideologiekritik," pp. 57–82, and "Replik," pp. 283–317.

62. In the vast historical literature on slavery the two books that have been of greatest value to me have been D. B. Davis, *The Problem of Slavery in Western Culture* (Cornell University Press, Ithaca, N.Y., 1967), in which the contradictory character of slavery serves as an explicit premise for the analyses of the relationships between slaveholders and slaves; and E. Genovese, *Roll, Jordan, Roll: The World the Slaves Made* (Random House, New York, 1974), in which an extraordinary and rare sensitivity is maintained to the way in which the principle of reciprocity reasserts itself even within relationships like those of the slave to the slaveowner that have to be defined primarily in terms of the violation of such reciprocity that they constitute.

Chapter 6

1. An essay by Jeremy Shapiro, "The Slime of History," in J. O'Neill, *On Critical Theory* (Seabury Press, New York, 1976), that deals among other things with the evolutionary significance of the emergence of language in the constitution of a human community has been helpful to me in connection with the matters under discussion here. For a treatment of the role of phenomenology in the creation of such a society and its relationship to Marxism, see Enzo Paci, *La funzione delle scienze e il significato de l'uomo* (Il Saggiatore, Milan, 1963), trans. P. Piccone and J. Hansen as *The Function of the Sciences and the Meaning of Man* (Northwestern University Press, Evanston, Ill., 1972).

2. The possibility of such a subterranean humanism was brought home to me with special force while visiting the Museo Antropologico in Mexico City where the statuettes and figurines from the Aztec and other pre-Columbian cultures exhibit such an acute sense of the variety and interest of *human* life in the midst of what must have been in most respects a profoundly repressive and antihuman society. The irony of the matter is that these remarkable recreations of the human scene were apparently all destined *ad usum mortuorum*.

3. A recent work that casts light on the kind of significance that dramatic representations of the archaic Greek world must have had in fifth-century Athens is Jean-Pierre Vernant and P. Vidal-Naquet, *Mythe et tragédie en Grèce ancienne* (F. Maspero, Paris, 1972).

4. See Josiah Royce, *The Problem of Christianity* (University of Chicago Press, Chicago, 1968), especially Lectures 9 and 13. An admirable contemporary exposition of a closely similar conception of society can be found in Wayne Booth, *Modern Dogma and the Rhetoric of Assent* (University of Chicago Press, Phoenix Books, Chicago, 1974).

5. In placing this strong emphasis on the interest in the present that motivates historical inquiry, I am implicitly endorsing much of what Benedetto Croce has said on this subject, as for example in *History as the Story of Liberty*, trans. by E. Spriggs (Allen and Unwin, London, 1941); but I would be much more cautious in endorsing Croce's more extreme formulations of his thesis than J. Meiland has been in his *Scepticism and Historical Knowledge*, chap. 1. Among these formulations are Croce's famous declaration that "every true

history is contemporary history''; in my view such statements are best regarded as paradoxes designed to counter the kind of nineteenth-century positivist dogma that identifies history with the assemblage of facts and fails to face up to questions about how these facts are conceptually constituted and thus to questions about conceptual differences between descriptions of these "facts" by those who were contemporary with the events they involve and by the historian who looks back on them from his "present." To take them literally would be to foster a fatal confusion.

6. This study deliberately limits itself to Western forms of humanism; but it is evident that the concept of humanism is susceptible to extension to other non-Western cultures and most notably to China. The account of Chinese humanism in Joseph Levinson, *Confucian China and Its Modern Fate* (University of California Press, Berkeley, 1958–65), is particularly useful in this connection, especially by reason of its discussions of specifically *historical* form assumed by the effort of the Chinese literati to understand the situation of their own civilization, with its claim to an absolute cultural validity, in the changing circumstances of the modern Western-dominated world.

7. Two important studies of the erosion that has taken place in our conception of the "public" sphere are Jürgen Habermas, *Struktur der Öffentlichkeit: Untersuchungen zu einer Kategorie der bürgerlichen Gesellschaft* (Luchterhand Verlag, Neuwied and Berlin, 1962) and—for the American scene—Richard Sennett, *The Fall of Public Man* (Random House, New York, 1977).

8. Some of the most eloquent and moving statements on the fate of humanistic culture in our time can be found in Nadezhda Mandelstam's memoirs, *Hope Against Hope* and *Hope Abandoned,* trans. Max Hayward (Atheneum, London and New York, 1970 and 1974).

Index

Abel, Theodore, 198–99, 212
Acham, Karl, 286 n. 40
Action: concept of, 22; explanation of, 12–15, 145–46, 155–56, 175–88; in imaginative literature, 47–49, 61–64, 66–67, 70; rationality of, 52–54, 146–52, 179–81, 238–40; description of, 57–58, 165–75, 193–94, 196–98, 213–19, 221, 284 n. 31; and historicity, 95–97, 259; types of, 114–17; institutional, 117–19, 148–49, 156–58, 276 n. 40; individual, 276 n. 39, 281 n. 61; in historical narrative, 137–44, 152–65, 232; legal analysis of, 155–56; as decisive cause, 155–56; dialectical character of, 158–65; consequences of, 160–61, 165–69, 171–72, 173–74; and violence, 161–62; and understanding, 192–94, 195–202, 213–19; as subject of interpretation, 227–28, 233; relation to rules, 279 n. 30
Adams, Henry, 236
Aristotle, 38–40, 59–60, 66
Author: creative freedom of, in imaginative literature, 41–46, 74–75; intentionality of, 45–46, 58, 68, 73–76; relation to reader, 46, 68; susceptibility to error, 73–76, 267 n. 8

Beardsley, Monroe, 70
Bouwsma, William, 164–65
Braudel, Ferdinand, 136, 140
Brentano, Franz, 16
Brown, Roger, 281 n. 61
Burke, Edmund, 126
Burke, Kenneth, 61–62, 165
Butterfield, Herbert, 286 n. 44

Cause: role in explanation, 13, 138, 282 n. 62; distinction of contributing and decisive, 48–49; human actions as decisive, 155–56; beliefs and intentions as, 181–83; in explanation of human action, 183–88
Collingwood, Robin G., 195–202, 223–25, 234–35

Covering-law theory. *See* Nomological-deductive theory of explanation
Croce, Benedetto, 288 n. 5

Danto, Arthur, 50, 82–83, 209, 278 n. 19
Davidson, Donald, 181–83
Descartes, René, 20–22
Dialectic: in Hegel's philosophy of history, 9–10; in imaginative literature, 46–48, 54, 55, 68; in historical action, 120–21, 128, 130, 158–65, 260; of master and slave, 243–44
Dray, William, 146–47
Droysen, Johann G., 134
Dualism, Cartesian, 20–23
Dummett, Michael, 283 n. 5

Eliade, Mircea, 113
Explanation: historical, 2–5, 135–43; nomological-deductive, 2–5, 179–88, 280 n. 44; teleological, 12–15, 24, 145–52, 198–99; belief as element in, 281 n. 58; in imaginative literature, 70–73; and narrative, 144–52; rational, 145–52; of collective actions, 281 n. 61; scientific, in history, 154–55, 187; and institutional roles, 156–58, 279 n. 30; and agents' descriptions, 165–75; of value conflicts, 286 n. 40; and intentions, 175–78, 184–86
Extensionality: principle of, 14–15; as applied to time, 51

Febvre, Lucien, 210–11
Fiction: as denoting imaginative literature, 267 n. 1; Robbe-Grillet's theory of, 269 n. 20
Frye, Northrop, 61–67

Gadamer, Hans-Georg, 162, 202–11, 251, 284 n. 25
Gallie, W. B., 146
Game theory, and dialectic of action, 159–60
Goldstein, Leon, 283 n. 5